"This overview of Luke and Acts will delight the reader with its accessible detail, helpful questions for discussion, and engaging Birdwinian turn of phrase. I encourage you to journey with Luke in one hand and this book in the other."
Sarah Harris, Carey Baptist College

"Mike Bird has opened the door wide to everyone wanting an entry into the world of Luke–Acts. Those reading Luke's two-part narrative will find themselves enriched by the way Bird follows Luke's story and attends to its themes. But he also follows the twists and turns of Lukan scholarship—discussing big ideas and principal controversies, as well as naming some key voices in contemporary study. What more could we ask for in an introduction to Luke–Acts?"
Joel B. Green, senior professor of New Testament interpretation at Fuller Theological Seminary

"Writing in the vein of I. Howard Marshall's classic *Luke: Historian and Theologian*, Bird provides an accessible yet rich journey through the historical and theological questions raised by the Lukan writings. This is a perfect volume for a seminary course or for preachers in a sermon series on Luke–Acts."
Joshua W. Jipp, professor of New Testament at Trinity Evangelical Divinity School

"Luke and Acts compose 28 percent of the New Testament. Bird is a reliable guide to the various issues and themes that arise in Luke. He carefully navigates nuanced debates while writing a brief but memorable overview. Students, pastors, and professors will be helped by this overview."
Patrick Schreiner, professor and author of *Acts: The Christian Standard Commentary*

"Michael Bird's thoughtful, thorough, engaging, and accessible study of Luke–Acts should be a go-to source for all New Testament readers. Bird treats theological themes (such as the holistic nature of salvation) and questions regarding Luke's historical accuracy (such as the Luke 2 census under Quirinius). By interacting with a range of sources—ancient as well as modern—and also referencing popular culture, Bird helps readers to understand what the ancient author Luke seemed to be doing in his two-volume work and also how he was doing it."
Dennis R. Edwards, dean of North Park Theological Seminary and author of *Humility Illuminated*

"We have come to expect from the pen of Michael Bird scholarship that is well grounded historically and theologically stimulating. This volume does not disappoint. It is thorough, thoughtful, and well written. I appreciate the special attention to the primary sources and his engagement with theology."
Osvaldo Padilla, professor of divinity at Beeson Divinity School and author of *The Acts of the Apostles: Interpretation, History and Theology*

"Michael Bird has the rare talent of communicating dense and often stodgy academic issues in an exuberant spirit and user-friendly fashion. Underlying the amiable tenor is expert knowledge derived from years of research and rumination. He has provided a much-needed service to the urgent need of the church (laity and leadership) to know more intimately the Word of God."

M. Sydney Park, Beeson Divinity School

Michael F. Bird

A Bird's-Eye View of Luke and Acts

Context, Story, and Themes

An imprint of InterVarsity Press
Downers Grove, Illinois

InterVarsity Press
P.O. Box 1400 | Downers Grove, IL 60515-1426
ivpress.com | email@ivpress.com

©2023 by Michael F. Bird

All rights reserved. No part of this book may be reproduced in any form without written permission from InterVarsity Press.

InterVarsity Press® is the publishing division of InterVarsity Christian Fellowship/USA®. For more information, visit intervarsity.org.

Scripture quotations, unless otherwise noted, are from the New Revised Standard Version Bible, copyright © 1989 National Council of the Churches of Christ in the United States of America. Used by permission. All rights reserved worldwide.

The publisher cannot verify the accuracy or functionality of website URLs used in this book beyond the date of publication.

Cover design: David Fassett
Interior design: Daniel van Loon
Cover images: © CSA Image / Getty Images, Wikimedia Commons

ISBN 978-1-5140-0809-6 (print) | ISBN 978-1-5140-0810-2 (digital)

Printed in the United States of America ∞

Library of Congress Cataloging-in-Publication Data
Names: Bird, Michael F., author.
Title: A bird's-eye view of Luke and Acts : context, story, and themes / Michael F. Bird.
Description: Downers Grove, IL : IVP Academic, [2023] | Includes bibliographical references and index.
Identifiers: LCCN 2023015432 (print) | LCCN 2023015433 (ebook) | ISBN 9781514008096 (print) | ISBN 9781514008102 (digital)
Subjects: LCSH: Bible. Luke–Criticism, interpretation, etc. | Bible. Acts–Criticism, interpretation, etc.
Classification: LCC BS2589 .B57 2023 (print) | LCC BS2589 (ebook) | DDC 226.4/06–dc23/eng/20230605
LC record available at https://lccn.loc.gov/2023015432
LC ebook record available at https://lccn.loc.gov/2023015433

| 29 | 28 | 27 | 26 | 25 | 24 | 23 | | 13 | 12 | 11 | 10 | 9 | 8 | 7 | 6 | 5 | 4 | 3 | 2 | 1 |

For Scott Harrower

Fellow follower in the Way!

Contents

	Preface	ix
	Abbreviations	xi
1	What's So Special About Luke–Acts?	1
2	Luke–Acts: The Origins Story	11
3	The Purposes of Luke–Acts	29
4	Luke: Historian or Theologian?	53
5	"This Jesus": The Christology of Luke–Acts	76
6	Luke and the Way of Salvation	105
7	"Beginning with Moses": The Old Testament in Luke–Acts	125
8	On the Road with Jesus: Lukan Discipleship	145
9	Luke the Feminist? Jesus, Women, and the Church	166
10	Luke the Socialist? Possessions and Poverty	185
11	The Promise of the Father: Luke and the Holy Spirit	200
12	Luke on Jesus, the Jews, and the Gentile Churches	217
13	Turning the World Upside Down: Luke and Empire	243
14	A Hope in God: Luke and the Future	270
	Bibliography	293
	General Index	313
	Scripture Index	319

Preface

THIS VOLUME IS THE PRODUCT of many years of teaching Luke–Acts to students across the UK, United States, and Australia. It is also the result of periodic forays in and out of Lukan scholarship. It is designed as an accompaniment to a class on the themes and text of Luke–Acts. It is certainly no replacement for a decent commentary on Luke and Acts but hopefully complements them, as it introduces students to the various debates and discussions in Luke–Acts. Yet it is also written with an eye on contemporary application, as people of Christian faith and communities of faith must constantly strive to discern in the precincts of their own consciences how Luke–Acts applies to them today. I hope the book will prove to be useful to researchers, instructors, students, seminaries, and anyone interested in Luke's testimony to Jesus and his history of the early church.

There are several people I need to thank. First and foremost, the editorial team at InterVarsity Press for the patience of Job in allowing me to deliver this manuscript after displaying what can only be described as rude contempt for deadlines and deadline extensions. Thanks to Anna Gissing for ensuring that I finally did get to this project, and thanks, too, to Rachel Hastings for seeing this book through its editing and production process.

Second, this volume is also indebted to my colleagues and students at Ridley College among whom these ideas were worked out.

Several of my colleagues have made their own forays into Luke–Acts, taught it themselves, preached on it, and modeled its pastoral and moral imperatives in our community. The team of librarians, ably led by Ruth Weatherlake, helped to track down several volumes and articles I needed to complete this book, so I am naturally thankful to them, especially Alison Foster and Harriet Sabarez. Also thanks to Mrs. Alison Flynn for doing the indices. Decades of students have also endured my teaching through Luke–Acts and slowly but surely working out my own ideas as to how to understand and grasp this important New Testament subcorpus. The Australian College of Theology also generously supported the research for this volume with a senior research fellowship grant.

Finally, this book is dedicated to my colleague and friend Scott Harrower, who has been the John to my Peter and the Barnabas to my Paul. Scott is a great theologian, teacher, pastor, sounding board, collaborator, and friend with whom to do the sort of things that the church did in Acts 2:42. Thank you, Scott!

Abbreviations

Ant.	Josephus, *Jewish Antiquities*
BDAG	Danker, Frederick W., Walter Bauer, William F. Arndt, and F. Wilbur Gingrich. *Greek-English Lexicon of the New Testament and Other Early Christian Literature*. 3rd ed. Chicago: University of Chicago Press, 2000
BIS	Biblical Interpretation Series
BZNW	Beihefte zur Zeitschrift für die neutestamentliche Wissenschaft
CBQ	*Catholic Biblical Quarterly*
CITM	Christianity in the Making
COQG	Christian Origins and the Question of God
CurBR	*Currents in Biblical Research*
EvQ	*Evangelical Quarterly*
ICC	International Critical Commentary
Int	*Interpretation*
JETS	*Journal of the Evangelical Theological Society*
JSNTSup	Journal for the Study of the New Testament Supplement Series
JTS	*Journal of Theological Studies*
J.W.	Josephus, *Jewish War*
LES	Lexham English Septuagint
LNTS	Library of New Testament Studies
NCCS	New Covenant Commentary Series

NovT	*Novum Testamentum*
NovTSup	Supplements to Novum Testamentum
NTT	New Testament Theology
Pol. *Phil.*	Polycarp, *To the Philippians*
SNTSMS	Society for New Testament Studies Monograph Series
TynBul	*Tyndale Bulletin*
WUNT	Wissenschaftliche Untersuchungen zum Neuen Testament

What's So Special About Luke–Acts?

WHY THE GOSPEL OF LUKE AND ACTS OF THE APOSTLES DESERVE YOUR TIME

Often when I'm thinking about a holiday destination, I must convince my family that we should journey to a particular place, especially if they are not familiar with it. After all, what is there to see in the Bunya Mountains, in northern Tasmania, in the mountains of Colorado, or the seaside of Cornwall? This volume is about a journey, a journey into the Gospel of Luke and the Acts of the Apostles (i.e., Luke–Acts). Maybe you are already up for it, maybe you think it will be boring, maybe you think it will be just cute stories about Jesus and quaint tales about the apostles. Well, as your tour-guide-in-chief through Luke–Acts, I want you to know that there are several reasons why Luke–Acts is a great read, a terrific study, and sumptuous feast of history, theology, and biblical insights. I offer six reasons why you should make Luke–Acts one of your top destinations for biblical study:

First, Luke–Acts forms a distinct corpus within the New Testament. Both books are written by "Luke," an evangelist and the church's first historian. Luke–Acts comprises a unified two-volume work with a distinctive approach to telling the story of Jesus, and it is one of our best sources about first-century Christianity.

Second, Luke–Acts makes up 28 percent of the New Testament. That is significant because Paul's epistles are only 24 percent of the New Testament, while John's Gospel, epistles, and apocalypse comprise 20 percent of the New Testament. Luke, then, is by far the biggest contributor to the New Testament.[1]

Third, by marrying a biography of Jesus to the history of the early church, Luke has effectively written a New Testament in miniature. His two-volume work is the story of Jesus and the mission of the apostles. Luke–Acts is the New Testament in a nutshell.[2]

Fourth, Luke–Acts contains some unique materials and unforgettable stories. Luke provides famous passages such as Mary's Magnificat (Luke 1:46-55), Zechariah's Benedictus (Luke 1:67-79), Jesus' Nazareth sermon (Luke 4:16-31), the parable of the prodigal son (Luke 15:1-32), the parable of the good Samaritan (Luke 10:30-37), the two disciples on the road to Emmaus (Luke 24:13-35), the ascension (Luke 24:50-53; Acts 1:1-11), the beginning of the church at Pentecost (Acts 2:1-47), the division between the Hebrews and Hellenists (Acts 6:1-6), Paul's conversion (Acts 9:1-30; 22:1-21; 26:2-23), and the Jerusalem Council (Acts 15:1-33). And that is just the tip of the iceberg.

Fifth, Luke–Acts emphasizes several key things:

- Jesus' concern for the poor and outcasts
- the rigorous nature of discipleship
- the importance of prayer and attitudes toward possessions
- the place of women among Jesus' disciples
- an emphasis on Israel's hopes fulfilled in Jesus
- the identity of Jesus as the messianic Lord

---

[1] Some scholars think Luke *might* have written Hebrews and had a hand in compiling Paul's pastoral letters (1–2 Timothy and Titus). This is far from certain, but if true, it would mean that Luke wrote close to 50 percent of the New Testament.

[2] C. K. Barrett, "The First New Testament?," *NovT* 38 (1996): 94-104.

- the importance of the Holy Spirit in the mission of the church
- the apostolic preaching of Jesus
- the beginnings of the Christian mission to the nations
- the beginnings of Paul's apostolic ministry
- the church's contentious relationship with the Jews and the Roman Empire

Sixth, Luke–Acts is valuable for your devotional life and in a church's preaching cycle. For a start, the Gospel of Luke shows what it means to be a follower of Jesus. The Lukan travel narrative (Luke 9:51–19:44) contains most of Luke's teaching about discipleship and urges disciples to a manner of life that separates the followers from the fans (see esp. Luke 9:57-62 about three would-be disciples). The book of Acts tells us of the beginnings of the church and gives an ideal picture of the church as committed "to the apostles' teaching and fellowship, to the breaking of bread and the prayers" (Acts 2:42).

> **Why Read Luke?**
>
> "The most important reason to study Luke's Gospel is captured in the words of Cleopas and another, unnamed disciple. After an encounter with the resurrected Jesus, they say to each other, 'Did not our hearts burn within us . . . while he opened to us the Scriptures?' (Luke 24:32). Jesus had been teaching them that all of Scripture has always been centered on him as the fulfillment of God's plan of redemption (Luke 24:26–27). When we study Luke's Gospel, we see Jesus, the Redeemer. We hear the words of Jesus, the friend of sinners. We feel the heartbeat of Jesus, who seeks and saves the lost. When we study this book, will not our hearts burn within us with love for him? And will not this love overflow for the salvation of the world?"[a]
>
> [a] C. D. "Jimmy" Agan III, "Why Study the Book of Luke?," Crossway, May 28, 2019, www.crossway.org/articles/why-study-the-book-of-luke/.

> **Why Read Acts?**
>
> "The book of Acts offers something unique in the Christian canon. It has no rival in terms of a book spanning so many different lands. Its references to the Spirit far outpace any other work. It functions as a hinge canonically, bridging the Gospels and Epistles. It recounts the birth of the church age, and its content has no parallel in the New Testament. Acts is also unparalleled in that it recounts a new stage in Christian history: post-Jesus life. Everything (canonically) before this has been either pre-Jesus or with Jesus. No longer are readers and characters looking forward to a Messiah, or following him on the dusty roads of Galilee. Now, readers get a glimpse of Jesus's followers as they seek to be faithful to Jesus after he has departed."[a]
>
> ---
> [a] Patrick Schreiner, *The Mission of the Triune God: A Theology of Acts* (Wheaton, IL: Crossway, 2022), 19-20.

All this is to say, going deeper into Luke–Acts is a great way to be reminded of authentic discipleship and a terrific refresher on the church's mission.

WRESTLING WITH LUKE

Reading Luke–Acts brings up some thorny questions and knotty challenges for us to consider in our thinking about the contents of this two-volume work and how to apply it. What follows is a list of what I intend to cover in each chapter of this volume with an explanation of why it matters for understanding Luke–Acts.

First, origins story. This includes exactly who was Luke, why he wrote his two-volume work, the details about date, genre, outline, and all that scholarly preamble. I know it is not exactly riveting theater, but we cannot afford to skip this part because we do need to place Luke in his social and historical context. We must have a working hypothesis about Luke's sources, we should try to figure out what is motivating him, and we need to at least consider how Luke–Acts holds together as a story.

Second, granted that Luke and Acts can both stand alone, if we read them together, can we discern a particular purpose that Luke has in mind? What makes someone write a biography of Jesus and the history of the church? Is the Lukan Gospel for the social justice–loving churches of the region of Achaia in Greece? Was Acts composed as kind of friend-of-the-court brief to help Paul during his trial in Rome? Assuming that Luke is not writing his two-volume story purely for the curiosity of posterity, it is incumbent on us to ask what impact he wanted his writings to have, both immediately and in the long haul.

Third, should we think of Luke as mainly a historian or a theologian? Scholars crank out huge tomes on these questions. It is a dense topic but a necessary one. That is because there are a few places where one wonders whether Luke has the details quite right (e.g., the census under Quirinius in Luke 2:1-5), but there are other places where Luke seems to be a historian of the first rank (e.g., the man really knows his ancient nautical travel itineraries in Acts 21–28). History aside, if Luke is principally a theologian, then what is driving his theological agenda? Is Luke trying to compensate for the failure of Jesus to return as quickly as everyone thought by telling the church to get comfy and hang in for the long haul in the "times of the Gentiles" (Luke 21:24)? Or is Luke simply a Jesus-freak and Paul fanboy who wants everyone to know the "way of salvation" (Acts 16:17)?

Fourth, who is Jesus, according to Luke? Luke has some unique material about Jesus that gives us Luke's own perspective about who Jesus is. Spoiler alert: in Luke's testimony Jesus is the messianic herald of salvation, Lord of the church, the anointed Spirit bearer, the exalted Spirit dispenser, and the only name in whom salvation can be found. While Luke's portrayal of Jesus operates differently in the Gospel (through the story of Jesus' life) versus in Acts (through Jesus heralded as the exalted Lord), Luke has a consistent and well-rounded view of Jesus as the Messiah of God in whom the nations find their hope.

Fifth, Luke is very big on the theme of salvation (Greek σωτηρία), with people attaining wholeness or deliverance from sinful deeds, dispossession, dishonor, disease, disability, demons, death, and despotic powers. Jesus is the prophesied "horn of salvation" from David's house (Luke 1:69 NIV), and "There is salvation in no one else" other than Jesus, "for there is no other name under heaven given among mortals by which we must be saved" (Acts 4:12). We must unpack the theme of salvation with its holistic and wide-ranging scope of meaning.

Sixth, Luke is a biblical theologian concerned with the how Israel's sacred Scriptures find their fulfillment in Jesus and the early church (see esp. Acts 13:32-34). Luke kicks off his Gospel by stating that his purpose is to provide "an orderly account of the events that have been fulfilled among us" (Luke 1:1). At the end of his Gospel, the risen Jesus gives the two travelers to Emmaus a lesson in christological readings of the Old Testament: "beginning with Moses and all the Prophets, he explained to them what was said in all the Scriptures concerning himself" (Luke 24:27 NIV). We'll see how Luke considers his Jesus-church story as built with the scaffolding of Israel's Scriptures.

Seventh, Luke has a lot to say about Jesus' disciples and what it means to be his disciple. The travel narrative (Luke 9:51–19:44) is filled with many episodes, encounters, parables, and sayings that demonstrate how nothing less than total commitment to Jesus and his kingdom is required for true disciples. The strenuous nature of discipleship is illustrated in Jesus' encounter with would-be disciples who are challenged as to whether they are really devoted to God's kingdom and Israel's sacred traditions or are only committed to the point of convenience. Acts provides a lot of details about how the early church cultivated its own pattern of devotion to Jesus and the God of Israel. The challenge is for us, too, to forsake possessions, luxury, family expectations, and career and to follow the risen and exalted Jesus.

Eighth, women are far more prominent in Luke–Acts than in any other part of the New Testament. Women have key voices and roles from the infancy narrative (Luke 1–2) all the way through to the churches of the eastern Mediterranean with those such as Lydia (Acts 16:14-15). However, if you are expecting Luke to be a fourth-wave feminist, then you are going to be disappointed. Luke is writing from within the Greco-Roman world, where female roles were still socially limited. At no point does Luke demand that we burn the patriarchal barn to the ground. Accordingly, feminist interpreters dispute whether Luke is truly pro-women or merely reiterates patriarchal power and privilege with slight modifications. For example, in Luke 10:38-42, does Luke commend Mary for sitting at Jesus' feet and listening to his teaching (unlike her sister Martha, who is irate that she has to do all the housework herself)? Or does Luke have Jesus commend Mary because she sits down and shuts up rather than actively serves?

Ninth, some parts of Luke–Acts sound a bit like socialism. Luke records John the Baptist telling someone, "Whoever has two coats must share with anyone who has none; and whoever has food must do likewise" (Luke 3:11), while the early church's members "would sell their possessions and goods and distribute the proceeds to all, as any had need" (Acts 2:45). To cut to the chase, Luke is not calling for state control of the means of production and for the abolishment of private property by a politburo on behalf of some industrial urbanized proletariat. However, Luke does have a lot—I mean a *lot*—to say about possessions and wealth, which is challenging as it is jarring. If your thing is based on your things, then you are going to find the Lukan Jesus' teachings about wealth quite disturbing. Luke may not be a political Marxist, but he's not exactly thrilled, either, at the prospect of the rich getting richer and the poor getting poorer. In Luke's view, the first will be last and the last will be first (Luke 13:30). This is unsettling stuff for those of us who live in a consumerist and affluent society.

Tenth, Luke was the first "Pentecostal" theologian, with his emphasis on the Holy Spirit. Jesus is both the bearer of the Spirit (Luke 3:22) and the dispenser of the Spirit (Luke 3:16). The Spirit is the "promise of the Father" (Acts 1:4) and "power from on high" (Luke 24:49). But don't get the wrong impression—the Spirit is not some kind of divine fog or a performance-enhancing drug for preachers. The Spirit really does not like being lied to (Acts 5:3, 9), and he directs the apostles toward missionary ventures (Acts 13:2). While not every church today is Pentecostal in the denominational sense, if it were not for Pentecost, there would not be any churches (see Acts 2).

Eleventh, Luke in many ways is trying to hold together the church's Jewish heritage while simultaneously affirming that the full inclusion of Gentiles in the church is a very Jewish thing to do. Luke gives us a Jewish Jesus who operates as the living Lord of a largely Gentile church. Luke tells a complicated story on that front, full of surprising twists, debates, setbacks, and controversy. At the same time, Luke knew that Jesus and Paul had some big religious showdowns with the Jews of Judea and the Diaspora, and some scholars wonder whether Luke had an anti-Jewish inclination born of sectarian debates between Jews and Christians. So there are lots of things to discuss here on Luke, Jesus, Jews, and Gentiles.

Twelfth, what did Luke think of the Roman Empire? Did Luke think the empire was inherently evil, useful but dangerous, or a good thing that facilitated the spread of Christianity? Luke appears so eager to blame the Jews for Jesus' death and for anti-Christian riots that he can sometimes make Roman officials look good in comparison. Other times, however, Luke portrays Roman officials as greedy, corrupt, indifferent to injustice, idolatrous, murderous, or even plain incompetent. It will be useful to see what Luke really thinks about Rome and its supporters out in the provinces of the empire.

Thirteenth and finally, we need to look at Luke's conception of hope. An older line of scholarship argued that Luke was trying to compensate for the failure of Jesus to return as soon as the first generation thought he would. Luke, so the argument goes, is trying to explain what happened and what the church was going to do in this long, long interim period. Even beyond that dry discussion, there is the matter of what Luke thinks will happen on earth when the Son of Man comes (Luke 18:8) and what it means that to believe that "it is through many persecutions that we must enter the kingdom of God" (Acts 14:22). In Luke's telling, Paul declares that he is on trial for "my hope in the promise made by God to our ancestors" (Acts 26:6). This hope is based on Jesus as God's expression of his faithfulness to Israel and his invitation for everyone to "eat in the kingdom of God" (Luke 13:29; see Luke 14:12).

These are the questions, or perhaps the challenges, that Luke sets before us, and we will carefully address them in the following chapters. At the end I hope that readers will know Luke's two-volume work better and will be more equipped to follow Jesus as the prince of life.

REVIEW QUESTIONS

1. What percentage of the New Testament is Luke–Acts?
2. To whom did Luke address his Gospel and Acts?
3. Luke 9:51–19:44 is known as what section of the Gospel of Luke?
4. How does Luke challenge the affluence and consumerism of our society?
5. What do you think Luke means by "salvation"?

FURTHER READING

Bock, Darrell. *A Theology of Luke and Acts: God's Promised Program, Realized for All Nations*. Grand Rapids, MI: Zondervan, 2012.

Carroll, John T. "The Gospel of Luke: A Contemporary Cartography." *Int* 68 (2014): 366-75.

Gaventa, Beverly R. *Acts*. Abingdon New Testament Commentaries. Nashville: Abingdon, 2003.

Green, Joel B. *Discovering Luke: Content, Interpretation, Reception*. London: SPCK, 2021.

Jipp, Joshua W. "The Acts of the Apostles." In *The State of New Testament Studies*, edited by Scot McKnight and Nijay Gupta, 350-67. Grand Rapids, MI: Baker, 2019.

Padilla, Osvaldo. *The Acts of the Apostles: Interpretation, History, and Theology*. Downers Grove, IL: InterVarsity Press, 2016.

Parsons, Mikeal C. *Luke: Storyteller, Evangelist, Interpreter*. Peabody, MA: Hendrickson, 2007.

Reid, Barbara E., and Shelly Matthews. *Luke 1–9*. Minneapolis: Liturgical, 2021.

Spencer, F. Scott. *The Gospel of Luke and Acts of the Apostles*. Nashville: Abingdon, 2011.

Strait, Drew J. "The Gospel of Luke." In *The State of New Testament Studies*, edited by Scot McKnight and Nijay Gupta, 315-33. Grand Rapids, MI: Baker Academic, 2019.

Tannehill, Robert. *The Narrative Unity of Luke–Acts: A Literary Interpretation*. 2 vols. Philadelphia: Fortress, 1991–1994.

2

Luke–Acts

The Origins Story

LUKE BEHIND THE CURTAIN

Whenever I'm invited to speak somewhere, whether a church, college, university, or prison, I'm normally introduced with a summary of who I am, where I'm from, and why people should bother listening to me. Or I'm interviewed by an emcee, and the audience gets to hear a little bit about who I am and what I do before they have to endure a grueling forty-five-minute lecture or twenty-five-minute sermon from me. I think such an introduction helps because you want to know something of the person you're listening to, as that adds context, color, texture, and realism to the person's talk. I really, really wish that before we delved into Luke–Acts we could interview Luke himself, perhaps watch an interview with him from two thousand years ago or even read his autobiography. I'd love to know about the man himself, how he wrote Luke–Acts, to question him about this bit or that part, to try to understand his motivations, and to inquire about the key motifs in his two-volume work. But alas, Luke is not with us; all we have is the text inside our New Testaments. But those big questions remain. We still desire to know the author and to try to grasp the backstory to Luke–Acts. Consequently, before we get into the story *within* Luke–Acts, we must first look at the story *behind* Luke–Acts.

Here we are exploring several things: Who was Saint Luke? When did he write? Whom was he writing for? What kind of work was he writing? Where did he get his material from? How do we know Luke and Acts go together?

These topics are not just throat-clearing exercises; they provide useful background information that will help us as we read through Luke–Acts. It will enable us to situate Luke–Acts in the context of ancient Judaism, emerging Christianity, and the Greco-Roman world. Covering these topics will help us later when we wrestle with hairy questions about Luke and his surrounding environment and his account of the birth of the early church.

WHO WAS LUKE?

Luke according to the New Testament. The superscription or title of the Third Gospel, "The Gospel according to Luke" (ΕΥΑΓΓΕΛΙΟΝ ΚΑΤΑ ΛΟΥΚΑΝ), appears at the end of one of our earliest manuscripts of Luke, designated as P[75] and dated to AD 175–225. The title itself was probably not part of the original composition because, we suspect, the titles were added later by copyists in order to distinguish the individual Gospels from each other after they began to circulate as part of a single collection (i.e., the Tetraevangelim or Four Gospels). However, the attributions of the canonical Gospels to Matthew, Mark, Luke, and John respectively were unanimous in the early church from Alexandria to Lyons, and this probably counts against the view that the Gospels ever circulated anonymously. The Gospels, prior to being put together into one literary collection, may well have had some indication of authorship inscribed on them, such as a reference on the reverse side of a papyrus scroll or a marginal note inside a small codex.[1] The attribution of the Third Gospel,

---

[1]See Martin Hengel, *The Four Gospels and the One Gospel of Jesus Christ*, trans. J. Bowden (Harrisburg, PA: Trinity Press International, 2000), 50-56.

and by extension Acts, to Luke, then, is probably a lot earlier than the late second century.

According to the Pauline letters, Luke (Λουκᾶς) was a prominent member of the Pauline circle, a "coworker" (συνεργός), a physician (ἰατρός), who assisted Paul during his captivities in Ephesus and Rome (see Colossians 4:14; Philemon 23-24; 2 Timothy 4:11). Some have tried to identify Luke with one of the characters in Luke–Acts, such as one of the seventy(-two) sent out on a mission by Jesus (Luke 10:1-17), the unnamed disciple on the road to Emmaus with Cleopas (Luke 24:13-35), or even Lucius of Cyrene (Acts 13:1; Romans 16:21).[2] These are interesting ideas, perhaps, but purely speculative.

An important observation is that during Paul's second missionary journey, the author suddenly switches to the first-person plural (i.e., *we* and *us*) beginning with Paul's stay in Troas (Acts 16:7-17) and continuing thereafter up to his arrival in Rome (Acts 20:5-15; 21:1-18; 27:1–28:16). These are usually referred to as the "we" passages and could indicate that the author of Acts accompanied Paul during part of his missionary travels. This would neatly correspond to the presence of Luke in several of the Pauline letters. Alternatively, the "we" passages might reflect the testimony of the author's sources, such as a travel diary, or else comprise a type of literary device to make the narrative seem more vivid. Such options are theoretically possible, but I see no reason not to take the "we"/"us" passages as genuine firsthand accounts of someone who accompanied Paul in his travels as narrated in the later chapters of Acts.

Luke according to patristic sources. Christian authors of the second, third, and fourth centuries identified the author of the Third

---

[2] See John Wenham, "The Identification of Luke," *EvQ* 63 (1991): 3-44.

Gospel and the Acts of the Apostles with Paul's traveling companion, the physician Luke.

> **Was the Author of Luke–Acts *Really* a Traveling Companion of Paul?**
>
> "In some cases it almost appears to be regarded as a test of critical integrity, a proof of critical virility, to find an explanation for these passages which can provide a believable alternative to the most obvious solution (that the narrator was personally involved in the episodes related). In fact, none of the alternatives has proved so credible as the most obvious solution. And the most probable solution remains that the author of Acts was indeed personally involved in the 'we/us' episodes, and so provides an eye-witness and near third-hand authority for most of at least the second half of Acts."[a]
>
> ---
> [a] James D. G. Dunn, *Beginning from Jerusalem*, CITM 2 (Grand Rapids, MI: Eerdmans, 2009), 58.

Bishop Irenaeus of Lyons (ca. AD 130–200) regarded Luke as a companion of Paul who wrote a Gospel during the Pauline mission (Irenaeus, *Against Heresies* 3.1.1; 3.10.1; 3.11.8; 3.14.1; 3.15.1). The connection between Paul and Luke was so close that it was commonly thought that Luke's Gospel was a collection of Paul's preaching about Jesus. Luke's Gospel is literally the "my gospel" Paul refers to in his letters (see Romans 2:16; 16:25; 2 Timothy 2:8; Irenaeus, *Against Heresies* 3.1.1; Tertullian, *Against Marcion* 4.5.3; Eusebius, *Ecclesiastical History* 3.4.8; 5.8.3).

> **Luke the Marcionite Gospel?**
>
> The connection between Luke and Paul was particularly important for Marcion of Sinope (ca. AD 85–160), an heretical Christian from the southern coast of the Black Sea who established his own congregations in Rome. For Marcion, Luke's Gospel, once shorn of its Jewish

elements, was the only authentic Gospel of the apostle Paul. Some scholars argue that Marcion edited a proto-Lukan text as his Gospel and that our canonical Luke–Acts is a subsequent edition largely written in response to Marcion's Gospel.[a] Marcion came to Rome in the 140s AD with hopes of attaining leadership in the Roman churches. He rejected the Old Testament for its ethics and its purportedly vengeful God, wrote a book called *Antitheses* pointing to alleged contradictions between the Old Testament and the teaching of Jesus, accepted only ten of Paul's letters (excluding the pastoral epistles), and used only the Gospel of Luke (shorn of its Jewish elements, which he regarded as corruptions). Marcion was excommunicated, so he split off and founded his own network of churches, which became popular and persisted for some centuries. Marcionism was attractive because (1) it resolved the ethical problems presented by the Old Testament; (2) it resonated with the anti-Jewish rhetoric in Christian tradition and the anti-Jewish prejudice of pagan civic leaders; (3) it amplified Paul's strong statements about discontinuity between the old and the new in Galatians 2–5; 2 Corinthians 3; and Romans 9; and (4) it made Christianity more palatable to pagans by turning Christianity into a pagan religion with Jesus at the center.

As to what Marcion did to the Gospel of Luke, Irenaeus writes, "He mutilates the Gospel which is according to Luke, removes all that is written respecting the generation of the Lord [i.e., birth and infancy], and sets aside a great deal of the teaching of the Lord's discourses in which the Lord is recorded most clearly confessing that the creator of this universe is his Father" (Irenaeus, *Against Heresies* 1.25.1). It is far more likely than not that Marcion was editing a version of Luke not too dissimilar from canonical Luke.[b]

---

[a] See Markus Vinzent, *Marcion and the Dating of the Synoptic Gospels* (Leuven: Peeters, 2014); Dieter T. Roth, *The Text of Marcion's Gospel* (Leiden: Brill, 2015); Roth, "Marcion's Gospel and Luke: The History of Research in Current Debate," *Journal of Biblical Literature* 127 (2008): 513-27.

[b] Judith Lieu, *Marcion and the Making of a Heretic: God and Scripture in the Second Century* (New York: Cambridge University Press, 2017), 209.

The Muratorian Canon (or Fragment) is a description of the origins of several New Testament books. It stems from a fourth-century codex that is a collection of Latin texts, including quotes from key church leaders, an exposition of the catholic creed, and a fragment of eighty-five lines of text listing the recognized books of the New Testament and explaining how they relate to the catholic faith of the church. Concerning the Gospel of Luke and Acts of the Apostles, the fragment says:

> The third book of the Gospel is that according to Luke. Luke, the well-known physician, after the ascension of Christ, when Paul had taken with him as one zealous for the law, composed it in his own name, according to [the general] belief. Yet he himself had not seen the Lord in the flesh; and therefore, as he was able to ascertain events, so indeed he begins to tell the story from the birth of John [the Baptist]. . . . Moreover, the Acts of all the Apostles were written in one book. For "most excellent Theophilus" Luke compiled the individual events that took place in his presence—as he plainly shows by omitting the martyrdom of Peter as well as the departure of Paul from the city [of Rome] when he journeyed to Spain.[3]

This listing of the books probably stems from the late second century, and the fragment names the author of the Third Gospel and Acts as Luke the physician, not an eyewitness to Jesus' life but a companion of Paul, who wrote his works prior to Paul's and Peter's deaths.[4]

Information about the Evangelists is also found in the prologues to several Gospel collections of Latin manuscripts of later

---

[3] Cited in Bruce M. Metzger, *The Canon of the New Testament: Its Origin, Development, and Significance* (Oxford: Clarendon, 1987), 305-7.
[4] Although some date the Muratorian Canon to the fourth century, the interest in the Shepherd of Hermas and the defense of the apostolicity of John's Gospel all suit a second-century date. See further Graham Stanton, "The Fourfold Gospel," *New Testament Studies* 43 (1997): 332-35; Eckhard J. Schnabel, "The Muratorian Fragment: The State of Research," *JETS* 57 (2014): 231-64.

centuries. While these are based predominantly on church tradition, they tell us at least what the current thinking was about the origins, purpose, and background of each Gospel in the second to fourth centuries. The anti-Marcionite prologue to Luke's Gospel says:

> Luke is a Syrian of Antioch, a Syrian by race, a doctor by profession. He had become a disciple of the Apostles and later followed Paul until his [Paul's] martyrdom, having served the Lord continuously, unmarried, without children, filled with the Holy Spirit, he died at the age of eighty-four in [Thebes of] Boeotia. . . . And indeed afterwards the same Luke wrote the Acts of the Apostles.[5]

We observe here perhaps the first indication of Luke's origins in Antioch, a proposed Gentile audience for his Gospel, and a setting in the Greek province of Achaia for his place of writing.

Church historian Eusebius (ca. AD 263–339) comments, "Luke, an Antiochene by birth and a physician by profession, was long a companion of Paul and was closely associated also with the other Apostles" (*Ecclesiastical History* 3.4). Eusebius goes on to say that Luke's Gospel was written on the basis of the testimony of others and Acts was based on his own experience. The great Bible scholar and translator Jerome (ca. AD 343–420) writes:

> Luke a physician of Antioch as his writings indicate was not unskilled in the Greek language. An adherent of the apostle Paul, and companion of all his journeying, he wrote a Gospel, concerning which the same Paul says, "We send with him a brother whose praise in the gospel is among all the churches" and to the Colossians "Luke the beloved

---

[5]Helmut Koester assigns the first portion of this prologue to the end of the second century and the second half to the fourth century. His rationale is that the first part is the only element preserved in Greek, and the rest depends on later Latin manuscripts. See Koester, *Ancient Christian Gospels* (Philadelphia: Trinity Press International, 1990), 335.

physician salutes you," and to Timothy "Luke only is with me." He also wrote another excellent volume to which he prefixed the title Acts of the Apostles, a history which extends to the second year of Paul's residence at Rome, that is to the fourth year of Nero, from which we learn that the book was composed in that same city. (Jerome, *De viris illustribus* 7)[6]

> **Luke the Doctor?**
>
> W. K. Hobart popularized the notion that the author of Luke–Acts was a physician, given the presence of medical terminology and vivid descriptions of illnesses in his two-volume work (e.g., Luke 4:38; 5:12; 8:43-44; 14:2; Acts 3:7; 28:8).[a] However, the verbal similarities between Luke and Greco-Roman medical writers only prove that Luke was well-educated and perhaps even well-read in medical literature. Hobart overlooked the fact that many non-medically trained contemporaries of Luke used similar language in their writings.[b] Although the author could well have been a physician, there is nothing in the text that explicitly and without ambiguity suggests that the author had an unusual grasp of medical terminology.
>
> [a]W. K. Hobart, *The Medical Language of St. Luke* (Grand Rapids, MI: Baker, 1954); also Adolf von Harnack, *Luke the Physician* (New York: Putnam, 1907).
> [b]H. J. Cadbury, *The Style and Literary Method of Luke* (Cambridge, MA: Harvard University Press, 1920), 39-72.

So who was Luke? Thus, in the traditions across the centuries, the Third Evangelist was thought to be the physician Luke, a native Antiochene, not an eyewitness to Jesus' life but a traveling companion of Paul. Luke's Gospel was the "my gospel" that Paul himself referred to, Luke was associated with the Greek province of Achaia, and he allegedly wrote for Gentiles.

---

[6]Cited in Rick Strelan, *Luke the Priest: The Authority of the Author of the Third Gospel* (Aldershot, UK: Ashgate, 2007), 80.

Much of this is probably based on what the New Testament says about Luke and from evolving legends about the apostles and their companions.

Based on the text of Luke–Acts itself, the author self-identifies as a second-generation Greek-speaking Christian (Luke 1:1-2). He wrote under the sponsorship of his patron Theophilus, for whom this two-volume work provided instruction in the way of Jesus Christ (Luke 1:3; Acts 1:1). The author was highly literate, familiar with Greek rhetoric, biography, and historiography, while also immersed in the Greek version of the Old Testament Scriptures (i.e., the Greek Bible, sometimes called the Septuagint). He was conversant with Jewish interpretive schemes and messianic expectations. The author probably had access to the Gospel of Mark, perhaps the Gospel of Matthew. It is not out of the realm of possibility that he knew of Paul's letters, and some even wonder whether he knew the works of the late first-century Jewish historian Josephus. He seems to have had contact with other Christians in Judea, Syria, Asia Minor, Greece, and Rome, from whom he has garnered information about the church's beginnings. In light of the "we" passages in Acts, the author was quite likely at one time a traveling companion of Paul. His own theology represents a post-Pauline position that ultimately stands on the shoulders of Paul but does not feel constrained to mimic Paul's own theology and language at every turn. Although there were many coworkers in the Pauline circle, Martin Hengel's conclusion on authorship may not be too far off the mark: "The author of the two-volume work is probably Luke the physician (Col. 4.14; cf. Philemon 24)."[7]

---

[7] Martin Hengel, *Earliest Christianity*, trans. John Bowden (London: SCM Press, 1986), 66.

> **Was Luke Gentile or Jewish?**
>
> Luke is normally regarded as having been a Gentile, but there is nothing in Luke–Acts or Paul's letters that explicitly requires that he was a Gentile. According to Jacob Jervell, "Luke's stylistic home was the synagogue. He was a Jewish Christian. Maybe he was born a Gentile, but then he came from God-fearers, having his roots in a Hellenistic-Jewish Christianity."[a] Others have found that view persuasive. More acutely, Rick Strelan argues that Luke was perhaps a convert from the priestly class to the Jesus movement and was among the many priests that converted and joined the church: "The word of God continued to spread; the number of the disciples increased greatly in Jerusalem, and a great many of the priests became obedient to the faith" (Acts 6:7).[b]
>
> ---
>
> [a]Jacob Jervell, *The Theology of the Acts of the Apostles* (Cambridge: Cambridge University Press, 1996), 5. See also Michael Fuller: "Luke may very well have been a Diaspora Jew or God-fearer. If Luke was a Gentile (convert), as many scholars contend, he has been educated in Israel's history and Scriptures, and feels compelled to situate the story of Jesus within this interpretative frame." Fuller, *The Restoration of Israel: Israel's Re-gathering and the Fate of the Nations in Early Jewish Literature and Luke–Acts*, BZNW 138 (Berlin: de Gruyter, 2006), 198n5. See similarly David A. Smith, "The Jewishness of Luke–Acts: Locating Lukan Christianity Amidst the Parting of the Ways," *JTS* (2021): 738-68.
> [b]Rick Strelan, *Luke the Priest: The Authority of the Author of the Third Gospel* (Aldershot, UK: Ashgate: 2007).

DATE

When did Luke write his two-volume work? Well, as per everything in biblical studies, it is disputed. Here are the factors that affect dating.

- Luke records Paul's visit to Rome in Acts 28, so it was written no earlier than circa AD 62, depending on how one reconstructs Pauline chronology.
- Luke is probably dependent on the Gospel of Mark (ca. AD 70) and possibly on the Gospel of Matthew (ca. AD 80).

Luke–Acts

- The Gospel of Luke is first alluded to by the bishop Clement of Rome in his letter to the Corinthians circa AD 95 (see *1 Clement* 46.8 = Luke 17:2; *1 Clement* 13.2 = Luke 6:31, 36-38).

- The book of Acts is probably first alluded to by the bishop Polycarp of Smyrna in his letter to the Philippians circa AD 115–135 (see Pol. *Phil.* 2.1 = Acts 10:42; *Phil.* 2.3 = Acts 20:35; *Phil.* 3.2 = Acts 16:12-40; *Phil.* 6.3 = Acts 7:52; *Phil.* 12.2 = Acts 26:18; 8:21).

- Some scholars think Luke is dependent on a collection of Paul's letters for his reconstruction of Paul's career (compiled ca. AD 65–140) and dependent on Josephus for his account of the destruction of the Jerusalem temple and for information about the various uprisings that took place in Judea by Judas the Galilean, Theudas, and the Egyptian (*Jewish Wars* ca. AD 75 and *Antiquities* ca. AD 93–94). Alternatively, maybe Luke simply knew from oral reports about the Roman siege of Jerusalem, had heard about the tumultuous history of Judea under the Romans, and knew of Paul's letters directly from Paul himself.

- Our earliest manuscripts of Luke (P^{75}) and Acts (P^{29}) both come from the third century.

Some try to date Luke–Acts very early (ca. AD 65–70) based on the observation that when Acts ends, Paul is in house arrest in Rome, and if Luke knew about Paul's trial and martyrdom, he would surely have told his readers about it. I see the attraction of that view, but it is sadly pushing a big rock up a steep hill. Scholars tend to date the Gospel of Mark to circa AD 70, and Luke is clearly dependent on Mark's outline for his own Jesus story. Plus, it helps if we remember that Acts is not a Pauline biography; it is about the beginnings of the church, the spread of the Christian mission, the proclamation of Jesus to the ends of the earth, how things began in Jerusalem and arrived in the streets of Rome.

Therefore, the Gospel of Luke was probably composed circa AD 75–95. The book of Acts could have been written immediately after or else separated by some decades, with an upper limit of circa AD 115. To be more precise, I'd opt for a date for Luke–Acts between AD 80-90.

AUDIENCE

Whom did Luke write his Gospel and Acts for? Well, at one level the answer is quite obvious: Theophilus. I tend to think that Theophilus was not a fictive figure but a real person. Theophilus was probably the patron sponsoring Luke's literary endeavors, perhaps a pagan convert to Christianity or a leader in the church wanting a fresh account of the story of Jesus and the story of how the church began.

Of course, I doubt Luke thought that the only person to read his Gospel and Acts would be Theophilus. Undoubtedly Luke intended his own circle of fellow believers and like-minded networks of churches to be interested in his literary endeavors. Yet what impact did Luke think his Gospel was going to have on them? This brings us to the question of purpose, which deserves and will receive a chapter of its own—the very next one. Suffice it to say for now that Luke's Gospel edges toward emphasizing Jesus' concern for the outcasts and marginalized, while Acts has a very clear apologetic edge, especially in terms of Paul's legacy and the status of Gentile Christians.

Beyond Theophilus, we can imagine Luke's Gospel being intended for—in different ways—Jewish Christians, Gentile Christians, perhaps even pagan inquirers of Christianity, or even non-Christ-believing Jews of the Diaspora. These audiences are not mutually exclusive and Luke might have envisaged his two-volume work as finding a home among a variety of audiences who had a variety of responses to it. I'm partial to what François Bovon wrote: "Among this readership, Luke, who writes with the care of a historian, the apologetic enthusiasm of a convert, and the earnest appeal of a missionary, envisages three target groups: educated Gentiles, Hellenistic Jews, and Christians unsettled by rumors (Luke 1:4; Acts 22:30)."[8]

GENRE

Luke's Gospel and the Acts of the Apostles are different texts. They tell united albeit distinguishable stories, they move from Jesus to the early church, and they are arguably intended to function in different ways. So we will deal with the genre of each one separately.

First, we have to ask: What is genre? It might seem like a mundane question, but it is a necessary one. Genre is kind of like an implied contract between author and readers on how a text relates to reality, the rules for understanding it, and how it should be received. In other words, the reality, rules, and reception of a text that begins, "Once upon a time" are different from a text that begins, "You can expect scattered showers and light northeasterly breezes." Scholars debate whether genre is based on a family of characteristics that texts share (types of narrator, use of symbolism, written in first or third person, etc.) or on the social function of a text (morality tale, apologetic, polemic, etc.). Just note for now that the meaning of genre is disputed.

Second, when it comes to the genre of the Gospel of Luke, the consensus is that it is a form of ancient biography, similar to

---

[8]François Bovon, *Luke 1: A Commentary on the Gospel of Luke 1:1–9:50* (Minneapolis: Fortress, 2002), 9.

Xenophon's *Memoirs of Socrates* or Philo's *Life of Moses*.[9] Ancient biography was a very flexible genre and could be written differently. In the case of the Gospel of Luke, it is tied very closely to Israel's sacred history and literature, it puts the Jesus tradition (i.e., teaching given by Jesus and stories about Jesus) into a biographical literary form, it marries together ancient rhetorical devices with Jewish schemes of scriptural interpretation, and it is connected to Christian evangelistic and apologetic preaching. For those reason I tend to think of the canonical Gospels, including Luke, as a type of *kerygmatic biography* (*kerygma* means "preaching").

Third, the genre of the Acts of the Apostles is a more challenging problem. In fact, there are some days where it feels as if every second PhD candidate in New Testament in the English-speaking world is writing their dissertation on the genre of Acts. We could think of Acts as historiography, a telling of history albeit with rhetorical and religious interests.[10] Or Acts could be a succession narrative or collected biography dealing with a preeminent figure and his later followers.[11] Or again, maybe Acts is a Hellenistic writing of sorts, but one strongly influenced by Israel's Scriptures, a new piece of "biblical history."[12]

---

[9]See Michael F. Bird, *The Gospel of the Lord: How the Early Church Wrote the Story of Jesus* (Grand Rapids, MI: Eerdmans, 2014), 222-40; Michael F. Bird and N. T. Wright, *The New Testament in Its World* (Grand Rapids, MI: Zondervan, 2019), 682-83.

[10]See, e.g., Clare K. Rothschild, *Luke–Acts and the Rhetoric of History: An Investigation of Early Christian Historiography*, WUNT 2/175 (Tübingen: Mohr Siebeck, 2004), 16-23; Eve-Marie Becker, *The Birth of Christian History: Memory and Time from Mark to Luke–Acts*, Anchor Yale Bible Reference Library (New Haven, CT: Yale University Press, 2017); Andrew W. Pitts, *History, Biography, and the Genre of Luke–Acts* (Leiden: Brill, 2019).

[11]Charles H. Talbert, *Literary Patterns, Theological Themes, and the Genre of Luke–Acts*, Society of Biblical Literature Monograph Series 20 (Missoula, MT: Scholars Press, 1974), 125-34; Sean A. Adams, *The Genre of Acts and Collected Biography*, SNTSMS 156 (Cambridge: Cambridge University Press, 2014), 116-256.

[12]Brian S. Rosner, "Acts and Biblical History," in *The Book of Acts in Its Ancient Literary Setting*, ed. Bruce W. Winter and Andrew D. Clarke (Grand Rapids, MI: Eerdmans, 1994), 65-82; James D. G. Dunn, "The Book of Acts as Salvation History," in *Heil und Geschichte: Die Geschichtsbezogenheit des Heils und das Problem der Heilsgeschichte in der biblischen Tradition und in der theologischen Deutung*, ed. Jörg Frey, Stefan Krauter, and Hermann Lichtenberger, WUNT 248

More likely than not, Acts is something like an apologetic historical work written up according to Greco-Roman literary conventions, as a conscious extension of Israel's sacred history, with a key focus on the lives of Jesus' followers, especially the apostles Peter and Paul.

UNITY

By now some readers will be wondering why Luke–Acts is being treated as one literary item rather than as two separate things, that is, Luke and Acts. Normally we read Luke beside the other three Gospels, while Acts gets read as a kind of preamble to the Pauline and Catholic epistles. Yes, they have the same author and some common themes, but the truth is that there is a something of a debate about the unity of Luke–Acts. While scholars today assume the unity of Luke and Acts and treat Luke–Acts as a single literary entity, this has not always been the case. Believe it or not, "Luke–Acts" with the hyphen or dash was not used by anyone until Henry Cadbury in 1927.[13] In other words, scholars have been thinking about Luke–Acts for less than a century. Across church history, in patristic, medieval, and early modern biblical interpretation, Luke was normally studied beside the other three canonical Gospels, while Acts was set beside the Pauline or Catholic epistles. Thus, Luke–Acts, with the notable hyphen or dash, is something of a recent novelty. In fact, Mikael Parsons and his coauthor wonder whether the hyphen in Luke–Acts needs to be loosened because each book represents "very distinct narratives

---

(Tübingen: Mohr Siebeck, 2009), 385-401; Samson Uytanlet, *Luke–Acts and Jewish Historiography: A Study on the Theology, Literature, and Ideology of Luke–Acts*, WUNT 2/340 (Tübingen: Mohr Siebeck, 2014), 21-23. Nils A. Dahl says that Luke betrays a "conscious intention . . . to write history in biblical style or, rather, to write the continuation of the biblical history." See Dahl, "The Story of Abraham in Luke–Acts," in *Studies in Luke–Acts*, ed. Leander E. Keck and J. L. Martyn (London: SPCK, 1968), 152-53.

[13]Henry Cadbury, *The Formation of Luke–Acts* (London: Macmiilan, 1927).

embodying different literary devices, generic conventions, and perhaps even theological concerns."[14] We have to remember that Luke and Acts can be read independently of each other, they were read independently of each other until relatively recently, they possess different genres, they can have different purposes, and they focus on different persons in different situations. Maybe Luke and Acts should go their own ways?

While a caveat about the reception of Luke and Acts is necessary, it is more probable than not that Luke wrote his Gospel with Acts in mind and that Acts was intended to be read by someone familiar with the Lukan Gospel. Evidence for that is (1) the prologues in Luke 1:1-4 and Acts 1:1 indicate that we have two parts of the one work, and Theophilus, the real reader, is expected to integrate both works in his own reading; (2) the consistent development of themes across Luke–Acts, such as promise and fulfillment, Gentile inclusion, Jesus as prophetic Messiah, Holy Spirit as promise and power, are indicative of a rhetorical, narrative, and theological unity; (3) material in the Lukan Gospel has been organized and distilled in light of what follows in Acts. For instance, Luke appears to omit material found in Mark (like the story of the Syro-Phoenician woman in Mark 7:24-30) because he is saving-up his best pro-Gentile stories for later. Some events in the Gospel anticipate what is to happen in Acts by giving attention to groups like the Samaritans who figure in the early Christian mission; (4) the ending of the Gospel is specifically drawn up with a view to the book of Acts as an intended sequel as apparent from the disciples being told to wait in Jerusalem until they receive the Holy Spirit (Lk 24:49).

---

[14]Mikael C. Parsons and Richard I. Pervo, *Rethinking the Unity of Luke and Acts* (Minneapolis: Fortress, 1993), 18; see also Patricia Walters, *The Assumed Authorial Unity of Luke and Acts: A Reassessment of the Evidence*, SNTSMS 145 (Cambridge: Cambridge University Press, 2009).

In sum, Joel B. Green is correct that Luke's purposes require him to write both his Gospel and the book of Acts. According to Green: "Luke's agenda is not to write the story of Jesus, followed by the story of the early church. . . . Rather, his design is to write the story of the continuation and fulfillment of God's project—a story that embraces both the work of Jesus and of the followers of Jesus after his ascension. From start to finish, Luke–Acts brings to the fore one narrative aim, the one aim of God."[15]

REVIEW QUESTIONS

1. What can be known about the author "Luke" from the text of Luke–Acts?
2. Whom did the early church think wrote the Third Gospel?
3. When were Luke and Acts probably written?
4. What genre are Luke and Acts?
5. What are the benefits of reading Luke and Acts together?

FURTHER READING

Alexander, Loveday. *Acts in Its Ancient Literary Context*. London: T&T Clark, 2007.

Armstrong, Karl L. *Dating Acts in Its Jewish and Greco-Roman Contexts*. LNTS 637. London: T&T Clark, 2021.

Bernier, Jonathan. *Rethinking the Dates of the New Testament: The Evidence for Early Composition*. Grand Rapids, MI: Baker, 2022.

Bird, Michael F. "The Unity of Luke–Acts in Recent Discussion." In *Rethinking the Unity and Reception of Luke–Acts*, ed. Andrew F. Gregory and C. Kavin Rowe, 3-22. Columbia: University of South Carolina Press, 2010.

Seccombe, David. "Dating Luke–Acts: Further Arguments for an Early Date." *TynBul* 71 (2021): 207-27.

---

[15] Joel B. Green, *The Theology of the Gospel of Luke*, NTT (Cambridge: Cambridge University Press, 1995), 47.

Spencer, Patrick E. "The Unity of Luke–Acts: A Four-Bolted Hermeneutical Hinge." *CurBR* 5 (2007): 341-66.

Strelan, Rick. *Luke the Priest: The Authority of the Author of the Third Gospel.* Aldershot, UK: Ashgate: 2007.

Wenham, John. "The Identification of Luke." *EvQ* 63 (1991): 3-44.

3

The Purposes of Luke–Acts

THE PROBLEM OF FINDING LUKE'S PURPOSE

People write for a reason. There is a reason I'm writing this book, this chapter, and this paragraph. There is a reason Julius Caesar wrote his *Gallic Wars* (i.e., to celebrate Caesar's Gallic campaign and to defend himself from criticisms of his character), and there is a reason Ralph Ellison wrote *Invisible Man* (i.e., to expose the hardships of African Americans in the 1950s). Luke's literary achievement is remarkable, taking us from Nazareth to Rome, encompassing a biography of Jesus and an historiographical narration of the beginnings of the early church. We must ask, Why? Why did Luke write Luke–Acts, and what was he trying to achieve? The problem is that, apart from the preface (Luke 1:1-4), Luke is not explicit about his literary intentions, so we have to infer them or work them out from a close reading of Luke–Acts.

At one level the genres of Luke and Acts tell us something about Luke's purposes. The Gospel of Luke, as a biography, narrates the story of Jesus to inform an audience who Jesus is, what he said and did, why he matters, why he died, how he died, and what about Jesus is admirable. The book of Acts, as historiography, narrates the beginnings of the early church and its spread from Jerusalem to Rome in order to present the church as an idealized community and to offer a positive account of the apostles Peter and especially Paul.

But even beyond the generalities of purpose associated with genre, we can identify Luke's stated purpose from his own words. Luke tells us in his prologue that he writes for Theophilus an "orderly account" (διήγησις, Luke 1:1) as a continuation and complement to the works of others (Mark and maybe Matthew). Luke writes not for the sake of posterity but so that Theophilus will have a sense of assurance about the things he has been told about Jesus and the apostles (Luke 1:1-4; Acts 1:1-2). Diane Chen comments that Luke intends to assure Theophilus and his circle that what they have "learned about Jesus is true and trustworthy, and that they must stay firm in their bold witness and faithful discipleship [even] in spite of persecution and rejection."[1] Similar is Alan Thompson: "Luke is writing to provide reassurance to believers about the nature of the events surrounding Jesus' life, death, resurrection, the spread of the message about Jesus, and the nature of God's people following Jesus' ascension."[2] Thus, Luke–Acts is a kind of advanced catechism for Theophilus and others like him, for people who desire to know more about Jesus and the apostles, who want to be rooted in the gospel story and understand the beginnings of the church.

There might also be several unstated purposes that Luke intends to achieve, or types of effects he wishes to have on an audience even if they are not plainly stated. The most obvious is, as we will see, the apologetic aspect. Luke has one eye on smears against Jesus, the early church, and the apostle Paul. Luke might also have his own response to Jewish objections to the Jesus movement, a scheme of Christian hope that he desires to advocate, a particular perspective

---

[1] Diane G. Chen, *Luke*, NCCS (Eugene, OR: Cascade, 2017), 8.
[2] Alan J. Thompson, *The Acts of the Risen Lord Jesus: Luke's Account of God's Unfolding Plan*, New Studies in Biblical Theology 27 (Downers Grove, IL: InterVarsity Press, 2011), 19.

on the Roman Empire that he weaves in, and a few erroneous views he intends to correct. Luke might have intended to achieve far more than what he materially says.

Otherwise, we need to also consider several utilities for Luke–Acts. That is, what Luke–Acts was used for, even if these uses were not specifically intended. For instance, Luke's Gospel, alongside the other Gospels, was used in Christian worship, as missionary literature, and as instruction for converts to the faith. The book of Acts was used as a refutation of heretics such as Marcion and also as a literary companion beside the general epistles to form a literary collection known as the Apostolos. Even up to the present time, Luke–Acts has several uses that Luke perhaps did not envisage, ranging from a manifesto for Christian socialism all the way through to a church-planting manual.[3] Luke–Acts has many utilities, a life beyond and beside anything Luke could have even imagined himself.

To recap, there are purposes for Luke–Acts associated with the genre of both books, Luke's stated aims to Theophilus, and his unstated aims, and there are also several utilities for Luke–Acts. The unstated aims are the most controversial. There scholars have to do some detective work or literary archaeology to find clues as to what Luke was up to beyond giving Theophilus and friends an advanced adult Sunday school class. This is what we'll explore in some depth.

PROPOSED PURPOSES FOR LUKE–ACTS

The various proposals for the purpose of Luke–Acts, with numerous variations, include the following:[4]

---

[3]See John C. Cort, *Christian Socialism: An Informal History* (Maryknoll, NY: Orbis, 1988); E. Elbert Smith, *Church Planting by the Book* (Alresford, UK: CLC International, 2015).

[4]Robert Maddox, *The Purpose of Luke-Acts* (Edinburgh: T&T Clark, 1982), 20-22; Jacob Jervell, *The Theology of the Acts of the Apostles*, NTT (Cambridge: Cambridge University

- to defend Paul at his trial
- to legally defend Christianity as a *religio licita* (i.e., legal religion)
- to defend Christianity to Romans
- to defend Christianity to Jews
- to defend Pauline Christianity to Jewish Christians
- to explain the persecution of Christians
- to attempt to unify the apostle Paul with Jerusalem traditions
- to combat certain heresies by means of telling a story
- to explain why Jesus has not returned by appeal to salvation history
- to provide a piece of missionary literature for either Jews or Gentiles
- to defend and confirm the message of salvation
- to show how Jesus and the early church embody the plan and purpose of God
- to explain the existence of a Jewish messianic sect in a Gentile world
- to provide sociological legitimation for the full inclusion of Gentiles in the church
- to attempt to reconcile Christian faith with common Judaism
- to prevent Jewish Christians from relapsing into Judaism
- to provide a polemical document against the Jews

Press, 1996), 11-17; Mark L. Strauss, "The Purpose of Luke–Acts: Reaching a Consensus," in *New Testament Theology in Light of the Church's Mission*, ed. J. C. Laansma, Grant Osborne, and R. Van Neste (Eugene, OR: Cascade, 2011), 135; Karl Allen Kuhn, *The Kingdom According to Luke and Acts: A Social, Literary, and Theological Introduction* (Grand Rapids, MI: Baker, 2015), 256-57.

Most of these views have something going for them; they seem at least partially right, so it is difficult to discern between them. That said, some views are probably more right than others, and some have a bit more explanatory power than others. I think it is reasonable to suggest that when it comes identifying the purposes of Luke–Acts we need to pay attention to four aspects: (1) the story of salvation, (2) the apologetic edge, (3) the polemical thrust, and (4) the matter of legitimacy. We can explore all four aspects to come to an informed view of the purposes of Luke–Acts.

THE STORY OF SALVATION IN LUKE'S GOSPEL

Luke has a rich and multifaceted understanding of God's salvation wrought in Jesus. This emphasis on salvation and deliverance is apparent from a cursory reading of Luke–Acts as the various horizons of salvation are set out. Notably, there is far more to Lukan salvation than the forgiveness of sins and something like going to heaven after death. Luke's notion of salvation covers various aspects ranging from Israel's own rescue, the problem of paganism for Gentiles, human frailty in a fallen world, and even spiritual and physical oppression. One might want to jump to the book of Acts and launch into the apostolic gospel sermons to explore the topic of salvation, but that would be premature, since there's much in Luke's Gospel on salvation. Luke takes his readers through a biography of Jesus because he wants to make four things about salvation abundantly clear.

God remembers Israel. First, God's salvation is seen in God's faithfulness to Israel as demonstrated in Jesus. The birth stories of John the Baptist and Jesus bristle with unexpected excitement that God at last is about to do something dramatic for his people. An angel tells Zechariah, "He [John] will turn many of the people of Israel to the Lord their God. With the spirit and power of Elijah he will go before him, to turn the hearts of parents to their children, and the disobedient to the wisdom of the righteous, to make ready a people prepared for the Lord" (Luke 1:16-17). Later, an angel tells Mary that through her the messianic deliverer is coming: "He will be great, and will be called the Son of the Most High, and the Lord God will give to him the throne of his ancestor David. He will reign over the house of Jacob forever, and of his kingdom there will be no end" (Luke 1:32-33). We have here the coming Elijah (Malachi 4:5) and the Davidic King (Isaiah 9:7; Jeremiah 23:5; Ezekiel 34:23-24).

In Mary's *Magnificat* (Luke 1:46-55) and Zechariah's *Benedictus* (Luke 1:67-79) there is a chorus of praise to "God my savior" (Luke 1:47), who has raised up a "horn of salvation for us in the house of his servant David" (Luke 1:69 NIV). All this transpires in relation to God's past, present, and future: his mercy, mighty deeds of deliverance, bringing down the mighty, lifting up the humble, remembering his servant Israel, remembering his covenant, agricultural abundance, making good his promises to Abraham, and the forgiveness of sins. The celebration is because the God of Israel has come to redeem his people (Luke 1:69). When Simeon meets the baby Jesus in the temple, he rejoices in finally seeing God's salvation, just as the prophetess Anna gives thanks to God for the child and for the "redemption of Jerusalem" (Luke 2:38).

We could easily take parts of Luke 1–2 and add them to the end of Malachi, and it would make perfect sense as an Old Testament story about Israel's God bringing forth a couple of new prophets to bring deliverance once again to Israel, this time under Roman rule. The major motifs are: God is coming, God is bringing his salvation, and this means redemption for Israel and a reordering of power for Israel's enemies. But there's a twist, as Simeon declares to the holy couple, "This child is destined for the falling and the rising of many in Israel, and to be a sign that will be opposed so that the inner thoughts of many will be revealed—and a sword will pierce your own soul too" (Luke 2:34-35). Salvation is coming, but perhaps not as people thought, perhaps not for whom some people thought, and maybe not everyone in Israel will receive it with gladness. So, while Luke narrates the story of salvation, the salvation that comes will be contested; there will be opposition from those within and around Israel.

Much of the Gospel of Luke is about Jesus dispensing salvation. Importantly, in Luke–Acts, salvation is holistic. It is not the immortality of the soul in a disembodied eternity. Rather, salvation includes healing (from illness, disability, demonic oppression, social ostracism, shame, and disgrace), cleansing, physical restoration, relational reconciliation with family and to God, escaping divine judgment, finding divine mercy, the liberation of a people group from foreign domination, and the forgiveness of sins. This salvation is in many ways coterminous with entering the kingdom of God, which is a mixture of destination, deliverance, and discipleship. If entrance into the kingdom entails the presence of salvation, then the kingdom must be entered and pursued, even if it costs a person their possessions or even their own mortal life. At several points, Jesus' kingdom preaching is married to acts of healing and exorcisms, so that the saving word and saving power are joined together (Luke 8:1-2; 9:2, 11; 11:20). Importantly, it is by placing faith in Jesus that many people are healed of their infirmities (Luke 7:50; 8:48-50; 17:19; 18:42). It is by believing and heeding Jesus' words that one is saved (Luke 8:12). This salvation is also universal, for the high and mighty as well as the lowly and humble (Luke 14:7-23; 19:2-10). Wherever Jesus goes, healing and hope follow, and this is what Israel's God promised his people and is now delivering on.

Jesus as Savior. In brief, "the story of Jesus," says Chen, "is the centrepiece of the plan of salvation ordained by the sovereign God, a plan that began with Israel but is intended for the nations."[5] Mary, in her famous song, rejoices in "God my savior" (Luke 1:47), a terrific reminder that Luke's Jesus story is fundamentally a God story about how God's redemptive reign and saving power hinge on the life, death, and resurrection of Jesus. Jesus too, is called "savior," prophesied from before his birth as "mighty savior" from the house of David (Luke 1:69), and acclaimed by angels as the Savior and messianic Lord (Luke 2:11). Furthermore, when Jesus explains his own prophetic vocation, he roots it in the scriptural promises of deliverance. In the "Nazareth Manifesto" the Lukan Jesus regards Isaiah 61:1 as his own job description: "The Spirit of the Lord is upon me, because he has anointed me to bring good news to the poor. He has sent me to proclaim release to the captives and recovery of sight to the blind, to let the oppressed go free, to proclaim the year of the Lord's favor" (Luke 4:18-19). Jesus believes he is following the Isaianic script to make Israel's postexilic deliverance a reality, and the healings he performs are the concrete proof of it (Luke 7:22-23). In addition, Jesus declares that he has come not to call the righteous "but sinners to repentance" (Luke 5:32) and "to seek out and to save the lost" (Luke 19:10).

Community of the saved. To follow Jesus is to join those being saved. This is clear in the parable of the narrow door (Luke 13:22-30). Salvation means experiencing the kingdom of God, both its current manifestation and its future consummation. Because this salvation is contested, opposed, doubted, chided, and sometimes abandoned, only a few will be saved. Salvation is like a narrow gate; many might consider it, try it, start it, but few will see it through to the end.

---

[5]Chen, *Luke*, 8.

Even though this salvation is universally offered, few embrace it. Many might claim familiarity with the master, but only those who have faith will receive him.

Salvation for outsiders. If the Jews reject the offer of salvation, then "others" will be saved. Salvation is clearly intended for Israel, that much is clear from Luke 1 to Luke 24. However, Jesus' preaching of the kingdom brings a rupture within Israel; some believe in him, some sneer at him, some earnestly oppose him. The Lukan Jesus does not come offering Israel grace over religion, morality over purity, much less a universalism to overcome their particularism. He comes to Israel bringing glad tidings of a new exodus where God's kingship is bristling and burgeoning in their midst, to warn of a judgment coming on all, to set forth an alternative way of being Israel, and to urge people to follow him as the last chance for Israel. He claims to speak for God, yet others say that this is not what God has told them. One can observe a distinct pattern beginning in Luke 4:16-30, one that continues in Paul's missionary career in Acts 13 and 17. This pattern goes synagogue sermon, scriptural fulfillment, initial acceptance, eventual rejection, and lethal attack.[6] While there is much joy in that God's salvation is reaching the covenant people, there is also deep lament that many Jews are turning their backs on it.

THE STORY OF SALVATION IN THE BOOK OF ACTS

Switching our attention to Acts, we find that the story of salvation continues unabated, albeit in the context of the postascension situation of the early church and its mission.

First, in the earliest days of the Jerusalem church, the people are urged to call on the name of the Lord and be saved (Acts 2:21). God

---

[6]John Dominic Crossan and Jonathan L. Reed, *Excavating Jesus: Beneath the Stones, Behind the Texts* (New York: HarperCollins, 2009), 63.

sent Jesus to Israel so that there would be "times of refreshing" and that "universal restoration" could come on Israel, as God announced long ago through his holy prophets (Acts 3:20-21). There is a strong sense in Acts that salvation does not bypass Israel or come despite Israel but comes through Israel to the Gentiles. Peter and Paul both remained fixated on sharing the gospel with their fellow Judeans and Diasporan Jews. Jews and Gentiles are both saved "through the grace of the Lord Jesus" (Acts 15:11).

Second, the proof of God's faithfulness is that Jesus was sent to Israel as their Savior for their repentance and forgiveness of sins (Acts 5:31; 13:23). Jesus is from God and for Israel; irrespective of how Gentiles are included, Jesus is Israel's own prince and deliverer. In fact, there's a certain degree of exclusivity in operation, a sort of Christofinality, as there is "no other name under heaven given among mortals by which we must be saved" (Acts 4:12) than that of Jesus.

Third, there are a couple of points where the message of salvation is considered the very purpose of the apostolic ministry. We see this especially in the account of Paul's ministry in Philippi. A slave girl with a pythonic spirit of divination pesters Paul by crying out to the people, "These men are slaves of the Most High God, who proclaim to you a way of salvation" (Acts 16:17), illustrating that even the spiritually afflicted can grasp the significance of the apostles' work. Also in Philippi, when the local jailer realizes that all the prisoners have been unchained, he asks Paul and Silas, "Sirs, what must I do to be saved?" to which they answer, "Believe on the Lord Jesus, and you will be saved, you and your household" (Acts 16:30-31).

Whatever we think of the story behind Luke–Acts, we have to admit that it is a story about salvation. Luke proclaims salvation for Jew and Gentile alike, by grace and through faith, a salvation of body and soul, a salvation that cuts across ethnic and economic distinctions, brought by Jesus the Savior and a God who is mighty to save. It is not salvation history—a demarcation of Israel, Jesus, and the church age—that is foremost but salvation itself. One of Luke's purposes is to declare and describe how God's saving purposes are worked out through Israel, in Jesus, and among Christ-believers in the Greco-Roman world.

> **God's Purpose Across Redemptive History According to Luke**
>
> "Luke's agenda is not to write the story of Jesus, followed by the story of the early church . . . Rather, his design is to write the story of the continuation and fulfillment of God's project—a story that embraces both the work of Jesus and of the followers of Jesus after his ascension. From start to finish, Luke–Acts brings to the fore one narrative aim, the one aim of God."[a]
>
> [a] Joel B. Green, *The Theology of the Gospel of Luke*, NTT (Cambridge: Cambridge University Press, 1995), 47.

THE APOLOGETIC CONCERN

Sometimes it is the last thing that someone mentions that gives you the best indication of their main concerns. One verse I regard as crucial in locating Luke's purpose is Acts 28:21-22, where the Jewish leaders in Rome say to Paul: "We have not received any letters from Judea concerning you, and none of our people who have come from there has reported or said anything bad about you. But we want to hear what your views are, *for we know that people everywhere are talking against this sect*" (NIV, emphasis added). Luke is aware that many people, Jews, Greeks, and Romans, are speaking against this peculiar sect of Christians for all sorts of reasons. Jews might be concerned that followers of Jesus are disloyal to the Scriptures, institutions, and traditions of Judaism. Greeks might think that

Christians are introducing strange and foreign gods into their cities. Romans might believe that Christians are a threat to the peace, security, and order of the Roman Empire. Luke, in different ways, tries to deflect these criticisms of Jesus and the early church. The purpose is, in the end, *an apologia pro evangelio*, a defense of the gospel.[7] Various aspects of Luke–Acts suggest this apologetic dimension.[8]

In defense of Jesus. To begin with, the preface to Luke's Gospel opens with Luke declaring that his aims include, among other things, Theophilus having a "secure knowledge" (NTE; ἀσφάλεια) about these matters, for he has been previously instructed (Luke 1:4). In other words, Luke's apologetic narrative for the gospel includes giving assurance that Jesus is the divine prophetic agent (Gospel of Luke) and that the apostolic testimony is the divinely approved message of a man who was "attested . . . by God" (Acts 2:22).

A person showing interest in the Christian religion, irrespective of whether they were a Jew or Gentile, would have been puzzled and perhaps put off by the fact that Jesus was executed as a criminal by a Roman governor.[9] The Lukan account of Jesus' trial and execution is accordingly filled with emphasis on his innocence. Luke weaves a narrative to portray Jesus as a victim of the scheming of the Judean priests, unjustly executed by Pilate, who is grotesquely indifferent to injustice, while Jesus himself is portrayed as a righteous man who dies a noble death.[10]

At the preliminary hearing before the Sanhedrin, Jesus is brought before the elders of the people, chief priests, and scribes, an assembly that is austere as much as representative of the Jerusalem

---

[7]Alexanderu Neagoe, *The Trial of the Gospel: An Apologetic Reading of Luke's Trial Narratives*, SNTSMS 116 (Cambridge: Cambridge University Press, 2002), 219-21.
[8]See survey in Philip F. Esler, *Community and Gospel in Luke–Acts: The Social and Political Motivations of Lucan Theology* (Cambridge: Cambridge University Press, 1989), 205-19.
[9]Neagoe, *Trial of the Gospel*, 83-84.
[10]On Jesus' noble death, see Jerome H. Neyrey, *An Encomium for Jesus: Luke, Rhetoric, and the Story of Jesus* (Sheffield: Sheffield Phoenix, 2020), 162-92.

The Purposes of Luke–Acts 41

leadership (Luke 22:66). Luke, in contrast to Mark, omits reference to the search for false witnesses (Mark 14:55-59) and splits the Markan version of Caiaphas's question whether Jesus is the Messiah into two parts (Mark 14:61; Luke 22:67-71).

As Jesus is led out before Pilate, the Sanhedrin's representatives accuse Jesus of seditious antitaxation views: "We found this man perverting our nation, forbidding us to pay taxes to the emperor, and saying that he himself is the Messiah, a king" (Luke 23:2). The reader knows this is patently false because earlier Jesus declared that taxes should be paid to Caesar (Luke 20:21-26). When Jesus is sent to Herod Antipas, Herod is amused and then bemused by Jesus, so Herod sends him back to Pilate, indicating that Herod thought he had no need to dispense with Jesus (Luke 23:8-11).

It is notable that no less than three times Pilate declares that he finds no basis for a punishment of Jesus (Luke 23:4, 14-15, 22). Pilate considers Jesus deranged but not worthy of death, so he has him scourged in the hope that such a penalty will satisfy the demands for his punishment (Luke 23:16). Yet Pilate, through either weakness or vacillation, eventually gives into the requests and hands Jesus over to be crucified (Luke 23:24). Jesus is then a victim of injustice by a weak Roman official. Even worse, the high priests accuse Jesus of sedition (Luke 23:2), yet they urge the release of Barabbas, a man accused of insurrection and murder. They free a man who has committed the very crime they accuse Jesus of committing (Luke 23:18-19).

Luke also presents a more intricate account of Jesus' interaction with the bandits crucified with him. Whereas Mark reports that the two bandits joined in the derision of Jesus (Mark 15:32), Luke tells us that one bandit mocked Jesus, while the other bandit rebukes the first one on the grounds that they are both guilty, whereas "this man has done nothing wrong" (Luke 23:41). To this Jesus replies that both he and his confessor will be united in paradise, the blissful part of the place for the righteous dead (Luke 23:39-43). Thereafter, Luke also alters Mark's material when, rather than having the centurion confess that Jesus is a son of a god (Mark 15:39), has him declare about Jesus, "Surely this was a righteous man" (Luke 23:47 NIV).

In the end, Jesus is not a rebel (Luke 23:2), bandit (Luke 22:52), enemy of Caesar (Luke 23:4), or enemy of Herod (Luke 23:15). Plus, he's hailed as innocent by the co-executed (Luke 23:41) and by his very executioner (Luke 23:47).

The emphasis on Jesus' innocence is not really about the uprightness of his character as much as his identity and legitimacy. Jesus really is Israel's Messiah (despite the howling protests of the high priests), and he really did nothing wrong (which even Pilate knew full well). Beyond the judicial defense of Jesus as innocent are a cluster of christological claims. In Luke's testimony, Jesus really is the Lord's Messiah (Luke 2:11, 26), a "man attested to you by God" (Acts 2:22), and the divinely appointed agent for the restoration of Israel (Luke 2:25; 24:21; Acts 1:6; 3:20-21). Jesus' death is not evidence against that claim; rather, Jesus' death is part of the purpose of God—things divinely determined and that must be fulfilled—to bring salvation to Israel and the Gentiles (Luke 9:22, 44; 18:31; 22:22; 24:7). Jesus was neither a bandit nor a victim of unfortunate circumstances.

While those who killed Jesus remain culpable for their actions, nonetheless behind the cross stands neither the high priest's jealously nor Pilate's vacillation but the "definite plan and foreknowledge of God" (Acts 2:23). Jesus' death was according to God's plan as given in Scripture. Plus, whatever ignominy was inflicted on Jesus, God reversed it by raising him from the dead and exalting him to his right hand. Hence Peter's claim: "Therefore let the entire house of Israel know with certainty that God has made him both Lord and Messiah, this Jesus whom you crucified" (Acts 2:36). The point is emphasized at length, that the Judean leaders hung him on a tree, "but God raised him" (Acts 2:24; 10:40; 13:30; see also Acts 13:37). If God's raising up of Jesus reverses the unjust and cruel death that Jesus was subjected to, then Jesus' exaltation to his right hand reverses his status from the shallows of shame and places him on the podium of divine glory. The purpose is reversal for redemptive history, because Jesus' exalted status—for Israel's redemption and as a revelation to the Gentiles—is bound up with God undoing what was done to Jesus. What is more, if God has reversed what the Judeans did to Jesus, then the Judeans need to repent, to reverse their verdict on who Jesus is.

In defense of the early church. The apologetic angle is continued in Acts with several episodes exonerating the Christians from various allegations.

The story of the early church is replete with incidents and stories designed to show that the church is not a rabble of religious fanatics, but in fact God is behind the whole Jesus movement. For a start, the risen Jesus appeared to his disciples and "presented himself alive to them by many convincing proofs" (Acts 1:3). Next, Peter's speech at Pentecost invokes a mixture of testimony and proof from prophecy to show that Jesus was a "a man attested to you by God with deeds of power, wonders, and signs that God did through him among you" (Acts 2:22). Jesus' resurrection is God's reversal of what the Judean leadership and Romans did to Jesus, and Jesus' exaltation is God's reversal of his status from shame to heavenly supremacy (Acts 2:32-36).

There is an idealized account of the church in Acts 2:43-47, where there is a marked increase of those being saved. Luke shows that Christians embody true *philanthropia* by how they treat each other and outsiders. There are various accounts of healings in Jesus' name to underscore its divine and almost mystical power (Acts 3:16; 4:10, 30). There is the Christian community's handling of divisions within its constituency (Acts 6:1-7), and Stephen is the model martyr who continues the message of Jesus in virtue of his opposition to the temple and his willingness to challenge the place of the Mosaic tradition (Acts 6:13-14). Everywhere Christian leaders go there are healings, courageous stands for faith, and multiple converts. Luke's intention is to declare that the reason Jesus and his followers are so successful is that they act according to the plan and purpose of God (Acts 2:23). Hence Rabbi Gamaliel's remarks to the Sanhedrin:

> A Pharisee named Gamaliel stood up in the Sanhedrin. He was a teacher of the law. He was honored by all the people. He ordered the apostles to be taken outside for a little while. Then Gamaliel spoke to the Sanhedrin. "Men of Israel," he said, "think carefully about what you plan to do to these men. Some time ago Theudas appeared. He claimed he was really somebody. About 400 people followed him. But he was killed. All his followers were scattered. So they accomplished nothing. After this, Judas from Galilee came along. This was in the days when the Romans made a list of all the people. Judas led a gang of men against the Romans. He too was killed. All his followers were scattered. So let me give you some advice. Leave these men alone! Let them go! If their plans and actions only come from people, they will fail. But if their plans come from God, you won't be able to stop these men. You will only find yourselves fighting against God." (Acts 5:34-39 NIRV)

The reason nobody can stop the Christians, neither the Sanhedrin, nor local officials, nor Roman proconsuls, is that God is with them and behind them.

Paul's testimony and ministry come up for repeated scrutiny. Luke presents, no fewer than three times, Paul's conversion story and his call by God to go to the Gentiles (Acts 9:1-19; 22:6-21; 26:12-23). Luke clearly accentuates Paul's Jewish credentials, ministry to Jews, and commitment to the traditions of Israel (Acts 18:6; 21:17-26; 23:1-11; 26:4-23). While Paul runs afoul of Roman authorities every so often, the depiction of the Roman officials ranges from the positive (Acts 13:7, 12; 27:1), to indifferent (Acts 18:17), to corrupt (Acts 24:26), to partisan (Acts 24:27). Paul protests his own innocence before Jewish and Roman authorities (Acts 23:1; 24:10-20; 25:8; 26:2-29; 28:17-22), and even the Judean monarch Herod Agrippa II affirms Paul's innocence to the governor Festus (Acts 26:31-32). In fact, the exchange between Festus and Agrippa II is comical. Paul has appealed to the emperor to hear his case, but Festus is still at a loss as to what the charge against him even is. We could imagine Paul's reception in Rome as something like, "'Sir, this man was sent by the Procurator in Judaea, because he is a citizen who appealed to Caesar in his defence.' 'Defense against what charge?' 'Well, sir, there is no charge.'"[11] Paul and his mission are not against God's purposes, Roman peace and security, or even against Israel's sacred traditions, but run aground on Jewish obstinacy and Roman injustice.

The apologetic dimension does not mean that Luke craves acceptance in the halls of Greek philosophy, in the forum of the Roman senate, or behind the doors of Jewish synagogues. But Luke does seek to address rumors and falsehoods raised by Gentile inquirers and Jewish detractors. He urges that Christians are neither troublemakers that civic officials should be wary of nor traitors to the Judean religion that synagogue leaders should excommunicate on sight. Luke's point is that Christians are faithful in the context of messianic fulfillment, and they exemplify true piety and true

---

[11]Steve Mason, "Speech-Making in Ancient Rhetoric, Josephus, and Acts: Messages and Playfulness, Part II," *Early Christianity* 3 (2012): 169.

philosophy by refusing idolatry. The utility of apologetic writings is that they can be useful both for internal consumption by adherents and as literature shared with outsiders.

> **Was Luke the First Apologist?**
>
> "The author of Acts has the right to ... be recognised as the first Christian apologist. The great age of Christian apologetic was the second century, but of the three main types of defence represented among the second-century Christian apologists Luke provides first-century proto-types: defence against pagan religion (Christianity is true; paganism is false), defence against Judaism (Christianity is the fulfilment of true Judaism), defence against political accusations (Christianity is innocent of any offence against Roman law)."[a]
>
> [a] F. F. Bruce, *The Book of Acts*, New International Commentary on the New Testament (Grand Rapids, MI: Eerdmans, 1988), 22.

THE POLEMICAL EDGE

In addition to proclaiming salvation and defending Christians against multiple allegations, Luke does have something of a polemical edge in places.

Luke is aware that the coming of Jesus brings a division within Israel. Simeon tells the holy parents, "This child is destined to cause the falling and rising of many in Israel" (Luke 2:34 NIV). The Lukan Jesus testifies that he has come to "bring fire to the earth," which will result in a division among Jewish families (Luke 12:49). His rejection at Nazareth, his hometown, is typical of the negative reception he gets from his fellow Judeans (Luke 4:14-30). Jesus' critiques of the Herodians, Sadducees, scribes, and Pharisees place himself in opposition to the official and unofficial leaders of the Jewish people. Luke clearly has an issue with Judean rejection of Jesus as a prophet (Luke 13:34) and Messiah (Luke 22:67). He raises the charge against the people of Israel that they are the ones who crucified Jesus (Acts 2:23, 36; 4:10). Acts ends with a quotation from Isaiah 6:9-10 about Israel's unwillingness or inability to believe in Jesus as their Messiah. Luke polemicizes against Judean opposition to Jesus, Jewish persecution of the church in the eastern Mediterranean, and Jewish resistance to the message of the gospel. This subject will require a chapter of its own, but for now we can note that Luke both laments and criticizes Jewish antagonism toward Jesus and the church.

Luke also has an axe to grind against the rich and powerful. Mary's Magnificat includes the memorable words that God "has brought down rulers from their thrones but has lifted up the humble" (Luke 1:52 NIV). Across the Gospel, there is a lot of material on wealth and the rich, how possessions and power are a snare, leaving some caught in destruction. Luke believes that the rich are greedy (Luke 12:15) and the powerful are tyrannical (Luke 19:27). For them, there is to be a reordering of power where the first will be last and the last will be first (Luke 13:30). In a world where the rich got richer and the poor got poorer, where might made right, Luke tells a story where there is a great reversal, for in the kingdom of God status and states are reversed.

It is also likely that Luke polemicizes against the Roman Empire. Luke–Acts is fertile ground for counterimperial and postcolonial readings. Luke's Gospel begins by setting up the coming of the prophesied Son of David in a world dominated militarily, politically, and socially by the son of Augustus. Much can be said about Luke and the Roman Empire; suffice it for now to say that Luke does not see Jesus or the apostles setting up something like the Judean People's Front. Luke is fully aware of the predatory and pernicious nature of Roman power. The kingdom of God is in a sense a rival empire, because the vestiges of Roman power will one day be swept aside. But for the moment, the church is not trying to overthrow the empire as much as set up a rival and subversive colony inside it. There are some noble Romans in the story (e.g., Sergius Paulus), but Rome is simply a symptom of a wider problem, a world caught in the thrall of evil powers.

It might not be clear at first, but Luke does along the way take a dig at certain other Christian groups. To begin with, Luke emphasizes the physicality of Jesus' resurrection by having Jesus declare, "Touch me and see; a ghost does not have flesh and bones, as you see I have" (Luke 24:39 NIV). Such a view might be a tacit attack on those who believed that Jesus' resurrection was nonphysical, that it was immaterial or purely spiritual. Such things were known in early Christianity by those steeped in Hellenistic antipathy toward the physical body, or at least the prospect of a postmortem physical body (see 1 Corinthians 15:35-49). Also, the Samaritan convert to Christianity Simon, a magician thought to be inhabited by "the power of God that is called great," ends up trying to purchase spiritual power from Peter, which Peter rebuffs (Acts 8:20). When the later church wrote the history of heresy, Simon the Magician (i.e., Magus) was considered the arch-heretic behind all heresies, including Gnosticism.[12] Luke probably has no little disgust with antigospel Jewish Christians from the party of Pharisees who wanted to compel Gentile converts to obey the Torah alongside faith in Christ (Acts 15:1-5). Luke–Acts is not an antiheresy tract, but it does show that some forms of Christian faith are, from Luke's perspective at least, considered unwholesome or even deviant.

Finally, Luke arguably has a polemical orientation against paganism, that is, Greco-Roman religion. Luke shares Jewish antipathy to idols. Stephen points out the dark moment in Israel's

---

[12] Stephen Haar, *Simon Magus: The First Gnostic?* BZNW 119 (Berlin: de Gruyter, 2003).

history when it engaged in idol worship during the exodus (Acts 7:41). In the city of Paphos (on the island of Cyprus), Paul and Barnabas are able to show up a magician and false prophet named Bar-Jesus before the proconsul (Acts 13:5-12). When Paul arrived in Athens, he walked around the city and he was positively disgusted by the idols in the city, like a germaphobe walking around a sewer (Acts 17:16). Luke reports with great joy the number of people who burned magic scrolls following Paul's successful preaching in Ephesus (Acts 19:19). It is no wonder that the main opponents of the Christians in Ephesus were the idol makers, because they had the most to lose with the success of Christian preaching, which included a denunciation of idols and an affirmation of an immaterial and translocal God (see Acts 14:15-18; 17:22-31).

THE LEGITIMATING FUNCTION

We could probably combine the salvific, apologetic, and polemic aspects if we see one of Luke's central purposes as to legitimate the Christian movement as an authentically, divinely established phenomenon. Luke writes to validate Jesus as God's agent par excellence and to extol the early church as an ideal society that exemplifies true piety and is made up of genuine heirs of Israel's religious heritage. Accordingly, Luke accents the ministry of Jesus as the fulfillment of God's plan (Luke 4:14-16). He affirms that Jesus' death and resurrection happened because the Messiah had to suffer and enter his glory (Luke 24:26). God poured out his Spirit on the church, precisely through Jesus, which vindicates Jesus and empowers the church for their mission (Acts 2). The Gentile mission was launched not because of human ingenuity but because of God's purposes (Acts 13:2; 15:14-18). In the three accounts of Paul's conversion and his call to go to the Gentiles, what is stressed is God's intervention in Paul's life to make him the apostle to the Gentiles (Acts 9:15-16; 22:2-5, 23:6; 24:14-16; 26:1-18). In fact, the conversion stories as a whole are not just random reports from the mission field; rather, they buttress the idea that God is for them, moving among them, calling Jews and Gentiles into this new community. As Mark Strauss puts it:

> The conversion accounts in Acts, while certainly models for unbelievers to follow, are, more importantly, evidence for the unrelenting progress of the gospel, proof that Jesus is the Messiah, and confirmation that the church made up of Jews and Gentiles represents the true people of God. This theme fits a legitimizing purpose better than an evangelistic one.[13]

Because this is the case, Luke's apologetics are intended to reassure believers in the truth they've been taught; his polemics are meant to reinforce distinctions from outsiders, with the overall effect of reaffirming for readers the inerasable worth of their shared group identity in a complex and contested sociopolitical and religious world. Gentile believers, perhaps such as Theophilus, can be assured that they are part of God's people, they are rooted in Israel's ancient religious tradition, they have turned from superstition to the true and living God, and they have experienced the fresh power of God's Holy Spirit.

THE PURPOSE OF LUKE–ACTS REVISITED

Why did Luke write Luke and Acts? The problem is that Luke may have had more than one purpose in mind. These purposes seem to involve a proclamation of salvation, an apologetic concern, a polemical edge, and a legitimating function. Yet Luke's intentions may have been even more comprehensive. Luke may have intended

---

[13]Strauss, "Purpose of Luke–Acts," 140.

his Gospel to function similar to how Mark's Gospel functioned in churches, something for private edification, public reading, or even missional literature. Luke may have wanted to amplify elements of Mark's story, to take the same story in a new direction, based on his own discrete interests and concerns. Maybe Luke thought his history of the church was a literary accomplishment similar to the history of the Romans or the history of the Pythagoreans, a history intended to inform as much as inspire and edify. Beyond that, Luke's two-volume work may have surplus utility and function in ways he did not envisage: as a foundational narrative, a manifesto for the church vis-à-vis the synagogue and state, or as a political apology for Christianity in the empire.

REVIEW QUESTIONS

1. How is a text's purpose different from its utility?
2. Does the genre of Luke and Acts indicate Luke's purpose?
3. To what extent does telling the story of salvation explain Luke's purpose?
4. In what senses are Luke and Acts apologetic writings?
5. Why does Luke emphasize the noble death of Jesus and the innocence of the apostle Paul?
6. What do we learn from Luke's purpose if we compare his account of the passion story with Mark's version?
7. What parts of Luke–Acts make us suspect that Luke might be polemicizing against certain ideas or groups?

FURTHER READING

Alexander, Loveday. "The Acts of the Apostles as an Apologetic Text." In *Apologetics in the Roman Empire*, 15-44. Oxford: Oxford University Press, 1999.

Maddox, Robert. *The Purpose of Luke–Acts*. Studies of the New Testament and Its World. Edinburgh: T&T Clark, 1982.

Marguerat, Daniel. *The First Christian Historian: Writing the "Acts of the Apostles."* SNTSMS 121. Cambridge: Cambridge University Press, 2002.

Neagoe, Alexandru. *The Trial of the Gospel: An Apologetic Reading of Luke's Trial Narratives*. SNTSMS 116. Cambridge: Cambridge University Press, 2002.

Shellard, Barbara. *New Light on Luke: Its Purpose, Sources, and Literary Context*. London: T&T Clark, 2004.

Strauss, Mark L. "The Purpose of Luke–Acts: Reaching a Consensus." In *New Testament Theology in Light of the Church's Mission*, edited J. C. Laansma, Grant Osborne, and R. Van Neste, 135-50. Eugene, OR: Cascade, 2011.

Wenham, David. "The Purpose of Luke–Acts: Israel's Story in the Context of the Roman Empire." In *Reading Luke: Interpretation, Reflection, Formation*, edited by Craig G. Bartholomew, Joel B. Green, and Anthony C. Thiselton, 79-103. Grand Rapids, MI: Zondervan, 2005.

4

Luke

Historian or Theologian?

IS LUKE MORE LIKE WILLIAM RAMSAY OR C. S. LEWIS?

Sir William M. Ramsay (1851–1939) was a Scottish archaeologist and New Testament scholar. When everyone was drunk on new wine from nineteenth-century Tübingen with its skepticism toward the historicity of the New Testament, Ramsay displayed some Scottish common sense realism and demonstrated from his archaeological digs in Turkey ample evidence to historically corroborate a great deal of the missionary journeys of the apostle Paul.[1] We could think of Luke as a prototype of Ramsay, a true historian, interrogating eyewitnesses, weighing up evidence, and excavating texts to get to the bottom of the stories of Jesus, Paul, and the apostles.

But Luke's purpose lies far beyond proving naked historical facts. Luke is not wishing to merely show that Jesus really said *x*, Peter really did *y*, or Paul truly visited *z*. Luke's apologetic approach might vouchsafe the historical trustworthiness of his account, but he is interested in more than setting the historical record straight. Luke's purpose is not to establish the truthfulness of what happened as much as it is to show the

---

[1] W. Ward Gasque, *Sir William M. Ramsay, Archaeologist and New Testament Scholar: A Survey of His Contribution to the Study of the New Testament* (Grand Rapids, MI: Baker, 1966).

truthfulness of the way of Jesus and the apostles. In other words, Luke doesn't want to prove the history of Jesus as much as inspire people to follow Jesus and join the community that worships him.

Maybe, then, Luke was more like C. S. Lewis (1898–1963), a literary theorist, Christian convert, and amazing storyteller who wrote the *Chronicles of Narnia*. Lewis had a simple yet elegant writing style, full of symbolism and informed by classical and medieval literature, that helped people imagine a world that made the truth of Christianity attractive through the genre of fantasy. Obviously, Luke was not a young adult fantasy novelist, but he does have a flair for the dramatic, a gift for creating tension, building characters, and showing us a world behind the one in front of us. Perhaps Luke was the C. S. Lewis of his own day, using artful storytelling to defend and proclaim the truth of the Christian message.

My suggestion, as you can probably guess, is that Luke has a bit of both Ramsay and Lewis in him. Yes, Luke is a historian, writing his account of Jesus and the early church according to the historiographical conventions of his day. But Luke is also a literary artist; he writes to persuade, to rouse, to surprise, and to imagine a world where Jesus is Lord and Caesar is a sideshow. So in this chapter we are going to look at how Luke is both a historian and a theologian.

LUKE AS HISTORIAN

Luke is commonly regarded as the first historian of the church. This is certainly true, and much of what we know about the beginnings of early Christianity is indebted to Luke. A historical purpose and historical consciousness on the part of Luke is clearly implied by his preface in Luke 1:1-4 (NRSV modified):

> Since *many* have undertaken to set down an orderly account of the events that have been fulfilled among us, just as they were *handed on to us* by those who from the beginning were *eyewitnesses* and servants of the word, I too decided, after *carefully gaining familiarity with everything* from the very first, to write an orderly account for you, most excellent Theophilus, so that you may know the *reliability* of the things about which you have been instructed.

In the words italicized above I highlight aspects that underscore the historical quality of Luke's narrative. This preface introduces both the Gospel and Acts in much the same way as Josephus's preface in book 1 of *Against Apion* (1.1-5) introduces the whole work, with the preface of book 2 recapitulating the same preface from the previous book (2.1-2).

The verisimilitude of the multivolume work is emphasized by Luke through a number of elements. To begin with, Luke locates his work in a chain of transmission running from the "eyewitnesses and servants of the word" → the "many" who have written an "orderly account" previously → Luke himself, and finally → Theophilus. Luke acknowledges that he is a second- or third-generation believer in Jesus and is himself dependent on others in his narration. The material that he is working with comes from "eyewitnesses" and "servants of the word" and denotes a proximity to the events themselves.[2] Through this mention of eyewitnesses, Luke is arguably emphasizing his work as an autopsy, which is the visual means of gathering information concerning an object of inquiry.[3] E. Earle Ellis contends, "The reference to 'eyewitnesses' is a

---

[2] The designation of "eyewitnesses" and "servants" probably indicates one group rather than two separate and successive groups, and it is this initial layer of persons who testified about and transmitted further the tradition as well as providing the leadership function in the nascent Jesus movement.

[3] Samuel Byrskog, *Story as History, History as Story: The Gospel Tradition in the Context of Ancient Oral History* (Leiden: Brill, 2002), 48-49, 228-32; Richard Bauckham, *Jesus and the Eyewitnesses: The Gospels as Eyewitness Testimony* (Grand Rapids, MI: Eerdmans, 2006), 116-24.

calculated answer to an explicit concern. It reflects the conviction that the Christian faith is rooted not in speculative creation but in historical reality."[4]

The material has also been "handed on" (παραδίδωμι), which is a near technical term for the faithful transmission of traditions about one's religious beliefs and practices (e.g., 1 Corinthians 11:2, 23; 15:3; Mark 7:13; Acts 6:14; Jude 3). That the traditions have been passed on "just as they were handed on to us" implies a consciousness of the possibility of false or inaccurate transmission, which Luke insinuates that he is avoiding.[5] Luke also states that he has undertaken this literary task only after "investigating everything carefully," and the word παρακολουθέω means not so much "investigating" as it means "following with the mind." Luke sets forth his credentials as one who has thoroughly understood the accounts that he has received.[6]

Luke ends his preface, quite deliberately, with assurances that what Theophilus has been instructed in is "reliable," and the Greek word (ἀσφάλεια) has connotations of security, firmness, and assurety.[7] That assurance extends to both the actual events referred to and the meaning Luke has attributed to the events through his storied account of the God of Israel. He is intending, like others before him, to write an "orderly account" (διήγησις) of the events transmitted to him by his sources. On the one hand, in historiographical works this word means a well-ordered and polished feat of historical writing, but on the other hand the

---

[4] E. Earle Ellis, *The Gospel of Luke* (London: Thomas Nelson, 1966), 63.
[5] François Bovon, *Luke 1: A Commentary on the Gospel of Luke 1:1–9:50* (Minneapolis: Fortress, 2002), 21.
[6] David P. Moessner, "The Appeal and Power of Poetics (Luke 1:1-4): Luke's Superior Credentials (παρηκολουθηκότι), Narrative Sequence (καθεξῆς), and Firmness of Understanding (ἀσφάλειαν) for the Reader," in *Jesus and the Heritage of Israel: Luke's Narrative Claim upon Israel's Legacy* (Harrisburg, PA: Trinity Press International, 1999), 84-123.
[7] BDAG, 147. See also Rick Strelan, "A Note on ἀσφαλεια (Luke 1.4)," *JSNT* 30 (2007): 163-71.

word is also used in the New Testament in the sense of recounting the mighty deeds of God (Mark 5:16; 9:9; Luke 9:10; Acts 9:27; 12:17; Hebrews 11:32). As an "orderly account," then, Luke's literary enterprise is touted as accurate, arranged in such a way as to be persuasive, and also aims to recount the very deeds of God. H. C. Kee comments:

> Obviously taking a position in the historical tradition, the author of this gospel is keenly interested in historical evidence, the reliability of the witnesses to whom he has turned for evidence, the preparation of a systematic record of the events and testimony, and convincing readers of the veracity of his report. Thus, concern for historicity is not a modern innovation, but is as old as the New Testament writings themselves.[8]

However, to grant that Luke has a historical intent brings to the surface a number of important questions. For a start, what we mean by *history* in our age might not be the same as what Luke and writers of antiquity thought about history. G. E. Sterling writes:

> To place Luke–Acts into the framework of ancient historiography does not presuppose a settlement of the issue of veracity. The relevance of this to that question is to ask what we mean by the category of history into which we place Luke–Acts. The issue of reliability can only be fully addressed once we understand the historiographical tradition of Luke–Acts and comprehend what the tasks and expectations of that tradition were.[9]

What kind of history was Luke writing, and exactly how historical was it? In certain pockets of New Testament research, it has been common to regard Luke–Acts as of limited historical value and

---

[8] Howard Clark Kee, *The Beginnings of Christianity: An Introduction to the New Testament* (New York: T&T Clark, 2005), 2.
[9] G. E. Sterling, *Historiography and Self-Definition: Josephus, Luke–Acts, and Apologetic Historiography*, NovTSup 64 (Leiden: Brill, 1992), 3.

more of a theological work.¹⁰ Luke "is not a historian but a preacher," argues Martin Dibelius, so "we must not allow our attempts to prove the authenticity of the speeches to cloud our perception of their kerygmatic nature."¹¹ Other scholars who have approached Luke and Acts in light of archaeology, papyrology, numismatics, inscriptions, and literary works of antiquity have urged that Luke be taken seriously as a historian.¹² Still others take more of a mediating position and argue that, all things being equal, Luke is well versed in the geographical, political, social, and religious realities of his day, but he is not necessarily accurate at every point and often is more concerned with the truth of Christianity than with its historical accuracy. But while Luke might be biased or was not always as informed as he could have been, his narration might still be close to what happened or at least the best educated guess that one could expect a historian to make.¹³ Let me give three examples of why Luke's accuracy as a historian is often questioned.

The census under Quirinius. In the midst of the Lukan infancy narrative we read:

> In those days a decree went out from Caesar Augustus that all the world should be registered. This was the first registration and was taken while Quirinius was governor of Syria. All went to their own towns to be registered. Joseph also went from the town of Nazareth in

---

¹⁰Todd Penner, *In Praise of Christian Origins: Stephen and the Hellenistic Apologetic Historiography* (New York: T&T Clark, 2004), 1-59.
¹¹Martin Dibelius, *Studies in the Acts of the Apostles* (London: SCM Press, 1956), 184.
¹²William M. Ramsay, *The Bearing of Recent Discovery on the Trustworthiness of the New Testament* (London: Hodder & Stoughton, 1953); Ramsay, *Pictures of the Apostolic Church: Studies in the Book of Acts* (Grand Rapids, MI: Baker, 1959); F. F. Bruce, *The Acts of the Apostles: The Greek Text with Introduction and Commentary* (Grand Rapids, MI: Eerdmans, 1951); A. N. Sherwin-White, *Roman Society and Roman Law in the New Testament* (Oxford: Clarendon, 1963); Colin Hemer, *The Book of Acts in the Setting of Hellenistic History* (Tübingen: Mohr Siebeck, 1989).
¹³C. K. Barrett, *Acts of the Apostles*, ICC (Edinburgh: T&T Clark, 1994–1998), 2:xxxiii-lxii; Barrett, "The Historicity of Acts," *JTS* 50 (1999): 515-34; Joseph A. Fitzmyer, *The Acts of the Apostles*, Anchor Bible (New York: Doubleday, 1998), 124-52.

Galilee to Judea, to the city of David called Bethlehem, because he was descended from the house and family of David. He went to be registered with Mary, to whom he was engaged and who was expecting a child. (Luke 2:1-5 NRSVUE)

The historicity of this account is disputed on several grounds: (1) there is no record of an empire-wide census carried out by Augustus; (2) Quirinius was not the governor of Syria in 4 BC, when Jesus was born, but later in AD 6, after the death of Herod the Great and after Archelaus was deposed as tetrarch of Judea (Josephus, *Ant.* 17.342-344; 17.354–18.2; 18.26; Tacitus, *Annales* 3.48); (3) Quirinius instigated a census, and this act precipitated a revolt (Josephus, *Ant.* 18.1-10); (4) it is unreasonable that a census would require everyone in the empire or even in Palestine to return to their hometowns in order to be registered; and (5) the account is said to be an imaginative story made up by Luke to have Jesus born in Bethlehem in order to fulfill biblical prophecy in retrospect (i.e., Micah 5:2), when in reality he was probably born in the same place he grew up: Nazareth of the Galilee.

The evidence above would not seem to bode well for the historicity of Luke's account. But there are other factors to consider as well:[14] (1) Although there is no evidence for an empire-wide census, Augustus did demonstrate an unprecedented zeal for fiscal rationalization, and he set up a register of resources for the whole empire (Tacitus, *Annales* 1.11; Dio Cassius, *Roman History* 53.30.2). Several provinces in the empire, such as Egypt, Syria, Gaul, and Spain, were on various yearly cycles for registration. The reference to such a census by Luke may have expressed the fact of a coordinated empire-wide financial policy of Augustus, in which case

---

[14] See Wayne A. Brindle, "The Census and Quirinius: Luke 2:2," *JETS* 27 (1984): 43–52.

Luke captures perfectly the mood of the economic policies of the Augustan regime.[15] (2) A census may have been instigated by Herod the Great or else by Syrian governors Saturinus (10–7 BC) or Varus (7–4 BC), who reported the findings of the census to Augustus. (3) Joseph may have returned to Bethlehem to register inheritance so as not to forfeit his claim on ancestral lands. In AD 104, C. Vibius Maximus required absentee landlords in Egypt to return to their hometowns for a census in Egypt, and a similar thing may have happened in Palestine. (4) Although some argue that Quirinius held an earlier governorship of Syria during the reign of Herod the Great, this is unlikely as far as the sources tell us.[16] Quirinius was consul of Rome in 12 BC, appointed adviser to Gaius Caesar (Augustus's adopted son) in Armenia in AD 1, and made governor of Syria in AD 6–7. The fact is that we do not know for sure what Quirinius was doing between 12 BC and AD 1. He may have held some kind of administrative position in the East when putting down a revolt in Cilicia (Tacitus, *Annales* 3.48).[17] Another possibility is that he was procurator (i.e., the emperor's personal representative) in Syria while Saturinus or Varus was governor of Syria.[18]

The speeches of Acts. The speeches in Acts are significant because they take up 25 percent of the entire book and represent one of the chief means through which Luke communicates his theological point of view. While there is some debate as to exactly how many speeches there are in Acts, there are approximately twenty-four

---

[15] Alfred Plummer, *The Gospel According to St. Luke*, ICC (Edinburgh: T&T Clark, 1896), 48 (esp. n1); John Nolland, *Luke*, Word Biblical Commentary (Dallas: Word, 1989–1993), 1:99; Bovon, *Luke 1*, 83.
[16] Ramsay, *Bearing of Recent Discovery*, 275-300.
[17] See Nolland, *Luke*, 1:99-103; Darrell L. Bock, *Luke*, Baker Exegetical Commentary on the New Testament (Grand Rapids, MI: Baker, 1994–1996), 1:903-9; Paul Barnett, *Jesus and the Rise of Early Christianity* (Downers Grove, IL: InterVarsity Press, 1999), 97-99.
[18] Nathanael Andrade, *Tried by Pontius Pilate: Why Did Jesus Die?* (Oxford: Oxford University Press, forthcoming).

speeches in only twenty-eight chapters. The speeches are frequent, even if brief.[19]

From a historical vantage point, the problem is of course to what degree Luke has faithfully represented these speeches in their original delivery, given that

- He was not an eyewitness to many of them (esp. those delivered in Jerusalem).

- The speeches have a somewhat uniform character in line with Luke's theology, and some of their contents could be said to have an acute repetitiveness in the recapitulation of themes and motifs.[20] These themes include (1) the transcendent God who acts out his purposes in the world, (2) God's purposes as made known in Jesus, (3) the fulfillment of God's plan and purposes, (4) the advent of the age of salvation, and (5) witness.[21]

- In some instances, the Pauline speeches seem to diverge from the theology of Paul's letters. For instance, contrast the

Table 4.1. The primary speeches in Acts

SPEAKER	REFERENCE
Peter	Acts 1:16-22
Peter	Acts 2:14-36, 38-39
Peter	Acts 3:12-16
Peter	Acts 4:8-12, 19-20
Peter	Acts 5:29-32
Gamaliel	Acts 5:35-39
Stephen	Acts 7:2-53
Peter	Acts 10:34-43
Peter	Acts 11:5-17
Paul	Acts 13:16-41
Paul	Acts 14:15-17
Peter	Acts 15:7-11
James	Acts 15:13-21
Paul	Acts 17:22-31
Demetrius	Acts 19:25-27
Ephesian town clerk	Acts 19:35-40
Paul	Acts 20:18-35
Paul	Acts 22:1-21
Tertullus	Acts 24:2-8
Paul	Acts 24:10-21
Festus	Acts 25:24-27
Paul	Acts 26:2-3
Paul	Acts 27:21-26
Paul	Acts 28:17-20

---

[19]Dibelius, *Studies in the Acts*, 150; Gerhard Schneider, *Die Apostelgeschichte* (Freiburg: Herder, 1980–1982), 1:96.
[20]Marion L. Soards, *The Speeches in Acts: Their Content, Context, and Concerns* (Louisville, KY: Westminster John Knox, 1994), 162-83.
[21]Soards, *Speeches in Acts*, 184-200.

reference to the God of creation being known through nature and Greco-Roman philosophy in the Areopagus speech of Acts 17:22-31 with Paul's statements in Romans 1:18-32, concerning the inadequacy of natural knowledge of God to lead to repentance, and his rejection of philosophy in 1 Corinthians 1:18–2:5.

What is more, in historiographical works of antiquity, speeches could be fabricated for the purposes of propaganda and for venerating the speaker. In a Hellenistic setting, written speeches were unlikely to be based on verbatim reports, epitomes, or prewritten transcripts. This is evident by a mere comparison of alternative versions of some recorded speeches, which are often unlike each other (even when both versions come from the same author!).[22]

Table 4.2. Comparative accounts of ancient speeches

SPEAKER	VERSION 1	VERSION 2
Mattathias	Josephus, *Ant.* 12.279-284	Josephus, *J.W.* 1.373-379
Herod	Josephus, *Ant.* 15.127-146	1 Maccabees 2:50-68
Otho	Plutarch, *Otho* 15	Tacitus, *Historiae* 2.47
Julius Caesar	Dio Cassius, *Roman History* 38.36-46	Caesar, *Gallic War* 1.40

In many cases what ancient historians aimed for in reporting speeches was not verbatim accuracy or even generalized approximations but a composition that, if possible, was based on sources and on ensuring the appropriateness of the words of the speaker to the occasion to which they spoke. Thucydides in his *History of the Peloponnesian War* (fifth century BC) writes:

> As to the speeches that were made by different men, either when they were about to begin the war or when they were already engaged therein, it has been difficult to recall with strict accuracy the words actually spoken, both for me as regards that which I myself heard, and

---

[22]Charles H. Talbert, *Reading Acts: A Literary and Theological Commentary on the Acts of the Apostles* (New York: Crossroads, 1997), 45-47.

for those who from various other sources have brought me reports. Therefore, the speeches are given in the language which, as it seemed to me, the several speakers would express, on the subjects under consideration, the sentiments most befitting the occasion, though at the same time I have adhered as closely as possible to the general sense of what was actually said. (1.22.1)[23]

The same view is found in Lucian's *How to Write History* (second century BC): "If a person has to be introduced to make a speech above all let his language suit his person and his subject. . . . It is then, however, that you can play the orator and show your eloquence" (58).[24]

The crucial elements in Thucydides's statement are his intent to write that which was "befitting the occasion" and his comment that there are limits to which his authorial creativity could go. While this might not have been true of all ancient historical writers (Polybius and Lucian object to sensationalist and inaccurate accounts by other writers), it shows that many authors did aim for verisimilitude and veracity.[25] At the same time, Thucydides and Lucian both recognize that authors are free to write so as to show their own style and literary eloquence. Conrad Gempf also argues that recorded speeches were more concerned with events than with verbatim reportage. Fidelity to the sources meant faithfulness to the speech-event and to present it in an exciting and penetrating way.[26] Eckhard Schnabel comments, "Speeches in

---

[23]Thucydides, *History of the Peloponnesian War*, vol. 1, *Books 1–2*, trans. C. F. Smith, Loeb Classical Library (Cambridge, MA: Harvard University Press, 1919), xvi-xvii.

[24]Lucian, *How to Write History; The Dipsads; Saturnalia; Herodotus or Aetion; Zeuxis or Antiochus; A Slip of the Tongue in Greeting; Apology for the "Salaried Posts in Great Houses"; Harmonides; A Conversation with Hesiod; The Scythian or The Consul; Hermotimus or Concerning the Sects; To One Who Said "You're a Prometheus in Words"; The Ship or The Wishes*, trans. K. Kilburn, Loeb Classical Library (Cambridge, MA: Harvard University Press, 1959), 58.

[25]See further on Thucydides, Hemer, *Book of Acts*, 421-26; Stanley E. Porter, "Thucydides 1.22.1 and Speeches in Acts: Is There a Thucydidean View?," *NovT* 32 (1990): 121-42.

[26]Conrad H. Gempf, "Public Speaking and Published Accounts," in *The Book of Acts in Its Literary Context*, ed. B. W. Winter and A. Clark (Grand Rapids, MI: Eerdmans, 1993), 262-64.

historical narrative rarely reproduce the actual words that were spoken. However, the speeches were not free inventions but provided an approximation of what was said, even if sometimes imaginative reconstruction was necessary."[27] Luke, then, like a Thucydides or Lucian, gives his audience the gist of what was said, preserves any critical decisions, writes to befit the occasion, and captures the ethos of a speech; but on the whole he was free to create, arrange, and adapt a speech in line with his own theological and rhetorical strategies. This explains why there is some variation in Luke's three accounts of Paul's conversion and call to go to the Gentiles (Acts 9; 22; 26). It was convention not to repeat material without variation and originality, balancing fidelity to the event with creativity in the elaboration. Speech writing was about earning trust, offering testimony, and showing off one's literary talent.

Luke may have combined information gleaned from his acquaintance with the original speakers and their audiences, his own memory, and a degree of free composition in his representation of the speeches in Acts. The speeches in Acts serve to develop Luke's own theological ideas, but he uses older traditions and gives appropriate characterization of individual speakers.[28] In one or two instances we can point out close parallels between a speech in Acts and an external source. Steve Walton points out the affinities between Paul's farewell address to the elders in his Miletus speech of Acts 20:18-35 and his exhortations in 1 Thessalonians.[29]

The Lukan portrait of Paul. Another test case for Luke's reliability as a historian is his representation of Paul. To what extent

---

[27]Eckhard J. Schnabel, *Acts* (Grand Rapids, MI: Zondervan, 2012), 35.
[28]Martin Hengel, *Earliest Christianity*, trans. John Bowden (London: SCM Press, 1986), 61.
[29]Steve Walton, *Leadership and Lifestyle: The Portrait of Paul in the Miletus Speech and 1 Thessalonians*, SNTSMS 106 (Cambridge: Cambridge University Press, 2000).

does Luke adequately reflect Paul's preaching and Paul's itinerary? Several disparities are evident here, and this has led some scholars to use Acts very cautiously in relation to constructing Paul's biography, missionary itinerary, and theology.

We've already touched briefly on some of the differences between the preaching of the Lukan Paul in Acts and the theology of Paul in the epistles. The Paul of Acts is a brilliant and eloquent orator, while the Paul of his epistles acknowledges that his preaching was deliberately lacking in any ornamented rhetoric (e.g., 1 Corinthians 2:1-5). The Paul of Acts scarcely mentions the death of Christ and focuses more on Jesus' resurrection and exaltation, whereas Paul's epistles convey a resolute focus on the crucicentric gospel (e.g., 1 Corinthians 1:17-18; 2:2; 5:7; Galatians 5:11; 6:12, 14). Paul Vielhauer argues that the Pauline speeches of Acts diverge from Paul's epistles in several areas, including attitudes toward natural revelation, Torah, Christology, and eschatology.[30] One could say that the Paul of Acts seems far more Torah observant than the Paul of the epistles.

At the same time, the similarities are often striking. In Acts (Acts 14:15) and in Paul's letters (1 Thessalonians 1:9-10), Gentiles are to turn away from idolatry and turn toward God. There are references to Paul's gospel as fulfilling the divine promises made to Israel (Acts 13:32; 2 Corinthians 1:20) and similar links between gospel and grace (Acts 20:24; Galatians 1:6; Philippians 1:7; Colossians 1:6). In both sets of writings Paul's gospel is for Jews and Gentiles (Acts 20:21; Romans 1:16). The differences may be attributed to Luke's summarizing of Paul and from Luke interpreting Paul's preaching through his own literary and theological goals.

---

[30]Philipp Vielhauer, "The 'Paulinism' of Acts," *Perkins (School of Theology) Journal* 17 (1963): 5-17.

Regarding Paul's chronology, things seem equally complex as well. A reading of Acts 17-18 and 1 Thessalonians 2:17-3:6 creates some apparent tensions as to where exactly Timothy and Silas parted company with Paul (in Thessalonica versus Athens). Does Galatians 2:1-10 correspond with the Jerusalem Council in Acts 15 or with the famine-relief visit in Acts 11:27-30?[31] Another topic is why Luke never mentions certain significant events from Paul's life, such as the Antioch episode (Galatians 2:11-14) and Paul's collection for the saints in Jerusalem (1 Corinthians 16:1-3; 2 Corinthians 9:1-15; Romans 15:25-27). We also have to acknowledge that Luke presents three different renditions of Paul's conversion (Acts 9:1-21; 22:1-21; 26:2-23). When did Paul receive his commission to go to the Gentiles? His own account in Galatians 1:16 is quite ambiguous. In the final Lukan version, Paul reports that he received his apostolic commission during his Christophany on the road to Damascus (Acts 26:16-18; see Acts 9:15). Alternatively, in Acts 22:15-21, it seems that the revelation to go to the Gentiles was based on a subsequent revelation that Paul received in Jerusalem and was an aspect of his calling that only became apparent to him later on.[32] So it seems that the pieces here do not always fit neatly together.

Luke's account of Paul's missionary career should not be too readily discounted, though. In fact, he provides information about Paul that is not found in the letters but is undoubtedly correct, such as Paul's origins in Tarsus and that he was a Roman citizen (Acts 21:39; 22:25-29; 23:27). We might do well to also consider those aspects of Luke's narrative about Paul that can be safely related to Paul's epistles.

---

[31]David A. deSilva, *An Introduction to the New Testament: Contexts, Methods and Ministry Formation* (Downers Grove, IL: InterVarsity Press, 2004), 377-78.
[32]See Fitzmyer, *Acts*, 141-44.

Table 4.3. Pauline parallels between Paul's epistles and the book of Acts[a]

EVENT	ACTS	PAULINE LETTERS
Paul's Christophany on road to Damascus	Acts 9:1-22	Galatians 1:17
Paul's escape from Damascus	Acts 9:22-25	2 Corinthians 11:32
Paul's first trip to Jerusalem	Acts 9:26-27	Galatians 1:18-20
Paul's time in regions of Syria and Cilicia	Acts 9:30	Galatians 1:21-22
Paul's meeting in Jerusalem	Acts 11:27-30 / Acts 15:1-22	Galatians 2:1-10
Paul's mission in Philippi and Thessalonica	Acts 16:11-40; 17:1-9	1 Thessalonians 2:2; 2 Corinthians 11:9; Philippians 4:15-16
Paul's trip to Athens	Acts 17:15-34	1 Thessalonians 3:1
Paul's mission in Corinth	Acts 18:1-18	2 Corinthians 1:19; 11:7-9
expulsion of Jews from Rome under Claudius	Acts 18:2	occasion for Romans
Timothy arrives in Corinth	Acts 18:5	1 Thessalonians 3:6
Paul urges Apollos to go to Corinth	Acts 19:1	1 Corinthians 16:12
Paul's lengthy period in Ephesus	Acts 19:1–20:1, 31	1 Corinthians 16:1-8
Paul's plan to visit Macedonia	Acts 19:21	2 Corinthians 2:13; 7:5; 9:2-4
Paul's plan to go to Rome after journey to Jerusalem	Acts 19:21	Romans 15:22-25
Paul earns his living through work	Acts 18:3; 20:34	1 Thessalonians 2:9; 1 Corinthians 9:15; 2 Corinthians 11:7-8

[a]Based on Joseph A. Fitzmyer, *The Acts of the Apostles*, Anchor Bible (New York: Doubleday, 1998), 134-35.

In light of the foregoing discussion, we should conclude that the portraits of Paul in Acts and Paul in the epistles are at times different but eminently compatible.[33]

Is Luke a good historian? Luke is indeed a historian; he can be rooted in the ancient practices of historiography, and he is interested in excavating appropriate sources, constrained and motivated like other historians of his time. Luke is as historically accurate as ancient historical method permitted and as much as his living and textual sources preserved reliable

---

[33]See Stanley E. Porter, *The Paul of Acts: Essays in Literary Criticism, Rhetoric and Theology*, WUNT 115 (Tübingen: Mohr Siebeck, 1999); Hemer, *Book of Acts*, 244-47.

information.³⁴ He has an impressive grasp of people, places, nautical travel, Jewish customs, Roman government, and the church's internecine conflicts. What is more, Luke's interest is not in cataloging facts for posterity but in God's revelation in Christ and the church. Accordingly, if we combine Luke's historical interest with his focus on God's actions in history, we might better label his work "theography."³⁵ At the end of the day, Luke stands with the very giants of his discipline. He is one of our most valuable sources for the history of the early Christian mission and an important source for the first-century eastern Mediterranean. I concur again with the words of Martin Hengel:

> Luke is no less trustworthy than other historian of antiquity. People have done him a great injustice in comparing him too closely with the edifying, largely fictitious, romance-like writings in the style of the later acts of the apostles, which freely invent facts as they like and when they need them.... His account remains within the limits of what was considered reliable by the standards of antiquity. That means that the author's assurance in Luke 1.3 is more than mere convention; it contains a real theological and historical programme, though this cannot be measured by the standards of a modern critical historian.³⁶

LUKE AS THEOLOGIAN

I have always found it fiercely ironic that the same generation of early to mid-twentieth-century German scholarship that regarded Luke–Acts as theologically freighted and of little historical value

---

³⁴I should acknowledge my debt to Benjamin Sutton, "Formulations of the Gospel in the Speeches of Acts: Memory and Historiography" (PhD diss., Australian College of Theology, 2015), whose work stimulated much of my thinking in this area.

³⁵Bock, *Acts*, 15. See Steve Walton, "The Acts—of God? What Is the 'Acts of the Apostles' All About?," *EvQ* 80 (2008): 291-306; Richard B. Vinson, "The God of Luke–Acts," *Int* 68 (2014): 376-88; Joshua W. Jipp, "The Beginnings of a Theology of Luke–Acts: Divine Activity and Human Response," *JTI* 8 (2014): 23-43.

³⁶Hengel, *Earliest Christianity*, 60-61.

paid relatively little notice to Luke as a theologian.[37] For example, I know of two so-called New Testament theology volumes that focus on Jesus, Paul, and John, with no mention of Luke.[38] German great Rudolf Bultmann and American scholar G. E. Ladd in their respective New Testament theologies place Acts within a broader study of the *kerygma* (i.e., proclamation) of the early church, while the theological contribution of the Gospel of Luke is either ignored (by Bultmann) or situated within a more general theological appraisal of the Synoptic Gospels (by Ladd).[39] This is disconcerting because Luke is a theologian who easily ranks beside Paul, John, Justin Martyr, Tertullian, or Augustine. In fact, Luke's theological interests are equally as apparent as his historical interests if we closely reread the prologue:

> Since many have undertaken to set down an orderly account of the events that have been *fulfilled* among us, just as they were handed on to us by those who from the beginning were eyewitnesses and *servants of the word*, I too decided, after investigating everything carefully from the very first, to write an orderly account for you, most excellent Theophilus, so that you may know the truth concerning the things about which you have been *instructed*. (Luke 1:1-4)

Notice the words that I have deliberately italicized here. First, *fulfilled* carries the sense of promises and prophecies coming to their divinely appointed goal. Second, *servants of the word* might mean those who originally proclaimed the gospel of Jesus Christ, or it could have a Christocentric element, much like the Gospel of John,

---

[37] The exception here of course is Hans Conzelmann and his highly influential work *The Theology of Saint Luke*, trans. G. Buswell (London: Faber and Faber, 1960).

[38] W. G. Kümmel, *Theology of the New Testament: According to Its Major Witnesses: Jesus—Paul—John*, trans. J. E. Steely (London: SCM Press, 1974); Larry R. Helyer, *The Witness of Jesus, Paul, and John* (Downers Grove, IL: InterVarsity Press, 2008).

[39] Rudolf Bultmann, *Theology of the New Testament*, trans. K. Grobel, 2 vols. (London: SCM Press, 1952-1955); G. E. Ladd, *A Theology of the New Testament*, rev. and ed. D. A. Hagner (Grand Rapids, MI: Eerdmans, 1993).

where *word* refers to Jesus the eternal and incarnate Word of God (John 1:1). Third, *instructed* has the connotation of "catechize" and involves learning the sacred truths of God among God's sacred people, the church. This illustrates that Luke's purposes are equally theological as they are historical. Luke is focused not on the mere factuality of Jesus and the origins of the church as a historical artifact but on the significance of Jesus for the church through the execution of his appointed mission. There is much more to follow about Luke's theology, but for the moment we might want to note several basic themes that he is concerned with.

The purposes and plan of God. Although Jesus is the central figure in the Gospel of Luke, and Peter and then Paul are the chief protagonists in the Acts of Apostles, nonetheless Luke's theological narration places God at the center of all things. God is not a benign Father lurking in the background, nor a one-dimensional character on the edge of a movie set. God is the director and author of the entire story, who makes cameo appearances in his own theodrama, where he executes his plan in glorious power.

God works out his saving purposes through Jesus and the apostles. This purpose is mentioned a number of times: John the Baptist came according to the foretelling of Scripture (Luke 7:27), Jesus' death is divinely determined (Luke 24:44), the Scriptures testify that the Messiah had to suffer and rise from the dead (Luke 24:46), Jesus was handed over according to the plan and foreknowledge of God (Acts 2:23; 4:28), Jesus is the Messiah appointed for Israel (Acts 3:18-20) and for Gentiles (Acts 13:48). The proclamation and realization of the kingdom of God constitutes the purpose for Jesus' coming (Luke 4:43), and as God's anointed King Jesus serves the purpose of God in much the same way that David did in his time (Acts 13:36-37). Luke describes Paul as stating that his teaching ministry focused on setting forth the whole purposes of God (Acts 20:27).

The primary purpose of God is to bring the long-awaited salvation to Israel and to include the Gentiles in the one people of God. This is why Jesus must die in Jerusalem and Paul must testify in Rome, for God's purposes to be displayed through Israel and to the world—this is the working out of God's plan. God is faithful to the covenant people, but also impartial when it comes to holding the world to account. This explains why Jesus tries to reconfigure the view of God as held by the disciples, followers, and contemporaries. The Lukan narrative essentially lays out a story of how *God's* Son proclaims and implements *God's* kingdom in order to achieve *God's purposes* for making salvation a reality for Jews and Gentiles.[40]

Jesus as Messiah and Lord. There are dangers if one tries to reduce Christology to mere titles, because Lukan Christology is shaped by narrative sequences, characterization, dramatic actions, divine functions and prerogatives, and the interplay of God and Jesus. That said, we cannot neglect the titles either, especially "Messiah" and "Lord." Luke emphasizes in the Gospel narrative and in apostolic preaching that Jesus is the Messiah, he is Israel's Messiah, he is the Lord's Messiah, and he is the "Messiah of God." As Frank Matera puts it:

> The Messiah of God comes to his people Israel as the Spirit-anointed Son of God with a gracious offer of salvation: the forgiveness of sins. Despite this gracious offer, Israel does not repent. Nonetheless, its rejection of the Messiah paradoxically fulfils God's plan that the Messiah must suffer in order to enter into his glory so that repentance and forgiveness can be preached in his name to all nations.[41]

Jesus is the risen and exalted Lord, honored by God and honored by the renewed Israel of God. The Petrine speech of Acts 2 describes

---

[40]See further Joel B. Green, *The Theology of the Gospel of Luke*, NTT (Cambridge: Cambridge University Press, 1995).

[41]Frank J. Matera, *New Testament Christology* (Louisville, KY: Westminster John Knox, 1999), 51.

how "this Jesus, whom you crucified," is now installed as Lord and Messiah by virtue of his resurrection by God and his role as dispenser of the promised Holy Spirit. Thus, there is an indelible connection between Jesus of Nazareth and the risen and exalted Lord. As the story progresses, the apostles operate as emissaries of this Jesus; indeed, they continue his service to Israel and open up new horizons to include Gentiles in the kingdom that Jesus himself inaugurated.

The Jewish roots of Christianity and its continuity with Israel's Scriptures. Luke is very clear that salvation only comes to and through Israel. Jesus' mission to redeem Israel (Luke 24:21) and to be a light of revelation to the Gentiles (Luke 2:32) are not two separate missions but part of the one interlocking mission. The good news is good for Israel and the Gentiles, and their deliverance and unity is part of God's purposes. Luke knows that there is something "new" in the "new covenant" (Luke 22:20) so that not everything from the prior epoch of redemptive history carries over into the new age of the kingdom (Luke 5:27; 16:16). Even so, that does not mean abandoning the old to the scrapheap. Luke speaks of Israel's God fulfilling his scriptural promises to redeem and renew Israel and to extend salvation to the Gentiles, as Israel was always intended to be a "light to the nations" (Isaiah 42:6; 49:6). Yes, Jesus' teachings about the Torah and temple conflict with some Jewish attitudes (Acts 6:14), and there are intramural debates about the Torah and Gentiles within the church (Acts 15:1-5, 10), but the Jewish Torah is never disparaged or denied (Acts 21:21-24). The church is not intended as a parallel chapter to Israel or as a replacement of Israel but as a continuation and fulfillment of what Israel is supposed to be in the new era, during the "times of the Gentiles" (Luke 21:24).

Holy Spirit. Luke is the Evangelist most focused on the Holy Spirit in the New Testament. The Holy Spirit animates prophecy at several points in the opening chapters of Luke's infancy narrative.

Luke

John the Baptist announces the coming one as charged with baptizing with the "the Holy Spirit and fire," which might be idiomatic for plunging people in the fiery breath of God as an act of eschatological cleansing (Luke 3:16). Jesus also receives the Holy Spirit at his baptism (Luke 3:22), which empowers him to face temptations and to conduct his own prophetic mission (Luke 4:1; Acts 10:38). Indeed, Jesus' miracles done in the power of the Spirit are evidence that kingdom of God has truly arrived (Luke 11:20). According to Jesus' teaching, the Holy Spirit is to be a gift (Luke 11:13). The Lukan Jesus reports that the disciples will be clothed with "power from on high" in their mission that is soon to come (Luke 24:49).

The Acts of the Apostles is perhaps best called "The Acts of the Holy Spirit *through* the Apostles and even *despite* the Apostles." The apostles do receive God's power at Pentecost, where they are baptized into the Holy Spirit, and this leads to miraculous acts and the proclamation of the gospel (Acts 2:1-43). This goes to show that the Holy Spirit is at a certain level salvific but primarily about empowerment for mission. The sign that God has accepted those beyond the borders of Israel is their reception of the Holy Spirit, and that includes both Samaritans (Acts 8:15-17) and Gentiles (Acts 10:44-48).

Discipleship. In Luke–Acts, to follow Jesus is to be a follower of "the Way" (Acts 9:2; 16:17; 18:25-26; 19:9, 23; 22:4; 24:14, 22). "The Way," says Joel Green, "designates a people who align themselves with and serve God's plan, especially as witnessed in the Scriptures and manifest in Jesus (cf. Acts 18:24-25; cf., e.g., Luke 1:6; 20:21)."[42] The Way is, then, a summary of what Jesus himself taught (Luke 20:21) and the hermeneutical framework for interpreting the Scriptures in light of their fulfillment in Jesus (Acts 18:26; 24:14). Above all,

---

[42]Green, *Theology of the Gospel of Luke*, 102.

discipleship in Luke–Acts means to embrace the teaching of Jesus and the pattern of Jesus in taking up one's cross (Luke 9:23-25) and being committed to the mission of the kingdom (Luke 9:57-62). Followers of Jesus also have a special concern for the poor, have no affection for wealth and possessions, express love for one's enemies, are committed to the Scriptures, persevere in prayer, witness to the gospel, and engage in authentic worship of God through Jesus in the joy of the Holy Spirit. Most of all, they align themselves with the purpose and plan of God in bringing the kingdom to fruition on earth through the church of God, made up of Jews and Gentiles.[43]

> **Luke's Project of Narrating and Interpreting the Memory of Jesus and the Acts of God**
>
> Do we have to choose between Luke as a historian or as a theologian? No. As Howard Marshall puts it, because "Luke was a theologian he had to be a historian."[a] For Luke, there is no story of salvation, no gospel, without the God who acts in history to work out his saving purposes.
>
> [a] I. Howard Marshall, *Luke: Historian and Theologian*, 3rd ed. (Carlisle, UK: Paternoster, 1988), 72.

The dichotomy of Luke–Acts as *either* history *or* theology owes much to the assumptions of previous generations. Yet Luke is just as much a historian as he is a theologian. He's not bequeathing naked facts, nor inventing things from whole cloth. There is no such thing as uninterpreted history, and Luke reports events as much as he interprets them. Luke combines a deposit of firsthand memory and secondhand testimony with his own hermeneutical intentions, interpretive glosses, and rhetorical crafting fit for his medium.

---

[43] See further C. H. Talbert, "Discipleship in Luke–Acts," in *Discipleship in the New Testament*, ed. F. Segovia (Philadelphia: Fortress, 1985), 62-75.

REVIEW QUESTIONS

1. How does Luke 1:1-4 exhibit Luke's historical interests?
2. How does Luke 1:1-4 exhibit Luke's theological interests?
3. What leads some scholars to question Luke's value as historian?
4. What are some good reasons for thinking that Luke should be taken seriously as a historian?
5. What are some of Luke's main theological themes?
6. Should a New Testament theology include Luke alongside Paul and John as the main witnesses?

FURTHER READING

Bird, Michael F., and Ben Sutton. "Social Memory in Acts." In *Jesus, Skepticism, and the Problem of History: Criteria and Context in the Study of Christian Origins*, edited by Ed Komoszewski and D. Bock, 305-19. Grand Rapids, MI: Zondervan, 2019.

Green, Gene L. "Luke: Historian, Rhetor, and Theologian. Historiography and the Theology of the Speeches in Acts." In *New Testament Theology in Light of the Church's Mission*, edited by J. C. Laansma, G. Osborne, and R. van Neste, 161-80. Eugene, OR: Cascade, 2011.

Hemer, Colin. *The Book of Acts in the Setting of Hellenistic History*. Tübingen: Mohr Siebeck, 1989.

Hengel, Martin. *Earliest Christianity*. Translated by John Bowden. London: SCM Press, 1986.

Rothschild, Clare K. *Luke–Acts and the Rhetoric of History: An Investigation of Early Christian Historiography*. WUNT 2/175. Tübingen: Mohr Siebeck, 2019.

5

"This Jesus"

The Christology of Luke–Acts

THE JESUS QUESTION

Luke's account of Jesus is not merely a minor variation of a wider Christology of the Synoptic Gospels. Nor is Luke's narration of Jesus a haphazard stitching together of disparate sources. Luke does have a perspective on Jesus, a powerful one, a poignant one. The Lukan Jesus appears as the centerpiece of a new redemptive event; however, his role within it and his precise identity is only gradually disclosed in the narrative of Luke–Acts. While the reader is slowly introduced to Jesus' mission and identity, for the characters in the story things are more obscure, and questions abound about him. The Pharisees want to know who this man is who thinks he can forgive sins (Luke 5:21; 7:49). The disciples are terrified by Jesus' power over the elements and wonder who can command the wind and water (Luke 8:25). Herod Antipas is curiously perplexed about Jesus and wants to see him (Luke 9:9). The chief priests want to know whether he thinks he is the Messiah (Luke 22:66-71), while Pilate is concerned with whether Jesus thinks of himself as a royal pretender (Luke 23:3). Yet these characters are merely grasping around the edges of the story, responding to snippets, acting in self-protective ways, oblivious to who Jesus really is. They act as if the game is *Guess who is Jesus*. But more properly, they should be asking, *What is God doing in Jesus? What does Jesus mean for Israel? What does Jesus tell us about God?* This is why the first sermon in Acts is not about providing an introduction to Jesus but getting the Jerusalemites to change their verdict about who Jesus really is, discovering who God has declared him to be, and what God has done, is doing, and will yet do through him (Acts 2:22-36).

Luke does, then, have a distinctive Christology, not the least in his emphasis on Jesus' prophetic ministry and his identity as Lord of the church. Unique to Luke–Acts is that Jesus is the "Lord's Messiah" (Luke 2:26; see Luke 2:11; Acts 2:36) and "Messiah of God" (Luke 9:20; 23:35; see Acts 4:26), the "dayspring" (Luke 1:78 KJV), and "Prince and Savior" (Acts 5:31 NIV). Beyond that, we must get away from the commonly held assumption that the Gospel of Luke has a functional Christology (i.e., Jesus is the protagonist in the Gospel), which yields a titular Christology in the book of Acts (i.e., Jesus is reduced to the titles used for him in his absence such as "Lord" or "Prince").[1] Under such an assumption, it is as if Jesus is a prophetic actor and then becomes present only as an object of proclamation thereafter. The reality is far more complex. Jesus appears as the messianic Lord, animated by the Spirit, who discloses the divine purpose and then, after his crucifixion-resurrection-exaltation, continues his work and witness through the apostles. Accordingly, in a fuller account of Lukan Christology, several important motifs require exposition.

SAVIOR

The infancy narratives drip with incandescent joy that salvation has risen over the horizon and is happening extraordinarily and

---

[1] So, e.g., Jacob Jervell, *The Theology of the Acts of the Apostles* (Cambridge: Cambridge University Press, 1996), 26.

unexpectedly through the births of John and Jesus. John will bear the spirit and power of Elijah (Luke 1:17), while Jesus will fulfill the role of Davidic savior (Luke 2:11). The births of the two infants are signs of deliverance given by "God my Savior," declares Mary (Luke 1:47), while Zechariah rejoices that God "has raised up a horn of salvation for us in the house of his servant David," which refers to Jesus (Luke 1:69 NIV). What is interesting is that Jesus is normally called "Savior" (σωτήρ) in the context of the proclamation of Israel's deliverance in Luke–Acts (Luke 2:11; Acts 5:31; 13:23). Among the Gospels, the title "Savior" is unique to Luke's writings and is often used in association with Jesus' messianic mission toward Israel (Luke 2:11; Acts 5:31). Jesus is, then, God's salvation, Israel's messianic Savior, the royal Lord of Israel. He is sent to bring deliverance to the people of Judea and Galilee who see themselves in continuity with God's sacred people Israel. According to Darrell Bock, "So for Luke the title savior has particular reference to God's whole program of promised deliverance, in addition to being tied to Israel, to exaltation, to forgiveness, and to the offer of the Spirit."[2]

ISRAEL'S MESSIAH

In Luke. I think it is fair to say that Lukan Christology has to be regarded principally as Jewish messianic discourse about an anointed deliverer. Yes, the Lukan Jesus reflects and enacts the traits of many scriptural and Second Temple redeemer figures. Luke's Jesus resembles various intermediary figures in antiquity, too, divine men who performed wondrous deeds; he's like a mighty prophet, a noble martyr, even like a deified emperor in some sense. But Jesus is above all the Messiah, Israel's Messiah, God's Messiah. He is the anointed king of the Davidic line, whom many Jews believed

---

[2]Darrell L. Bock, *A Theology of Luke and Acts: God's Promised Program, Realized for All Nations* (Grand Rapids, MI: Zondervan, 2012), 185.

would one day rescue the people from foreign domination, death, disease, and their transgression of the covenant. Frank Matera is correct in his conclusion that in Luke–Acts "the central concept for identifying Jesus is *messiahship*.... Of the many terms that Luke employs to identify Jesus, then, 'Messiah' is among the most important. Indeed, one could argue that it is *the* title in reference to which all others are to be understood."[3] Although John the Baptist is celebrated as a prophet, even the last of the prophets (Luke 7:24-28; 9:19; 16:16), Jesus exceeds him, for Jesus is both a prophet and the one to come (Luke 3:16; 7:20), the messianic Lord (Luke 2:11).

The angel's announcement to Mary includes the riveting promise about her baby: "He will be great, and will be called the Son of the Most High, and the Lord God will give to him the throne of his ancestor David. He will reign over the house of Jacob forever, and of his kingdom there will be no end" (Luke 1:32-33). This obviously reflects the Davidic covenant in 2 Samuel 7:8-16, which concerns God's giving the descendants of David a throne that endures for the ages. It is from the Davidic house that a horn of salvation is raised up for Israel, as "said through his holy prophets long ago" (Luke 1:70 NIV). Zechariah celebrates the arrival of the ἀνατολή (Luke 1:78), which means the "dawn" (NRSV), "dayspring" (KJV), or "rising sun" (NIV). The word ἀνατολή is a messianic metaphor used in the LXX (i.e., the Greek translation of the Old Testament used by many Jews and later by Christians) to translate "branch" (צֶמַח), a designation for the coming Davidic leader (Zechariah 3:8; 6:12), since a Davidic Messiah is one who "rises" like the sun to reign (Numbers 24:17 LXX).[4] It means that "God sends his Messiah

---

[3] Frank J. Matera, *New Testament Christology* (Louisville, KY: Westminster John Knox, 1999), 68-89, emphasis original.
[4] François Bovon, *Luke 1: A Commentary on the Gospel of Luke 1:1–9:50* (Minneapolis: Fortress, 2002), 76. See further David Wenkel, *Jesus the Dayspring: The Sunrise and Visitation of Israel's Messiah* (Sheffield: Sheffield Phoenix, 2021).

as the bright dawn of salvation shining on the face of people."[5] Taken together, these royal-messianic categories begun in the birth narratives will eventually occupy a key role in the apostolic proclamation of Jesus (Acts 2:25, 29, 31, 34; 13:22, 34, 36; 15:16).[6] In fact, Davidic messiahship is programmatic for Luke's christological purpose in Luke–Acts. Jesus is *introduced* and *explained* precisely as the one who will fulfill the scriptural promises made about David's kingdom and is destined to occupy his throne.[7] Yet in his messianic office, Jesus will create a division within Israel over his very identity (Luke 2:34; 22:66-71), and an inevitable clash will result with another house of kings, the family of Caesar Augustus (Luke 2:1-3; Acts 17:6-7).

Later, when Jesus is in Nazareth, he identifies himself with the prophetic figure anointed by the Lord for a prophetic ministry (Luke 4:18-21; Isaiah 61:1). The Davidic and Isaianic senses of "anointed one" (i.e., Messiah) converge at a key juncture in the Gospel. Jesus appears to obliquely affirm his messianic identity when questioned by followers of John the Baptist. John, languishing in prison, perhaps starts to doubt whether Jesus really is the prophesied messianic agent, so he sends his followers to ask Jesus, "Are you the one who is to come, or are we to wait for another?" (Luke 7:19-20). Luke carefully sets the scene by noting, "Jesus had just then cured many people of diseases, plagues, and evil spirits, and had given sight to many who were blind" (Luke 7:21). Jesus responds to the question: "Go and tell John what you have seen and heard: the blind receive their sight, the lame walk, the lepers are cleansed, the deaf hear, the dead are raised, the poor have good news brought to them. And blessed is anyone who takes no offense

---

[5]Bock, *Theology of Luke and Acts*, 155.
[6]Mark L. Strauss, *The Davidic Messiah in Luke–Acts: The Promise and Fulfilment in Luke's Christology*, JSNTSup 110 (Sheffield: Sheffield Academic Press, 1995), 76-125.
[7]Strauss, *Davidic Messiah*, 124.

at me" (Luke 7:22-23). In effect, Jesus tells John not to mistake the reception of the kingdom with its reality. No revolution has broken out, but the signs of the kingdom are still there; the ministry of Jesus proves it. What is important to note here is that Jesus' answer draws on a compilation of texts from Isaiah that refer the signs of Israel's restoration:

- blind receive sight (Isaiah 29:18; 35:5; 42:7, 18)
- lame walk (Isaiah 35:6)
- lepers are cleansed (Isaiah 53:4)
- deaf hear (Isaiah 29:18-19; 35:5; 42:18)
- dead are raised (Isaiah 26:19)
- poor have the good news preached to them (Isaiah 61:1)

Furthermore, Jesus is doing precisely what the Messiah was expected to do according to the Messianic Apocalypse (4Q521) from the Qumran scrolls.[8] The Messianic Apocalypse is an apocalyptic poem, and it describes God's Messiah performing the same deeds ascribed to Jesus in Luke 7:19-23. Column 2 reads:

> [For the hea]vens and the earth shall listen to His Messiah [and all w]hich is in them shall not turn away from the commandments of the holy ones. Strengthen yourselves, O you who seek the Lord, in His service. Will you not find the Lord in this, all those who hope in their heart? For the Lord seeks the pious and calls the righteous by name. Over the humble His Spirit hovers, and He renews the faithful in His strength. For He will honour the pious upon the th[ro]ne of His eternal kingdom, setting prisoners free, opening the eyes of the blind, raising up those who are bo[wed down]. And for [ev]er I shall hold fast [to] the [ho]peful and pious [. . .][. . .] shall not be delayed [. . .] and the

---

[8] For an introduction see Daniel Zacharias, "Dead Sea Scrolls: Messianic Apocalypse," in *Encyclopedia of the Historical Jesus*, ed. C. A. Evans (New York: Routledge, 2008), 138-39.

Lord shall do glorious things which have not been done, just as He said. For He shall heal the critically wounded, He shall revive the dead, He shall send good news to the afflicted, He shall [... the ...], He shall lead the [...], and the hungry He shall enrich. (4Q521 2.1-10; trans. Wise, Abegg, Cook)[9]

When viewed side by side, 4Q521 2.12-13 and Luke 7:22 both describe the Messiah performing a series of mighty deeds drawn from Isaiah, in particular Isaiah 35:5-6; 61:1. These signs of restoration from Isaiah indicate that the messianic salvation is indeed underway and form a sufficient answer to the Baptist's question. This demonstrates that, in addition to hopes for a coming Davidic deliverer, Isaiah looms large in shaping Luke's messianic Christology.[10] Markus Bockmuehl appropriately concludes: "In light of the prophecy of Isaiah 61, Jesus' healings and preaching have a self-authenticating messianic significance, especially given the contemporary interpretations [at Qumran] of the Isaianic prophecy."[11]

Another key moment is Luke's account of Peter's confession that Jesus is the "Messiah of God" (Luke 9:20). Luke's phrase is a genitive of origin (τὸν χριστὸν τοῦ θεοῦ), that is, it means "the Messiah who has come from God." Luke, like the other Synoptic Evangelists, relates this confession to Jesus' identifying himself as the Son of Man who suffers and rises, to the necessity of taking up one's own cross and following him (Luke 9:22-25), and to the Son of Man coming in the glory of the Father with the holy angels (Luke 9:26). This is the path and promise for the advent of the kingdom's coming (Luke 9:27). This confessional and confrontational scene is married

---

[9]Michael Owen Wise, Martin G. Abegg, and Edward M. Cook, trans. and eds., *The Dead Sea Scrolls: A New Translation* (San Francisco: HarperSanFrancisco, 1996).
[10]See Michael Labahn, "The Significance of Signs in Luke 7:22-23 in Light of Isaiah 61 and the Messianic Apocalypse," in *From Prophecy to Testament*, ed. Craig A. Evans (Peabody, MA: Hendrickson, 2004), 146-68.
[11]Markus Bockmuehl, *This Jesus: Martyr, Lord, Messiah* (Edinburgh: T&T Clark, 1994), 53.

to Luke's version of the transfiguration episode, where the temporary glorification of Jesus in the manner of Moses and Elijah is a glimpse of the heavenly enthronement of the Messiah, which will transpire after his "departure" that is "about to bring to fulfillment in Jerusalem" (Luke 9:31 NIV). Thus, in Luke's narrative, the messiahship of Jesus follows a pattern of suffering and glory.

The scheme of Jesus as the Messiah/Son of God and suffering Son of Man come together at his trial before the Sanhedrin. In response to questions and accusations, Jesus affirms, somewhat obliquely, that he is the Messiah and Son of God, which the reader, too, knows. However, Jesus adds, "But from now on the Son of Man will be seated at the right hand of the power of God" (Luke 22:69). The addition of "from now" (ἀπὸ τοῦ νῦν) sets Luke apart from Mark's version (Mark 14:62) and signifies that Jesus' exaltation and enthronement is already beginning, precisely through his crucifixion and death. The allusions in these words to Psalm 110:1 hark back to Jesus' challenge to the scribes where he asks, in light of Psalm 110:1, how the Messiah can be David's son when David calls him "Lord" (Luke 20:41-44). The answer, repeated here, is that the Messiah is no mere human descendant but a figure destined to sit and share in the orbit of divine sovereignty. More importantly, the Messiah is, through the crucible of suffering, preparing even now to enter his glory and to reign with the Father as vice regent.

By the time of Jesus' resurrection and ascension (Luke 24), the Davidic hope has come to pass, the Isaianic anointed one has been revealed, the Son of Man has suffered and risen, and the Messiah has entered his glory. The story of the crucified and glorified Messiah (Luke 24:26, 46-47), his redemption for Israel (Luke 24:21), and the offer of forgiveness of sins to all nations (Luke 24:47) thereafter becomes programmatic for the messianic discourse of apostolic proclamation (e.g., Acts 2:25-31).

In Acts. Jesus as Messiah is at the heart of Christian preaching to the Jews in Acts.[12] In Acts 2, Peter's Pentecost speech includes the summary that "Jesus of Nazareth was a man accredited by God to you by miracles, wonders and signs" (Acts 2:22 NIV), along with the assertion that Jesus' death was divinely ordained, though the Jerusalem leadership is still culpable (Acts 2:23). Next is a citation of Psalm 16, which is taken as a messianic prophecy whereby David "spoke of the resurrection of the Messiah, that he was not abandoned to the realm of the dead, nor did his body see decay" (Acts 2:31 NIV). Instead, "God has raised this Jesus to life, and we are all witnesses of it" (Acts 2:32 NIV). Beyond that, "Exalted to the right hand of God," Jesus "has received from the Father the promised Holy Spirit and has poured out what you now see and hear," explained in light of Psalm 110 (Acts 2:33 NIV). This leads to Peter's dramatic announcement, a declaration and warning, "Therefore let all Israel be assured of this: God has made this Jesus, whom you crucified, both Lord and Messiah" (Acts 2:36 NIV). The reason for the warning, says C. K. Barrett, is that "the crucifixion of one who shares the throne of God is a sin against God; hence the force of the appeal for repentance which follows."[13] By consenting to Jesus' death, the Jerusalemites joined the nations who rage against the Lord's anointed (Psalm 2:1-3; Acts 4:25-26). This is why the audience needs to repent and be baptized—for the forgiveness of sins and to save themselves from a wicked generation (Acts 2:38-41).

A similar cluster of themes appears in Peter's speech in Solomon's Portico (Acts 3:11-26), Peter's speech before the high-priestly

---

[12]I. Howard Marshall, "The Christology of Luke's Gospel and Acts," in *Contours of Christology in the New Testament*, ed. Richard N. Longenecker (Grand Rapids, MI: Eerdmans, 2005), 143.
[13]C. K. Barrett, *Acts of the Apostles*, ICC (London: T&T Clark, 1994–1998), 1:152.

family (Acts 4:8-12), and Peter and the apostles before the Sanhedrin (Acts 5:29-31). The primary motifs are

- that the Jerusalem leaders and their supporters killed Jesus (Acts 3:13-15, 17; 4:25-27)
- Jesus' description with exalted titles such as "author of life," "Prince and Savior," the appointed Messiah sent for Israel's restoration (Acts 3:15, 20; 5:31 NIV)
- that God raised him from the dead and glorified him (Acts 3:15; 4:10)
- that the Messiah's suffering and resurrection were part of God's plan foretold in the prophets (Acts 3:18, 21-22, 24-25)
- that the apostles are witnesses of these things (Acts 3:15; 5:32)
- that in Jesus' name forgiveness, healing, salvation, and national restoration are offered (Acts 3:16, 18; 4:10, 12; 5:31)
- that the Spirit is given from/through Jesus (Acts 5:32)
- that now is the time for repentance if they are to avoid disaster (Acts 3:23)

A summary of apostolic preaching in Jerusalem is, "And every day in the temple and at home they did not cease to teach and proclaim Jesus as the Messiah" (Acts 5:42). The apostles' proclaim that everything about Jesus' life, death, and resurrection is part of God's plan, that God reversed Jesus' state (death) and status (shame) by raising him from the dead and exalting him to his right hand. According to Jacob Jervell, the burden of the speeches in the initial chapters of Acts is to claim, "The suffering Messiah is not an invention of the church, but the testimony of old from God himself."[14]

---

[14]Jervell, *Theology of the Acts of the Apostles*, 28.

Outside the Jerusalem environs, Luke's story has messianic proclamation strewn throughout the larger narrative, including by Philip, who proclaims the Messiah to Samaritans (Acts 8:5). After his conversion, Saul of Tarsus "grew more and more powerful and baffled the Jews living in Damascus by proving that Jesus is the Messiah" (Acts 9:22 NIV). At the Jerusalem Council, the church appears to have understood itself as the restoration of David's kingdom as promised in Amos 9:11, which makes it a self-consciously messianic movement (Acts 15:15-18). The same thing happens when Paul enters a synagogue in Thessalonica, where he is "explaining and proving that it was necessary for the Messiah to suffer and to rise from the dead, and saying, 'This is the Messiah, Jesus whom I am proclaiming to you'" (Acts 17:3). Similarly, in Corinth: "Paul was occupied with proclaiming the word, testifying to the Jews that the Messiah was Jesus" (Acts 18:5). In Paul's speech before King Agrippa II, Paul reports that he has declared his message to "those in Damascus, then in Jerusalem and throughout the countryside of Judea, and also to the Gentiles, that they should repent and turn to God and do deeds consistent with repentance . . . that the Messiah must suffer, and that, by being the first to rise from the dead, he would proclaim light both to our people and to the Gentiles" (Acts 26:20, 23). When Paul finally arrives in Rome, he summons the local Jewish leadership, and Luke says, "From morning until evening he explained the matter to them, testifying to the kingdom of God and trying to convince them about Jesus both from the law of Moses and from the prophets. Some were convinced by what he had said, while others refused to believe" (Acts 28:23-24).

Luke carefully curates a picture of Jesus as the messianic fulfillment of the prophetic hopes for a Davidic deliverer, Isaiah's anointed one, whose destiny is to be crucified, raised, and exalted as the Son of Man. The messianic aspect of Jesus' work is most acute in relation to Israel, as their Savior, the Messiah, who is destined to bring them into the great renewal of the covenant. So strong is this emphasis that one has to wonder whether Luke, even as a Gentile, even if writing for a mostly Gentile church, still has one eye on evangelism, trying to convince the Jews of the Diaspora that Jesus is the Messiah, their Messiah. According to Rebecca Denova, one might conclude from the narrative of Luke–Acts that it was written "to persuade other Jews that Jesus of Nazareth was the messiah of Scripture and that the words of the prophets concerning 'restoration' have been 'fulfilled.'"[15]

> **Minor Christological Titles in Luke–Acts**
> Holy One (Acts 2:27; 3:14)
> Righteous One (Luke 23:47 NIV; Acts 3:14; 7:52; 22:14)
> Judge (Acts 10:42; 17:31)
> King (Luke 19:12, 38; 23:2-3, 37-38; Acts 17:7)
> Servant (Acts 3:13, 26; 4:25-27, 30)
> Leader/Prince (Acts 3:15; 5:31)

GALILEAN PROPHET

One thing that stands out in Luke is the prophetic character of Jesus' ministry and how he is clearly recognized and venerated as a prophet. What is more, the entire range of his life, death, resurrection, and exaltation is immersed in prophetic fulfillment. Luke tells us from the prologue about the fulfillment (Luke 1:1) as it

---

[15]Rebecca I. Denova, *The Things Accomplished Among Us: Prophetic Tradition in the Structural Pattern of Luke–Acts* (Sheffield: Sheffield Academic Press, 1997), 230-31. See similarly David A. Smith, "The Jewishness of Luke–Acts: Locating Lukan Christianity Amidst the Parting of the Ways," *JTS* (2021): 738-68.

transpired in Jesus' preaching (Luke 4:21), crucifixion (Luke 18:31; 22:37; Acts 3:18; 13:27), and his entire messianic mission (Luke 24:44). This is a fulfillment that will extend beyond Jesus and even into the "things" surrounding the early church (Luke 1:1).

To begin with, Jesus calls himself a prophet when he says, "No prophet is accepted in his hometown" (Luke 4:24 NIV), he compares himself to the prophet Elijah (Luke 4:27), and he declares that no prophet can die outside Jerusalem (Luke 13:33-34). Those who witness his healing powers are convinced that a "great prophet has appeared among us" (Luke 7:16 NIV), and the general consensus about him is that he is a prophet (Luke 7:39; 9:8, 19). Even among his followers and in the Jerusalem church, he is remembered as a "prophet, powerful in word and deed before God and all the people" (Luke 24:19 NIV). Peter challenges the Jerusalemites that "Jesus of Nazareth was a man accredited by God to you by miracles, wonders and signs, which God did among you through him, as you yourselves know" (Acts 2:22 NIV), and Peter and Stephen both later state that he was a prophet like the one Moses prophesied would come (Acts 3:22-23; 7:37).

> **Jesus, the Prophet like Moses**
>
> "Jesus embodies—'fulfils,' if one desires—the qualities of a very specific sort of prophetic figure. Readers are to understand Jesus not as a court advisor or person of letters, like an Isaiah or Jeremiah, but as a leader of the people who works wonders through the power of the Holy Spirit. For this reason, Luke draws the strongest connection between Jesus, his followers, and the figure who was the first and greatest of the prophets of this type, Moses."[a]
>
> ---
> [a] Luke Timothy Johnson, *Prophetic Jesus, Prophetic Church: The Challenge of Luke–Acts to Contemporary Christians* (Grand Rapids, MI: Eerdmans, 2011), 31.

What elicits the designation of Jesus as a prophet is the very things he says and does. Like Elijah, he performs mighty deeds as he speaks truth to power (Luke 7:11-15; 13:32). Like Amos, he announces the need for repentance if judgment is to be averted (Luke 10:13; 11:32; 13:1-5). Like Isaiah, he looks ahead to God's kingship being announced and revealed and notes how God is truly becoming king in their midst (Luke 4:43; 11:20, 29-32). Like Jeremiah, he runs the risk of being called a traitor to the national cause because he dares to challenge its official and unofficial leaders even while he claims to speak for God (Luke 20:1-26). Like Ezekiel, he warns that the temple will be abandoned and left to desolation (Luke 21:1-38). Like Zechariah and Daniel, he explains in symbols and stories Israel's coming tribulation, reconstitution, and vindication (Luke 13:6-9, 28-29; 20:9-19).[16]

In general, the Lukan Jesus enacts a prophetic praxis, especially in the travel narrative, where he undertakes a variety of prophetic activities. Jesus preaches God's kingship, warns of judgment, calls for repentance, speaks for the poor and marginalized, denounces wealth and injustice, shows compassion, performs mighty deeds of healing, calls for committed followers, and looks ahead to the redemption of Israel. This is not a "low" Christology; it is a Christology for those on the lower rungs of the social order. God sends the prophet Jesus with the promise of his reign, his healing, his redemption, and a reordering of power.

DIVINE SON

An important designation for Jesus is God's Son. In the annunciation, the angel Gabriel tells Mary that the child she will bear

---

[16] Here I'm largely following N. T. Wright, *Jesus and the Victory of God*, COQG 2 (London: SPCK, 1996), 164-68.

"will be called the Son of the Most High" and that "the holy one to be born will be called the Son of God" (Luke 1:32, 35 NIV). Jesus is described as a divine son in that he fulfills the promise of God to raise up a Davidic ruler to sit on David's throne. Consequently, the title "Son of God" is correlated with Jesus' Davidic enthronement (see 2 Samuel 7:14; Psalm 2:7; 4Q174 3.7-13). Luke depicts Jesus as the Davidic Son of God, anointed for his reign, something that continues in apostolic preaching of Jesus as the messianic son (Acts 9:20-22). Here divine sonship is messianic rather than metaphysical, yet Luke builds on this Davidic foundation and goes beyond the conventional messianic understanding of the designation by drawing Jesus' divine sonship around his mission in language that includes Jesus' unique filial relationship to God the Father.[17]

When Jesus is baptized, he prays, heaven opens, the Holy Spirit descends on him, and "a voice came from heaven: 'You are my Son, whom I love; with you I am well pleased'" (Luke 3:22 NIV). This is important because we have here allusions to Psalm 2:7 and Isaiah 42:1. The words "You are my son" are taken from Psalm 2:7 in the context of the coronation and metaphorical begetting of Israel's king by Yahweh. The words "in/with you I am well pleased" hark back to the Isaianic servant, "Here is my servant, whom I uphold, my chosen one in whom I delight; I will put my Spirit on him, and he will bring justice to the nations" (Isaiah 42:1 NIV). This event is clearly an empowerment of Jesus for his messianic mission, but also his anointing with the Spirit as the Davidic Messiah and Suffering Servant. Jesus' divine sonship, then, is a royal status and a spirit-empowered vocation to serve Israel.

---

[17]Brendan Byrne, "Jesus as Messiah in the Gospel of Luke: Discerning a Pattern of Correction," *CBQ* 65 (2003): 85.

In the genealogy, Jesus is designated as the "son"—so it was thought—"of Joseph." But Luke offers his own version of Jesus' genealogy somewhat different from Matthew's (Luke 3:23-38). It is notable that in Jesus' ancestry there is David (Luke 3:31), Abraham (Luke 3:34), and Adam, who is "son of God" (Luke 3:38). Jesus, then, is by heritage connected to David's reign, Abraham's promises, and Adam's lineage. This speaks to the simultaneous particularity and universality of Jesus' sonship. Jesus' species of sonship is universal as he is one with all people as a son of Adam, bonded with Abraham the forefather of all monotheists, and Israel's deliverer as a son of David. Jesus' sonship makes him the true human being, a fitting object of Abrahamic promises, the Israelite Messiah, and Savior of the world.

That Jesus' sonship belongs to the heavenly realm is affirmed by unexpected witnesses including Satan (Luke 4:3, 9) and even demons (Luke 4:41; 8:28). Further, Jesus himself accents his unique filial relationship with God the Father and his unique prerogative to reveal the Father as only he can as God's Son: "All things have been committed to me by my Father. No one knows who the Son is except the Father, and no one knows who the Father is except the Son and those to whom the Son chooses to reveal him" (Luke 10:22 NIV). The heavenly voice from the baptism is heard again at the transfiguration scene, where Jesus is made visually resplendent before the very eyes of a trio of disciples and is joined by Moses and Elijah. It is repeated, "This is my Son, whom I have chosen; listen to him" (Luke 9:35 NIV). This scene is important, as it reaffirms the divine sanction of Jesus' mission and adds that he is to be obeyed as he speaks and acts with divine authority as the divine Son. But importantly, this follows right on the back of the episode where Jesus predicts his suffering and death as the Son of Man (Luke 9:21-27). While Jesus is seen in glory and appears beside glorified saints such as Moses and Elijah (Luke 9:30-31), it is a glory that destines him for his exodus, his fateful journey to Jerusalem, where "he must be killed and on the third day be raised to life" (Luke 9:22 NIV). In other words, the Son of God, born of a virgin, who sacks the demonic realm, who uniquely knows God and makes him known, who stands in glory beside Moses and Elijah, this Son of God must become the Son of Man and lead his people in a new exodus through waters of his baptism, which is his death (Luke 12:50).

Jesus' identity as Davidic Messiah, heavenly Son of God, and suffering Son of Man are telescoped together at his trial before Caiaphas:

> "If you are the Messiah," they said, "tell us."
> Jesus answered, "If I tell you, you will not believe me, and if I asked you, you would not answer. But from now on, the Son of Man will be seated at the right hand of the mighty God."
> They all asked, "Are you then the Son of God?"
> He replied, "You say that I am." (Luke 22:67-70 NIV)

When presented with a point-blank messianic question, Jesus at first appears to obfuscate, but then he changes tack and declares that the Messiah is none other than a heavenly figure destined to be co-enthroned with God. Quite strikingly, Jesus' answer is a conflation of Psalm 110:1 and Daniel 7:13, texts that refer to a Davidic king and a mysterious heavenly man co-enthroned with God becoming a σύνθρονος. This term refers to a throne sharer with a deity, a superlative position that meant holding a certain type of equality in regency and power, to share in the orbit of divine sovereignty.[18] Jesus does not say that he will one day possess

---

[18] See D. Clint Burnett, *Christ's Enthronement at God's Right Hand and Its Greco-Roman Cultural Context* (Berlin: de Gruyter, 2021).

such power but that he has it "from now on" (Greek ἀπὸ τοῦ νῦν). In other words, in audacious provocation, he claims that he already exercises this authority as God's vice regent, as the true Adam, the embodiment of Israel, the anointed Davidic king, the divine Son of God, who is meant to rule and reign on God's behalf. But . . . this reign is only realized if Jesus, as the Son of Man, enters into the waters of his baptism, if he takes up the cross, suffers the flames of the fire, dies a prophet's death, and drinks the cup of wrath.

SON OF MAN

When it comes to christological titles, there is none more disputed, more technical, more contested, and more confusing than "Son of Man" (ὁ υἱὸς τοῦ ἀνθρώπου). In Luke–Acts, "Son of Man" is a self-reference by Jesus and title for Jesus, found twenty-three times in the Gospel yet only once in Acts. To understand "Son of Man," we have to look at the Jewish background to this self-designation/title, general usage in the Synoptics, and particular Lukan usage of the saying.

The Jewish background to "Son of Man." Jesus' self-designation as "Son of Man" is prominent in all four Gospels and must be situated in its Jewish context.

First, it is possible that Jesus' self-reference as Son of Man is a scriptural idiom for humanity in general. In the Hebrew Bible (i.e., Old Testament), we read in Psalm 8:4 (author's translation): "What is a human being [אֱנוֹשׁ] that you are mindful of him, a son of man [בֶּן־אָדָם] that you care for him?" Note that בֶּן־אָדָם can be translated, literally, as "son of Adam," and it is set in parallel to אֱנוֹשׁ, for "human being" or "humankind." So בֶּן־אָדָם is just a way of referring to humanity in general as descendants of Adam. Similarly, in Ezekiel, the Hebrew בֶּן־אָדָם, is used for God's address to

Ezekiel, and it seems to mean something like "mere mortal man" (e.g., Ezekiel 2:1-3). Seeing this scriptural idiom בֶּן־אָדָם behind Jesus' self-reference as "Son of Man," some scholars translate the Greek ὁ υἱὸς τοῦ ἀνθρώπου (literally, "the Son of the Man") as either "Son of Adam" (Scholar's Version) or "the Human One" (CEB). Jesus, as Son of Man, is perhaps referring to his humanity or to humanity in its proper state and function under God. Jesus, as the son of Adam (Luke 3:38), exercises authority as the "Son of Man is lord of the Sabbath" (Luke 6:5 NIV).

Second, several Son of Man sayings very probably have a connection to the mysterious "one like a Son of Man" in Daniel 7. Daniel 7 is a vision report about four beasts symbolizing four successive empires. At the climax of the vision is a mysterious figure, "one like a son of man" who receives power and authority from the Ancient of Days.

> In my vision at night I looked, and there before me was one *like a son of man* [כְּבַר אֱנָשׁ], coming with the clouds of heaven. He approached the Ancient of Days and was led into his presence. He was given authority, glory and sovereign power; all nations and peoples of every language worshiped him. His dominion is an everlasting dominion that will not pass away, and his kingdom is one that will never be destroyed. (Daniel 7:13-14 NIV)

This mysterious man is perhaps an angel (see the human qualities of angels in Daniel 10:5-6), a heavenly representative of God's people (see Daniel 7:22, 27), or is a symbol of God's kingship who stands against the arrogant horn (Daniel 7:8). So, this son of man could be a heavenly, angelic, messianic, and corporate figure all at once. That would mean that the Lukan Jesus would be referring to himself as this quasi-divine messianic son of man who is enthroned with God in places such as Luke 9:26; 12:40; 17:24-30; 18:8; 21:27;

22:69, where the Son of Man comes with angels, comes on a cloud, or is exalted with God (see also Acts 7:56).

Third, "Son of Man" may also reflect an Aramaic idiom of self-reference. The Gospels have Jesus refer to himself as ὁ υἱὸς τοῦ ἀνθρώπου in Greek. But if Jesus spoke Aramaic, what would "son of man" mean in first-century Aramaic? Well, it takes a bit of guesswork, but Jesus probably referred to himself in Aramaic as בֶּן־אָדָם or some variation thereof. What is debated is whether בֶּן־אָדָם is a generic reference to "man" or whether it can have particular sense of "this man." On the one hand, seeing "Son of Man" as a kind of indirect form of self-reference makes sense in places such as Luke 9:58, where Jesus says, "Foxes have holes, and birds of the air have nests; but the Son of Man has nowhere to lay his head." If we change "Son of Man" to "I," "me," or "someone in my position," it still makes sense. My hunch is that Jesus probably referred to himself as בֶּן־אָדָם but did so with a particularizing connotation, that is, "the man among men," which is why the first people to translate Jesus' Aramaic idiomatic self-reference into Greek decided to adopt the awkward Greek expression ὁ υἱὸς τοῦ ἀνθρώπου, to convey the particular emphasis that Jesus used to describe himself as *the* man.

So, in a Jewish context, "Son of Man" can mean "human being," refer to a mysterious heavenly figure exalted by God, or constitute an Aramaic idiom for indirect self-reference.

Son of Man in the Synoptic Gospels. In the Synoptic Gospels, it is generally recognized that Jesus refers to himself as Son of Man in three basic ways: a man of authority, a man destined to suffer, and a man who will be exalted and appear in glory.[19] Applied to Luke, we could tabulate it this way:

---

[19]Rudolf Bultmann, *Theology of the New Testament*, trans. K. Grobel (London: SCM Press, 1952–1955), 1:30.

Table 5.1. The three types of Son of Man sayings in the Synoptic tradition

AUTHORITY		SUFFERING/SHAME/REJECTION		EXALTATION/COMING	
Luke 5:24	Son of Man can forgive sins	Luke 6:22	Excluded because of Son of Man	Luke 9:26	Son of Man will come in glory of Father
Luke 6:5	Son of Man is lord of the Sabbath	Luke 7:34	Son of Man is friend of sinners	Luke 12:8	Son of Man will acknowledge you before angels
Luke 19:10	Son of Man comes to seek and save the lost	Luke 9:22	Son of Man must suffer many things	Luke 12:40	Son of Man will come at unexpected hour
		Luke 9:44	Son of Man handed over to men	Luke 17:22	Some long to see the days of the Son of Man
		Luke 9:58	Son of Man has no permanent home	Luke 17:24	Son of Man will appear like lightning
		Luke 12:10	Son of Man is blasphemed	Luke 17:26	Son of Man will come unexpectedly as in the days of Noah
		Luke 18:31	Prophecies about the Son of Man will be fulfilled	Luke 17:30	Son of Man will be revealed at inopportune moment
		Luke 22:22	Son of Man goes to his fate, but woe to his betrayer	Luke. 18.8	Will there be faith on earth when Son of Man comes?
		Luke 22:48	Judas betrays Son of Man with a kiss	Luke 21:27	Son of Man comes with clouds in power and glory
		Luke 24:7	Son of Man had to be handed over, crucified, and raised on third day	Luke 22:69	From now on Son of Man will be seated at the right hand of Mighty God
				Acts 7:56	Stephen sees heaven opened and Son of Man standing at right hand of the power

Luke largely inherits this taxonomy from Mark, but he clearly amplifies it and augments it with his own emphases. Luke accents that following the Son of Man will entail being mocked and maligned with the Son of Man and taunted and tainted with the same brush as the Son of Man; it means shame and suffering (Luke 6:22; 7:34; 9:58; 12:10). Luke stresses, too, that the Son of Man's coming in glory will be sudden and unexpected and lead to dire consequences for the unprepared (Luke 12:35-40; 17:22-35; 18:8).

In addition, Jesus' response to Zacchaeus's contrition and penitence is quite striking: "Jesus said to him, 'Today salvation has come to this house, because he too is a son of Abraham. For the Son of Man came to seek out and to save the lost'" (Luke 19:9-10). I'd aver, apart from maybe Luke 4:18-21, that Luke 19:10 is the most programmatic summary in Luke–Acts of Jesus' mission. In fact, Luke 4:16-30 and Luke 19:1-10 bookend the story of Jesus' public ministry to usher in the kingdom and to seek and save the lost. Jesus, as Son of Man, comes to bring salvation to the lost and lowly. Thus, salvation and Christology are intertwined. Zacchaeus, the arch–tax collector, the epitome of greed and avarice, is the lost son who comes home. This rich man doesn't walk away in grief but gives away his possessions and follows Jesus, makes it through the eye of the needle, comes back into the family of Abraham. So, instead of sneering at him, there is rejoicing over him. Jesus' journey to Jerusalem ends on the note that Jesus, as Son of Man, is the Savior of sinners.

Finally, Luke also majors on Jesus' exaltation. Luke, like Mark, applies the Psalm 110:1/Daniel 7:13 synthesis to Jesus as a throne sharer at God's right hand (Luke 22:69), but he repeats it again in Stephen's vision just ahead of his martyrdom (Acts 7:56). Luke will always mention Jesus' crucifixion in apostolic preaching, but he doesn't major on it; instead, the center of gravity lies with Jesus' exaltation, the undoing of death with resurrection, the contrast of degradation with divine honor, the reversal of rejection with exaltation to the highest position imaginable. Just as Jesus was unjustly killed and then co-enthroned with God, so now the risen and exalted Jesus stands ready to receive Stephen into his heavenly entourage. Jesus, the Messiah murdered by men out of malice, is neither absent nor indifferent to his disciples but continues to minister to his disciples even in their deaths.

DIVINE LORD OF THE CHURCH

Some accounts of Lukan Christology identify Jesus as a Spirit-anointed prophet, an ideal human figure, one adopted into the Davidic line, a teacher of wisdom, and a righteous martyr. Plus, because John has a truly divine Christology, and Luke is not John, therefore Lukan Christology is earthly, mundane, or even "low." But that will not do. God's saving acts are announced in the arrival of Jesus, performed by Jesus, and in the end are identified with Jesus. Israel's Lord sends Jesus as his prophet and servant, but in another sense as "Son of the Most High"; as the "messianic Lord," Jesus is identified with God. The question is how Israel's God is manifested in and through the figure of Jesus.[20]

First, there is an emphasis on divine sonship, both Jesus' Davidic office and his unique filial relationship with Israel's God. About Jesus it is said, "He will be great and will be called the Son of the Most High. The Lord God will give him the throne of his father David" (Luke 1:32 NIV). Yet, the boy Jesus speaks about God as if God is his Father (Luke 2:49), not in the sense that God is everybody's Father but as his true Father, making him a chosen son (Luke 23:5). Added to that, the birth of Jesus is superintended and supernatural, mysterious as it is marvelous. It means that his sonship is not a matter of adoption or honorific attribution but a divine begetting (Luke 1:35).[21]

Second, Luke places particular stress on Jesus as "Lord" (κύριος). Israel's God is Lord, and Jesus serves this Lord, which is precisely

---

[20]Richard B. Hays, *Reading Backwards: Figural Christology and the Fourfold Gospel Witness* (Waco, TX: Baylor University Press, 2014), 59.
[21]Hays, *Reading Backwards*, 60.

why the "Lord God" grants Jesus a throne (Luke 1:32), why Jesus operates in the "power of the Lord" (Luke 5:17), why Jesus appeals to the "Lord of the harvest" (Luke 10:2), and why he rebukes Satan, as one must worship only the "Lord your God" and "not put the Lord your God to the test" (Luke 4:8, 12). Jesus is anointed with the "Spirit of the Lord" (Luke 4:18 = Isaiah 61:1), he tells people to "love the Lord your God" (Luke 10:27 = Deuteronomy 6:5), and he enters Jerusalem in the "name of the Lord" (Luke 13:35; 19:28 = Psalm 118:26).

Yet Jesus himself is the "messianic Lord" (Luke 2:11, my translation) and "lord of the Sabbath" (Luke 6:5). In the infancy narrative, Elizabeth calls Mary "the mother of my Lord" (Luke 1:43). John the Baptist prepares the way for the Lord, who is the Lord of Isaiah 40, and the person he is anticipating in none other than Jesus (Luke 1:17, 76; 3:4). Across the narrative, disciples and supplicants of healings address Jesus as "Lord" (Luke 5:8, 12; 6:46; 9:54; 18:41; 22:33, 38, 49). When the news of the resurrection gets out, the disciples report, "The Lord has risen indeed, and he has appeared to Simon" (Luke 24:34), and he is thereafter referred to as the "Lord Jesus" by the apostles (Acts 1:21; 4:33; 11:20). In the confession of the church, he is installed as "Lord and Messiah" (Acts 2:36). He is called on as "Lord" in the early church, with deliberate allusions to scriptural texts referring to Israel's Lord, Yahweh (Acts 2:20 = Joel 2:31). That Jesus shares in the lordship of Israel's Lord is made clear with the application of Psalm 110:1 ("The Lord says to my lord, 'Sit at my right hand until I make your enemies your footstool'") to him (Luke 20:42-44; Acts 2:33-35; 5:31; 7:55-56), making Jesus God's own vice regent, so that Jesus is "Lord of all" (Acts 10:36).

Although Jesus has returned to heaven, he is not absent, as he remains in relationship with his disciples and the churches they establish. Salvation is by the grace of the Lord Jesus (Acts 15:11) and comes by believing in the Lord Jesus (Acts 16:31; 20:21), and baptisms are administered in the name of the Lord Jesus (Acts 8:16; 19:5). Discipleship means to follow the "Way" of the Lord (Acts 18:25), and the mission is to complete the task the Lord gives people such as Paul (Acts 20:24). In many cases, the Lord Jesus' presence is personal and revelatory. Just before his martyrdom, Stephen has a vision of the exalted Jesus and prays to the Lord Jesus to receive his spirit (Acts 7:55-56, 59-60). Paul meets the risen and glorious Lord Jesus on the road to Damascus (Acts 9:5; 22:8; 26:15). Jesus even appears to prevent Paul from going to Asia and instead into Macedonia (Acts 16:6-9) and comes to Paul strengthen him during his confinement (Acts 23:11).

"Through the narrative," says Kavin Rowe, "Luke uses κύριος [Lord] to make an essential claim about the relation between Jesus and the God of Israel: Jesus of Nazareth is the movement of God in one human life so much so that it is possible to speak of God and Jesus together as κύριος." Luke stresses neither the words, nor even his deeds, but the "totality of the life of Jesus . . . as the embodied revelation of κύριος ὁ θεὸς [the Lord God]." Ultimately what Theophilus is instructed in is a matter of "divine disclosure," a revelation that is *through* Jesus as much as it *is* Jesus.[22]

Third, Luke also stresses how the events surrounding Jesus are bound up with God's visitation to his people. Zechariah's Benedictus erupts with celebration, "Praise be to the Lord, the God of Israel, because *he has come* to his people and redeemed them" (Luke 1:68 NIV); "because of the tender mercy of our God . . . the rising sun *will come to us* from heaven" (Luke 1:78 NIV). When Jesus raises a widow's son, the crowd sees it as an act of

---

[22]C. Kavin Rowe, *Early Narrative Christology: The Lord in the Gospel of Luke* (Grand Rapids, MI: Baker, 2006), 217-18.

divine visitation, that "A great prophet has appeared among us. . . . God has *come to help* his people" (Luke 7:16 NIV). The Greek word here is ἐπισκέπτομαι, which has the sense of close inspection with a view to assistance. The same word is used in the LXX in celebration that God visited with concern the Hebrews who toiled under Egyptian oppression (Exodus 4:31). In the Psalter there are prayerful pleas, "O God of mighty powers, return now, look down from heaven and see, and visit this vine [i.e., Judah], and restore that which your right hand planted, and for the son of humanity whom you strengthened for yourself" (Psalm 79:15 LES [MT 80:15]), and "Remember us, O Lord, with the good pleasure of your people, to visit us with your salvation" (Psalm 105:4 LES [MT 106:5]). Luke describes how, in the advent of the new Davidic king and the prophet Jesus, God is again visiting his people to show mercy and bring salvation.

Jesus, on entering Jerusalem, engages in a moment of prophetic lament for the city, knowing that it is destined to be besieged and broken by a Roman army in the future. The tragedy comes, he says, because they did not reckon with their time of visitation.

> As he approached Jerusalem and saw the city, he wept over it and said, "If you, even you, had only known on this day what would bring you peace—but now it is hidden from your eyes. The days will come upon you when your enemies will build an embankment against you and encircle you and hem you in on every side. They will dash you to the ground, you and the children within your walls. They will not leave one stone on another, because you did not recognize the time of God's coming to you." (Luke 19:41-44 NIV)

The word *God* is not in the Greek text, but it is implied as the one whose "visitation" (NRSV) or "coming" (NIV) is referred to. The precise word used in Luke 19:44 is ἐπισκοπή, which refers to the

"the coming of divine power, either for benefit or judgment."[23] In this case, Jesus identifies himself as a divine visitation to bring peace and redemption (Luke 2:38), yet, because he is rejected, there will be another visitation of judgment against Jerusalem (Luke 10:8-16). Later authors use the same language to refer to the return of Jesus to visit judgment on the world (1 Peter 2:12; *1 Clement* 50.3). This meshes with the Qumran scrolls, which deploy the language of divine visitation in association with divine judgment (e.g., CD 8.2-3; 19.9-10). But Luke's point is that Jesus' entry into Jerusalem is the very coming of God in peace and mercy.

Fourth, we need to note as well Jesus' relationship to the Spirit. On the one hand, Jesus is led by the Spirit, with the Spirit as the driving force and dominant partner in Jesus' prophetic ministry (Luke 4:1, 14; 10:21). Jesus, then, is the Spirit-anointed prophet of Isaiah 61:1, and this is the basis for a type of Spirit Christology. However, Jesus is more than the bearer of the Spirit; he is also the baptizer with the Spirit. John the Baptist prophesies, "I baptize you with water; but one who is more powerful than I is coming; I am not worthy to untie the thong of his sandals. He will baptize you with the Holy Spirit and fire" (Luke 3:16). Jesus will, in other words, give the Spirit to those who need its purifying power as a way to escape a purgation of evil at the final judgment. The risen Jesus tells his disciples that he will send them "the promise of the Father," which is "power from on high" (Luke 24:49). Or again, later, they are to wait for the "promise of the Father," and they will be "baptized with the Holy Spirit" (Acts 1:5). Jesus will plunge them into the holiness and cleansing power of the Spirit so that they will be indwelled by a divine power as the Father promised. This is why the Spirit is given in Jesus' name (Acts 2:38).

---

[23]Johannes P. Louw and Eugene A. Nida, eds., *Greek-English Lexicon of the New Testament: Based on Semantic Domains*, 2nd ed. (New York: United Bible Societies, 1989), 1:452.

What is significant is that giving the Spirit is something that Israel's God performs as part of Israel's restoration. In the prophets, Yahweh promises to dispense his Spirit in a new, dynamic, and universal way on all flesh (Psalm 104:30; Isaiah 44:3; Ezekiel 39:29; Joel 2:28-29; Acts 2:17-18). Luke, however, while nominating the Spirit as the promise/gift/power from the Father, nonetheless puts Jesus in the position as the dispenser of the Spirit, from whom and for whom it is given. This puts Jesus in a position analogous to Yahweh in the prophetic writings since dispensing the Spirit as part of Israel's redemption and restoration is a task that properly belongs to Yahweh.

REVIEW QUESTIONS

1. How is Jesus the Savior of Israel and Gentiles?
2. To what extent is "Lord's Messiah" (see Luke 2:11) a good summary of the Christology of Luke–Acts?
3. How is Jesus' prophetic ministry continued in the church?
4. In your own words, summarize who the Son of Man is.
5. What does it mean for us today to confess Jesus as the Lord of the church?

RECOMMENDED READING

Bird, Michael F. *Jesus Is the Christ: The Messianic Testimony of the Gospels*. Milton Keynes, UK: Paternoster, 2012. Pages 79-96.

Grindheim, Sigurd. *Christology in the Synoptic Gospels: God or God's Servant?* London: T&T Clark, 2012. Pages 118-47.

Harris, Sarah. *The Davidic Shepherd King in the Lukan Narrative*. London: Bloomsbury T&T Clark, 2016.

Henrichs-Tarasenkova, Nina. *Luke's Christology of Divine Identity*. LNTS 542. London: T&T Clark, 2016.

Marshall, I. Howard. "The Christology of Luke's Gospel and Acts." In *Contours of Christology in the New Testament*, edited by Richard N. Longenecker, 122-47. Grand Rapids, MI: Eerdmans, 2005.

Matera, Frank. *New Testament Christology*. Louisville, KY: Westminster John Knox, 1999. Pages 49-82.

Rowe, C. Kavin. *Early Narrative Christology: The Lord in the Gospel of Luke*. Grand Rapids, MI: Baker, 2006.

Strauss, Mark L. *The Davidic Messiah in Luke–Acts: The Promise and Its Fulfilment in Lukan Christology*. JSNTSup 110. Sheffield: Sheffield Academic Press, 1995.

Luke and the Way of Salvation

6

SAVED?

The 2004 movie *Saved* is a religious satire and teen flick about the dangers of Christian girls fraternizing with boys who are not "saved." I never went to a Christian high school, but some of my students who attended a Christian high school and who have seen the movie tell me that it is funny for its realism in its teeth-grinding cringiness. In Christian subcultures, especially the evangelical kind, there is a whole insider vocabulary of terms, taboos, and traditions about being saved. How to pray for it, how to get it, how to not lose it, how to stop worrying about losing it, and so forth.

I suspect that Saint Luke would understand very little of evangelical pop culture and its various idiosyncrasies of being saved, whether making a decision, being destined for immortal bliss, or expecting to escape a coming rapture. I doubt he'd be terribly thrilled, either, with mainline Christianity's mixture of self-help moralism and offering social activities for the elderly as the limit of the church's work for salvation. To be sure, Luke uses the language of "salvation" and "being saved" with great frequency and intensity. Luke dually stresses God as Savior (Luke 1:47) and Jesus as Savior (Luke 2:11; Acts 5:31; 13:23), for to see Jesus is to see God's salvation (Luke 2:30), Jesus comes to "to seek and to save the lost" (Luke 19:10 NIV), his people are those "being saved" (Acts 2:47), and their mission is telling people how anyone can be saved (Acts 4:12; 15:1, 11; 16:17, 30-31). Salvation, as we'll soon see, has many dimensions and permeates Luke and Acts. Indeed, for any topic we touch on in Luke–Acts, whether Christology, Israel, Holy Spirit, the church, or use of the Old Testament, we will find that Lukan salvation in some sense is connected to it. So it is a very important topic and one that bears close scrutiny. Luke is if anything the theologian of salvation.

Accordingly, I'll explore Luke's theology of salvation in terms of salvation within the world, salvation and the future, and salvation as a way of mission and praxis.

> **Lukan Theology as Salvation Theology**
>
> "It is our thesis that the idea of salvation supplies the key to the theology of Luke. Not salvation-history but salvation itself is the theme which occupied the mind of Luke in both parts of his work."[a]
>
> [a] I. Howard Marshall, *Luke: Historian and Theologian*, 3rd ed. (Carlisle, UK: Paternoster, 1988), 92.

SALVATION WITHIN THE WORLD

> **Salvation in This Life or the Next?**
>
> "For Luke, salvation means freedom from exile and all forms of oppression—spiritual, yes, but also physical, political, social, and economic. Although Luke, like many other Jews, believed in an afterlife (Luke 16:20-21), he did not confuse the hereafter with the divine promises of national restoration concerning Israel that were supposed to take place in this world. Salvation in Luke–Acts is not completely diluted into a spiritual concept."[a]
>
> [a] Isaac W. Oliver, *Luke's Jewish Eschatology: The National Restoration of Israel in Luke–Acts* (Cambridge: Cambridge University Press, 2021), 140.

Lukan salvation is a matter of deliverance from the travails *within* this world, that is, from sociopolitical oppression, illness, death, debt, disease, despair, and the demonic. For a start, consider Mary's Magnificat.

> His mercy is for those who fear him,
> > from generation to generation.
> He has shown strength with his arm;
> > he has scattered the proud in the thoughts of their hearts.
> He has brought down the powerful from their thrones,
> > and lifted up the lowly;
> he has filled the hungry with good things,
> > and sent the rich away empty.
> He has helped his servant Israel,
> > in remembrance of his mercy,
> according to the promise he made to our ancestors,
> > to Abraham and to his descendants forever. (Luke 1:50-55)

Even though this song takes place during the infancy narrative and is part of Christian readings during Christmas celebrations, I cannot think of a single Christmas hymn that sings about God bringing down the mighty or sending the rich away hungry. What is more, you could probably take those lines and insert them into the middle of a pamphlet by a Marxist with a zealous faith, and you might not notice the interpolation.

Mary's Magnificat proclaims that God has remembered his promises to the patriarch Abraham and is faithful to Israel, along with an inversion of the social pyramid, a great reversal between the mighty and the powerless. The future kingdom will not be characterized by egalitarian equality but by a reversal of positions: Jesus says, "Indeed, some are last who will be first, and some are first who will be last" (Luke 13:30). Many persons, especially the rich, who assume they are going to have the best seats in the messianic banquet, will not even be let in, while those thought to be unworthy will have places of honor (Luke 13:22-30; 14:7-11, 15-23; 16:19-31).

Lest I be misunderstood, Luke is not calling for a Marxist revolution, with the seizure of all private property and the nationalization of state resources. Yet, Luke expounds a salvation that includes upending the social, political, and economic order in its oppressive expression, at least in the final reckoning, with some anticipation in the present. Also, Luke is not expecting guillotines to be erected to eradicate those with too much disposable cash or a nice property portfolio. Riches are a dangerous temptation and a snare that many get caught in, but even the rich and powerful need salvation, and there are positive examples of rich men who repent of their greed and avarice (Luke 18:9-14; 19:1-10). As John the Baptist points out, the wealthy and powerful will be welcomed if they refrain from extortion and exploitation of others (Luke 3:10-14). As such, Jesus' followers and devotees include tax collectors, priests, merchants, centurions, and proconsuls. Salvation has economic expressions in terms of deliverance from deprivation, destitution, and debt, but it also embraces everyone on all levels of the economic pyramid.

In Lukan terms, salvation is indeed for Israel, their redemption, rescue, and refreshment (Luke 1:68; 2:38; 24:21; Acts 3:19), through a "horn of salvation" (Luke 1:69 NIV), the coming Davidic king (Luke 1:68-75), and the centerpiece of a restored Davidic kingdom (Luke 22:30; Acts 15:15-18 = Amos 9:11-12). But it spills over to the Gentiles (Luke 2:32; 7:1-10; 24:47; Acts 1:8; 10:45; 11:18; 13:47; 20:21; 28:28) because a transformed Israel is to transform the world, to be, like Jesus, a light to the nations (Acts 13:47; Isaiah 42:6; 49:6). The great act of liberation for Israel will not overthrow the Herodians or the Romans, but it will create a renewed Israel, a society within a society, bearing the Spirit, carrying each other's burdens, preaching in truth and power the truth to the powerful. It will be a new covenant, as a foretaste of the new age, and bring Gentiles into David's renewed house. Seen through an Isaianic lens, Luke is telling the story of how "all people will see God's salvation," as the Baptist proclaims from Isaiah (Luke 3:6 NIV = Isaiah 40:5). The messianic light shining on Israel reflects toward the Gentiles and all who live in darkness (Luke 1:79; Acts 26:18), as Paul testifies, "I am saying nothing beyond what the prophets and Moses said would happen—the Messiah would suffer and, as the first to rise from the dead, would bring the message of light to his own people and to the Gentiles" (Acts 26:22-23 NIV).

Luke also associates salvation (σῴζω) with healing from illness and demonic affliction (Luke 6:9; 8:36). This salvation often takes place on account of faith. Hence the refrain by Jesus to a supplicant of healing, "your faith has saved you" (Luke 7:50; 8:48, 50; 17:19; 18:42). There is a running theme of Jesus' concern for the poor (Luke 4:18; 6:20; 7:22; 11:41; 12:33; 14:13, 21; 18:22) and of releasing those afflicted with demons (Luke 4:31-37; 7:22; 8:2, 26-39; 9:37-43) and various illnesses (Luke 5:12-20; 7:22; 8:40-56; 13:10-14; 17:11-19; 18:35-43). Particular to Luke is Jesus' special concern for the welfare of widows, who were always vulnerable and often victimized (Luke 2:37; 7:11-12; 18:1-8; 20:47; 21:1-3). This theme of healing is more than acts of random mercy, as it is programmatically set out in the Nazareth Manifesto (Luke 4:18-21) as part of Israel's restoration. Jesus, following the prophetic script of Isaiah 61:1, makes it his mission to liberate the oppressed, restore sight to the blind, set the captives free, and bring good news to the poor (Luke 4:18). Indeed, such healings, liberations, and declarations are proof that Jesus is the coming messianic deliver, and the signs of Israel's restoration are apparent in his miraculous deeds even if the messenger is rejected (Luke 7:18-23).

Another important element in the Lukan scope of salvation is how it pertains to a reversal of status for outsiders, that is, restoration and inclusion. When Mary sings that God has "lifted up the lowly," this does not mean God looks with favor on those who do not brag (true though this may be, as per Luke 14:11; 18:14). Rather, it means that God reverses their status as he exalts the humiliated. Elizabeth, in bearing a child in her old age in a culture where women were prized for fertility, rejoices that "In these days he has shown his favor and taken away my disgrace among the people" (Luke 1:25 NIV). Jesus healed women whose illnesses were associated with impurity, shame, and exclusion (Luke 8:42-48; 13:10-16); even women who are "sinful" or prostitutes find a warm welcome from Jesus (Luke 7:37). Jesus offers a scope of inclusion that is truly scandalous, breaking bread with the immoral and impure, making him a "friend of . . . sinners" (Luke 7:34) such as tax collectors. The invitation to the kingdom is open to those whom many supposed would be excluded (Luke 13:28-29; 14:1-23).

Jesus also challenges ethnic prejudices and rivalries. He is inclusive of ethnic "others," such as Samaritans and Gentiles. Jesus subverts ethnic stereotypes by making a Samaritan an exemplar of the scriptural command to love one's neighbor in the parable of the good Samaritan (Luke 10:25-37). In another episode, a Samaritan is an exemplar of faith, since out of the ten lepers Jesus heals the only one to come back and thank him is a Samaritan (Luke 17:11-19). Jesus also refuses to indulge the fantasy of apocalyptic violence by James and John against a Samaritan village that would not welcome him (Luke 9:51-56). While Luke does not incorporate Mark's material about Gentiles, such as the Syro-Phoenician woman (Mark 7:24-30), Jesus does heal a centurion's servant and commend his faith (Luke 7:1-10), as well as the Gerasene demoniac in the Decapolis (Luke 8:26-39). Such episodes, I argue elsewhere, foreshadow the Gentile mission of the later church (Luke 24:47; Acts 1:8).[1]

The early church implements Jesus' teachings with a holistic vision of salvation and takes care of the spiritual and material needs of church members. People sell possessions to support those in need and assist the church in its provisions (Acts 2:45; 4:32-37; see Luke 3:10-11). This sharing of provisions takes place between the regional churches of Antioch and Jerusalem (Acts 11:27-30). There is a daily distribution of food for the vulnerable, including widows, leading to the establishment of the office of deacon (Acts 6:1-4). The apostles, just like Jesus, perform several healings, many of which outrage local Jerusalem officials (Acts 3:1-16; 5:12-16). Peter performs a couple of healings for believers in the coastal cities of Lydda and Joppa (Acts 9:32-43). Paul also heals a lame man in Lystra (Acts 14:8-10). Paul even develops a reputation as a healer and exorcist in Ephesus (Acts 20:11-12). Philip casts out many unclean spirits while in Samaria (Acts 8:7).

The early church follows Jesus in clearly dismantling ethnic barriers. Paul releases a slave girl possessed by a pythonic spirit (Acts 16:18), and he breaks bread with sailors and passengers in the midst of a terrifying storm to encourage them and strengthen them (Acts 27:33-38). The church breaks with tribal loyalties and historic hostilities by establishing churches among Samaritans (Acts 8:4-25) and Greeks (Acts 11:19-21). Peter faces serious criticism and censure from within the church because he enters the house of a Gentile and even eats with him (Acts 10-11). Peter says the Spirit taught him through this encounter that "God shows no

---

[1] See Michael F. Bird, *Jesus and the Origins of the Gentile Mission*, LNTS 331 (Edinburgh: T&T Clark, 2006).

partiality, but in every nation anyone who fears him and does what is right is acceptable to him" (Acts 10:34), because "God gave them the same gift that he gave us when we believed in the Lord Jesus Christ" (Acts 11:17; see Acts 15:8). This proves that God "did not discriminate between us and them, for he purified their hearts by faith" (Acts 15:9 NIV), which leads to the rightful conclusion, "So then, even to Gentiles God has granted repentance that leads to life" (Acts 11:18 NIV).

The early church, in its idealized state as Luke presents it, was a place where the prophetic work of Jesus was continued by the apostles. They strove to continue Jesus' kingdom mission and do what was right before God and all people, showing Jesus' concern for the poor, vulnerable, and outcast as well as breaking down ethnic barriers.

SALVATION AND THE FUTURE

Luke is rightly thought of as the Evangelist with an evident concern for the poor, women, widows, outsiders, and outcasts. This emphasis translates into an obvious application for similar concerns today and even amounts to support for projects we might call works of charity and social justice. However, Luke also believed in eternal life, the future kingdom of God, deliverance from the demonic, the dangers of a final judgment, saving one's soul from hell, and the need to have one's sins pardoned. So, for Luke, salvation has a great deal to do with one's standing before God. It is about an eternal future equally as much as the present body.

Salvation as the kingdom of God. Much of Jesus' message (Luke 4:43; 8:1; 16:16) and that of the church (Acts 8:12; 19:8; 20:25; 28:23) focuses on the kingdom of God. In the Lukan account, the kingdom of God is the coming of God as king, in and through Jesus and the Spirit; it is a present reality (Luke 10:9; 11:20; 17:21) but also has a future consummation (Luke 11:2; 13:28; 14:15; 21:31; 22:16-18, 29-30; 23:42; Acts 1:6). The kingdom is God's present reign and a future realm. The kingdom is present in healings and longed for as a future hope (see esp. Luke 9:2, 11). The kingdom of God is the present restoration and a coming redemption. The kingdom is embryonic in its present state but eschatological in its final fulfillment. The kingdom is the forgiveness of sins ahead of a future judgment. In other words, the kingdom is both now and not yet. The kingdom of God is, Luke stresses, something that must be apprehended with a sense of desperation, like a defendant trying to reconcile with his accuser before going to court (Luke 12:57-59), like a person trying to get into a house before the door is shut on a freezing night (Luke 13:24-27), like a steward trying to hurriedly play off his master against his clients to keep his position (Luke 16:9), like a rich man trying to get rid of ill-gotten wealth before a day of judgment (Luke 12:13-21). The kingdom must be sought after (Luke 12:31-32), entered (Luke 18:24-29), with childlike faith (Luke 18:17), and doing so requires persevering through hardships (Acts 14:22).

Salvation as life. Closely related to the kingdom of God is eternal life, which is the life that will characterize the kingdom in the future (note the explicit parallel between "eternal life" and "kingdom of God" in Luke 18:18, 24). It does not have quite the same currency that it has in John's Gospel, but the promise of eternal life is part of the preaching of the early church (Acts 13:46-47). Eternal life, or the future aspect of the kingdom, can be described as a great banquet or wedding feast (Luke 13:29; 14:15; 22:27). It a place where people receive the homes they lost, the family members they left behind, and the security they surrendered for the sake of the kingdom (Luke 18:29-30). Eternal life is not disembodied bliss but resurrection life, a reconstituted bodily existence, where one is repaid for righteous acts (Luke 14:14), an existence comparable to that of the angels where death is no more (Luke 20:36). The nature of eternal life is paradise, a reconstituted people of God, a restored creation, a reversal of injustice and suffering, a resurrected body, and life with God and his Messiah. That is what is offered, to be gained or spurned by how someone responds to Jesus and his message.

Salvation from sins and the need for judgment. If the kingdom of God and eternal life are the ultimate endpoint in salvation, then what is it that lays between and can stop our attaining it? To begin with, people have "sins." Now, Luke never defines for us what sin is, nor does he lay out a hierarchy of sinful acts. But we can infer that sin relates to several things: greed (Luke 11:39; 12:21; 18:22-25; 20:47), lawlessness (Acts 7:53; 13:39), sexual impropriety (Luke 7:37-39; Acts 15:20, 29; 21:25), self-righteousness and hypocrisy (Luke 6:42; 11:37-52; 12:1, 56; 13:15; 18:11), lust for power and greatness (Luke 20:46; 22:24-26; Acts 8:18-23), a refusal to fear God and not having regard for anyone (Luke 18:2), rejecting God's saving purposes in Jesus and blaspheming the Holy Spirit (Luke 4:22-30; 7:30; 10:3-16; 11:14-15, 53-54; 20:17-19; Acts 2:36; 5:39; 7:51-52; 9:5), neglecting justice (Luke 11:42), idolatry (Acts 7:41-43; 15:20, 29; 17:16; 21:25), magic and witchcraft (Acts 13:6-11; 19:19-20), or just the run-of-the-mill "wickedness" of the contemporary generation (Luke 9:41; 11:29-32; Acts 2:40; 3:26). Simon Peter, realizing Jesus is a holy man, bemoans his own sins (Luke 5:8); likewise does the tax collector in the temple in one parable (Luke 18:13). Sin is something that is done to us and done to others, but above all sin is an offense against God. In Luke's telling, everyone is villain and victim; they sin as much as they are sinned against, whether Jew, Samaritan, Greek, or Roman, whether rich or poor, man or woman. Everyone brings up evil things out of their hearts (Luke 6:45).

But it gets worse. People are not just morally sick, society is not merely unjust, the Romans are not just a political nuisance, systems of debt and exploitation are not merely predatory, the Jerusalem priesthood is not only nakedly self-interested. Things are bad because people live in darkness (Luke 1:79), a darkness that permeates their body and being (Luke 11:34-35; Acts 26:18), a darkness that sometimes feels like it holds sway and reigns over the whole edifice of human affairs (Luke 22:53). Then there is the Satan, the sum and symbol of the spiritual and earthly powers of all cosmic evil in its rebellion against God and his people. Satan (or the devil) vainly tries to thwart God's plan in Jesus through the temptation (Luke 4:1-13) but fails and needs to wait until an "opportune time" to launch a further sortie against Jesus (Luke 4:13). Satan is the power that keeps a person in the misery of affliction (Luke 13:16), the one who takes the word from the hearts of people to deprive them of salvation (Luke 8:12), who enters and occupies Judas the way someone might enter a building for the purpose of carrying out an assassination (Luke 22:3), who fills the hearts of pseudo-disciples such as Ananias with lies to the Holy Spirit (Acts 5:3), who desires to sift and chastise those who are faithful to Jesus such as Simon Peter (Luke 22:31), and a "strong man" (Luke 11:21-22) who keeps Jews and Gentiles under the aegis of his malevolent power (Acts 26:18).

In Luke's moral universe there cannot be a "restoration of all things" (Acts 3:21 CEB; ἀποκατάστασις) until there is a judgment of the evil within it. The Lukan Jesus exhorts the hearts of the oppressed that God will "grant justice to his chosen ones who cry to him day and night" (Luke 18:7) because he judges the wicked and vindicates the innocent. Indeed, judgment is a prominent theme in Luke–Acts, something that is both national and individual.

Israel's deliverance means rescue from the hands of enemies by bringing down the mighty (Luke 1:52, 74). John the Baptist warns of a coming wrath that draws near like an axe preparing to fell a tree if there is not massive repentance (Luke 3:7-9). Furthermore, if Israel rejects God's prophetic envoy (Luke 4:21-23; 10:16), the power of salvation will go to "sinners," outsiders within Israel, the poor and "wicked" who seek God's mercy rather than spurn it (Luke 5:32; 7:34; 19:10; 20:9-18). Or salvation will be offered even to those beyond Israel, just like it was in the times of Elijah and Elisha, who were themselves mistreated and turned to help the widow of Zarephath and Naaman the Syrian (Luke 4:24-27). Examples of this extension of salvation include the centurion at Capernaum (Luke 7:1-10) and the Gerasene demoniac (Luke 8:26-39). Paul, similarly, turns not once but twice from preaching to the Jews, deciding to go to the Gentiles after encountering Jewish recalcitrance to the gospel (Acts 13:46; 18:6). If Israel rejects the call to repent and believe (Luke 13:1-5), then the nation's condition will be worse than that of Sodom and Gomorrah (Luke 10:8-16; 11:29-32). If the nation does not give up its way of being Israel, if it does not heed Jesus' exhortations and warnings, and if it continues to follow instead the Pharisees, scribes, or priests, then the nation will tragically end up in a bloody, brutal, and futile rebellion against Rome, in which even the temple will be destroyed (Luke 19:41-44; 21:5-38).

Individuals, too, must repent of their sins, for if they do not repent and bear good fruit (Luke 3:9; 13:6-9), they risk being cast into hell, a place of final judgment (Luke 12:5). A warning of judgment is repeatedly made against the rich, those who hoard wealth (Luke 12:13-21), in one case in an eschatologically charged parable comparing their fate to that of the poor and the righteous in Hades, the waiting place of the dead (Luke 16:19-31). Those who are unwilling to act or are unprepared for the mysterious coming of the Son of Man will find that it is too late for them (Luke 17:26-37). Even though Jesus is condemned by others, he is, it turns out, the appointed judge (Acts 10:42; 17:31; 24:25).

Salvation as mercy, forgiveness, justification, and sanctification. For Israel, repentance is for the sin of transgressing the law, being stiff-necked, rejecting the messianic deliverer, while for Gentiles, repentance is from the sin of immorality, idolatry, and wickedness. If sin is what separates peoples, Jew and Gentile, from God, then what do they need in order to enter the kingdom of God and attain eternal life? On this subject, Luke is positively bursting with joyous energy to tell us that God is eager to save his elect, shepherd his flock, and be reconciled to his people, and bring those who were far off into the family of the Messiah. God's deliverance, Luke tells us, consists of several things.

The infancy narrative mentions over and over God's mercy (Luke 1:50, 54, 58, 72, 78). At one level, considering Israel's Scriptures, this mercy is God's חֶסֶד, his covenant love for his people in their darkness and despair, his refusal to walk away, and his determination to be faithful. At another level, God hears the cries of those who call out for mercy, like a penitent tax collector who knows he is unworthy (Luke 18:13) or a blind man begging for healing (Luke 18:38). The ocean of God's mercy extends to the depths where people thought God could not find them, and it runs wide to include all the peoples of the earth, even those who do not know the God who is rich in mercy.

If Luke has one favorite image for what people need, one word that sums up salvation, it would be *forgiveness*. The Greek word ἀφίημι can have a broad range of meanings, such as "release," "set free," and "dismiss," but connected with a judicial setting pertaining to sin, it has a sense of "to acquit, absolve, pardon, or release."[2] In fact, "forgiveness of sins" is effectively a synonym for salvation in Luke–Acts. This is why John the Baptist's ministry is to give people

---

[2]BDAG, 156.

"knowledge of salvation" in the form of the "forgiveness of their sins" (Luke 1:77) and the Lukan Great Commission includes that "repentance for the forgiveness of sins will be preached in his name to all nations" (Luke 24:47 NIV). The parable of the prodigal son provides something of a paradigm for the forgiveness of the sinner (Luke 15:11-32). The parable demonstrates the Father's scandalous eagerness to forgive an undeserving sinner if they are repentant even if onlookers sneer. Similarly, the story of Jesus being anointed by a sinful woman in the company of the Pharisees also demonstrates the scandalous nature of forgiveness as it grants a release from the weight of condemnation, both divine and social, to those who have lived lives of disrepute (Luke 7:36-50). In apostolic preaching, the forgiveness of sins is emphasized in several sermons and is a basic summary of the gospel, whether presented to Jews or to Greeks (Acts 2:38, 5:31, 10:43, 13:38, 26:18).

Luke also uses the language of "justification," but not quite with the precise nuance that Paul deploys in such language. Luke uses the verb δικαιόω largely in the sense of vindication (Luke 7:29, 35), but it can also refer to someone asserting their own covenantal righteousness (Luke 10:29; 16:15). The haughty Pharisee praying in the temple asserts his superiority over other sinners, yet it is the humble and penitent tax collector who goes away "justified," in the sense that he is righteous, not of his own accord but because of God's mercy, to which he appeals. This mercy restores him to divine favor, to covenant standing (Luke 18:9-14). Pauline language for justification does appear at one point in Acts. In Paul's evangelistic sermon in Pisidian Antioch, Paul tells a Jewish audience, "Therefore, my friends, I want you to know that through Jesus the forgiveness of sins is proclaimed to you. Through him everyone who believes is set free [literally, "justified by," δικαιωθῆναι] from every sin, a justification [δικαιοῦται] you were not able to obtain under the law of Moses" (Acts 13:38-39 NIV). This shows Paul's own approach, which treats justification as parallel to forgiveness (Romans 4:6-8) and associates justification with liberation from sin's mastery (Romans 6:7).

An underappreciated Lukan image for salvation is being "purified" and "sanctified." The church consists of all those who are "sanctified" (ἁγιάζω; Acts 20:32; 26:18) and "purified" by faith (καθαρίζω; Acts 10:15; 15:9), which means to be made holy from their former state of impurity. This is important, because Luke's images for salvation are not just juridical but moral and cultic. God cleanses and sanctifies those considered tainted by sin, idolatry, social prejudice, or tribal rivalries. A Jewish priest who believes in Jesus is just as holy as the prostitute who casts herself before Jesus' feet or the Roman centurion who seeks God's mercy.

Salvation and human response. Salvation is part of God's plan and purpose, largely at God's initiative and invitation, but it has a human element of appropriation. People, whether Jew or Gentile, are called to repent and believe. John the Baptist proclaims a baptism for repentance with an implicit trust in a coming messianic deliver (Luke 3:3, 8, 16). In the church's memory of John, "John's baptism was a baptism of repentance. He told the people to believe in the one coming after him, that is, in Jesus" (Acts 19:4 NIV). Jesus himself calls sinners to repentance (Luke 5:32, 19:10), and there are several episodes about repentance, including a vivid warning that Israel's options are to repent or to perish (Luke 13:1-5). God is eager to forgive the repentant like a sheep who has wandered away, and of course there is the parable of the prodigal son (Luke 15). The rich need to repent if they are rapacious (Luke 16:30).

Repentance is closely related to the forgiveness of sins (Luke 24:47), for Jews as for Gentiles, which entails belief that Jesus is messianic mediator of divine forgiveness. In the post-Easter period, repentance is what the Jerusalem populace must do because of its consent, implicit or otherwise, in Jesus' unlawful execution (Acts 2:38) and as the precursor to Israel's restoration (Acts 3:19). The Jews must express sorrow for their sins and change their verdict about who Jesus is and what their leaders did to Jesus. As the story unfolds, it becomes clear that, with some surprise, "Even to Gentiles God has granted repentance that leads to life" (Acts 11:18 NIV). Gentiles need to repent of their idolatry, ignorance, and immorality, as Paul tells the Athenians (Acts 17:30). For Gentiles such as the Philippian jailer, salvation means, "Believe on the Lord Jesus, and you will be saved" (Acts 16:31), but also that Gentiles "should repent and turn to God and do deeds consistent with repentance" (Acts 26:20). Probably the best summary of the human response to the gospel is what Paul tells the Ephesians about his decades of apostolic ministry: "I have declared to both Jews and Greeks that they must turn to God in repentance and have faith in our Lord Jesus" (Acts 20:21 NIV).

> **What Is Salvation?**
>
> "To come to God for salvation is to let Him deal with one's sin through Christ."[a]
>
> ---
>
> [a] Darrell L. Bock, "Jesus as Lord in Acts and in the Gospel Message," *Bibliotheca Sacra* 143 (1986): 153.

SALVATION AS CULTURE

One could argue that in Luke–Acts, salvation is *past* in having been determined in the purpose and plan of God, *present* in the life of faith by following the way of Jesus, and *future* as one perseveres to enter the kingdom of God. To be a Christian is to join those who are "being saved" (σῳζομένους), as Luke describes the church in Acts 2:47. Salvation is in the present tense a work in process. The church is a place where, we could say, there is a salvation culture, which manifests itself in several ways.

First, there is a common experience of salvation, where people know God as Savior and the salvation that comes from Jesus. It means a communion of those who repent of sins, who believe in the Lord Jesus, who rest in God's forgiveness, who enjoy the cleansing of the heart, and find consolation in the mercy of God. It means, too, that one's identity and one's values are determined by the story of the life, death, resurrection, and exaltation of Jesus. It means some have decided to take up their cross *daily* and follow Jesus, looking ahead to the day of their redemption.

Second, a salvation culture emerges in the mission of church. The followers of Jesus continue to enact and declare the kingdom of God, about which Jesus and the apostles spoke. It means that the Nazareth Manifesto (Luke 4:18-21) becomes the church's manifesto. It means that the ideal apostolic community of Spirit, word, and sacrament should be normal as it is nourishing (Acts 2:42-47). This salvific culture is holistic, concerned with gospel proclamation as much as discipleship, meeting the bodily needs of its members and its community. Where Christians gather, there should be faith, financial generosity, human flourishing, and evangelical zeal.

Third, a salvation culture is pneumatic (or charismatic, if you are so inclined) because the Holy Spirit animates believers for making this culture of salvation a reality. The Holy Spirit is poured out so that we might bring fresh wind and fire to those who need it. The Spirit compels us to take risks, to transgress boundaries, to go beyond our natural limits, to bury old grievances, to find new alliances, and to forge new paths. The Spirit is a gift and guide, a promise and power, who compels churches to translate the gospel into innovative proclamation and courageous actions that show that we live what we believe.

Fourth, salvation culture is inclusive. It is inclusive in the sense that Jesus is to be proclaimed to all nations. Christianity is neither a feminist cult nor a boys' club. It is not a tribal or ethnic religion. Neither death nor despair discriminates; all people sin and stumble in the darkness, and everyone needs God's light in Christ and the joy of the Spirit. Where Christianity becomes gendered, siloed by class, segregated by race, or tribalized by politics or profession, it is the church's duty to bring those divisions down. The church is a place, too, where the disabled are not tolerated but valued for their contribution, where those mocked and maligned for the sexed nature of their bodies, such as the Ethiopian eunuch, are welcomed for baptism. Here we must be careful, as inclusivity can also be a modern secular value, and the church of Jesus is not infinitely inclusive. Yes, Jesus is for everyone, but the church is for followers, not fans (see Luke 9:57-62). Evil forces must be confronted as Paul and Barnabas confronted Elymas/Bar-Jesus (Acts 13:6-11), and those who want to peddle the word for profit must be sternly warned like Simon Magus (Acts 8:9-25). Yet it cannot be stressed enough that Luke's vision for churches is to transcend differences that divided people in his day and no doubt ours.

LUKE AND HIS TWO-PART SALVATION STORY

Luke's story of salvation begins in rural Galilee with an angelic appearance to a teenage girl and ends with a middle-aged Jewish Christian man testifying to other Jews in the urban metropolis of Rome about Jesus and the kingdom of God. In Luke's telling, Jesus and the kingdom adequately describe the agent and end of salvation, deliverance from the anti-God and anticreation powers that put their feet on Israel's throat and even draw Gentiles into the vice-like grip of their dark claws. In Luke's narrative, salvation consists principally of release and restoration. This is release from suffering, sins, and shame, and restoration of body, social inclusion, covenant standing, and rightness before God. Luke's view of salvation, then, is comprehensive; it includes freedom from political oppression (Luke 1:68-71), demonic possession (Luke 8:48), physical affliction (e.g., Luke 8:50; 17:19; 18:42; Acts 4:9), economic destitution (Luke 4:18; 6:20; 7:22), and even judgment (Luke 10:14; 11:31-32). This salvation comes through repentance and faith (e.g., Luke 7:50; 8:48, 50; 17:19; 18:42), specifically through calling on the name of the "Lord" Jesus (Acts 2:21) since Jesus is the only name by which persons can be saved (Acts 4:12), even excluding the Mosaic law (Acts 15:1, 11). In Luke–Acts, the ultimate source of salvation is God the Savior and his Son, Jesus, who is born into the world to bring salvation to Jew and Gentile alike in fulfillment of Israel's sacred Scriptures.

REVIEW QUESTIONS

1. In Lukan terms, what does it mean to be saved?
2. How is salvation manifested in Jesus' ministry to the poor, sick, outcast, and oppressed?
3. What does Jesus save people from?
4. What are the debates about salvation in Acts 15 about?
5. How might your church replicate Luke's salvation culture?

RECOMMENDED READING

Bock, Darrell L. *A Theology of Luke and Acts: God's Promised Program, Realized for All Nations.* Grand Rapids, MI: Zondervan, 2012. Pages 227-77.
Marshall, I. Howard. *Luke: Historian and Theologian.* 3rd ed. Carlisle, UK: Paternoster, 1988. Pages 77-102.
Steyn, Gert J. "Soteriological Perspectives in Luke's Gospel." In *Salvation in the New Testament: Perspectives on Soteriology*, edited by Jan G. van der Watt, 67-99. Leiden: Brill, 2005.

Wi, MiJa. *The Path to Salvation in Luke's Gospel: What Must We Do?* London: T&T Clark, 2019.

Zyl, Hermie C. van. "The Soteriology of Acts: Restoration to Life." In *Salvation in the New Testament: Perspectives on Soteriology*, edited by Jan G. van der Watt, 133-60. Leiden: Brill, 2005.

7

"Beginning with Moses"

The Old Testament in Luke–Acts

ACCORDING TO SCRIPTURE

There is a climactic moment in Luke's resurrection narrative where Cleopas, one of the two travelers to Emmaus, laments to the risen-yet-unrecognized Jesus that he hoped that Jesus would be the one "to redeem Israel" (Luke 24:21). Yet such a hope was dashed by Jesus' crucifixion and confused by women claiming that his tomb was empty and that they had a vision of angels declaring that Jesus was alive (Luke 24:17-24). Ironically, Cleopas chides the stranger (i.e., Jesus) when he feigns ignorance of the recent turmoil that engulfed Jerusalem and crushed Jesus under its weight. Then, in turn, the risen Jesus chides the two travelers for not knowing that the "the Messiah" had to "suffer these things and then enter into his glory" (Luke 24:26). Then Jesus, "beginning with Moses and all the prophets . . . interpreted to them the things about himself in all the scriptures" (Luke 24:26-27). Jesus' pretended ignorance of current events is eclipsed by the duo's ignorance as to how Jesus is indeed the one to redeem Israel precisely because the Messiah's death and resurrection are part of the story of Scripture. Jesus in effect offers a new way of reading Scripture, rereading it in light of the Messiah's passion and glory, so that the hopes of the despairing are not dashed but ignited by grasping how the identity and mission of Jesus as the Messiah are prefigured in Israel's Scriptures.[1]

Now, Jesus' explanation of "the things about himself in all the scriptures" must have been one epic exegetical exposition as to how the Jewish Scriptures, the Torah and Prophets, find their fulfillment in him. Of course, myriad questions immediately enter our minds. Which Scriptures? What kind of interpretation? How do they all fit together? We are sadly not told. But, as Luke promised in his prologue, the events surrounding Jesus pertain to "the events that have been fulfilled among us" (Luke 1:1). The Lukan Paul says something similar in a sermon in Pisidian Antioch, where he declares to a Jewish audience, "We bring you the good news that what God promised to our ancestors he has fulfilled for us, their children, by raising Jesus" (Acts 13:32-33), followed immediately with quotations of Psalm 2:7; Isaiah 55:3; and Psalm 16:10. Luke–Acts is concerned with the Jewish Scriptures, what we call the "Old Testament," precisely because it represents the fulfillment of messianic prophecies.

But here is the thing: there is far more to the presence and influence of the Old Testament in Luke–Acts than Jesus as the fulfillment of messianic prophecies. The Old Testament is present in many different ways. Yes, messianic prophecies for sure, but in other ways, too, such as thematic motifs that run through the two books, several different citations of Old Testament texts that are not messianic, particular interpretive devices common in ancient Judaism that are deployed, and Luke's particular integration of the Old Testament into his narratives about Jesus and the apostles. Luke, while aware of Greco-Roman rhetorical and historiographical conventions, tethers his testimony to the substructure of the Jewish Scriptures, and he ties in various scriptural themes at

---

[1]Richard B. Hays, *Reading Backwards: Figural Christology and the Fourfold Gospel Witness* (Waco, TX: Baylor University Press, 2014), 55-56.

key points. So reading Luke–Acts really does require a knowledge of the Jewish Scriptures and attention to how Luke is incorporating various texts, topics, and interpretive techniques.

> "The influence, whether literary or theological, of the Old Testament upon the Lucan writings . . . is profound and pervasive."[a]
>
> [a] C. K. Barrett, "Luke/Acts," in *It Is Written: Scripture Citing Scripture: Essays in Honor of Barnabas Lindars*, ed. D. A. Carson and H. G. M. Williamson (Cambridge: Cambridge University Press, 1988), 231.

As we cover this subject of Luke and Scripture, hopefully our hearts will also be "burning within us" as we learn how Luke weaves the Jewish Scriptures into his gospel of Jesus and narrative of the early church (Luke 24:32).

A CRASH COURSE ON SCRIPTURE CITING SCRIPTURE

When it comes to understanding the Old Testament in the New Testament, there are a few things to know.

1. All texts are intertextual. By that I mean that all texts interact with and rehearse previous texts, whether explicitly or implicitly. This is true whether you are reading Shakespeare's *Romeo and Juliet*, a biography of Winston Churchill, a novel about teenage vampires, or a messianic fragment from the Dead Sea Scrolls. All texts are influenced by prior texts. This influence might be at the level of genre, style, contents, conventions, quotations, imitation, refutation, or a repetition of themes. Even early Old Testament books influence later Old Testament books. For example, the story of the Hebrews leaving Egypt in the book of Exodus has a big impact on Isaiah 40–55. Jeremiah's seventy years of exile (Jeremiah 25:1-14) is taken up by Daniel and translated into 490 years of exile (Daniel 9:2, 20-27).[2] It is then,

---

[2] See Gary Edward Schnittjer, *Old Testament Use of the Old Testament: A Book by Book Guide* (Grand Rapids, MI: Zondervan, 2021).

no surprise, that when you read something such as Romans 9–11, the book of Hebrews, or the book of Revelation, you'll find a Christian text replete with various kinds of influences from the Old Testament. The same applies to Luke–Acts: it is intensely intertextual, and there is a pattern of influence from the Old Testament that is absolutely crucial to the various subsections and the overall message. The Gospel of Luke opens with the story of Zechariah and Elizabeth in their childlessness in a way reminiscent of Hannah and her childlessness in 1 Samuel 1–2. The book of Acts closes with a quotation of Isaiah 6:9-10 about Israel's obstinacy, a passage with its own unique reception history in Jewish and Christian literature. So, Luke–Acts is intertextual from Luke 1 to Acts 28.

2. New Testament writers used the Septuagint to cite the Old Testament. When Luke cites the Old Testament, he cites it not from the Hebrew but from a preexisting Greek translation we call the Septuagint, abbreviated LXX. According to legend, a group of seventy Jewish scribes in Alexandria translated the Hebrew Torah into Greek in the third century BC under the sponsorship of the Ptolemaic dynasty. The remainder of the Hebrew Bible was translated into Greek later in Alexandria and Palestine. When Luke cites "Scriptures" it is normally the case that he is citing a Greek text, the Septuagint, as this was "the Bible" for the Greek-speaking church, especially in the eastern Mediterranean.[3]

---

[3]It is important to note that the LXX in the form of the standard critical edition (Rahlfs-Hanhart) is an eclectic text based largely on Christian compilations of the Old Testament in Greek (e.g., Codices Vaticanus, Sinaiticus, and Alexandrinus). However, note the following: (1) In the first century, there was no standardized Greek text of the Old Testament, nor a standard list of books to be included in a Greek Old Testament canon. Instead, there was a fluid stream of texts and translations of the Jewish Scriptures into Greek, as evidenced by a Greek scroll of the Minor Prophets called Nahal Hever (8HevXII gr) found in the Judean desert, and scholars call these texts the Old Greek. (2) The earliest translations of the Hebrew Bible into Greek were somewhat hasty and have various errors and emendations, which were gradually corrected by later translators, such as Aquila, Symmachus, and Theodotion. They strove to conform the Greek Old Testament to be closer to the Hebrew Old Testament. What is important to understand here is that Luke's Bible, his access to the Jewish Scriptures, came from a form of the Old Greek that

It is notable that sometimes the LXX differs markedly from the Hebrew text (i.e., the Masoretic Text), and Luke's Old Testament citations are normally—but not completely or not always—closer to the LXX version. This is apparent with James's quotation of Amos 9:11-12 in Acts 15.

Table 7.1. Amos 9:11-12 in Hebrew Bible, Septuagint, and Acts 15 with English translations

AMOS 9:11-12 (NIV)	AMOS 9:11-12 (Masoretic Text)
11 In that day I will restore David's fallen shelter— I will repair its broken walls and restore its ruins— and will rebuild it as it used to be, 12 so that they may possess the remnant of Edom and all the nations that bear my name, declares the LORD, who will do these things.	11 בַּיּוֹם הַהוּא אָקִים אֶת־סֻכַּת דָּוִיד הַנֹּפֶלֶת וְגָדַרְתִּי אֶת־פִּרְצֵיהֶן וַהֲרִסֹתָיו אָקִים וּבְנִיתִיהָ כִּימֵי עוֹלָם׃ 12 לְמַעַן יִירְשׁוּ אֶת־שְׁאֵרִית אֱדוֹם וְכָל־הַגּוֹיִם אֲשֶׁר־נִקְרָא שְׁמִי עֲלֵיהֶם נְאֻם־יְהוָה עֹשֶׂה זֹּאת׃
AMOS 9:11-12 (Lexham English Septuagint)	**AMOS 9:11-12 (Greek)**
11 On that day I will raise up the tent of David that has fallen, and I will rebuild its things that have fallen, and I will raise up its things that have been destroyed, and I will rebuild it just as the days of the age, 12 so that the remnant of the people, and all the nations upon whom my name was invoked upon them, will search for me," says the Lord who is making these things.	11 ἐν τῇ ἡμέρᾳ ἐκείνῃ ἀναστήσω τὴν σκηνὴν Δαυιδ τὴν πεπτωκυῖαν καὶ ἀνοικοδομήσω τὰ πεπτωκότα αὐτῆς καὶ τὰ κατεσκαμμένα αὐτῆς ἀναστήσω καὶ ἀνοικοδομήσω αὐτὴν καθὼς αἱ ἡμέραι τοῦ αἰῶνος,† 12 ὅπως ἐκζητήσωσιν οἱ κατάλοιποι τῶν ἀνθρώπων καὶ πάντα τὰ ἔθνη, ἐφ' οὓς ἐπικέκληται τὸ ὄνομά μου ἐπ' αὐτούς, λέγει κύριος ὁ θεὸς ὁ ποιῶν ταῦτα.
ACTS 15:15-18 (NIV)	**ACTS 15:15-18 (Greek)**
15 The words of the prophets are in agreement with this, as it is written: 16 "After this I will return and rebuild David's fallen tent. Its ruins I will rebuild, and I will restore it, 17 that the rest of mankind may seek the Lord, even all the Gentiles who bear my name, says the Lord, who does these things." 18 things known from long ago.	15 καὶ τούτῳ συμφωνοῦσιν οἱ λόγοι τῶν προφητῶν καθὼς γέγραπται· 16 μετὰ ταῦτα ἀναστρέψω καὶ ἀνοικοδομήσω τὴν σκηνὴν Δαυὶδ τὴν πεπτωκυῖαν καὶ τὰ κατεσκαμμένα αὐτῆς ἀνοικοδομήσω καὶ ἀνορθώσω αὐτήν, 17 ὅπως ἂν ἐκζητήσωσιν οἱ κατάλοιποι τῶν ἀνθρώπων τὸν κύριον καὶ πάντα τὰ ἔθνη ἐφ' οὓς ἐπικέκληται τὸ ὄνομά μου ἐπ' αὐτούς, λέγει κύριος ποιῶν ταῦτα 18 γνωστὰ ἀπ' αἰῶνος.

---

eventually contributed to the making of the Christian LXX. See further about the LXX, J. Ross Wagner, "The Septuagint and the 'Search for the Christian Bible,'" in *Scripture's Doctrine and Theology's Bible: How the New Testament Shapes Christian Dogmatics*, ed. Markus Bockmuehl and Alan J. Torrance (Grand Rapids, MI: Baker, 2008), 17-28; Timothy Michael Law, *When God Spoke Greek: The Septuagint and the Making of the Christian Bible* (Oxford: Oxford University Press, 2013).

The context of Amos 9 pertains to a vision of Israel's judgment (Amos 9:1-10) accompanied by a promise of a united Israel's restoration (Amos 9:11-15). Salient for our interests is the promise of restoration in Amos 9:11-12. Amos 9:11-12 was a text that stimulated creative imaginings of what Israel's restoration, the reestablishment of the Davidic monarchy, and the rebuilding of the temple meant for the nations (Amos 9:12 LXX; Daniel 11:14 [Old Greek]; CD 7.14-19; 4Q174 3.12; Babylonian Talmud Sanhedrin 96b-97a; Acts 15:12-21). Such a restoration could conceivably have meant militarily subjugating nearby nations such as Edom (Hebrew text) or implied the eschatological conversion of the nations to Yahweh (LXX text).

Luke, in Acts 15, incorporates Amos 9:11-12 from the LXX and places it on the lips of James in the deliberations about what to do with Gentile Messiah-believers. To back up for a moment, the context of Acts 15 is the Jerusalem Council (ca. AD 50) and the debate about whether Gentile Messiah-believers had to become proselytes to Judaism—which, for males, entailed circumcision and keeping the Torah—in order to be fully accepted by Jewish Messiah-believers in the assemblies of Antioch and Jerusalem. Peter argues that his encounter with Cornelius, who received the Spirit and had his heart cleansed by faith, shows that God accepts Gentiles on the basis of faith and does not discriminate. Peter also reasons that the Torah has been a burden on the Jews, and it would be wrong to impose this burden on Gentiles in the postmessianic period. Next, Paul and Barnabas talk about all the signs and wonders that God had performed through them among the Gentiles. Then, James offers some concluding thoughts based on Amos 9:11-12 that Israel's restoration, with the coming of a new David and the rebuilding of the temple, always had as its sequel the incorporation of Gentiles into a renewed Israel (see, e.g., Isaiah 2:2-4; 66:19-21; Micah 4:1-4;

Zechariah 8:21-23; Esther 8:17).[4] Here the assumption is that Jesus is the new David and the church is the new temple. According to Richard Bauckham: "The Jewish Christian exegete who created the text in Acts 15.16-18 [with Amos 9:11] understood the eschatological temple, not as a literal building, but as the eschatological people of God composed of both Jews and Gentiles."[5] Thus, Luke roots his theology of Gentile inclusion in a Septuagintal gloss on the Hebrew text that offers a vision for Gentile inclusion not on the basis of military subjugation but on the basis of Gentiles searching for God. In the words of Beverly Gaventa, "Taken together, the second half of the citation [from Amos 9:11-12] reinforces the claim that the Gentiles also belong to God's name and that God has always intended to bring about their inclusion. The language of seeking after God also recalls the Ethiopian who wants instruction (8:26-40), as well as Cornelius's unquestioning obedience (10:1-8)."[6]

3. New Testament writers used Jewish interpretive techniques. There existed various Jewish interpretive techniques, including paraphrase, pesher, typology, allegory, midrash, and more. We do not have time to explore this area in depth; however, it should be noted that "since the Christian *kerygma* was first formulated by Jews for Jews, using Jewish arguments and methods of exposition, it goes without saying that a thorough knowledge of contemporary Jewish exegesis is essential to the understanding (and not just a better understanding) of the message of the New Testament and, even more, of Jesus."[7] This is certainly true of Luke, immersed as

---

[4] See Bird, *Jesus and the Origins of the Gentile Mission*, 29-44.
[5] Richard Bauckham, "James and the Gentiles (Acts 15.13-21)," in *History, Literature and Society in the Book of Acts*, ed. Benjamin Witherington (Cambridge: Cambridge University Press, 1996), 164.
[6] Beverly Roberts Gaventa, *Acts*, Abingdon New Testament Commentaries (Nashville: Abingdon, 2003), 219-20.
[7] Geza Vermes, "Bible and Midrash: Early Old Testament Exegesis," in *The Cambridge History of the Bible*, vol. 1, *From Beginnings to Jerome*, ed. Peter R. Akroyd and Craig F. Evans (Cambridge: Cambridge University Press, 1975), 1:229.

he was in both Greek rhetoric and Jewish scriptural interpretation. Thus, when reading the works of Luke, who was a reader himself of Jewish Scripture, we should not judge him according to modern historical-critical standards but situate him closer to Jewish interpretive conventions.[8]

4. The Old Testament can appear in the New Testament in different forms. There are several ways that an Old Testament text can make itself present in the New Testament. The general taxonomy used in scholarship includes quotation, allusion, and echo.[9] While the definition of each is disputed, they approximate to the following explanations. *Citation* is when the words from an Old Testament text are given with an introductory formula such as "to fulfill what was said through the prophet Isaiah" (Matthew 4:14 NIV), followed up with an actual quotation from Isaiah 9:1-2. *Allusion* is where there is no introductory formula and perhaps not even an explicit quotation, but the wording is similar enough to indicate a throwback to an Old Testament text. For instance, a reference to Jesus "coming on the clouds" is a likely allusion to Daniel 7:13 (Matthew 24:30; 26:64; Mark 13:26; 14:62; Revelation 1:7). *Echo* is where there is a thematic resonance between some wording or description in the New Testament that can be loosely correlated with a text in the Old Testament. The difference between allusion and echo is not always clear, and identifying echoes can be somewhat subjective and lead to maximalist claims

---

[8]See Matthian Henze, ed., *A Companion to Biblical Interpretation in Early Judaism* (Grand Rapids, MI: Eerdmans, 2012); Karin Hedner Zetterholm, *Jewish Interpretation of the Bible: Ancient and Modern* (Minneapolis: Fortress, 2012).
[9]See Stanley E. Porter, "The Use of the Old Testament in the New Testament," in *Early Christian Interpretation of the Scriptures of Israel: Investigations and Proposals*, ed. Craig A. Evans and James A. Sanders, JSNTSup 148 (Sheffield: Sheffield Academic Press, 1997), 79-96; Porter, "Further Comments on the Use of the Old Testament in the New Testament," in *The Intertextuality of the Epistles: Explorations of Theory and Practice*, ed. Thomas L. Brodie, Dennis R. MacDonald, and Stanley E. Porter, New Testament Monographs 16 (Sheffield: Sheffield Phoenix, 2007), 98-107.

"Beginning with Moses"

of manifold echoes. As an example, you could argue that Jesus walking on the water is an echo of Psalm 77:19 about Yahweh leading the Hebrews through the Red Sea (Mark 6:45-52; Matthew 14:22-33; John 6:16-24), and Jesus calming the storm is a possible echo of Psalm 107:29, where Yahweh stills the storm with a whisper and forces the waves of the sea to be hushed (Mark 4:35-41; Matthew 8:23-27; Luke 8:22-25).

As to how this tripartite classification plays out in Luke–Acts, consider Luke 4:16-30:

Table 7.2. Examples of citation, allusion, and echo

OLD TESTAMENT INFLUENCE	LUKAN TEXT	OLD TESTAMENT TEXTS
CITATION	When he came to Nazareth, where he had been brought up, he went into the synagogue on the sabbath day, as was his custom. He stood up to read, and the scroll of the prophet Isaiah was given to him. He unrolled the scroll and found the place where it was written: "The Spirit of the Lord is upon me, because he has anointed me to bring good news to the poor. He has sent me to proclaim release to the captives and recovery of sight to the blind, to let the oppressed go free, to proclaim the year of the Lord's favor." (Luke 4:16-19)	Isaiah 61:1-2 Note that the Lukan text omits reference to divine vengeance found in the Hebrew and Greek versions of Isaiah 61:2.
ALLUSION	"Truly I tell you, no prophet is accepted in the prophet's hometown. But the truth is, there were many widows in Israel in the time of Elijah, when the heaven was shut up three years and six months, and there was a severe famine over all the land; yet Elijah was sent to none of them except to a widow at Zarephath in Sidon. There were also many lepers in Israel in the time of the prophet Elisha, and none of them was cleansed except Naaman the Syrian." (Luke 4:24-27)	1 Kings 17:8-24 (widow of Zarephath) 2 Kings 5:1-19 (Naaman in the Syrian) These two stories are invoked by the Lukan Jesus to make a startling claim: even during times of Israel's desperate need, if the prophetic messenger is rejected, like Elijah and Elisha were, then deliverance and blessings will be offered to persons of lowly status outside Israel's covenant, that is, a foreign widow and a leprous Gentile in the army of Israel's enemy

OLD TESTAMENT INFLUENCE	LUKAN TEXT	OLD TESTAMENT TEXTS
ECHO	When they heard this, all in the synagogue were filled with rage. They got up, drove him out of the town, and led him to the brow of the hill on which their town was built, so that they might hurl him off the cliff. But he passed through the midst of them and went on his way. (Luke 4:28-30)	Deuteronomy 13:1-11 The law of Moses commanded that people put false prophets to death, which perhaps motivated the men of Nazareth to try throw Jesus off a nearby cliff.

Hopefully by now you can see that when it comes to the influence and presence of the Old Testament in Luke-Acts, it is a bit more complicated than prophetic prediction and messianic fulfillment. There are a variety of ways that the Old Testament shapes and influences the Lukan narrative.

OLD TESTAMENT IN LUKE-ACTS

Let me give two examples of how Old Testament books influenced the shape and contents of Luke-Acts using the Psalter and the prophet Isaiah.

The Psalms. The Psalter looms large in Luke-Acts, particularly in relation to Lukan Christology with its focus on Jesus' messianic identity.[10] The Psalms, as a mixture of prophecy, and typology, furnish Luke with the christological tools he needs to demonstrate the things that have been fulfilled in Jesus.

- In the Gospel of Luke, the heavenly voice that calls Jesus "my son" at his baptism and at his transfiguration is an allusion to Psalm 2:7, which is about the enthronement of a Davidic king (Luke 3:22; 9:35).

- During Jesus' triumphal entry into Jerusalem, the crowd sings a verse from one of the *hallel* psalms, "Blessed is the

---

[10]See esp. Peter Doble, "The Psalms in Luke-Acts," in *The Psalms in the New Testament*, ed. Stephen Moyise and Maarten J. J. Menken (London: T&T Clark, 2004), 83-117; Doble, "Luke 24.26, 44—Songs of God's Servant: David and his Psalms in Luke-Acts," *Journal for the Study of the New Testament* 28 (2006): 267-83.

king who comes in the name of the Lord" (Luke 19:38; Psalm 118:26).

- After telling the parable of the wicked tenants, Jesus closes with the words, "The stone that the builders rejected has become the cornerstone," which obviously designates himself as the stone rejected by the builders, also mentioned in Psalm 118 (Luke 20:17; Psalm 118:22).

- Jesus directly challenges the scribes as to who the Messiah is, given that David, the speaker in Psalm 110, calls the Messiah his "Lord." But, if David calls the Messiah "Lord," then how can the Messiah be David's son? The answer, I think, is that while the Messiah is a Son of David, he is far more than a mere descendant of David; rather, the Messiah is a heavenly figure with divine authority (Luke 20:42-43; Psalm 110:1).

- There is a clear allusion to Psalm 110:1 (and Daniel 7:13) at Jesus' trial before Caiaphas, where Jesus claims, "From now on the Son of Man will be seated at the right hand of the power of God" (Luke 22:69).

- On the cross, as Jesus dies, he cries out, "Father, into your hands I commend my spirit," which is a clear reference to Psalm 31 about the suffering righteous one who entrusts himself to God's faithfulness (Luke 23:46; Psalm 31:5).

The influence of the Psalter continues in the book of Acts. There is a clear pattern that emerges where Jesus' rejection, death, resurrection, and exaltation are directly linked to the Psalter in apostolic preaching. Jesus' rejection by the Judean populace is explained by way of Psalm 118:22, with Jesus designated as stone the builders rejected (Acts 4:11). Similarly, the Judean and Roman leaders' opposition to Jesus is traced back to the kings who raged against the Lord and his anointed king in Psalm 2:1-2 (Acts 4:25-26).

Jesus' death and descent to the underworld are explained in light of Psalm 16:8-11, where God did not abandon his chosen one to the realm of the dead (Acts 2:25-31; 13:35). Jesus' resurrection is portrayed with reference to Psalm 2:7 as constituting proof of his divine sonship (Acts 13:33), and his exaltation is described in language drawn from Psalm 110:1 about sitting at God's right hand (Acts 2:33-34; 5:31; 7:55-56).

The conclusion we should draw from this survey is that in Luke's testimony, rooted itself in the church's corporate memory of Jesus' prophetic career and in the developing habits of apostolic hermeneutics, is that the Psalter attests Jesus as God's anointed king, as the rejected stone who became the cornerstone for a renewed Israel, as the suffering righteous one in his death, as the divine son in his resurrection, and as the messianic Lord in his exaltation. The Psalms provide the scriptural coordinates to speak of Jesus' rejection and reign.[11] In other words, when the early church tried to make sense of Jesus' mission, the opposition to him, his identity, his crucifixion, and the events surrounding Easter, their minds were immediately drawn to the Psalter. It was the Psalter that provided the imagery and language to explain who Jesus is, what happened to him, why, how this accorded with God's purpose, where Jesus is now, and what all that meant for Israel, Jesus' followers, and the nations. In other words, the early church's Christology as Luke describes it was principally shaped by its memory of Jesus, its experience of the risen Jesus, and an explicit messianic interpretation of the Psalter.

The book of Isaiah. A fascinating dimension to Luke–Acts is the way that the book of Isaiah looms large over the work, since Isaiah is the prophetic book that enables Luke to show how God's plan for

---

[11]See Jamie A. Grant, "Singing the Cover Versions: Psalms, Reinterpretation and Biblical Theology in Acts 3–4," *Scottish Bulletin of Evangelical Theology* 25 (2007): 27-49.

salvation to Israel and the nations takes place through Jesus and his disciples.

Luke clearly identifies Jesus with the Suffering Servant of Isaiah 53. At the Last Supper, the Lukan Jesus explicitly quotes Isaiah 53:12: "It is written: 'And he was numbered with the transgressors'; and I tell you that this must be fulfilled in me. Yes, what is written about me is reaching its fulfillment" (Luke 22:37 NIV). This immediately tells us that Luke understands Jesus' death in terms of Isaiah 53 and the suffering of the servant. It means, too, that Jesus' death is neither the tragic demise of a courageous prophet nor the just desserts of a fraudulent messiah but part of the divine plan when understood in Isaianic terms. Unsurprisingly, then, Jesus is explicitly called God's "servant" (παῖς) who was "handed over" (παραδίδωμι) to be killed, which is straight out of Isaiah 52:13; 53:6, 11-12 (Acts 3:13). Later in Acts, the Ethiopic eunuch is in his chariot reading Isaiah 53:7-8 about the servant who, just like a eunuch, faced humiliation and had no descendants, when Philip encounters him and explains to him the gospel about Jesus (Acts 8:26-35). Also, the title "Righteous One" given to Jesus (Acts 3:14; 7:52; 22:14) most likely derives from Isaiah 53:11. The resurrection of Jesus interconnects with the ambiguous reference to the servant, who will see the light after his sufferings also in Isaiah 52:11 (Acts 3:26). The exaltation of Jesus into glory may owe something to Isaiah 52:13 (LES), where it says that the servant will "be raised up and magnified exceedingly" (Luke 24:26; Acts 2:33; 5:31). Given that the Isaianic servant suffers for sins and carries sins away (Isaiah 53:4-6, 12), this passage may be alluded to in Peter's speech to Cornelius's household: "All the prophets testify about him that everyone who believes in him receives forgiveness of sins through his name" (Acts 10:43).

But Isaianic influence in Luke–Acts is far more than identifying Jesus as the servant. We might say that Isaiah, particularly Isaiah 40–55, influences a wide variety of themes and motifs related to God's purposes, Jesus' mission, and the ministry of the apostles. To begin with, John the Baptist's ministry is prefaced with a quotation from Isaiah 40:3-5 about the "way of the Lord" as a path leading "all people" to "see God's salvation" (Luke 3:4-6 NIV). In context, Isaiah 40 is the announcement of God coming to reign as king and to liberate the Babylonian exiles, and in Luke this passage constitutes something of a "hermeneutical key," as the rest of the story centers on this Isaianic "new exodus."[12] The Isaianic hope for the coming of the Lord segues into the coming of Jesus as the messianic Lord (Luke 2:11) and the Lord's Spirit-anointed prophet whose ministry is scripted according to Isaiah 61:1 (Luke 4:18-21; Acts 10:38). This is a ministry that included performing the signs of Israel's restoration drawn from Isaiah 35:5-6; 44:18 (Luke 7:22-23).

The Isaianic theme explains, too, why the early church referred to themselves as followers of "the Way." As they were the walking in the way of this new exodus, they saw God coming as king in Jesus, and they were the vanguard of Israel's restoration (Acts 9:2; 19:9, 23; 22:4; 24:14). In addition, Acts 1:8, where the church is to be a witness to Jerusalem, Judea, Samaria, and the ends of the earth, is perhaps drawn from the Isaianic program of Jerusalem's deliverance (Isaiah 44:24-28), Israel's restoration (Isaiah 40–44), and the extension of salvation to the ends of the earth (Isaiah 2:2-4; 25:6-8; 66:19).[13] Just as the Isaianic servant was called to be "a light to the nations" in Isaiah 42:6; 49:6, the same designation is applied to Jesus by Simeon (Luke 2:32) and Paul (Acts 26:23). But note how Paul applies the same Isaianic "light" text to himself and Barnabas:

---

[12] David W. Pao, *Acts and the Isaianic New Exodus* (Grand Rapids, MI: Baker, 2002), 249.
[13] Pao, *Acts and the Isaianic New Exodus*, 249-50.

"It was necessary that the word of God should be spoken first to you. Since you reject it and judge yourselves to be unworthy of eternal life, we are now turning to the Gentiles. For so the Lord has commanded us, saying, 'I have set you to be a light for the Gentiles, so that you may bring salvation to the ends of the earth'" (Acts 13:46-47). In the Lukan scheme, the Christian mission to the nations is a continuation of the work of Jesus, where the risen Messiah proclaims light through his apostles. Luke's readers, then, should be assured that Jesus and the apostles act according to Isaiah, but they should also be encouraged to take up the servant's unfinished acts for themselves in a new chapter of the church's mission.[14] Finally, Acts concludes with Paul under house arrest in Rome and quoting Isaiah 6:6-9 to describe how Israel's obduracy has paved the way for the Gentile mission (Acts 28:25-28). Paul does not castigate Israel as much as lament that they have rejected the servant and his servants because they have not received the revelation that he has.

> **How Does Luke Use Isaiah?**
>
> "These Isaianic references are used by Luke to interpret events in the narrative, showing that events are occurring in accordance with the plan and purposes of God. Hence the actions of the chief human characters in the narrative are explained and legitimated with reference to the divine plan. For Luke, important aspects of this plan are revealed in Isaiah, particularly in passages that speak of the mission to bring salvation to all people and the response to the proclaimed message by Israel and the nations. This appears to be Luke's characteristic use of Isaiah."[a]
>
> [a] Peter Mallen, *The Reading and Transformation of Isaiah in Luke–Acts*, LNTS 367 (London: T&T Clark, 2008), 199.

---

[14] Peter Mallen, *The Reading and Transformation of Isaiah in Luke–Acts*, LNTS 367 (London: T&T Clark, 2008), 201.

Luke and Scripture. Luke's use of Scripture is not as stark and as blatant as that of Matthew, who likes plain formulae such as "As it is written," nor is it as oblique as that of John, who makes tacit allusions to Old Testament stories, but the Old Testament is nonetheless crucial to Luke's account of Jesus and the early church. Luke places Jesus in relation to the prophetic hope and typological shape of Scripture, while also seeing Scripture as pointing to the church's own proclamation and activities. Luke's reading of Scripture is as Christocentric (i.e., focused on Jesus) as it is ecclesiocentric (i.e., related to the church's own mission and activities). Jesus is the true Adam, the Davidic Messiah, the prophet like Moses, the coming Son of Man, the Spirit-bearing prophet, the Suffering Servant, and the righteous one. The church is the people of God who experience the prophetic promise of God's Spirit poured on them. The church walks in "the Way" of Isaiah's new exodus, and continues the ministry of the servant. Jesus and his disciples are therefore part of the unfolding scriptural story of God's purpose and plans.

> **How Does Luke Use the Old Testament?**
> 1. Covenant and promise: God remembers his covenant and fulfils his prophetic promises.
> 2. Christology: Scripture shows that Jesus is the Davidic Messiah and Isaianic Servant.
> 3. Community mission: Scripture indicates that the church occupies a key place in God's purpose and plans.
> 4. Gentile mission: Scriptures testifies that salvation is intended for all nations to the very ends of the earth.
> 5. Warnings to Israel: If Israel rejects the messiah and his messengers they risk being waylaid.[a]
>
> [a]Darrell L. Bock, "Scripture and the Realisation of God's Promises," in *Witness to the Gospel: The Theology of Acts*, ed. I. Howard Marshall and David Peterson (Grand Rapids, MI: Eerdmans, 1998), 49.

MESSIANIC REVELATION AND MESSIANIC READING

If Jesus is the coming one who fulfilled messianic prophecies, who suffered and entered his glory as Moses and the prophets foretold, if Paul was compelling and competent at reasoning from Scriptures that Jesus is the risen and exalted Messiah, then why was Jesus crucified and why were the apostles rejected by their fellow Jews in Judea and the Diaspora? Jesus' own sermon on Isaiah 61:1 at Nazareth nearly got him thrown off a cliff, Stephen was stoned to death by an angry mob after giving a basic rundown on Israel's history, and Paul got shown the door at numerous synagogues after his homilies on messianic hope. If Jesus and the church are the true fulfillment of Scripture, then why the negative reception (without falling into some kind of anti-Jewish trope that blames the Jews for being *x*)?

The answer is that the rejection of the Messiah and his people is in fact part of the prophetic pattern of Scripture. Many of the prophets were ignored, rejected, and martyred. Elijah and Elisha got a frosty reception from various quarters. Jeremiah was thrown in a pit, and according to tradition Isaiah was cut in half. Jesus, as the Isaianic servant, suffers and is treated unjustly. While this implies the culpability of Judas and the Jerusalem leaders, nonetheless it was divinely "determined" and transpired according to God's "definite plan and foreknowledge" (Luke 22:22; Acts 2:23).

This is why Isaiah 6:9-10 (LXX) is prominent in Luke's account of Jesus, the apostles, and Scripture.

> And he said, "Go and tell this people, 'You will hear by hearing and not understand; and *although* looking, you will look and not see.' For the heart of this people has been thickened; and they have heard with difficulty *with* their ears, and they closed their eyes lest they see *with their* eyes and hear *with their* ears and understand *with their* heart and turn, and I will heal them." (LES)

Isaiah 6 is situated in the context of Isaiah's heavenly vision and commission to warn Israel of a coming judgment. He is told from the outset that they are unlikely to heed this divine warning, with the result that desolation and destruction will come on the land. Similarly, the Lukan version of the parable of the sower explains why the word sometimes fails with a quotation of Isaiah 6:9 by Jesus (Luke 8:1-10). Sometimes the prophet is rebuffed, and sometimes the prophetic word is met with hardheartedness. This rejection, far from casting aspersions on the prophet's authenticity, proves the prophet's credentials. Isaiah 6:9-10, then, is true of Jesus (Luke 4:24; 8:10) and the apostles (Acts 28:25-28). If that is the case, how can anyone, Jewish or Gentile, be saved?

Ultimately, believing a messianic reading of the Jewish Scriptures is a matter of messianic revelation. The risen Jesus' appearing to the disciples altered not just their view of Jesus but their view of Jesus and Scripture:

> He [Jesus] said to them [the disciples], "This is what I told you while I was still with you: Everything must be fulfilled that is written about me in the Law of Moses, the Prophets and the Psalms."
>
> Then he opened their minds so they could understand the Scriptures. He told them, "This is what is written: The Messiah will suffer and rise from the dead on the third day, and repentance for the forgiveness of sins will be preached in his name to all nations, beginning at Jerusalem. You are witnesses of these things." (Luke 24:44-48 NIV)

What is crucial here are the words, "Then he opened their minds so they could understand the Scriptures" (Luke 24:45). The gap between the disciples' knowledge of God's purposes for Israel and their ignorance of the Messiah's place in God's plan is closed when their minds are opened. In other words, a messianic reading requires a messianic revelation. It is the risen Jesus who appeals to Moses and the prophets to explain "what was said in all the Scriptures concerning himself" (Luke 24:27 NIV). The reason Luke recounts Paul's conversion story no fewer than three times (Acts 9; 22; 26) is that Paul's own message includes his own revelation of Jesus and a rereading of Scripture in light of that experience.

The Lukan way of reading Scripture is not about exegetical technique, giving texts an interpretive tweak, deploying the rhetorical devices of ancient Greek, but arises out of an event, an experience shrouded in messianic mystique. For Luke, the persuasive power of Scripture is less about method and logic than about the power and revelation of the risen and exalted Lord.[15] For Luke, the fulfillment of Scripture is a synthesis of the Easter event, religious experience, and illuminated exegesis, a confluence of text and testimony, a way of reading that sees and senses that Jesus Christ "is Lord of all" (Acts 10:36).

REVIEW QUESTIONS

1. How does biblical prophecy figure in Lukan themes about Jesus and salvation?

2. What is the Septuagint?

3. How would you define the terms *citation*, *allusion*, and *echo*?

4. Identify a passage in Luke and Acts influenced by the book of Isaiah.

5. What role does experience and revelation have in biblical interpretation?

RECOMMENDED READING

Beale, G. K. *Handbook on the New Testament Use of the Old Testament: Exegesis and Interpretation*. Grand Rapids, MI: Baker, 2012.

---

[15] E. B. Powery, *Jesus Reads Scripture: The Function of Jesus's Use of Scripture in the Synoptic Gospels*, BIS 63 (Leiden: Brill, 1999), 245.

Beers, Holly. *The Followers of Jesus as the "Servant": Luke's Model from Isaiah for the Disciples in Luke–Acts*. London: T&T Clark, 2016.

Denova, Rebecca I. *The Things Accomplished Among Us: Prophetic Tradition in the Structural Pattern of Luke–Acts*. Sheffield: Sheffield Academic Press, 1997.

Evans, Craig A., and James A. Sanders, eds. *Luke and Scripture: The Function of Sacred Tradition in Luke–Acts*. Eugene, OR: Wipf & Stock, 2001.

Litwak, Kenneth D. *Echoes of Scripture in Luke–Acts: Telling the History of God's People Intertextually*. London: T&T Clark, 2005.

Marshall, I. Howard. "Acts." In *Commentary on the New Testament Use of the Old Testament*, edited by G. K. Beale and D. A. Carson, 513-606. Grand Rapids, MI: Baker, 2007.

Pao, David W., and Eckhard J. Schnabel. "Luke." In *Commentary on the New Testament Use of the Old Testament*, edited by G. K. Beale and D. A. Carson. 251-414. Grand Rapids, MI: Baker, 2007.

8

On the Road with Jesus

Lukan Discipleship

WALKING IN THE WAY

There are many journey novels and movies. In recent memory, there is Cormac McCarthy's *The Road*, a postapocalyptic novel about a father and son. Recently I watched the World War I movie *1917*, directed by Sam Mendes, about two soldiers trying desperately to deliver an urgent message to the frontlines. The Lord of the Rings trilogy of books and movies is an epic narrative of the adventure of two hobbits to destroy the ring of power in Mount Doom in Mordor. For something a bit more highbrow, there is Jack Kerouac's *On The Road*, detailing the character's skit-skat life between San Francisco and New York. In all of these works, it's not so much the journey itself that is gripping, as if going from A to B somehow ushers in a character's transformation. It is the revelation of the struggle and transformation of the characters involved that really makes for an arresting story.

What does this trope of journey fiction have to do with Luke–Acts? Well, first, the bulk of Luke's Gospel and teaching on discipleship takes place in the travel narrative, Jesus' journey to Jerusalem in Luke 9:51–19:44. This section is more thematically organized than an actual travelogue; for instance, by Luke 17:11, Jesus is at the border of Galilee and Samaria, whereas Luke says he bypassed some Samaritan villages back in Luke 9:52-53. Yet in this section we find the bulk of Luke's unique material, key Lukan themes about discipleship, and how following Jesus entails following him to Jerusalem, where he must suffer, die, and enter his glory. Second, the book of Acts is a type of journey narrative. Acts 1:8 is commonly regarded as a table of contents as to how Jesus' witnesses will go, in the power of the Spirit, from Jerusalem into Judea, Samaria, and the ends of the earth. In that journey there is infighting, famines, shipwrecks, local opposition, imperial opposition, angry mobs, martyrs, heretics, magicians, miracles, conversions, and all sorts of theological convulsions. Yet, by the end of the story, the gospel has touched people as far east as Damascus, as far west as Rome, as far south as Ethiopia, and as far north as Macedonia. The gospel of Jesus has begun to spread to the ends of the earth. Along the way, there is much learned by characters and plenty to be learned by readers. For readers, the learning includes paradigms for preaching, the necessity of perseverance, negotiating Jewish scruples, navigating a way around Roman authorities, encouraging new converts, and cultivating the power of the Spirit.

If Luke intends his two-volume work to be not just informative but transformative for readers such as Theophilus and those who come after him, then we need to pay attention to the sections of Luke–Acts that speak to the nature and responsibilities of discipleship. What does it mean to follow Jesus? What separates a follower from an admirer? How does one enter the kingdom of God? What is authentic discipleship compared to the discipleship of those such as Ananias or Simon Magus, who fall or flounder? That is the task for us to explore in this chapter, to discover what it means to follow Jesus in "the Way," to figure out who is a true "disciple" (μαθητής).

One could argue that the true purpose of biblical instruction and theological reflection is not the accumulation of knowledge but the transformation of hearts and the readiness of hands to serve. It is how you live that shows what you truly believe. Luke's instruction on discipleship is inherently practical, challengingly so, even uncomfortable in some places. The Lukan Jesus gives strenuous commands, and discipleship can be costly. Luke, then, would have us know that those who bear Christ's name must learn to walk in Christ's way.[1]

HOW IT BEGINS: TURNING AND TRUSTING

Luke makes it clear that the following Jesus begins with repentance and faith. The problem is that we think we already know what repentance and faith are, and we read those ideas into Luke–Acts.

> **What Is Conversion in Luke–Acts?**
>
> "Converts are those who, enabled by God, have undergone a redirectional shift and now persist along the Way with the community of those faithfully serving God's eschatological purpose as this is evident in the life, death, and exaltation of the Lord Jesus Christ, and whose lives are continually being formed through the Spirit at work in and through practices constitutive of this community."[a]
>
> [a]Joel B. Green, *Conversion in Luke–Acts: Divine Action, Human Cognition, and the People of God* (Grand Rapids, MI: Baker, 2015), 78.

Granted repentance. Concerning repentance (μετάνοια, μετανοέω), while it includes an act of contrition, an admission of one's own sins, repentance/repenting is far more than that. Repentance includes a change of mind, a change of verdict, a change of life, and even a change of spiritual lordship.

The Baptist preaches a "baptism of repentance" and tells people to "bear fruits worthy of repentance" (Luke 3:3, 8; see also Acts 13:24;

---

[1]See Kevin J. Vanhoozer, *The Drama of Doctrine: A Canonical Linguistic Approach to Christian Theology* (Louisville, KY: Westminster John Knox, 2005), 16, 102, 442.

19:4). This message was about moral renewal but also "constitutes a prophetic appeal for people to turn their backs on previous loyalties and align themselves fundamentally with God's purpose."[2]

Jesus' ministry also has much to do with rehearsing the prophetic paradigm of repentance as abandoning personal sins and turning from national blindness in his call of sinners to repentance (Luke 5:32). God rejoices over sinners who repent (Luke 15:7, 10) and promises severe judgment to those who refuse to repent (Luke 10:13; 11:32; 13:3-5). Jesus calls tax collectors and whole towns to repent because everyone's destiny is on the line, from greedy merchants to the whole nation. Repentance means changing one's behavior as well as one's aspirations and approach to being God's people. Repentance is individual as much as national; it is about personal ethics and the proper way of being Israel.

Among Luke's unique material is the extended story of Peter's "conversion" and call (Luke 5:1-11). Peter's conversion has a strong analogy with Paul's own Damascus road Christophany, as both events entail a turning and calling.[3] In Peter's case, the conversion is initial. I say *initial* because Peter goes on a journey, from his climactic confession of Jesus as "the Messiah of God" (Luke 9:20), to leaving everything to follow Jesus (Luke 18:28), to his denial of Jesus (Luke 22:54-61), to his weeping contrition (Luke 22:62), to his witness to the resurrection (Luke 24:34), to his boldness in subsequent proclamation (Acts 2:14-41; 3:11-26). Jesus predicts that Peter himself might fail, but once he has "turned back" he will strengthen his brothers (Luke 22:32). The story of Peter demonstrates that repentance is not a single event but an ongoing process; indeed, the Christian life is one of continual repentance.[4]

---

[2]Joel B. Green, *The Theology of the Gospel of Luke*, NTT (Cambridge: Cambridge University Press, 1995), 170.
[3]Markus Bockmuehl, *Simon Peter in Scripture and Memory* (Grand Rapids, MI: Baker, 2012), 156.
[4]See Bockmuehl, *Simon Peter*, 153-63.

In Acts, there is a great deal of repentance and turning to God. To begin with, on the day of Pentecost, Peter tells the Jerusalem populace to repent, which in context means they should change their verdict about Jesus. Repentance means submitting to baptism but also receiving the forgiveness of sins and gift of the Holy Spirit (Acts 2:38). The motif of Israel's repentance and forgiveness is reiterated in apostolic proclamation to Jewish audiences (Acts 3:19, 26; 5:31). Peter is again crucial when Gentiles begin to believe in Jesus and receive the Holy Spirit. Peter concludes in the case of Cornelius, "God has given even to the Gentiles the repentance that leads to life" (Acts 11:18). As the story of Paul's mission unfolds, we learn that many Gentiles were "turning" (ἐπιστρέφω) to the Lord (Acts 9:35; 11:21; 15:19). Later, Paul claims that the call to repentance is a consistent part of his message irrespective of geography or ethnicity: "First to those in Damascus, then to those in Jerusalem and in all Judea, and then to the Gentiles, I preached that they should repent and turn to God and demonstrate their repentance by their deeds" (Acts 26:20 NIV).

> **Luke's Summary of Paul's Preaching**
> "I have declared to both Jews and Greeks that they must turn to God in repentance and have faith in our Lord Jesus" (Acts 20:21 NIV).

Believe in the Lord Jesus Christ. The Greek noun πίστις and the verb πιστεύω have a semantic range wider that "faith/trust" and "believe." They refer to attitudes and actions that show "complete trust and reliance—to believe in, to have confidence in, to have faith in, to trust, faith, trust," with connotations of fidelity and allegiance toward something or someone that/who is reliable and trustworthy.[5]

---

[5]Johannes P. Louw and Eugene A. Nida, eds., *Greek-English Lexicon of the New Testament: Based on Semantic Domains*, 2nd ed. (New York: United Bible Societies, 1989), 1:376; BDAG, 818. See also Matthew Bates, *Salvation by Allegiance Alone: Rethinking Faith, Works, and the Gospel of Jesus*

A consistent motif across Luke–Acts is that salvation—in its rich and diverse sense—is by faith. This is particularly true for supplicants of healing, whom Jesus tells, "Your faith has saved you, go in peace" (e.g., Luke 7:50; see also Luke 8:48; 18:42). One who believes is "justified," made right with God, relationally and covenantally, whether a contrite tax collector (Luke 18:14) or the Jews of the Diaspora (Acts 13:26). A Philippian jailer can be saved by believing in the Lord Jesus (Acts 16:31). Salvation is by grace and through faith, for Jews and Gentiles (Acts 14:1; 17:4; 19:17), as Peter stresses at the apostolic council: "We believe that we [Jews] will be saved through the grace of the Lord Jesus, just as they [Gentiles] will" (Acts 15:11; see also Acts 18:27). Those who believe are forgiven, justified, saved, and receive the Holy Spirit.

Jesus' parables and encounters with various individuals underscore how faith works itself out in practice. By faith, the word sown grows a hundredfold. By faith, one is healed and saved. By faith, a helpless widow badgers a wicked judge until she gets justice. By faith, one knocks on a neighbor's door asking for some bread. By faith, one approaches Jesus and asks to follow him. By faith, one waits patiently for the Son of Man. By faith, a tax collector begs for mercy and gives away half his possessions. According to Teresa Morgan, "*Pistis* [faith], Luke indicates, takes the initiative. It not only trusts and endures: it seeks, asks, knocks, lobbies, and is not satisfied until it gets the *dikaiosynē* [righteousness] it longs for."[6]

Belief is emphasized in Acts. In fact, the followers of Jesus are called, among other things, "believers" (πιστεύοντας; Acts 2:44; 4:32; 5:14; 22:19). They are so named because they believe that Jesus is the Messiah prophesied in Scripture (Luke 24:25; Acts 10:43;

---

the King (Grand Rapids, MI: Baker, 2017); Nijay K. Gupta, *Paul and the Language of Faith* (Grand Rapids, MI: Eerdmans, 2020).

[6]Teresa Morgan, *Roman Faith and Christian Faith: Pistis and Fides in the Early Roman Empire and Early Churches* (Oxford: Oxford University Press, 2017), 377.

26:27), believe the word of the gospel (Acts 4:4; 8:12; 9:42; 13:12, 48; 15:7), believe Jesus is Lord and surrender to him as Lord (Acts 5:14; 11:21; 14:1; 18:8). We must understand that in Acts the church is united by belief, not by ethnicity or ancestral customs. Belief in Jesus, reception of the Spirit, and baptism—these are the marks of God's people, a people who find grace in Jesus and who by faith exercise a common allegiance to the same Lord. All this is overwhelming, notes Morgan: "Acts is a story of the power of the word evoking *pistis* in the Lord Jesus Christ."[7]

The Faith that is "Through" Jesus

Acts 3:16 is a peculiar verse where Peter tells onlookers that a lame beggar was healed by Jesus' name and literally by the faith that comes through him (ἡ πίστις ἡ δι' αὐτοῦ).

Table 8.1. Acts 3:16 in English translations

NIV	It is Jesus' name and the faith that comes through him that has completely healed him, as you can all see.
ESV	The faith that is through Jesus has given the man this perfect health in the presence of you all.
NRSV	The faith that is through Jesus has given him this perfect health in the presence of all of you.
CEB	The faith that comes through Jesus gave him complete health right before your eyes.

The expression "the *faith* through *him*" is grammatically odd, but it probably means that Jesus' name is the object of faith, while Jesus is also the author of faith. The man was not healed by Peter's own charisma or by magic but by Jesus and the faith he evokes. James Dunn puts it well: "The attitude of open trust is an important medium through which the healing power flows, but the faith itself is divinely enabled, and the effective power is the power of him whose name is named."[a]

[a] James D. G. Dunn, *The Acts of the Apostles* (Grand Rapids, MI: Eerdmans, 2016), 45.

---

[7] Morgan, *Roman Faith and Christian Faith*, 388.

Not to be forgotten is the chorus of faithful characters, major and minor, in Luke–Acts, who are often juxtaposed with bad or faulty characters. Zechariah is confounded by the angelic news that his wife, Elizabeth, will bear a son and retorts: "How can I be sure that this will happen?" (Luke 1:18-20 NLT). In contrast, Mary is told the angelic news of her pregnancy, yet her response is altogether different, "May your word to me be fulfilled" (Luke 1:38 NIV). There is the contrast of the Pharisee who invites Jesus to dinner with the sinful woman who washes his feet with her tears (Luke 7:36-50). The former exhibits hubris, the latter contrition. The same theme is repeated in the contrast of the Pharisee and the tax collector in the temple—presumption of status versus penitence for wrongdoing (Luke 18:9-14). Looking in Acts, when it comes to possessions, there's a big difference between Ananias and Sapphira, who lie and "kept back some of the proceeds" they promised to give to the church (Acts 5:1-10), and Barnabas, who "sold a field that belonged to him, then brought the money, and laid it at the apostles' feet" (Acts 4:36-37). In addition, many persons go on a long faith journey. Peter is an example of someone who is a repenter, confessor, denier, returner, and proclaimer of Jesus. Jesus prays that Peter's "faith may not fail" (Luke 22:32), yet it does, but later he turns back to Jesus. As Teresa Morgan points out, "*Pistis* is evidently something which can both fail and grow within discipleship."[8]

TAKING UP THE CROSS DAILY

Luke makes it clear that following Jesus is costly. Luke redacts Mark's account of Jesus calling disciples to take up their cross to follow him (Mark 8:34) by adding "daily" (καθ' ἡμέραν) in Luke 9:23. The adage is repeated later, only this time Jesus warns a crowd: "If anyone comes to me and does not hate father and mother, wife and children, brothers and sisters—yes, even their own life—such a

---

[8] Morgan, *Roman Faith and Christian Faith*, 375.

person cannot be my disciple. And whoever does not carry their cross and follow me cannot be my disciple" (Luke 14:26-27 NIV). A disciple must be willing to prioritize Jesus and his cause above all human obligations and earthly possessions. That is the cross one must carry, and it is the sine qua non of discipleship.

> **What Does It Mean to Take Up the Cross Daily?**
>
> "In the ancient Greco-Roman world, crucifixion signified the epitome of shame, over and above its cruelty as a means of capital punishment. Criminals were crucified naked, tied or nailed to a horizontal cross beam, with barely a piece of wood on the vertical beam to support their feet and their entire body weight. Many died by asphyxiation, if not severe loss of blood. It was such a slow and disgraceful death that even the word crucifixion was not to be mentioned in polite company. Cross-bearing as a requirement of discipleship meant ostracism and death. Condemned to death by crucifixion, the victim had to carry the cross beam to the place of execution. 'Taking up the cross implied 'a dead man (or woman) walking.' Jesus requires all would-be followers to take up their cross *daily*, dying repeatedly, day by day. Jesus is not interested in any masochistic glorification of shame and humiliation. Self-denial means letting go of everything that stands in opposition to God. It requires that one's identity, priorities, attitudes and actions be reshaped and reformed. It is the relinquishment of all worldly values, possessions, and habits that stand in the way of obedience and fidelity to Jesus. This level of commitment will invite ridicule, misunderstanding, and retaliation—hence a daily cross-bearing."[a]
>
> ---
> [a] Diane G. Chen, *Luke*, NCCS (Eugene, OR: Cascade, 2017), 129.

It is striking that, as Jesus begins his journey to Jerusalem, he immediately encounters three men. The first and third men are volunteers, looking to join Jesus, while the second is approached by Jesus (Luke 9:57-62). Jesus warns the first man that joining him means joining the ranks of the dispossessed. The second and third make excuses based on familial duties as to why they cannot join Jesus. These words are meant to be confronting. We might think to ourselves, "Surely Jesus would not object to someone observing burial duties for a deceased father or delaying so one can say a final farewell to parents." But no, Jesus does not grant seemingly reasonable delays precisely because of the urgency of the situation. If a wildfire is running down a hill and your job is to warn a nearby village of the approaching calamity, then you don't stop to water your mother's roses. That is why those who hold onto anything or anyone are not "fit for the kingdom of God" (Luke 9:62). Interestingly, Luke never tells us how these would-be disciples respond to Jesus' message, whether they turn away or follow him. Irrespective of what happened, Luke is making an important point: those who join Jesus in the Way, those who follow Jesus, must forsake all things.[9] In the words of Darío López Rodriguez: "Discipleship has a cost; it demands real renunciations; it calls for a radical reorientation of values. This cost, requirement, and demand cannot be and should never be lowered."[10]

A duo of parables shows that there is a cost to be borne in following Jesus, and one must calculate the sacrifice against the gain. The examples given include a man beginning to build a tower or a king considering whether to go to war (Luke 14:28-33). One must be willing to give up family (Luke 14:26) and possessions (Luke 14:33) in order to follow Jesus; this is what it means to carry the cross. True disciples do exactly that. They leave "everything" to follow Jesus, just as Peter (Luke 5:11) and Levi do (Luke 5:28). The

---

[9]Frank Matera, *New Testament Ethics: The Legacies of Jesus and Paul* (Louisville, KY: Westminster John Knox, 1999), 80.
[10]Darío López Rodriguez, *The Liberating Message of Jesus: The Message of the Gospel of Luke* (Eugene, OR: Pickwick, 2012), 55.

gain is that one gets through the narrow door (Luke 7:22-30), one finds the salvation of one's own soul (Luke 9:25). No one "will fail to receive many times as much [as they gave up] in this age, and in the age to come eternal life" (Luke 18:30 NIV).

The same thing plays out in the church. Following Jesus entails persecution from one's own people and family, a sharing of one' possessions, and embracing the shame of the cross and the foolishness of the resurrection. The followers of the Way are harassed and persecuted from Jerusalem all the way through to Rome. This is why Paul admonishes disciples with the words, "It is through many persecutions that we must enter the kingdom of God" (Acts 14:22).

The Lukan pattern of discipleship involves repentance and renunciation, forsaking all things and following Jesus in the way of the kingdom.

THE MARKS OF A DISCIPLE

There is much to be learned about discipleship from the many exemplary disciples in Luke–Acts who exhibit traits, attitudes, and actions that benefit others, even at their own expense. Many of Jesus' women followers are paragons of generosity, such as the three women who support Jesus financially (Luke 8:2-3); of boldness, such as the woman who anoints Jesus' feet (Luke 7:36-50); and of devotion, such as Mary (Luke 10:38-42) and the widow in the temple (Luke 21:1-4). Female apostles are the first preachers of the resurrection (Luke 24:9-12). A Samaritan leper who is cleansed by Jesus demonstrates faith as thankfulness (Luke 17:11-19). Tax collectors such as Levi and Zacchaeus heed the call to follow Jesus by joining him and obeying his instructions (Luke 5:27-28; 19:1-10). In the early church, many figures who are not apostles are no less vital in the church's life, whether the courageous Stephen, the first martyr (Acts 7), or Philip the evangelist of Samaritans and Ethiopians (Acts 8). Barnabas is an encourager, reconciler, and the person you send to spearhead innovative church practices such as multiethnic churches (Acts 4:37; 9:27, 11:22-27). Then there is James, who functions as a mediator between disparate groups within the church, evidenced by the Jerusalem Council and Paul's return to Jerusalem (Acts 15:12-21; 21:17-25). Persons such as Cornelius in Caesarea (Acts 10) and Lydia in Philippi represents model Gentile converts who are pious, generous, and receptive to the word (Acts 16:11-15, 40). A reader of Luke–Acts is meant to learn from these characters and imitate their better traits and replicate their actions. Accordingly, there are several marks, perhaps even virtues, that characterize disciples. They not only turn to the Lord, believe in him, and forsake all attachments and relationships, but they are to think and behave in a certain way.

Equality. Luke's Sermon on the Plain (Luke 6:17-49) is ordinarily neglected in favor of its sibling, Matthew's Sermon on the Mount (Matthew 5–7). But Luke's sermon is more than a derivative and shorter version of the Matthean sermon. Whereas Matthew's Jesus focuses on true covenant righteousness, Luke's Jesus centers his attention on true covenant love. The Lukan Jesus' sermon is given not on a mountain but on a "level place" (Luke 6:17), indicative of an equality among the disciples. These disciples, in Luke's telling, include people from Judea, Jerusalem, Tyre, and Sidon—in other words, a mixed audience (Luke 6:17-19).

Hope. The Lukan beatitudes celebrate the radical reversal that the kingdom brings and how disciples will share in that reversal from poverty to kingship, from hunger to feasting, from weeping to laughter, from rejection to vindication (Luke 6:20-26). Disciples do not have to accept the current order of things with its inequalities and injustices because God has determined to overturn and reverse them. Disciples are blessed in the sense of being happy and hopeful that God is on the side of those who are the bottom of the pile. This announces a key point: discipleship is premised on the notion that God raises the poor and humble and brings down the rich and powerful (see Luke 1:52; 14:10-11; 16:9-31; 18:14). This is why the oppressed, those facing injustice or tyranny, can place their hope in God, because God is on their side and will reverse their fortunes.

Love. A central motif is that of love, in particular love of enemies (Luke 6:27-32). Instead of revenge, disciples must love their enemies, do good to those who hate them, pray for those who curse them, and be kind to those who mistreat them. They are to show restraint, respect, generosity, and mercy to those who oppose them. Instead of repaying violence or hatred in its own coin, we have the golden rule, to treat others the way you would have them treat you. This love for enemies is for those who cannot or will not show love in return. In many ways, this is a commentary on the covenantal requirement to love one's own neighbor (Leviticus 19:18) which Jesus will expand on later (Luke 10:27, 37).

Forgiveness. Another mark of discipleship is that instead of judging others, disciples should be forgiving and generous toward others (Luke 6:37-38). Now, the injunction against judgment does not mean that disciples should be morally vacuous and keep all negative opinions to themselves. Jesus knows and teaches against many things and condemns them to hell. What Jesus censures are "spiteful snap judgments in the heat of the moment, with no redemptive aim."[11] Added to that, Jesus warns against hypocrisy, correcting others without self-awareness of one's own faults. All teachers must themselves be taught. There is no license for self-justifying judges who sit in judgment of others but consider

---

[11] F. Scott Spencer, *Luke*, Two Horizons New Testament Commentary (Grand Rapids, MI: Eerdmans, 2019), 176.

themselves immune to criticism, which is like the blind leading the blind, as a result of which both stumble (Luke 6:39-42).

Fruitfulness. Luke switches to agricultural and architectural imagery (Luke 6:43-49). Good trees produce good fruit. Jesus states that speech shows what one harbors in one's heart, whether good or bad. In addition, holding to Jesus' words, obeying them and keeping them, is like a sturdy house built on strong foundations that can endure the torrents of life. In effect, if you keep Jesus' words, harbor them in your heart, then you will be fruitful and faithful in the long term.

Willingness to learn. Finally, disciples are learners. They store up the words of Jesus in the granary of their minds for a fruitful faith (Luke 6:47-49) and commit themselves to the apostles' teachings (Acts 2:42). The office of teacher serves specifically this purpose, to encourage and equip believers in their faith (Acts 11:23; 13:1; 14:22; 16:40; 18:11, 26; 20:7-12). Teachers exercise the "ministry of the word of God" (Acts 6:2 NIV), teach from "house to house" (Acts 20:20), and instruct disciples in the "whole purpose of God" and the "message of his grace" (Acts 20:27, 32). This way, all believers, like Theophilus, can be fully assured of the things they have been taught (Luke 1:4).

The marks of a disciple plainly put. If we were to summarize the Sermon on the Plain, we could say: play your part in God's turning of the tables, let go of inclinations toward revenge and systems of exploitation, love those who refuse to love you back, leave judgment to God, sow seeds of good fruit into your heart, and don't call Jesus "Lord" without doing what he says. These are the marks of a true disciple.

MISSIONAL DISCIPLES

A story of mission for a missional community. Missional readings of the New Testament are all the rage, and quite rightly so. The story of the New Testament cannot be told without the mission and expansion of the early church.[12] The Gospel of Luke is about the mission of Jesus to Israel, and the Acts of the Apostles is the history of the early church's mission from Jerusalem to Rome. To follow Jesus is to participate in his mission to proclaim and embody the kingdom of God. To be part of the apostolic church is to promote the gospel of the kingdom and Jesus the Messiah in local, regional, and foreign environs.

> "As Luke sees it, God is a missionary, Jesus is a missionary and so is the church. Embodying Jesus so that he continues his mission is, for Luke, the prime function of the church. Though not the light itself, the Church reflects the light of Christ for the world. Therefore, not to be 'on mission' is to cease being the Church."[a]
>
> [a]Graham H. Twelftree, *People of the Spirit: Exploring Luke's View of the Church* (London: SPCK, 2009), 214.

Luke's interest in mission is evident from the fact that he records several missionary tasks. The Father's mission is mercy—to extend mercy to those who fear him (Luke 1:50), to mercifully embrace a wayward son (Luke 15:20), and to show mercy to miserable sinners (Luke 18:13). Disciples are to be merciful precisely because their heavenly Father is merciful (Luke 6:36). There is Jesus' own mission to call sinners, preach good news to the poor and oppressed, to seek and save the lost (Luke 4:18-21; 5:31; 19:10), and to give his body and pour out his blood for the forgiveness of sins (Luke 22:19-20). Jesus sends the Twelve apostles to preach the kingdom of God and heal the sick (Luke 9:1-6, 10-11), dispatches messengers to enter a hostile Samaritan village (Luke 9:52-56), and commissions seventy-two followers to again heal the sick and

---

[12]See N. T. Wright, "Reading the New Testament Missionally," in *Reading the Bible Missionally*, ed. Michael Goheen (Grand Rapids, MI: Eerdmans, 2016), 175-93.

proclaim the kingdom (Luke 10:1-12, 17-20). Then there is the Lukan Great Commission, where the risen Jesus tells his disciples, "The Messiah will suffer and rise from the dead on the third day, and repentance for the forgiveness of sins will be preached in his name to all nations, beginning at Jerusalem. You are witnesses of these things" (Luke 24:46-48 NIV). That witness motif is rehearsed in the book of Acts, where the risen Jesus' commission to his disciples is remembered with a slight variation but a similar thrust: "You will be my witnesses in Jerusalem, in all Judea and Samaria, and to the ends of the earth" (Acts 1:8). According to F. Scott Spencer:

> The good news of Christ's restoration, reconciling death and resurrection is not for private, elite, or ethnocentric consumption, but rather for the whole world. It is multinational or global in scope, as it *always has been* in the mind of the Creator-Redeemer God. And it is intentionally collaborative, co-missional, in active partnership with the living Lord, not accomplished by him alone. Accordingly, Christ commissions (co-missions) his followers to proclaim God's saving word through the world—the gospel word rooted not only in scriptural revelation, but also in *personal experience,* Jesus adds "You are *witnesses* of these things" (24:48). Jesus's ambassadors can speak with authority, authenticity, and compassion only concerning *what they know intellectually and experientially* from God's inscribed and incarnate word fulfilled in the suffering and living Christ.[13]

Luke–Acts is part of one redemptive story about how God's plan and purpose for Israel is worked out in Jesus, through the church, to all nations of the world. Luke–Acts is the unfolding story of the *missio Dei* in the *missio ecclesiae* in order to bring about the restoration of Israel and the rescue of creation. Acts

---

[13]Spencer, *Luke*, 633, emphasis original.

is about how the church took up Jesus' gospel and continued his message albeit with him as the centerpiece of the kingdom of God and as God's definitive agent of salvation. According to Dean Flemming:

> If any New Testament writing could be called a "mission book," it is the book of Acts. The story of the church's beginnings is in reality a story of the mission of God. Luke's narrative is not so much "the Acts of the Apostles" as the acts of the triune God, who sends, empowers and guides his people on a journey of mission that spans from Jerusalem to Rome. In Acts, the church's identity is formed only as it engages in mission. If there's no mission, there's no church.[14]

If mission is part of the story, if mission is the reason why the church exists, then mission will be instrumental to discipleship and be imperative for the community of Jesus' followers.

Discipleship is missional in that disciples must continue the prophetic mission of Jesus and the apostles to be a "light to the nations" (Isaiah 42:6; 49:6; Luke 2:32; Acts 13:47). For a case in point, Paul, when appearing before King Agrippa II, declares that everything he proclaims is in accordance with the prophets and Moses, whereby the Messiah, after his sufferings and resurrection, would "proclaim light both to our people and to the Gentiles" (Acts 26:22-23). Spencer explains the logic of the passage as it relates to the motif of light in Acts 26:

1. The risen Jesus originally revealed himself to Paul as blinding, enveloping "*light* from heaven" (26.13).

2. The risen Jesus commissioned Paul to testify to what he had seen before Gentiles (as well as Jews) in order that "they may turn from darkness to *light*," as Paul had done (26.16-17).

---

[14]Dean Flemming, *Recovering the Full Mission of God: A Biblical Perspective on Being, Doing and Telling* (Downers Grove, IL: InterVarsity Press, 2013), 133.

3. The risen Jesus continued to "proclaim *light*" to both Jews and Gentiles—the same mission he had assigned to Paul (26.23).[15]

In a world where people live in darkness, under the shadow of death (Luke 1:79), where bodies are permeated by the darkness hidden in their hearts (Luke 11:34-35), where satanic darkness seems to reign without limit (Luke 22:53), where people live in ignorance about injustice (Acts 26:18), Jesus comes as light. This light shines through the apostles and their disciples like a prism so that it reflects on the wider world to dispel the darkness in its moral ugliness, spiritual impoverishment, unjust inequalities, and alienation from God. This is the mission of Jesus, the apostles, and the church. In the mission of Jesus' followers, Satan falls "like lightning" (Luke 10:18 NIV), sins are forgiven (Acts 10:43; 26:16), hearts are cleansed by faith (Acts 15:9; 26:18), amazing communities of faith are created in unexpected places such as Antioch (Acts 11:19-21), the gospel is heard by the mighty such as Sergius Paulus (Acts 13:4-12), and the marginalized are freed, such as the slave girl in Philippi, from demonic possession (Acts 16:18). Wherever the apostles proclaim the gospel and offer testimony, there they make disciples and establish churches, and those churches brim over with liberation, light, love, hope, unity, generosity, and redemption.

For God's mission through the church to take place, for the commission to be fulfilled, four points are important to note.

The Holy Spirit drives mission. The Holy Spirit is the engine driving mission. Jesus does no ministry or miracles until he receives the Holy Spirit at his baptism (Luke 3:21-22), and Jesus roots his prophetic ministry in his anointing with the Holy Spirit as the Isaianic servant (Luke 4:18). Jesus also tells the disciples that the Spirit will provide them with words and wisdom for their witness before

---

[15]F. Scott Spencer, *Acts* (Sheffield: Sheffield Academic Press, 1997), 228.

rulers and judges (Luke 12:11-12; 21:15). Most important of all, the risen Jesus instructs his disciples that their mission to proclaim the forgiveness of sins will not happen until they receive the Father's promise and "power from on high," which is the Holy Spirit (Luke 24:48-49; Acts 1:4, 8). This is precisely why Luke repeats how a person is "filled" with the "Spirit" and then begins to proclaim the word of the gospel. That is specifically true of Peter (Acts 4:8) and Paul (Acts 13:9), but it also applies to the whole church, as Luke notes in one instance: "When they had prayed, the place in which they were gathered together was shaken; and they were all filled with the Holy Spirit and spoke the word of God with boldness" (Acts 4:31).

Beyond the Twelve, there are leading evangelists and proclaimers including Philip, Paul, Barnabas, John Mark, Silas, Timothy, Apollos, Priscilla and Aquila and many others who share the word of God when scattered by persecution (Acts 8:4; 11:20). Luke presents the gospel being shared in a variety of places: the Jerusalem temple, synagogues, lavish homes, markets, crammed apartments, amphitheaters, courtrooms, corridors of power, prisons, lecture halls, boats, and the street. Michael Goheen rightly comments that the church's witness "begins with this small apostolic group but extends as the calling of the whole church."[16] The Holy Spirit is the fire behind the testimony of disciples. Without such fire the church's words are empty rather than evangelistic, propaganda rather than proclamation, superstition rather than salvation, religionizing rather than redeeming.

The Spirit actively directs the church in its mission. At Antioch, the Spirit speaks through a prophet to commission Paul and Barnabas for their innovative mission to Cyprus and Phrygia: "Set apart for me Barnabas and Saul for the work to which I have called

---

[16]Michael Goheen, *A Light to the Nations: The Missional Church and the Biblical Story* (Grand Rapids, MI: Baker, 2011), 127.

them" (Acts 13:2). Later Paul intends to go into Bithynia, but Luke reports that "the Spirit of Jesus did not allow them," and they go instead into Macedonia (Acts 16:7). The Holy Spirit is the divine person who authorizes and animates the mission of disciples in their testimony to Jesus as part of God's mission.

Mission is fueled by prayer. There is much prayer involved in mission. This is precisely why Jesus prays and calls his disciples to persistent prayer. Jesus teaches, "The harvest is plentiful, but the laborers are few; therefore ask the Lord of the harvest to send out laborers into his harvest" (Luke 10:2). Paul testifies with great pathos and devotion to his captors, "I pray to God that not only you but also all who are listening to me today might become such as I am—except for these chains" (Acts 26:29). Prayer accompanies the apostles as they engage in mission; therefore, prayer is imperative in the continuation of the mission.

There is no mission without provision. Mission only happens with material support. Whether we are talking about Roman Antioch or American Puerto Rico, mission needs money. A number of wealthy women supported Jesus in his ministry (Luke 8:3), and churches used their common funds to support the apostolic mission, as is certainly the case with the Antiochene church and the first missionary journey of Paul (Acts 13:1). Paul and coworkers certainly worked as tentmakers to pay their way; however, they were also supported by the generosity and commitment of the congregations they established. This means that mission requires adjusting one's spending habits, church budgets, and financial priorities to align with the plan and purpose of God.

Mission requires courage. The testimony of the apostles often takes place in the context of adversity, whether before the hostile Jerusalem Sanhedrin, a skeptical synagogue, or a group of philosophers. What characterizes the church's testimony to Jesus is that they speak the word of God with "boldness" (παρρησία), that is, without fear of consequence.

Table 8.2. A summary of mission in Luke and Acts[a]

GOSPEL OF LUKE	BOOK OF ACTS
<ul><li>preaching the gospel and healing the sick</li><li>extending forgiveness to sinners and justice to the oppressed</li><li>delivering from Satan's powers and bearing witness to the nations</li><li>confronting insiders and embracing outsiders</li><li>touching the poor with compassion and liberating the rich from addiction to money</li><li>restoring the lost and loving one's enemies</li><li>explaining the Scriptures and enacting them through symbols</li><li>doing ministry in the company of Jesus and by the power of the Spirit</li><li>announcing and embodying the good news</li></ul>	<ul><li>speaking the gospel to Jews and Gentiles</li><li>performing mighty works of healing and confronting the powers of darkness</li><li>engaging in ministries of teaching, prayer, sharing, and serving</li><li>deploying flexibility and innovation in the church's witness to cross boundaries and discover new ways of articulating the faith as the church encounters new circumstances</li><li>following the Spirit's direction and resourcement in its evangelistic endeavors</li></ul>

[a]Dean Flemming, *Recovering the Full Mission of God: A Biblical Perspective on Being, Doing and Telling* (Downers Grove, IL: InterVarsity Press, 2013), 110-11, 155-57.

REVIEW QUESTIONS

1. What does it mean to "turn to the Lord" for Luke?
2. How would Luke define faith?
3. What are the marks of a true disciple?
4. What distinguishes Jesus-fans from Jesus-followers?
5. Where did the rich young ruler and Simon Magus go wrong?

RECOMMENDED READING

Fitzmyer, Joseph A. "Discipleship in Lucan Writings." In *Luke the Theologian: Aspects of His Teaching*, 117-45. New York: Paulist, 1989.

Longenecker, Richard N. "Taking Up the Cross Daily: Discipleship in Luke–Acts." In *Patterns of Discipleship in the New Testament*, edited by Richard N. Longenecker, 50-76. Grand Rapids, MI: Eerdmans, 1996.

Talbert, Charles H. "Discipleship in Luke–Acts." In *Discipleship in the New Testament*, edited by F. Segovia, 62-75. Philadelphia: Fortress, 1985.

9

Luke the Feminist?

Jesus, Women, and the Church

IS LUKE AN ALLY OF WOMEN?

When I read Luke–Acts, I cannot help but think that Luke deliberately intends to cast a spotlight on the important place of women in the life of Jesus and in the ministry of the church. In Luke's narration, women have prominent places in the purpose and plan of God, beginning with Mary and Elizabeth but also featuring other exemplary women such as Mary Magdalene, Tabitha, and Lydia. Furthermore, Luke also has a real concern for the vulnerability of women, especially widows, women who suffer from various afflictions and disgraces, the infertile, and prostitutes. Luke depicts the plight of women who experience injustice, deprivation, and shame. His two-volume work is in some sense a protest against a pernicious patriarchy and its exploitation of women. James Arlandson writes, "When Luke constantly esteems women in Luke–Acts, and especially six from the unclean and degraded and the expendable classes at the expense of wealthy, powerful, and prestigious men, then he is transmitting a value about women to the Christian community, especially about poor women."[1] This is a telltale sign that women were probably a majority of the early church's membership

---

[1] James Malcolm Arlandson, *Women, Class and Society in Early Christianity: Models from Luke–Acts* (Peabody, MA: Hendrickson, 1997), 188.

and the Christian message was slowly beginning a revolution of women's rights in the ancient world that would crystallize into the chivalric code of Christendom and the modern concern for gender equality. Luke, I believe, is on the side of women; however, the issue is not simple.

As much as we might like to think of Luke as the champion of women's roles, rights, and plights, Luke was still a product of his patriarchal age, and in many ways he simply assumes and rehearses patriarchal perspectives. Alas, Luke was no feminist like Simone de Beauvoir or Germaine Greer. In fact, some feminist scholars see Luke as more of a villain than a hero insofar as he (assuming the author was male) continues to depict women without agency, equality, and authority. Consider the scene where the Lukan Jesus commends Mary for sitting at his feet to learn from him and dismisses Martha's complaint that her sister is not helping her in their domestic chores (Luke 10:38-42). We can read this positively, as the Lukan Jesus commending Mary as a female disciple who wants to learn and who shuns the normal obligations of female domesticity. Or we can read this negatively, with Luke commending a woman who literally sits down and shuts up in contrast to Martha, who is actively serving and asserting her own perspective and the unfairness of her predicament.[2] It is legitimate to ask, as Barbara Reid does, "Does Luke silence women, or does he show them as faithfully responding to and proclaiming the word?"[3]

In this chapter, we'll explore Luke's depiction of women in the ministry of Jesus and in the beginnings of the early church. I hope we'll see that Luke is indeed an ally of women; however, we must be conscious of anachronism, as Luke might not be pro-women

---

[2]See discussion in Barbara E. Reid, *Choosing the Better Part? Women in the Gospel of Luke* (Collegeville, MN: Liturgical, 1996), 144-62.
[3]Barbara E. Reid, "The Gospel of Luke: Friend or Foe of Women Proclaimers of the Word?," *CBQ* 78 (2016): 3.

according to the metrics of our own modern age. An exhaustive survey here is impossible. Therefore, I will survey select figures in the form of Mary, Anna, Mary and Martha, Mary Magdalene, Lydia, Tabitha, and Priscilla.

MARY, BIRTHER OF HOPE

Luke depicts Mary, the mother of Jesus, as no ordinary peasant girl and no one-dimensional character. Mary has a significant place in God's purposes, and she is an exemplary disciple in many respects. Mary is also compared with the compliant Elizabeth and juxtaposed with the recalcitrant Zechariah, the two of whom also experience their own miraculous pregnancy. She is a herald of God's justice, a paragon of piety, the mother of the Lord, and even the church's first theologian.

In the annunciation (Luke 1:26-37), Mary is told by the angel Gabriel that she is God's "favored one" who has "found favor with God" (Luke 1:28, 30). She is both elected by grace and electable by her own devotion. She is the vessel by which the "Son of the Most High" will enter his realm and receive his Davidic throne. Mary is perplexed, not as to the truth of what she is told but its means. She is assured by Gabriel that, despite her virginity, she will become pregnant. For, if God can make her elderly relative Elizabeth pregnant through normal procreation, then surely God can make her fall pregnant without procreation. On hearing this, Mary responds like a prophet with the words, "Here am I, the servant of the Lord; let it be with me according to your word" (Luke 1:38). These words, contrasted with others such as Zechariah's dullness and Peter's denial, cast Mary as the exemplar by which all future disciples should be measured since she is the one who hears and obeys God's word.[4] "Mary is in many ways," write Gregory Forbes

---
[4] Reid, *Choosing the Better Part?*, 69.

and Scott Harrower, "a model of a desired response to the unexpected ways in which God may work in and through the lives of the faithful."[5]

Mary's Magnificat (Luke 1:46-56) stands beside the Song of Moses (Exodus 15:1-18) and the Song of Miriam (Exodus 15:20-21) as one of the most stirring scriptural celebrations of God's victory for his people. The song exudes worshipful joy as it celebrates God's faithfulness to the patriarchs and Israel, his mercy and power, and the reordering of powers and reversal of status that divine salvation brings. Mary here is the prophet heralding divine justice and judgment. Mary's song promises mercy and justice to all descendants, the family of faith, who will also sing the song that Mary did.

As the story continues, Mary gives birth to her son in Bethlehem, connecting the scriptural pattern of a young maiden bearing a new Davidide (Isaiah 7:14) with messianic prophecy of a Davidic Messiah born in the small Judean town (Micah 5:2-6). When the shepherds come to the holy family and explain their angelic visitation, Luke reports, "Mary treasured all these words and pondered them in her heart" (Luke 2:19). The sense is that Mary is processing, pondering, and putting all the pieces of the story together, and it leaves an indelible impression on her.

A week later, the family offers the relevant sacrifices in the Jerusalem temple for their purification after the birth. At that time, the prophet Simeon tells Mary about what the child will one day do. But also, to Mary herself he says, "a sword will pierce your own soul too" (Luke 2:35), which intimates that Mary herself will come to experience something of the pain of her son's own passion. Then, in Jesus' twelfth year, when his parents are anxiously searching for

---

[5] Gregory W. Forbes and Scott D. Harrower, *Raised from Obscurity: A Narrative and Theological Study of the Characterization of Women in Luke–Acts* (Eugene, OR: Pickwick, 2015), 44.

him in the temple, Jesus' answer is that he must be "in my Father's house" (Luke 2:49). Though neither Joseph nor Mary understands the boy's words, these words are prophetic, not presumptive, and his obedience to his parents furnishes proof of his devotion to them. To this Luke comments, "His mother treasured all these things in her heart" (Luke 2:51). Taken together, Luke 2:19 and Luke 2:51 indicate that the first person to meditate and marvel at Jesus, his identity and his words, was his mother.

Luke is clear that Mary is a vessel of divine grace, inimitably faithful, a prophet of God's justice as well as ponderous of God's purposes. She should rightly be called "blessed" by "all generations" and be acclaimed as "the mother of my Lord" (Luke 1:42-43, 48).

ANNA THE PROPHET

The prophetess Anna might seem like a minor character, but her short appearance underlies her piety and testimony to Jesus.

> There was also a prophet, Anna the daughter of Phanuel, of the tribe of Asher. She was of a great age, having lived with her husband seven years after her marriage, then as a widow to the age of eighty-four. She never left the temple but worshiped there with fasting and prayer night and day. At that moment she came, and began to praise God and to speak about the child to all who were looking for the redemption of Jerusalem. (Luke 2:36-38)

Anna is the first of many pious and righteous widows, socially disempowered and destitute but not without purpose. She is a commendable figure who devotes her time to worship in the temple with "fasting and prayer night and day," which evokes figures such as Daniel (Daniel 9:3) and Ezra (Ezra 9:5-9) and prefigures the early church, who also pray and fast (Acts 14:23). Her encounter with the holy family erupts in praise to God. Added to that, Luke reports how Anna began "to speak about the child to all who were looking for the redemption of Jerusalem," which implies her grasp of Jesus as the agent of redemption and demonstrates that she, a widow, is the first witness for Jesus to others. True, Luke appears to valorize Anna for her asceticism, celibacy, and refusal to seek a better situation. Nonetheless, Anna is not passive, and she is celebrated for her praise and her proclamation.

MARY AND MARTHA OF BETHANY

The story of Mary and Martha is ground zero for feminist interpretation of Luke and often determines whether one thinks of Luke as an ally or adversary of women.

> Now as they went on their way, he entered a certain village, where a woman named Martha welcomed him into her home. She had a sister named Mary, who sat at the Lord's feet and listened to what he was saying. But Martha was distracted by her many tasks; so she came to him and asked, "Lord, do you not care that my sister has left me to do all the work by myself? Tell her then to help me." But the Lord answered her, "Martha, Martha, you are worried and distracted by many things; there is need of only one thing. Mary has chosen the better part, which will not be taken away from her." (Luke 10:38-42)

In some creative and critical readings, Martha's service, her διακονία, is not housework but cryptically symbolizes a ministry of prayer and word just like that of the apostles (see Acts 1:25; 6:4). Such service, allegedly performed by women in Luke's own day, is supposedly denigrated by the Lukan Jesus in favor of Mary's silence and submissiveness. The message to women on such a reading is, "Dear Christian women, you are valued for your silence and subjection, not your service." Of course, even without a feminist hermeneutic of suspicion, many women find Jesus' dismissal of Martha's complaint hard to swallow. Every woman I know has found herself at one time or another left to do more than her fair share of household chores while everyone else, usually men, puts their feet up and says, "Can you get me some more Doritos?" or "You missed a spot!" in cleaning up a mess. Many women identify with the overwhelmed Martha rather than the superspiritual Mary. The problem is not the commendation of Mary for listening to Jesus; it is the dismissal of Martha's complaint about the unfair burden placed on her to provide for everyone. It is natural to ask: Must Mary's veneration come at the expense of Martha's consternation?[6] Thus, the suspicious feminist and the conservative homemaker can be belligerent allies in questioning Luke's view of women in the home and church.

Those are, I think, legitimate concerns from readers about the depiction of women, all the more so if this is a veiled reference to women in Luke's own day. That said, I'm a sympathetic reader of Luke; I doubt he is trying to put any woman down, and I think Luke's intention here is rather benign.

First, Luke's Gospel has much to say about the nature of service and its diversions, which provides the backdrop for the Martha/Mary episode.[7] Luke provides several examples of Jesus telling disciples not to be anxious (Luke 12:11-12) and to avoid distraction by centering themselves on God's power over their predicament, to rest in God's provision for their needs (Luke 12:22-34). Even the disciples who enjoy great success in their own local mission need to remember that service is not an end in and of itself but contributes to a greater purpose in advancing the kingdom, a kingdom they can reflect on and rejoice to be a part of (Luke 10:17-20). Luke labors the point that one must first "hear the word" (Luke 8:15) before one can "go and do likewise" (Luke 10:37). Thus, meditation

---

[6]See Loveday C. Alexander, "Sisters in Adversity: Retelling Martha's Story," in *A Feminist Companion to Luke*, ed. Amy-Jill Levine (Cleveland, OH: Pilgrim, 2001), 198.
[7]Warren Carter, "Getting Martha Out of the Kitchen: Luke 10.38-42 Again," in Levine, *Feminist Companion to Luke*, 227-30.

and action belong together. Action without meditation leads to pragmatism. Meditation without action yields inertia.

Second, Martha has a unique problem as the materfamilias of the household. Jesus and his disciples were welcomed by Martha into "her home." Martha is, from what it appears, the head of the house, and therefore she has the responsibility to provide hospitality for her guests, a task that might not be easy if a dozen men turn up unannounced and only meager provisions are on hand. Further, given ancient views about hospitality, if Martha does not prove to be a good hostess, then she will bring shame on her family and sully her reputation. To make matters worse, her sister Mary, rather than performing her dutiful female role in female space by assisting Martha, is acting like a male by sitting and listening to the teacher. So, in addition to struggling to be hospitable, Martha also has to deal with the reputational risk caused by Mary abandoning her traditional female role and transgressing male spaces. In other words, Martha's primary worry is not her uneven workload but her and her house's reputation for hospitality and upholding gender norms in an agrarian village where honor was a precious commodity. According to Bruce Malina and Richard Rohrbraugh, "Since a woman's honor and reputation depended on her ability to manage a household, Martha's complaint would be read by the culture as legitimate."[8]

Third, Martha's problem according to Jesus is not her service but her distraction and anxiety.[9] The women in Luke–Acts who provide hospitality and financial support are always treated positively (see

---

[8] Bruce J. Malina and Richard L. Rohrbraugh, *Social-Science Commentary on the Synoptic Gospels* (Minneapolis: Fortress, 1992), 348.
[9] Veronica Koperski, "Women and Discipleship in Luke 10.38-42 and Acts 6.1-7: The Literary Context of Luke–Acts," in Levine, *Feminist Companion to Luke*, 195. I don't think Martha's διακονία is a cipher for a women engaged in the work of apostolic ministry and prayer, as per Acts 6:4. I think this διακονία is just about domestic hospitality.

Luke 8:1-3; Acts 16:15). There's no way Luke is saying, "Thanks for the tea and cookies, Martha, but you shouldn't really be doing that. We don't want any man to feel usurped by your servant-heartedness." No, I think Luke is pro-women and has no problem with women as companions of Jesus and partners in church ministries. The proof of this is that Martha's service is never disparaged, and neither is her complaint dismissed; rather, the point seems to be that her contribution and concerns need to consider the perspective of a greater need than domesticity and a greater good, which is receiving the word. Without such a perspective, Martha, for all her sense of duty and decorum, runs the risk of being like the soil covered with thorns, which does not receive the word because the word is choked by anxieties over mundane matters (Luke 8:14).

Fourth, both women can be positive examples in their own way. On the one hand, Martha engages in genuine service, exercises generous hospitality, and arguably anticipates the diaconal ministry of Acts 6. Even if what Mary does is "better," this does not entail that what Martha is doing is bad. All service is important, but hearing the word is doubly important. For, although Martha's priorities and concerns need to be put into proper perspective, her service is appreciated and affirmed. On the other hand, Mary is a positive example of women as learners, worthy of instruction, worthy of investment. Sitting at a teacher's feet is the position of a disciple (Acts 22:3). Mary is one who chooses theological instruction and spiritual devotion over domestic duties even if it means defying gender boundaries and norms. Such a position validates women who choose a ministry career or monastic community over marriage and motherhood. For some women, Martha and Mary are times of the week or stages of life. Women may have times in life when they've swapped family responsibilities for theological education.

THE SINFUL WOMAN

In another episode (Luke 7:36-50), Jesus is the invited guest at the home of one of the Pharisees—who only ate with people they considered clean and kosher—when an unnamed "sinful woman" turns up:

> And a woman in the city, who was a sinner, having learned that he was eating in the Pharisee's house, brought an alabaster jar of ointment. She stood behind him at his feet, weeping, and began to bathe his feet with her tears and to dry them with her hair. Then she continued kissing his feet and anointing them with the ointment. Now when the Pharisee who had invited him saw it, he said to himself, "If this man were a prophet, he would have known who and what kind of woman this is who is touching him—that she is a sinner." (Luke 7:37-39)

Pharisees believed that Israel's renewal was contingent on keeping themselves morally and ceremonially clean, and yet this woman is transgressing public mores, defying domestic boundaries, contaminating the holiness of Simon and his guest, and even engaging in a quasi-sexual gesture of physical intimacy. Simon is scandalized that Jesus is completely unperturbed by her sacrilegious invasion, her salacious actions, and even the risk to his own reputation. If Jesus were a prophet, Simon reasons with himself, then he would know *who* she is and *how* affronting her actions are. Yet Jesus is a prophet, the proof of which is that he knows what Simon is thinking (or at least can read his body language).

In response, Jesus tells a parable about two creditors. The punchline is that those who, like Simon, are forgiven little show little love for Jesus. In contrast, those who, like the woman, are forgiven much show much love to Jesus. In Jewish fashion, sin is cast as a debt, and God is eager to erase that debt—not with reference to the worthiness of the debtor, but because God's nature is to be merciful and forgiving. According to Scott Spencer,

> The indebted/sinful woman's loving gesture toward Jesus does not precipitate (earn) his forgiveness; put another way, Jesus does not forgive *because the woman loves him*. Rather, she loves him *because he had already forgiven her*: Jesus's gracious action was primary and prompted her manifold love. Thus it appears that Jesus indeed *had known* this woman both/either in a prior confessional encounter (not in some illicit dalliance) and/or in the present engagement where he senses—as a prophet!—her sincere, heartfelt love. The woman may be intruding on Simon's event, but she has already been—and continues to be—welcomed by the loving-forgiving Jesus.[10]

Luke's story uses a woman of low status to one-up the Pharisees on the nature and extent of divine forgiveness. Jesus does not shrink back from the woman's almost intimate devotion and instead presents her as the ideal recipient of forgiveness.

MARY MAGDALENE: THE APOSTLE TO THE APOSTLES

Oh, the things that books and movies say about Mary Magdalene and Jesus. From salacious eroticism to creative conspiracy theories, audiences lap up inventive tales and tawdry gossip about the two figures. Sadly, the legend that Mary Magdalene was a prostitute began in the sixth century when Pope Gregory I conflated Mary Magdalene (Luke 8:2) with Mary of Bethany (Luke 10:39) and with the anonymous "sinful woman" who washes Jesus' feet (Luke 7:36-50). From there you get all sorts of things such as the song "I Don't Know How to Love Him" in *Jesus Christ Superstar* to the fanciful fiction in Dan Brown's *The Da Vinci Code*. The truth about Mary Magdalene is not dry; there is much to see here, but it is hardly sensational.

---

[10] F. Scott Spencer, *Luke*, Two Horizons New Testament Commentary (Grand Rapids, MI: Eerdmans, 2019), 198.

For a start, Mary, probably short for Miriam, was a common Jewish name for women. More disputed is the meaning of her family name, "Magdalene." It could designate her origins in the village of Magdala, derived from the Hebrew word מגדל, for "tower," located on the western shore of the Sea of Galilee (also known as the city of Tarichaea). Alternatively, given the nicknames that many of Jesus' followers are given by their teacher (see Mark 3:17; Matthew 16:17), maybe "Magdalene" means something like "Tower," for her towering faith and support.[11] This is speculation, of course, not implausible, but we do not know for sure.

Otherwise, Mary Magdalene is mentioned in two places in the Gospel of Luke, in association with Jesus' Galilean ministry and as a witness to his resurrection.

> Soon afterwards he went on through cities and villages, proclaiming and bringing the good news of the kingdom of God. The twelve were with him, as well as some women who had been cured of evil spirits and infirmities: Mary, called Magdalene, from whom seven demons had gone out, and Joanna, the wife of Herod's steward Chuza, and Susanna, and many others, who provided for them out of their resources (Luke 8:1-3)

It is little known but should be widely noted that Jesus was financially supported in his prophetic work by three prominent women: Mary Magdalene, Joanna, and Susanna, among others. These women were most likely financially well-off if not outright affluent in the case of Joanna, whose husband was Herod Antipas's chief administrator. Concerning Mary, just as Christians kept alive the memory of key disciples and their experience of Jesus, such as Peter's call, confession, and betrayal, so too, in the case of Mary,

---

[11] See Elizabeth Schrader and Joan E. Taylor, "The Meaning of 'Magdalene': A Review of Literary Evidence," *Journal of Biblical Literature* 140 (2021): 751-73.

they remembered her exceptional exorcism.[12] Mary was a demoniac—though what that precisely means we are not told—who then joined the Jesus movement, remaining faithful to Jesus even into his death.

> But on the first day of the week, at early dawn, they [i.e., some female disciples] came to the tomb, taking the spices that they had prepared. They found the stone rolled away from the tomb, but when they went in, they did not find the body. While they were perplexed about this, suddenly two men in dazzling clothes stood beside them. The women were terrified and bowed their faces to the ground, but the men said to them, "Why do you look for the living among the dead? He is not here, but has risen. Remember how he told you, while he was still in Galilee, that the Son of Man must be handed over to sinners, and be crucified, and on the third day rise again." Then they remembered his words, and returning from the tomb, they told all this to the eleven and to all the rest. Now it was Mary Magdalene, Joanna, Mary the mother of James, and the other women with them who told this to the apostles. But these words seemed to them an idle tale, and they did not believe them. (Luke 24:1-11)

Just as women are prominent in the Lukan birth and infancy narrative, so too are they prominent in the resurrection narrative. Luke is largely reworking Markan material about the women visiting the tomb and there encountering a glorious angel who announces the resurrection of Jesus, which leads them to flee, fearful and confused (Mark 16:1-8). However, Luke reports that these women "remembered his words" (Luke 24:8) and "told all this to the eleven and to all the rest" (Luke 24:9). In Luke's telling, the women, led by Mary Magdalene, are the first to connect Jesus' death with his passion prediction and the first to proclaim the

---

[12]François Bovon, *Luke 1: A Commentary on the Gospel of Luke 1:1–9:50* (Minneapolis: Fortress, 2002), 300.

resurrection to the apostles. This is precisely why, since Thomas Aquinas, Mary Magdalene has been known as the "apostle to the apostles."

TABITHA/DORCAS THE DISCIPLE

Turning to the book of Acts, we see many important women in Luke's narrative of the spread of the gospel and growth of the church.

The story of Tabitha (Aramaic) or Dorcas (Greek) is an amazing vignette as a miraculous resuscitation and its valorizing of a female disciple (Acts 9:36-43). The story is significant for a few reasons: (1) Compared to the preceding episode about Aeneas (Acts 9:32-35), Tabitha is given a more prominent résumé for her faith and piety. (2) This is the only place where a woman is called a disciple in Luke–Acts (Acts 9:36). (3) Tabitha is described as "devoted to good works and acts of charity," which is the quintessential description of piety for both men and women (Acts 9:36). (4) There are parallels with Jesus' healing of Jairus's daughter (Luke 8:40-42, 49-56). The story illustrates that Peter is continuing the role of Jesus, and Tabitha's revivification leads many people to becoming believers, which makes her story a medium for the apostolic message. According to Forbes and Harrower:

> The story of Tabitha contributes to Luke's broader understanding of female discipleship. Luke–Acts leaves no doubt that in the reader's mind that believing women are full members of Jesus' community and are rightly designated as disciples. This view is predicated upon the women's continual presence in the narrative as disciples, by Jesus' words and actions, by the nature of the kingdom of God and the coming of the Holy Spirit. Given the numerous examples of women being ideal disciples, ideal discipleship is not compromised by being female. Therefore, *female disciples may be disciples in the fullest sense.*[13]

---

[13]Forbes and Harrower, *Raised from Obscurity*, 173-74, emphasis original.

LYDIA THE CONVERT

Paul and his coworkers were compelled by a vision to travel from northwestern Asia Minor into Macedonia in Europe. Luke records that Paul and his friends quickly made their way to Philippi, a Roman colony in Macedonia (Acts 16:11-15). On the Sabbath, down by the river, they find some Jewish worshipers and begin to converse with them. Among them is a woman named Lydia, who is described as a "worshiper of God" (θεοσεβής, Acts 16:14), an elastic term often used for someone who is a Gentile adherent to some Jewish beliefs and practices and dwells on the fringes of a local Jewish community.[14]

Lydia is "from the city of Thyatira and a dealer in purple cloth" (Acts 16:14). Luke abbreviates the evangelistic conversation that Paul has with Lydia to, "The Lord opened her heart to listen eagerly to what was said by Paul" (Acts 16:14). Lydia becomes the first Christian convert to Christianity in Europe, at least in the Pauline mission, which is underscored by Luke's narrative: "When she and her household were baptized, she urged us, saying, 'If you have judged me to be faithful to the Lord, come and stay at my home.' And she prevailed upon us" (Acts 16:15). This is more than Lydia meeting a religious philosopher, taking a bath, and inviting him over for lunch. Just as Mary listened to words of Jesus (Luke 10:39), so Lydia listened to Paul. Just as the two travelers to Emmaus had "their eyes opened" to recognize Jesus (Luke 24:31), so Lydia had her heart opened by the Lord.[15] She submits to baptism, a symbol of believing, a ritual of belonging, and an oath for behaving according to Christ. Whereas Philippi had no synagogue or Jewish

---

[14]See Michael F. Bird, *Crossing Over Sea and Land: Jewish Missionary Activity in the Second Temple Period* (Peabody, MA: Hendrickson, 2010), 44-52.
[15]Joshua W. Jipp, *Divine Visitations and Hospitality to Strangers in Luke–Acts: An Interpretation of the Malta Episode in Acts 28:1-10*, NovTSup 153 (Leiden: Brill, 2013), 242.

prayer house, it now had a house church that met in Lydia's home, presumably under her leadership.

PRISCILLA THE MISSIONARY

According to Paul, Priscilla and Aquila work with him "in Christ Jesus" (Romans 16:3). More details are provided by Luke, who notes that Priscilla and Aquila met Paul in Corinth after they had been expelled from Rome by Claudius's edict (Acts 18:2). They are a Greek-speaking Jewish Christian couple, also tentmakers, who work among the Roman churches. They travel with Paul to Ephesus (Acts 18:18-19). There they meet Apollos, a Greek-speaking Jewish Christian from Alexandria who is learned in rhetoric and Scriptures and is also an evangelist for Jesus, albeit without a fully furnished knowledge of the early church and its practices such as baptism. Luke recounts that Priscilla and Aquila heard him speak in one of the Ephesian synagogues, and "they took him aside and explained the Way of God to him more accurately" (Acts 18:26).

Priscilla and Aquila were part of a network of traveling Greek-speaking Jewish Christians who were active and animated about their faith in the eastern Mediterranean and managed to connect with like-minded persons in Paul and Apollos. They were both, it seems, involved in service and ministry, and they both had a part in topping up Apollos on the belief and practices of the nascent church. Priscilla was a woman of significant service and work for the churches of Rome, Corinth, and Ephesus.

LUKE AND WOMEN: RETROSPECT

Is Luke just another one in a long history of men who write women out of history, diminish their contribution, and try to subjugate them to male domination? Some read Luke that way. As you can guess, I do not. I wonder whether there is no strict answer here because one's own presuppositions and experiences will determine whether and to what extent Luke is considered an advocate for women or just another privileged man who ignores them.

Barbara Reid, a pioneer in feminist interpretation of Luke, changed her mind about Luke. Whereas she once thought that Luke sought to lessen the contribution of women, Reid later altered her opinion in a subsequent article, where she adopts a more sanguine view of Luke and women. Reid acknowledges that in Luke's Gospel, "There are no narratives showing individual women as called, commissioned, enduring persecution, or ministering by the power of the spirit, as there are of men. Women in Luke and Acts do not imitate Jesus' mission of preaching, teaching, healing, exorcising, forgiving, or praying. Only men are depicted in these roles." However, Reid acknowledges that her earlier study had limitations, and if one looks at Luke 23:44–24:12, it is possible to see Luke as affirming women as preachers of the word. She concludes: "Luke's own use of the motif of 'memory' not only invites us to recall that in the past Jesus' women followers were faithful witnesses and proclaimers of the word but also impels us toward present enactment of this memory for the well-being of the church and world."[16]

I hasten to add that moral judgments about ancient authors are a matter of context: both theirs and ours. Luke was not one of us. He did not know of the UN Declaration of Human Rights or the suffragette movement. Nor was he a fourth-wave feminist. He was a first-century Greek-speaking Christ-believer with a flair for literary artistry who possessed a deep faith. His narrative was soaked in first-century presuppositions and immersed in the social

---

[16] Reid, "Gospel of Luke," 4, 23.

structures around him. I find it odd to condemn Luke for not being as liberal and progressive as we might be on women's rights in society and in the church. To those who sit in judgment over Luke, I would ask them to remember that when we finally get to tenth-wave feminism, feminists will probably look back on fourth-wave feminism with sneering contempt. To avoid the incessant and inevitable moralizing condemnation of everyone who came before us, we do better to judge people by the conventions of their own day and by the effects that their writing had in the advancement of society toward benevolent ends.

On this score, Luke–Acts was by the standards of its time a liberative work for women and very pro-women. Luke commends women, shows genuine concern for the plight of women, whether widows or prostitutes, and believes that women are significant in the story of Jesus and the growth of the Jesus movement. I think it is because of Luke that Christianity became a pro-woman, pro-child, and pro-slave religion. Second-century pagan philosopher Celsus condemned Christianity as religion of the *stulti*, the expendables and deplorables, "women, children, and slaves" (Origen, *Against Celsus* 3.44). Luke, I imagine, would reply, "Why, thank you!"

REVIEW QUESTIONS

1. Who is your favorite female character in Luke–Acts, and what characteristics stand out to you?
2. Would contemporary feminists and womanist advocates consider Luke an enemy or ally to their cause?
3. Is Luke a product of his own age concerning gender roles and women's limited rights, or is he a revolutionary?
4. How do women contribute to the growth of the church in the book of Acts?

RECOMMENDED READING

Forbes, Gregory W., and Scott D. Harrower. *Raised from Obscurity: A Narrative and Theological Study of the Characterization of Women in Luke–Acts*. Eugene, OR: Pickwick, 2015.

Levine, Amy-Jill, with Marianne Blickenstaff, eds. *A Feminist Companion to Luke*. Cleveland, OH: Pilgrim, 2001.

Reid, Barbara E. *Choosing the Better Part? Women in the Gospel of Luke*. Collegeville, MN: Liturgical, 1996.

Spencer, F. Scott. *Dancing Girls, Loose Ladies, and Women of the Cloth*. New York: T&T Clark, 2014.

———. *Salty Wives, Spirited Mothers and Savvy Widows: Capable Women of Purpose and Persistence in Luke's Gospel*. Grand Rapids, MI: Eerdmans, 2012.

10

Luke the Socialist?

Possessions and Poverty

LUKE AND THE ENGLISH DIGGERS

In 1649, shortly after the execution of Charles I in England, Gerrard Winstanley—a religious reformer, political agitator, and social activist—led a group of "True Levellers" or "Diggers" in pursuit of heavenly justice. This group of commoners wanted to level the laws of the land and portion out private land so that people could dig for their own crops, hence the designation "Diggers." Winstanley published a pamphlet titled *The New Law of Righteousness*, which took its inspiration from the vision of common property in the book of Acts. Winstanley complains that God made the earth as a "common Treasury for all to live comfortably upon," but it "is become through mans' unrighteous actions one over another, to be a place, wherein one torments another." The solution, he reasons, is, "The Earth becomes a Common Treasury again, as it must, for all the Prophesies of Scriptures and Reason are Circled here in this Community, and mankind must have the Law of Righteousness once more writ in his heart, and all must be made of one heart, and one mind."

Winstanley also makes reference to prophetic and ecstatic utterances of his followers, what people said in a "trance," namely, "Work together, Eate Bread together, Declare this all abroad," and "Whosoever labours the Earth for any Person or Persons, that are lifted up to rule over others, and doth not look upon themselves, as

Equal to others in the Creation: The hand of the Lord shall be upon that Laborer: I the Lord have spoke it, and I will do it."

The goal of the Diggers was that "we would have none live in Beggery, Poverty, or Sorrow, but that everyone might enjoy the benefit of his creation: we have peace in our hearts, and quiet rejoycing in our work, and filled with sweet content, though we have but a dish of roots and bread for our food." Also, styling the Diggers as a movement of the Spirit, Winstanley declares, "We are assured, that in the strength of this Spirit that hath manifested himself to us, we shall not be startled, neither at Prison nor Death, while we are about his work; and we have bin made to sit down and count what it may cost us in undertaking such a work, and we know the full sum, and are resolved to give all that we have to buy this Pearl which we see in the Field."[1]

Winstanley and the Diggers were directly inspired by texts that describe a sharing of community goods in Acts: "Now the whole group of those who believed were of one heart and soul, and no one claimed private ownership of any possessions, but everything they owned was held in common" (Acts 4:32). The Diggers, much like the early Jerusalem church, practiced a common sharing of property and a prophetic spirit that cultivated an egalitarian community. The key difference is that the Jerusalem church was not trying to mandate that their practices become common law in Judea, with the requirement to redistribute agricultural property to the poor. However, passages such as Acts 2:44-45 and Acts 4:32 have contributed to the rise of Christian socialism since the nineteenth century in both Catholic and Protestant circles. What if Christians, and a Christian society, really did live like the Jerusalem church did? What if Jesus' teachings about the dangers of

---

[1] Gerrard Winstanley, "The True Levellers Standard Advanced: Or, The State of Community Opened, and Presented to the Sons of Men," 1649, www.marxists.org/reference/archive/winstanley/1649/levellers-standard.htm.

wealth and the temptation of riches really should be heeded? What if preaching good news to the poor and ending poverty were real objectives for the church as it continues in the way of Jesus?

Scholarship, of course, has different views about Luke's approach to wealth and poverty, and whether Luke's account of the early church is actually prescriptive is another matter. That said, Luke has much to say about possessions and wealth and about how to live faithfully whether in poverty or flush with material goods. The topic thus warrants discussion precisely because Luke–Acts propels us to address matters of consumerism, greed, and social justice.

THE DANGERS OF WEALTH

Luke writes about wealth as if dollar bills should come with an alert, "WARNING: Money may erode your character, endanger your safety, and impair your eternal destiny." Riches are like swimming in an ocean with a big weight around your neck or holding a bomb that could explode at any moment. Riches are not a sign of blessing but a tempest of temptation. One can have money and use money, but one cannot serve both God and money (Luke 16:13).

> **Who Are the Rich?**
>
> The Greek word πλούσιος refers to those "having an abundance of earthly possessions that exceeds normal experience, *rich, wealthy*."[a] We might say that, in Lukan understanding, the rich are those whose consolation, purpose, and hope reside in the ever-increasing accumulation of wealth, power, and status, even if ill-gotten, and to the neglect of those in need.
>
> [a]BDAG, 831.

Luke's caution about the danger of riches begins early in his Gospel. Mary sings of a great reversal wherein God has "sent the rich away empty" (Luke 1:53). The rich here are castigated as powerful and predatory, those who oppress the poor in general and the pious in particular. Jesus offers blessings for the poor, to whom the kingdom belongs, but utters a word of warning to the rich: "But woe to you who are rich, for you have received your consolation" (Luke 6:24). Jesus, too, warns that sometimes the word of the kingdom does not bear fruit in a person because the word is choked by "the cares and riches and pleasures of life" (Luke 8:14), exemplified by the rich young ruler (Luke 18:23).

Jesus provides two particularly confronting examples of how riches are a seduction that can deceive someone and determine their eternal destiny.

First, the parable of the rich fool (Luke 12:13-21) is precipitated by a complaint by a member of a crowd about the division of an inheritance. To this Jesus replies with a warning about greed (Luke 12:15) and a parable about a "rich man" (Luke 12:16). The rich man's folly is that he is concerned only with the accumulation of more and more surplus so that he can eat, drink, and be merry. The rich man has traded covenant fidelity for fiscal security as he ignores the commands of God on him in his pursuit of luxury. His plans are futile because his life can disappear in a flash, and his accumulated possessions will pass to someone else. The man is foolish because he ignores God but also because he fails to understand a basic fact, that he who dies with the most stuff still dies and cannot take it with him. The rich man is rapacious, David Garland explains, because of "his greed, the ruthless appetite to have more and more of what one already has regardless of the consequences to others."[2]

Second, the parable of the rich man and Lazarus is a particularly striking vignette of greedy indulgence married with indifference to the suffering of others (Luke 16:19-31). It is something of a

---

[2] David E. Garland, *Luke*, ZECNT (Grand Rapids, MI: Zondervan, 2011), 515.

crescendo in the building critique of greed and the accumulation of riches.³ In the parable, the rich man is the paragon of wealth and affluence; his clothing speaks to his opulence. Meanwhile, Lazarus is a beggar on the bottom tier of society; he is destitute and disease-ridden. He receives pity, not from the rich man but from dogs. Then, in death, there is a reversal as the two men have contrasting post-mortem states. In Hades, Lazarus reclines on the bosom of Abraham, while the rich man is tormented. The rich man's punishment is not for his riches but his apparent refusal to use them for anything other than his own exorbitant indulgence. Abraham rebuffs his request to alleviate his suffering or to warn his brothers of what fate awaits them. The scene undoubtedly plays on Jewish views of the afterlife. It may not be intended literally, but the point remains. He who dies with the most things may suffer horrendous things in the hereafter. In the future, the first will be last, and the last will be first.

These two episodes, both unique to Luke, underscore Luke's interpretation of Jesus as one who taught that wealth and possessions, though not intrinsically evil, are nonetheless the cause of selfishness and callousness. This is why one must not become someone who loves money (Luke 16:14), for it is easier for a camel to go through the eye of a needle than for those who love money to enter the kingdom of God (Luke 18:25).

> ### Luke and the Poor
> "Luke's church does not see itself as the 'church of the poor,' for it awaits the reversal to come and does not campaign for it in the present, but the values it declares to be God's values may make that campaign inevitable."[a]
>
> [a] Judith Lieu, *The Gospel of Luke* (Eugene, OR: Wipf & Stock, 2012), 51.

---

[3] James A. Metzger, *Consumption and Wealth in Luke's Travel Narrative* (Leiden: Brill, 2007), 14.

FORSAKING POSSESSIONS

Luke makes it clear that one aspect of discipleship is forsaking possessions. Jesus' itinerant ministry meant relying on the hospitality of others and not establishing a residency with possessions, regular work, or even reliable income. He tells a would-be disciple, "Foxes have holes, and birds of the air have nests; but the Son of Man has nowhere to lay his head" (Luke 9:58). In other words, to accompany Jesus, to participate in his mission, to take up the yoke of the kingdom, means joining the ranks of the homeless and poor. Elsewhere, Jesus instructs his disciples that in their forays to other villages and towns they are to take no possessions with them, no purse, bag, sandals, staff, bread, or extra clothing. Their poverty and lack of possessions would, it seems, emblematize the urgency of the situation brought about by the kingdom's nearness (Luke 9:3; 10:4). Luke also goes out of his way to describe how the disciples Jesus calls literally leave everything behind and follow him, including Peter (Luke 5:11) and Levi (Luke 5:28) as paradigmatic examples. Also, the widow who gives two copper coins as an offering in the temple is an example of one who is generous not in one's disposable income but out of one's poverty (Luke 21:1-4).

The question is whether Jesus expects all disciples to forsake possessions and even family to follow him or whether this radical renunciation is discipleship for an elite few, perhaps an ideal level of discipleship. For would-be disciples who make excuses or offer conditions for following him, Jesus makes the choice very clear: "Jesus said to him, 'No one who puts a hand to the plow and looks back is fit for the kingdom of God'" (Luke 9:62). Jesus tells disciples not to fear about material needs but to be generous: "Do not be afraid, little flock, for it is your Father's good pleasure to give you the kingdom. Sell your possessions, and give alms. Make purses for yourselves that do not wear out, an unfailing treasure in heaven, where no thief comes near and no moth destroys. For where your treasure is, there your heart will be also" (Luke 12:32-34). In addition, the rich young ruler is challenged, "There is still one thing lacking. Sell all that you own and distribute the money to the poor, and you will have treasure in heaven; then come, follow me" (Luke 18:22). Finally, Jesus' commands for disciples are starker and blunter: "So therefore, none of you can become my disciple if you do not give up all your possessions" (Luke 14:33). This saying in particular makes one think that the call to forsake everything and everyone besides Jesus is normal and universal. But then again, not everyone who encounters Jesus sells all their possessions, kisses their family goodbye, and hits the road with Jesus, such as Mary and Martha (Luke 10:42) and Zacchaeus (Luke 19:8-10). Similarly, not every member of the Jerusalem church or convert from the Greek cities gives up all their possessions to become wandering vagabonds. Barnabas is noticeably generous for selling a field he owned (Acts 4:37), but Sergius Paulus, the proconsul of Cyprus, does not renounce wealth and privilege and becomes a prototypical model of Saint Ignatius of Loyola (Acts 13:12).

The solution, I suspect, is that Luke conceives of participation in the reversal of status and fortunes, in the renunciation of wealth and riches, and in the right response to Jesus' gospel as different for each person. As Christopher Hays observes, "One's *vocation* in the Kingdom of God and *relative affluence* determine the particular expression one gives to renunciation."[4] Every person, from a proconsul to a pauper, must discern what they must renounce, what must be reversed, and how best to respond to Jesus and his apostles. Whether barns of grain, silver, business partnerships, family obligations, prestige in a trade guild, or

---

[4]Christopher M. Hays, *Luke's Wealth Ethics: A Study of Their Coherence and Character*, WUNT 2/275 (Tübingen: Mohr Siebeck, 2010), 175, emphasis original.

status within a Jewish synagogue, everyone must give up sources of affluence, status, and identity as part of the kingdom's reordering of power. Viewed this way, the renunciation of wealth and even some relationships is not only for the Twelve or even for a more fully dedicated class of monastic disciples but applies to all followers of Jesus, albeit in different ways depending on their circumstances. "Every right response to God's work in Jesus," comments Rachel L. Coleman, "involves leaving behind the old relationship to wealth and possessions; this leaving is expressed variously as giving, selling, renouncing or using (to meet the needs of others).["][5]

THE RIGHTEOUS RICH?

Luke's picture of Jesus is not that of a Robin Hood who takes from the rich and gives to the poor, nor that of a Marxist revolutionary mobilizing the urban proletariat to revolt against their evil capitalist overlords. While Jesus is no doubt on the side of the economically impoverished and vulnerable, he spends much time with those who possess some degree of means and wealth. Further, the portrayal of the rich and well-off in Luke–Acts, though they are sometimes subject to critique and even judgment, is not universally negative.

To begin with, when the crowds ask John the Baptist what they should do to prepare for the coming one and the messianic judgment, his response to various groups does not require abandoning everything one owns. Rather, people are to share clothing and food with those who have none, tax collectors should harvest no more taxes than they need, and soldiers should not extort people for money (Luke 3:10-14). This is easily summarized as "be

---

[5]Rachel L. Coleman, *The Lukan Lens on Wealth and Possessions: A Perspective Shaped by the Themes of Reversal and Right Response*, BIS 180 (Leiden: Brill, 2020), 154-55.

generous to those in need and do not be greedy to the point of exploiting others."

There is clear continuity between the Baptist and Jesus on this theme of people who use riches in a righteous way. The practice of love, Jesus taught, means "Give to everyone who begs from you; and if anyone takes away your goods, do not ask for them again" (Luke 6:30). In addition, one must lend to those who cannot necessarily pay one back because one is to "love your enemies, do good, and lend, expecting nothing in return" (Luke 6:35). Jesus provides, it would strangely seem, a defense of begging, pilfering, and defaulting on loans. To be clear, this is not permission for everyone everywhere to do such things but dispensation for the vulnerable. Otherwise, one would have to beat down a beggar, prosecute a pauper who steals a loaf of bread, or foreclose on a widow's house if she cannot pay you back. Better to be wronged by the poor than to win compensation from them.

In uniquely Lukan material, Jesus tells parables wherein rich persons use their wealth generously. In a parable about forgiveness as gratitude, Jesus tells the tale of a certain creditor who had two debtors and forgave debts both small and great (Luke 7:40-43). Then, classically, the parable of the good Samaritan shows the generosity and mercy of a Samaritan outsider to a victim of a violent robbery (Luke 10:25-37). Also, in the parable of the banquet, Jesus urges the rich to invite not only their peers but the impoverished, telling them to "invite the poor, the crippled, the lame, and the blind" (Luke 14:13). If they do so, "you will be blessed, because they cannot repay you, for you will be repaid at the resurrection of the righteous" (Luke 14:14). The saying resonates with similar rabbinic teaching, "Let your house be wide open, let the poor be your house companions" (Mishnah Abot 1:5). The rich are to show hospitality with generosity, and those who do will be duly rewarded.

The parable of the dishonest manager (Luke 16:1-13) provides another instance of how wealth can be used or flat-out manipulated for good ends. In the parable, a household manager discovers that he is about to be dismissed from service by his master for squandering his master's possessions. So he reduces the amounts that some debtors owe his master, which does two things. First, it places the debtors into the debt of the manager and thus gives him a potential place of future employment by those who owe him. Second, if the master now sacks the manager or reverses his debt reductions, the master will be publicly shamed for retracting this gracious relief of debt issued by the manager. The master recognizes that his manager has, quite shrewdly, put the master in a difficult position (lose goods or lose face) and put himself in a win-win situation (find a new job with one of the master's debtors, or the master has to keep him employed to protect his own reputation). From the parable, Jesus makes the point that one must shrewdly use even ill-gotten wealth (i.e., mammon) to make God one's own debtor who will welcome people into his eternal home (Luke 16:9). Jesus then pivots to teach that one who is unfaithful with ill-gotten wealth cannot be faithful with true riches. One must either put wealth in service of God or one will be a servant of wealth. Such is the main point: no slave can serve two masters; you cannot serve God and mammon (Luke 16:10-13).

> **Messiah vs. Mammon**
>
> "Jesus attacks mammon with the utmost severity where it has captured men's hearts, because it has a demonic character by which it blinds men's eyes to God's will—in concrete terms, to their neighbour's needs."[a]
>
> ---
>
> [a] Martin Hengel, *Property and Riches in the Early Church*, trans. J. Bowden (London: SCM Press, 1974), 24.

Another factor for consideration is that tax collectors are treated as examples of rich outsiders who are welcomed in God's kingdom and demonstrate exemplary contrition and faith. The tax collectors who come to the Baptist are told to collect no more than required (Luke 3:12-13). The tax collector Levi abruptly accepts Jesus' call to follow him, and Jesus thereafter attends a banquet with Levi and other tax collectors, much to the consternation of the Pharisees (Luke 5:27-32). Jesus has such a reputation for sharing table fellowship with tax collectors and sinners (Luke 5:30; 7:34) that he tells the parable of the prodigal son to defend his habit of spending time with those of ill repute (Luke 15:1-2, 11-32). Further, the parable of the Pharisees and the tax collector presses the provocative point that a penitent tax collector is more in the right with God than a pretentious Pharisee (Luke 18:9-14). The character of Zacchaeus is the tax collector par excellence, who shows contrition, generosity, and makes restitution. Zacchaeus is the sinner who gets healed by the physician, the rich man who gets through the eye of the needle, the prodigal son who comes home to his father (Luke 19:1-10).

There are people who use their wealth and riches for kingdom ends. A trio of women support Jesus in his ministry and provide for his needs (Luke 8:2-3). Barnabas is generous in selling property (Acts 4:37), Dorcas/Tabitha is known for charity and patronage of widows (Acts 9:36-40), and Lydia takes the apostles into her home (Acts 16:15). What makes rich people righteous is that they use wealth wisely, neither hoarding it nor worshiping it. People of means can be generous, charitable, humble, and hospitable. Diane Chen captures Luke's ethos: "Earthly wealth will not last, but proper use of wealth that embodies God's values and salvific aims will yield eternal dividends."[6]

---

[6] Diane G. Chen, *Luke*, NCCS (Eugene, OR: Cascade, 2017), 224.

THE COMMUNITY GOODS

Luke's account of the Jerusalem church selling their possessions and sharing their wealth and goods is one of the most striking things we read about the earliest days of the disciples of Jesus.

> All who believed were together and had all things in common; they would sell their possessions and goods and distribute the proceeds to all, as any had need. (Acts 2:44-45)

> Now the whole group of those who believed were of one heart and soul, and no one claimed private ownership of any possessions, but everything they owned was held in common. . . . There was not a needy person among them, for as many as owned lands or houses sold them and brought the proceeds of what was sold. (Acts 4:32, 34)

On the one hand, Luke's account is undoubtedly attempting to portray the church as the ideal miniature society. For instance, when Luke reports, "There was not a needy person among them," it brings to mind the philosopher and politician Seneca, who reminisced of an idyllic time in humanity's past "before avarice and luxury had broken the bonds which held mortals together, and they, abandoning their communal existence, had separated and turned to plunder," a time when "you could not find a poor person among them" (*Ep.* 90.36, 38).[7] That does not mean, however, that Luke's account is an invented fiction written to merely make the church sound economically ideal. Some Jewish sects did indeed pool wealth and possessions into a common treasury, such as the Essences (CD 14.13; Philo, *Quod Omnis Probus*, 76-77, 85-87; *Hypothetica* 11.4-13; Josephus, *Ant.* 18.20-22; *J.W.* 2.122-127), as did the Pythagoreans in their school founded at Croton (Iamblichus, *Life* 6.29-30; Porphyry, *Life* 20). Various groups did on occasion try

---

[7]Seneca, *Seneca's Letters from a Stoic*, trans. Richard Mott Gummere (Mineola, NY: Dover, 2016), 296.

to escape poverty, pool possessions, and pursue common lives immersed in devotion to philosophy, community, and religion.

The practice of sharing possessions in the early church was voluntary and situational; people gave as there was need, indicated by Barnabas, who sells a field and gives the proceeds to the disciples (Acts 4:37). Barnabas stands in contrast to Ananias and Sapphira, who sell a piece of property and promise to give the proceeds to the struggling community but hold back a portion for themselves. They experience a dramatic and unexpected judgment for lying about their generosity. The point is that faithfulness in finances requires a healthy fear of the Lord (Acts 5:1-11).

A concern for the poor among the followers of Jesus is evident at several places. There is, initially at least, no needy person among them (Acts 4:34). However, as the Jerusalem church's ranks swell, there are problems of administration and complaints that some wings of the church are neglected, as in the case of Greek-speaking widows, which requires the appointment of deacons to oversee the fair distribution of food (Acts 6:1-6). The compulsion to assist those in need even happened between churches in different regions. During a famine in the 40s AD, the Antioch church sends aid to the churches in Judea: "The disciples determined that according to their ability, each would send relief to the believers living in Judea; this they did, sending it to the elders by Barnabas and Saul [i.e., Paul]" (Acts 11:29-30). The churches had a mutual concern for the welfare of their coreligionists despite the separation of language, social status, and geography.

LUKE-ACTS AND WEALTH: SUMMARY

Paul's exhortation to the Ephesian elders sums up the attitude toward possessions and poverty in Luke–Acts: "I coveted no one's silver or gold or clothing. You know for yourselves that I worked with my own hands to support myself and my companions. In all this I have given you an example that by such work we must support the weak, remembering the words of the Lord Jesus, for he himself said, 'It is more blessed to give than to receive'" (Acts 20:33-35). Among the followers of Jesus, there is to be no greed, and believers should follow the words of Jesus himself about generosity to others.

Beyond that, a good summary is offered by Brian Capper as to how Jesus and the early church's attitude toward possessions and generosity remains meaningful for us today:

> The renunciation of property by Jesus, his traveling disciples, and early believers in him in Jerusalem offers precedent for voluntary groups within the Christian church who renounce property and practice community of goods, a model especially suited for mission among the poor. This may not sound like an exciting conclusion to those eager to press a political case concerning world poverty or to encourage Christians to generosity. However, the significance of the actual model of the common purse of Jesus and his traveling party, and of their first social project in Jerusalem, teaches much. In the most difficult situations of poverty, groups achieve a great deal who together share property and channel resources to the most needy in the context of their whole witness and community life. Such groups act for the wider church and can be richly supported by it; their mode of life demonstrates a real identification with the plight of the poor.[8]

As I write these words in 2022, I'm reading accounts of how churches in Poland have opened their buildings and homes to refugees fleeing the war in Ukraine. Although Poland is mostly Catholic and Ukraine is mostly Orthodox, the barriers of language, geography, and even theology are set aside in a time of crisis. These

---

[8]Brian J. Capper, "Jesus, Virtuoso Religion, and the Community of Goods," in *Engaging Economics: New Testament Scenarios and Early Christian Reception*, ed. Bruce W. Longenecker and Kelly D. Liebengood (Grand Rapids, MI: Eerdmans, 2009), 80.

churches have put into practice Jesus' command to love their neighbors, to be good Samaritans, to show concern for those left homeless by war, and to share possessions for the sake of the kingdom. These are deeds that reflect obedience to the words of Jesus and replicate the ethos of the Jerusalem church.

REVIEW QUESTIONS

1. When someone says, "Christian socialism," what is your instinctive reaction?
2. What does Jesus teach about the allure and dangers of riches?
3. Why must riches and even some relationships be renounced for the sake of the kingdom?
4. How does Western consumerism and affluence make the teachings of Jesus difficult to swallow?
5. Can one live righteously as a "rich" person? If so, how?

RECOMMENDED READING

Coleman, Rachel L. *The Lukan Lens on Wealth and Possessions: A Perspective Shaped by the Themes of Reversal and Right Response*. BIS 180. Leiden: Brill, 2020.

Hays, Christopher M. *Luke's Wealth Ethics: A Study of Their Coherence and Character*. WUNT 2/275. Tübingen: Mohr Siebeck.

Johnson, Luke Timothy. *Sharing Possessions: What Faith Demands*. Grand Rapids, MI: Eerdmans, 2011.

Metzger, James A. *Consumption and Wealth in Luke's Travel Narrative*. Leiden: Brill, 2007.

Miller, Amanda C. "Bridge Work and Seating Charts: A Study of Luke's Ethics of Wealth, Poverty, and Reversal." *Int* 68 (2014): 416-27.

Pilgrim, Walter. *Good News to the Poor: Wealth and Poverty in Luke–Acts*. Eugene, OR: Wipf & Stock, 1981.

Walton, Steve. "Primitive Communism in Acts? Does Acts Present the Community of Goods (2:44-45; 4:32-35) as Mistaken?" *EvQ* 80 (2008): 99-111.

11

The Promise of the Father

Luke and the Holy Spirit

LUKE AS THE WORLD'S FIRST "PENTECOSTAL"

In terms of the probable order in which the Synoptic Gospels were composed, there is a pattern of escalating reference to the Holy Spirit. The Gospel of Mark has six references to the Holy Spirit. The Gospel of Matthew has twelve references to the Holy Spirit. In the Gospel of Luke there are sixteen references to the Holy Spirit, but that's not all; in the book of Acts there are almost sixty references to the Holy Spirit. While there is much said about Jesus, the Holy Spirit, and the believer in the Gospel of John and in the Pauline epistles, nonetheless, Luke is by both volume and emphasis the church's main narrator and theologian of the Holy Spirit. Justo González, then, is quite right to conclude, "Luke's contribution to the Christian doctrine of the Spirit is unparalleled in the New Testament."[1]

Luke also bequeaths to us several distinct questions. Is the Holy Spirit an impersonal force or a divine person? What does it mean to be "filled" or "baptized" with the Holy Spirit? Is the Lukan conception of the Holy Spirit purely about empowerment, or does it have a salvific aspect? How does the Holy Spirit figure in Luke's

---

[1] Justo L. González, *The Story Luke Tells: Luke's Unique Witness to the Gospel* (Grand Rapids, MI: Eerdmans, 2015), 116.

vision of the church's communal life and its mission? All that and more is there for us to mull over.

Yet as interesting as those questions are—and we will get to them in the fullness of time—it should not obscure the immediate impression Luke-Acts gives us. Jesus was a prophet animated by the Holy Spirit, and the early church was a movement driven by and even defined by its sense of the Spirit's presence and power. The Spirit was the driving force in Jesus' ministry, just as the Acts of the Apostles could be named the Acts of the Holy Spirit through the Apostles (and sometimes even despite them). Luke creates the impression that Jesus was a man of the Spirit and the church was a people of the Spirit.

At one level, this is not altogether dissimilar from other religious figures of antiquity. Various teachers, philosophers, healers, and seers claimed to have received the genius or power of their patron deity. Where Luke is perhaps different is that Jesus is a messianic Spirit-driven protagonist who operates in the domain of Israel's sacred promises and future hopes. Also, the Holy Spirit in the church's life is tied closely to the task of proclamation and creating a new type of community within Israel and yet also beyond it. Luke's pneumatology is tied closely to his messianism, to promise and fulfillment, to the church as the vanguard of Israel's renewal, and to the lead protagonist in the church's mission to the Gentiles.

The day of Pentecost in Acts 2 is promised in Luke's Gospel and then becomes programmatic for the book of Acts. Luke would be happy, I suspect, to accept the label "Pentecostal" for the character of his theology, Christology, ecclesiology, and missiology, pervaded as these are by the role of the Holy Spirit. Don't get me wrong; I think Luke would have more than a word or two to say about the prosperity gospel that is rife in some modern Pentecostal churches. But Luke would undoubtedly think that a church that is infused with the vitality of the Spirit's life, led into new and risky missional ventures by the Spirit's promoting, and filled with the Spirit's power in preaching is meant to be kind of, well, normal. Luke is for my mind the very first Pentecostal, if by that one means a theologian who regarded God's pouring out of the Holy Spirit as a proof of Jesus' messianic status, a sign of God's faithfulness to Israel, and an experience meant to be shared by everyone who calls on the Lord Jesus Christ. Thus, irrespective of one's denominational affiliation or lack thereof, Luke believed Pentecost happened because, for the church, Pentecost is constantly happening. It happens whenever the Spirit opens people's hearts to believe the gospel, whenever the Spirit prompts someone to exposit the word of God, or whenever people of diverse ethnicity break bread together in the name of the Lord Jesus Christ.

JESUS AS THE SPIRIT BEARER

An important facet of Luke's presentation of Jesus is that Jesus receives the Spirit as messianic Lord and as the Isaianic prophet.

The Davidic and messianic nature of Jesus' carrying the Holy Spirit is evident in several places. The angel Gabriel informs Mary that she will bear a child who "will be called the Son of the Most High, and the Lord God will give to him the throne of his ancestor David. He will reign over the house of Jacob forever, and of his kingdom there will be no end" (Luke 1:32-33). Yet this child is not born of ordinary procreation; rather, he is generated inside Mary by the Spirit's supernatural work: "The Holy Spirit will come upon you, and the power of the Most High will overshadow you; therefore the child to be born will be holy; he will be called Son of God" (Luke 1:35). In addition, Jesus' baptism is the moment where heaven opens and the Spirit descends into him in bodily form like a dove, along with a heavenly voice declaring about him, "You are my Son, the Beloved; with you I am well pleased" (Luke 3:22). The heavenly voice blends together two scriptural allusions, namely, Psalm 2:7, concerning the installment of the Judean king as God's Son, and Isaiah 42:1, concerning the servant who is chosen and has the Spirit placed on him. This meshes with other references to the Spirit resting on either David (1 Samuel 16:13; 2 Samuel 23:2) or on a future Davidic deliverer (Isaiah 11:2) and references to the Spirit anointing the Isaianic servant (Isaiah 61:1). What does the combination of Davidic identity and reception of the Spirit mean? It means that Jesus is the eschatological Davidic deliver, and as part of his vocation he receives the Holy Spirit to designate him as Israel's Anointed One, that is, the Messiah.

> Then Samuel took the horn of oil, and anointed him in the presence of his brothers; and the spirit of the Lord came mightily upon David from that day forward. (1 Samuel 16:13)
>
> I will tell of the decree of the Lord:
> He said to me, "You are my son;
>   today I have begotten you." (Psalm 2:7)
>
> A shoot shall come out from the stump of Jesse,
>   and a branch shall grow out of his roots.
> The spirit of the Lord shall rest on him,
>   the spirit of wisdom and understanding,
>   the spirit of counsel and might,
>   the spirit of knowledge and the fear of the Lord. (Isaiah 11:1-2)
>
> Here is my servant, whom I uphold,
>   my chosen, in whom my soul delights;
> I have put my spirit upon him;
>   he will bring forth justice to the nations. (Isaiah 42:1)
>
> The spirit of the Lord God is upon me,
>   because the Lord has anointed me;

> he has sent me to bring good news to the oppressed,
>> to bind up the brokenhearted,
> to proclaim liberty to the captives,
>> and release to the prisoners;
> to proclaim the year of the LORD's favor,
>> and the day of vengeance of our God;
> to comfort all who mourn. (Isaiah 61:1-2)

In addition, the Spirit clearly drives the prophetic side of Jesus' ministry. Luke accents the role of the Holy Spirit as the prophetic power that animates prophetic figures. By doing this, Luke is rehearsing Jewish tradition whereby God's Spirit is the energy and enablement of a prophet's voice and vision (e.g., Isaiah 48:16; 59:21; Ezekiel 2:1-2; Micah 3:8). Luke, then, sees the Spirit of prophecy at work in John the Baptist (Luke 1:15-17, 76), Zechariah (Luke 1:67-79), and Simeon (Luke 2:26-32). Jesus, too, is explicitly depicted as a prophetic figure carried along by a divine power. After his baptism, once Jesus is "full of the Holy Spirit," he is "led by the Spirit in the wilderness" to be tempted by Satan (Luke 4:1).

Luke uniquely introduces Jesus' Galilean ministry with Jesus "filled with the power of the Spirit" (Luke 4:14). Immediately, in his home village of Nazareth, he reads from Isaiah 61:1 about the Spirit of the Lord on the servant of the Lord in Isaiah and pronounces its fulfillment in the midst of the assembly (Luke 4:16-21). In Luke's précis of Peter's preaching in Caesarea, "God anointed Jesus of Nazareth with the Holy Spirit and with power; how he went about doing good and healing all who were oppressed by the devil, for God was with him" (Acts 10:38). It is because of the Spirit's anointing and unction (Luke 3:21-22; 4:18; Acts 4:27; 10:38), its authority and power operating through him (Luke 4:14, 36; 5:17; 6:19; 8:46), that Jesus is not merely a prophet; he is *the* prophet in the line of Moses (Acts 3:22-24), the Isaianic servant (Luke 4:16-21;

Acts 4:27), and the new David (Luke 1:32, 69; 2:11; 20:41-44; Acts 13:34-39). In theological terms, there is no Lukan Christology without Lukan pneumatology.

JESUS AS THE SPIRIT GIVER

A vital element in the Lukan narrative is that Jesus is not merely the bearer of the Spirit, the last of a long line of spiritually endowed prophets. He is also the giver of the Spirit. That is to say, Jordan is the necessary condition for Pentecost, for in the Jordan River Jesus receives the Spirit so that he might serve in its strength, suffer in its absence, be raised by its power, and then bestow the Spirit on his followers. The Spirit descends on Jesus so that Jesus can dispense the Spirit as part of God's promise to Israel and to the world.

The place to start is with John the Baptist's messianic testimony about the coming one, namely, "He will baptize you with the Holy Spirit and fire" (Luke 3:16). According to Darrell Bock, this is "the most important text on the Spirit and its central role in God's program," and Bock wishes that Luke 3:16 were just as well-known as John 3:16.[2] The entire statement may be idiomatic for something like plunging people into the fiery breath of God, a simultaneous purgation and purification of people, dividing humanity into those adequately prepared for the final judgment and those who will be exposed and engulfed by it.[3]

At one point, the Lukan Jesus teaches disciples to ask for the Holy Spirit the way a child asks for something from their father: "If you then, who are evil, know how to give good gifts to your children, how much more will the heavenly Father give the Holy Spirit to those who ask him!" (Luke 11:13). This is reiterated later

---

[2]Darrell L. Bock, *A Theology of Luke and Acts: God's Promised Program, Realized for All Nations* (Grand Rapids, MI: Zondervan, 2012), 213; Bock, *Recovering the Real Lost Gospel of Jesus* (Nashville: B&H, 2010), 12.
[3]James D. G. Dunn, *Baptism in the Spirit* (London: SCM Press, 1970), 13-14.

when the risen Jesus tells the disciples, "I am sending upon you what my Father promised; so stay here in the city until you have been clothed with power from on high" (Luke 24:49; Acts 1:4-5; 2:33). Then, on the eve of the ascension, he tells them, "But you will receive power when the Holy Spirit has come upon you; and you will be my witnesses in Jerusalem, in all Judea and Samaria, and to the ends of the earth" (Acts 1:8).

Later new believers receive the Spirit and experience this purification, promise, power, and presence. That is why apostolic preaching refers to the "forgiveness of sins" (Luke 24:47; Acts 2:38; 5:31; 10:43; 13:38), having a heart cleansed by faith (Acts 15:9), and the bestowal of God's own giftings through the Spirit (Luke 11:13; Acts 2:33, 38; 10:45). The Spirit is given as the Father's promise for a spiritual blessing to fall on all people of the earth as the Spirit is dispensed to and through Israel (Joel 2:28-32; Acts 2:1-42). It is devotion to God and Jesus, combined with belief in Jesus as the Spirit-anointed prophet and Lord's Messiah, that marks a person out as a follower of the Way and a participant in the salvation that Jesus achieved for his people. This is a salvation largely composed of and applied by the Holy Spirit.

That Jesus is the one who gives the Spirit is highly significant. The Spirit is given in the name of Jesus, which proves that Jesus is God's Son, the Spirit-anointed and now Spirit-dispensing Messiah. The Spirit, then, is bestowed on behalf of the Father by Jesus. This is startling because Jesus' dispensing of the Spirit entails his doing what only Israel's Lord does according to the Jewish Scriptures, since the Lord promised to pour out his Spirit in a full and fresh way (Psalm 104:30; Isaiah 44:3; Ezekiel 39:29; Joel 2:29-29; Acts 2:17-18). The other aspect that stands out is that the Spirit is not given to the religious elites, to the righteous, or to those reigning in palaces. Rather, God's Spirit is given to Jesus' disciples and their converts, be they Jewish, Samaritan, Syrian, Greek, or Roman. Jesus is the messianic agent who confers the Spirit, and the Jesus-people are the ones who experience the fullness of the Spirit's blessings and power.

> **Is the Holy Spirit Divine?**
>
> "How then can he who gives the Spirit not be God? Indeed how much must he who gives God be God? None of his disciples ever gave the Holy Spirit; they prayed that he might come upon those on whom they laid hands. . . . He received it as man, he poured it out as God."[a]
>
> [a] Augustine, *De Trinitate* 15.46, cited in Frank D. Macchia, *Jesus the Spirit Baptizer: Christology in Light of Pentecost* (Grand Rapids, MI: Eerdmans, 2020), 2.

THE HOLY SPIRIT AS POWER OR PERSON?

It has to be noted that Luke sometimes uses somewhat impersonal language and imagery to describe the Spirit. The Spirit appears to be something like a divine power that drives Jesus and the apostles (Luke 4:14; Acts 1:8), a gift (Luke 11:13; Acts 2:38; 10:45), a promise, a power one is clothed in (Luke 24:49; Acts 1:8; 2:33). The Spirit fills people like a liquid in a cup (Acts 4:31) and can be a virtual synonym for "wisdom" (Acts 6:3, 10). One could imagine the Holy Spirit as a Lukan version of the force from Star Wars or as an invisible gas that enables those who breathe it in to possess superhuman abilities in preaching and spiritual warfare. But that is only half the story. Luke can describe the Spirit as a person, as a divine person no less.

The qualities of personhood are attributed to the Spirit across Luke–Acts. For a start, the Spirit is able to reveal things and guide people, as the Spirit does for Simeon (Luke 2:26-27). The Holy Spirit speaks and predicts things through prophets such as David (Acts 1:16; 4:25) and Isaiah (Acts 28:25). The Spirit teaches people what to say at an important hour (Luke 12:12), the Spirit can "witness" to things (Acts 5:32; 20:23), and the Spirit tells people to say things, as is the case with Philip and Peter (Acts 8:29; 10:19; 11:12, 16). The Spirit tells Peter not to make a distinction in the sense of a discrimination between Jews and Gentiles (Acts 11:12). The Spirit can send people to places or even prevent people from going to some places (Acts 8:39; 13:4; 16:6-7). A ministry of the Spirit is to provide people with comfort (Acts 9:32). The Spirit commissions overseers in the church (Acts 20:28). The Spirit even predicts a famine in Judea (Acts 11:28) and speaks in the first person to set apart Saul and Barnabas for their missionary journey (Acts 13:1-2), as well as speaking through a prophet to warn Paul of his fate in Jerusalem (Acts 21:11). The church discerns difficult decisions in—it would appear—conversation with the Holy Spirit, when things appear "good to the Holy Spirit" (Acts 15:28). The Spirit can be opposed by people within Israel (Acts 7:51) and lied to, as Ananias and Sapphira do (Acts 5:3). If you take these qualities, interventions, prerogatives, declarations, and acts together, they are indicative of a person, not an impersonal power or force.

In addition, I would argue as well that the Holy Spirit is not only a person but a divine person.[4] Now, to be fair, one cannot expect the entire trinitarian package to be found in Luke–Acts, as if Luke were writing his narrative with the Councils of Nicaea (AD 325) and Constantinople (AD 381) in mind. However, Luke does provide some of the ingredients for what is later packaged as the church's trinitarian theology. The baptism of Jesus involves the Father's voice, Jesus the Son, and the Holy Spirit coming on him, which indicates the three divine actors as part of the drama of salvation (Luke 3:21-22). Similarly, Paul's farewell to the Ephesian

---

[4] See further Michael F. Bird, *Evangelical Theology*, 2nd ed. (Grand Rapids, MI: Zondervan, 2018), 676-86.

elders at Miletus mentions how the "Holy Spirit has made you overseers, to shepherd the church of God that he obtained with the blood of his own Son" (Acts 20:28), which intimates the tripartite yet united role of the persons in the church. Jesus warns about committing blasphemy against the Holy Spirit as the unforgivable sin, which indicates the sacred nature of the Spirit's person (Luke 12:10). It is interesting, too, that in the case of Ananias and Sapphira, lying to the Holy Spirit means lying to God (Acts 5:3-4). It is clear, then, that the Holy Spirit enacts the plan and purposes of God through Jesus, carries the voice of God in Scripture, and represents the prerogatives of God as the Spirit directs the church's mission.

BAPTIZED AND FILLED WITH THE SPIRIT OF GOD

One key thematic link across Luke's Gospel and Acts is Jesus as the bestower of the Holy Spirit to fulfill God's promises in the prophets. Just as Jesus was anointed with the Holy Spirit, believers later will be baptized with the Holy Spirit (Luke 3:16; Acts 1:4-5, 8). That event, reception of the Spirit, is described differently. For instance, on the day of Pentecost in Jerusalem, the Holy Spirit is "poured out" on the disciples (Acts 2:33). Later, in Caesarea, among Cornelius and his household, the Holy Spirit is said to be falling "upon all who heard the word," and they are all "baptized with the Holy Spirit" (Acts 10:44; 11:16). Also, in Ephesus, the disciples of John have the Holy Spirit "come upon them" (Acts 19:6). Elsewhere, the Spirit's sudden presence in a person is referred to as *receiving* the Holy Spirit (Acts 2:38; 8:15-17; 10:47).

Although the disciples receive the promised baptism of the Holy Spirit after waiting in Jerusalem for some time, this baptism/pouring/coming/receiving of the Spirit is something that happens normally in association with conversion. Yet even then it happens differently, in various ways and in diverse situations. Sometimes reception of the Spirit is connected to water baptism, as for the Jerusalemites (Acts 2:38); other times it is connected to the laying on of hands by the apostles, as for the Samaritans and followers of the Baptist (Acts 8:15-17; 19:6); and on other occasions it happens purely on the basis of faith itself (Acts 10:44). Whereas theologians like to posit an *ordo salutis*, in terms of the proper order of events in conversion understood as something like new birth/baptism, faith, and water baptism, Luke's narrative defies the postulation of any stringent sequence of events in conversion. The Spirit baptizes people or comes on people at different moments—at faith, at baptism, or later with the laying on of hands.[5] Irrespective of *when* or *how* it happens or the different words Luke uses to describe it, in Luke's narration baptism with the Holy Spirit is the infusion of spiritual life into a person, the shining of divine light to illuminate their heart, a purifying power that falls on someone, something that burns with belief in the God who is revealed in Jesus and the God who is experienced through the promise of the Holy Spirit.

Luke also refers to people being "filled" with the Spirit. The notion of the Spirit filling a person, usually as part of a specific calling, vocation, or task, is found in the Old Testament. Notably, in Micah, the prophet declares, "But as for me, I am filled with power, with the spirit of the LORD, and with justice and might, to declare to Jacob his transgression and to Israel his sin" (Micah 3:8). The prophet's power to declare a divine word of woe or deliverance is due to a special unction given by God's Spirit. Similarly, in Luke–Acts key characters are filled with the Spirit, as in the case of Elizabeth (Luke 1:41-44), Zechariah (Luke 1:67-79), John the Baptist (Luke 1:15), and Simeon (Luke 2:25-35), as they are all said

---

[5]See discussion in Bird, *Evangelical Theology*, 699-704; Craig S. Keener, *Gift and Giver: The Holy Spirit for Today* (Grand Rapids, MI: Baker, 2001), 147-68.

to be filled with the Holy Spirit in their prophetic pronouncements and celebrations.⁶ In addition, those who are baptized with the Spirit are later filled with the Spirit, including Jesus (Luke 4:1, 14) and the disciples (Acts 2:4). Thereafter, Luke narrates how at special junctures particular persons are filled with the Holy Spirit, usually in the context of enabling a bold proclamation of the gospel (Acts 4:8, 31; 7:55). Thus, being filled with the Holy Spirit is primarily about divine empowerment to declare the salvation of God. This takes the form of prophetic pronouncements of blessings such as that Elizabeth speaks to Mary (Luke 1:41-44) and prophetic declarations of salvation such as Zechariah's Benedictus (Luke 1:67-79) and Simeon's *nunc dimittis* (Luke 2:29-32).

Whereas the Lukan infancy narrative depicts the Spirit filling persons for "prophetically inspired speech and praise" or to animate Jesus' "future messianic mission," in the book of Acts the Spirit fills people largely for "cross-cultural prophetic witness and mission."⁷ The Spirit fills people so that they overflow with evangelical proclamation and recite the story of Jesus (Acts 4:8-22, 31). Or persons are filled with the Spirit to declare the sovereignty of Jesus over all things, such as Stephen (Acts 7:55-56), or to declare God's judgment over the wicked, such as Paul to the magician Elymas/Bar-Jesus (Acts 13:8-12). "From the beginning of Acts," notes Beverly Gaventa, "the Holy Spirit that empowers the witness into the future—a future replete with journeys among distant people and places—is also a major sign of God's faithfulness to Israel's past."⁸

---

⁶Concerning Simeon, it is never explicitly said that he is "filled" with the Holy Spirit; rather, "the Holy Spirit rested on him" (Luke 2:25), and he is "guided by the Spirit" when he sees in the infant Jesus (Luke 2:27).
⁷Youngmo Cho and Hyung Dae Park, *Acts*, NCCS (Eugene, OR: Cascade, 2019), 1:46.
⁸Beverly Roberts Gaventa, *Acts*, Abingdon New Testament Commentaries (Nashville: Abingdon, 2003), 36.

The other thing to note about being baptized or filled with the Holy Spirit is the element of eschatological fulfillment. The giving of the Holy Spirit is something the Father promises through prophets, including Joel (Joel 2:28-29) and John the Baptist (Luke 3:16), and is explicitly taught by Jesus (Luke 24:49; Acts 1:4). Hence, in apostolic preaching, the Spirit is given as the promise of God the Father for those who call on the name of Jesus (Acts 2:33, 38-39). Further, the Spirit's filling or fullness is also part of the religious experience of the early church. When Paul and Barnabas depart Pisidian Antioch for Iconium, Luke records how, by the time the apostles finish up their ministry there, "the disciples were filled with joy and with the Holy Spirit" (Acts 13:52). The giving of the Spirit is not merely a ticket for salvation or membership in a religious club; it is associated with joy, the infusion of divine life, which erupts into bursts of celebration at God's faithfulness and mercy. This joy itself marks a reversal of status and the fulfillment of prophetic promises of salvation (e.g., Isaiah 25:9; 35:2; 61:10).[9] The experience of the Spirit's anointing and abundance entails "an emotional or spiritual fullness that overflows outwardly."[10]

THE HOLY SPIRIT AS SALVATION

New Testament scholars continue to be vexed by what happens if you compare and contrast Luke and Paul on the Holy Spirit. Is Luke solely interested in the Spirit as divine power and enablement, or does he, like Paul, regard the Spirit as a source of divine life infused into the believer? Do Luke and Paul share contrary views of the Spirit, with Luke focused on personal experience and corporate mission, while Paul remains fixated on the Spirit as divine

---

[9]See David H. Wenkel, *Joy in Luke–Acts* (Milton Keynes, UK: Paternoster, 2015).
[10]González, *Story Luke Tells*, 115.

agent that applies the redemptive work of Christ to the believer?[11] I'd aver that whereas for Paul the Holy Spirit was a deposit or down payment of the kingdom (2 Corinthians 1:22-23; 5:5; Ephesians 1:13-14), for Luke the Holy Spirit is, somewhat analogously, the presence of the kingdom's power working in Jesus (Luke 11:20), and Israel's renewal is bound up with the giving of the Holy Spirit (Acts 1:6-8; 3:17-24).

Looking at issues beyond the Paul-Luke juxtaposition, Luke has a thick and holistic account of salvation, and the Holy Spirit is connected to that salvation in several ways.

First, the Holy Spirit brings empowerment and liberation. This is clear in the way that the Spirit empowers Jesus (Luke 4:1, 14) and the apostles (Acts 4:8, 31) in their preaching and ministry. The Spirit is the divine enablement to proclaim and embody the good news of God's love. But the Spirit is also a liberating power that rescues people from what afflicts them. Jesus makes this explicit in the "Nazareth Manifesto," where he declares that the Spirit anointed him to set people free from poverty, captivity, infirmity, and oppression (Luke 4:18-19; Isaiah 61:1). This liberation from evil and suffering is a form of "release" (ἄφεσις), a cognate for "forgiveness," which is available to Israel, any penitent person in Judea, and even the nations (Luke 1:77; 3:3; 24:47; Acts 5:31; 10:43; 13:38; 26:18). Thus, wherever the Spirit goes, through Jesus and his apostles, there is freedom and forgiveness wrought by the Spirit's enabling power.

Second, the Holy Spirit extends salvation to those beyond the boundaries of geographical Israel. The relationship between Israel and the nations is a complex topic in history, biblical theology, and Luke–Acts. Accordingly, we will tackle it at length in

---

[11] See Youngmo Cho, *Spirit and Kingdom in the Writings of Luke and Paul: An Attempt to Reconcile These Concepts* (Milton Keynes, UK: Paternoster, 2005).

the very next chapter—more anon. What we should note here is that the Holy Spirit is at the forefront of God's purpose and plan to bring "a light for revelation to the Gentiles" (Luke 2:32) by sending the apostles to share Israel's messianic faith with non-Jews. We see this especially in Acts 10–11 concerning the Gentile Pentecost, when Peter is "astounded that the gift of the Holy Spirit had been poured out even on the Gentiles" because it means that "these people . . . have received the Holy Spirit just as we have" (Acts 10:45, 47). This event is the proof, to both Peter and the Jerusalem church, that God does not discriminate between them (Gentiles) and us (Jews; Acts 11:12; 15:9). The Spirit is part of the Lukan scheme of mission because the Spirit prompts witnesses who extend the light of salvation beginning from Jerusalem unto the ends of the earth (Luke 2:32; 24:49; Acts 1:8; 13:47; 28:28).

Third, the Holy Spirit is a divine gift that brings internal transformation. The Holy Spirit empowers Israel's Messiah, guides the apostolic mission, energizes the charismatic life of the church, and brings freedom and forgiveness. The bestowal of the Spirit is an act of eschatological fulfillment. Yet the coming of the Holy Spirit, even as it rings out across the theater of redemptive history, is no less something for the individual. The Holy Spirit is freely given to those who put their faith in Jesus (Acts 2:38). In fact, looking at Peter's Pentecost sermon, González observes, "Peter seems to take for granted that the gift of the Holy Spirit is an almost automatic consequence of conversion and baptism."[12] When the Lord moves in someone's heart to bring them to faith, this faith cleanses their heart (Acts 15:8; 16:14). Thereafter, the Spirit brings joy to the life of believers (Acts 13:52).

---

[12] González, *Story Luke Tells*, 123.

LUKE THE PENTECOSTAL THEOLOGIAN

In Luke's story of Jesus and the early church, the Holy Spirit is not a silent partner, not scenery or stagehand but a central character in the drama. The Spirit is active in animating Jesus' messianic mission and the evangelical testimony of the nascent church. The Holy Spirit is the Father's promise and the Messiah's gift to bring renewal to Israel and light to the nations. The Holy Spirit cleanses believers' hearts and fills them with the fullness of joy. The Spirit is a person, a divine person, who speaks with wisdom, assists in discernment, warns of judgment, and puts an end to discrimination in the family of faith (Acts 11:12). The Spirit is the power from on high. God clothes people with that power so that they will go forth in the power of his presence and with the presence of his power.

After reading Luke–Acts, in particular after reading about the anointing of Jesus (Luke 3) and the day of Pentecost (Acts 2), it is clear that Luke presents the Spirit as an event and an experience, something we should liken to fresh wind and fire from heaven. This is a power that is invisible as it unstoppable, something that consumes everything in its wake, a purification from sin as well as a liberation from evil. The Holy Spirit who brought the divine life to creation, who gave the word of God to the prophets, who inspired Elizabeth and Zechariah with their songs of salvation, and who anointed the Messiah is now bestowed on those who call on the Messiah's name in faith so that they might have justice and joy, faith and forgiveness.

Because of this account of the Holy Spirit, Luke can be called, in the sense I've explained, a Pentecostal theologian. For Luke, what happened on the Jordan happened again at Pentecost, and Pentecost is the gift that keeps on giving. Where there is repentance, where the Spirit brings contrition, that is Pentecost. Where people of all ethnicities and languages come together in worship, where the Spirit brushes aside prejudice and partiality, that is Pentecost. Where there is good news to the poor and a proclamation of forgiveness for sins, where the Spirit provides unction to the speaker, that is Pentecost too. Where there are heavenly gifts poured out on men and women, where the Spirit is called on to give heavenly wisdom and power to our earthly endeavors, you know that is Pentecost too.

REVIEW QUESTIONS

1. What comes to your mind when you think of the day of Pentecost?
2. Explain the significance of Luke 3:16.
3. What does it mean to be filled with the Spirit?
4. Describe the role of the Spirit in the church's mission.
5. What does the Holy Spirit contribute to salvation?

RECOMMENDED READING

Atkinson, William P. *Baptism in the Spirit: Luke–Acts and the Dunn Debate.* Eugene, OR: Pickwick, 2011.

Bock, Darrell. *A Theology of Luke and Acts: God's Promised Program, Realized for All Nations.* Grand Rapids, MI: Zondervan, 2012. Pages 211-26.

González, Justo L. *The Story Luke Tells: Luke's Unique Witness to the Gospel.* Grand Rapids, MI: Eerdmans, 2015. Pages 111-25.

Varghese, P. V. "The Holy Spirit and the Risen Christ in Luke–Acts." *Indian Theological Studies* 44 (2007): 245-74.

12

Luke on Jesus, the Jews, and the Gentile Churches

LUKE BETWEEN SYNAGOGUE AND CHURCH

I have a distinct memory from my final year in high school where we needed to choose our seats for the high school formal (what is in America called "prom"). Along with all the other seventeen-year-olds, I rushed over to the wall with the clipboards and wrote my name in a slot to be seated next to my friends. But immediately, and right in front of me, a girl named Evelyn—the meanest of mean girls—walked up to the same clipboard, erased my name, and wrote in the name of one of her friends. I looked at her with shock and disbelief and asked, "Why would you do that? And right in front of me?" She just ignored me and walked away. I felt rejected and replaced, invisible and expendable.

Why am I telling you that story? What does it have to do with Luke–Acts? Well, when many people read Luke–Acts today they wonder whether Luke is trying to replace the "Jews" with Christians as God's people. On the one hand, Jesus is clearly a Jewish figure, a Galilean prophet, a messianic leader, who ministers among the Jewish people, bringing the salvation they have long desired. Plus, the apostles are all Jews; they do not invent a new religion, but rather they operate as a messianic sect within Judaism. In fact, the early church could be described as Christ-believing Judaism, a Jewish community who believed that the Jewish hopes for salvation in the

Jewish Scriptures had come on them. But, on the other hand, the Lukan Jesus engages in vicious polemics against the Pharisees, scribes, and priests. Then, later, in Acts, there is a strong emphasis on the culpability of the Jews for Jesus' death, and blame is heaped on the Jews for various riots and social disturbances. The book ends in Acts 28, describing the Jewish reaction to Paul's arrival in Rome, with a quotation of Isaiah 6:9-10 to the effect that Jewish unbelief is because they are dull of mind and hard of heart.

> **Scholarly Summaries on Luke and the Jews**
>
> "Luke has written the Jews off."[a]
>
> "Luke–Acts is one of the most pro-Jewish and one of the most anti-Jewish writings in the New Testament."[b]
>
> "Acts is by far the most anti-Jewish book in the New Testament, posing far more difficulties in the long run than the celebrated Fourth Gospel."[c]
>
> [a]Ernst Haenchen, "The Book of Acts as Source Material for the History of Early Christianity," in *Studies in Luke–Acts: Essays Presented in Honor of Paul Schubert*, ed. Leander E. Keck and J. Louis Martyn (Nashville: Abingdon, 1968), 278.
> [b]Lloyd Gaston, "Anti-Judaism and the Passion Narrative in Luke and Acts," in *Anti-Judaism in Early Christianity*, vol. 1, *Paul and the Gospels*, ed. Peter Richardson and David Granskou, Studies in Christianity and Judaism (Waterloo, ON: Wilfred Laurier University Press, 1986), 153.
> [c]John Pawlikowski, review of *Mature Christianity*, by Norman A. Beck, CBQ 49 (1987): 138, cited in Isaac W. Oliver, *Luke's Jewish Eschatology: The National Restoration of Israel in Luke–Acts* (Cambridge: Cambridge University Press, 2021), 131.

Some readers of Luke–Acts believe that Luke has contributed to a type of supersessionist theology whereby the Jews are rejected for their unbelief and replaced by the Gentile church. In many minds, Luke depicts Jewish institutions such as the temple as rejected and Jewish traditions such as circumcision as transcended; Jewish synagogues are little more than houses that harbor violent opposition to the apostles; and even the Jewish Scriptures are only salvaged by having them redrafted as witnesses to Jesus. Thus, many suspect that Luke roots the early church in its Jewish heritage, only to then denounce and discard the Jews for their opposition to Jesus and the apostles.[1] Indeed, such a view of Luke–Acts has been common for centuries—that Luke exonerates the church by excoriating the Jews, that Luke believes that Israel's light has been extinguished and God has lit his messianic lamp among the Gentiles.

Anti-Judaism in the New Testament and antisemitism in Christian history is a difficult and painful topic, but alas, it is one we must soberly face, especially in Luke–Acts.[2] So then, what did Luke say, believe, and hope concerning the Jewish people? Did he really think the Jews had had their bite of the apple and were now voted off redemptive-history island? Or is there more going on here? Well, much like my relationship with mean girls in high school, the answer is complicated.

"THIS JESUS, WHOM YOU CRUCIFIED"

We must observe how Luke puts the blame for Jesus' death squarely at the feet of the Jerusalem chief priests, scribes, elders, rulers, and even the people.

Luke's passion narrative accents the role of the Jerusalem priests, acting with the popular consent of the Jerusalem crowds, to petition Pilate to hand Jesus over to be crucified.

Luke's redactional activity (i.e., how he deliberately edits his Markan material) puts emphasis on the guilt of the official leaders of Judea and diminishes Pilate's role.

1. Luke gives prominence to the chief priests and scribes "vehemently accusing" Jesus of false charges related to stirring up sedition (Luke 23:10; see Luke 23:2, 14).

---

[1] See, e.g., Jack T. Sanders, *The Jews in Luke–Acts* (Philadelphia: Fortress, 1987); Amy-Jill Levine, "Luke and the Jewish Religion," *Int* 6 (2014): 389-402.

[2] See, e.g., Craig A. Evans and Donald A. Hagner, eds., *Anti-Semitism and Early Christianity: Issues of Polemic and Faith* (Minneapolis: Fortress, 1993); Paula Fredriksen and Adele Reinhartz, eds., *Jesus, Judaism and Christian Anti-Judaism: Reading the New Testament After the Holocaust* (Philadelphia: Westminster John Knox, 2002); Terence Donaldson, *Jews and Anti-Judaism in the New Testament: Decision Points and Divergent Interpretations* (Waco, TX: Baylor University Press, 2010).

2. Luke lumps together the chief priests, rulers, and people as campaigning for the crucifixion of Jesus (Luke 23:13). The leaders and Jerusalemites "found no cause for a sentence of death, [yet] they asked Pilate to have him killed" (Acts 13:28).

3. Luke has Pilate no less than three times declare that he found no charge against Jesus to be established (Luke 23:4, 14-16, 22; see Acts 3:13) and wants to release him (Luke 23:16, 20, 22).

4. Luke omits Mark's mention of Pilate's handing Jesus over to be crucified and the mocking of Jesus by the soldiers (Mk 15:15) yet accents Pilate's handing over Jesus to satisfy the demands and wishes of the chief priests (Luke 23:24-25).

It is hard not to see Luke laboring the point that Jesus was "innocent," even "righteous," buttressed by the testimony of the penitent bandit on the cross beside Jesus and the acclamation of the centurion at the foot of the cross (Luke 23:41, 47). Luke magnifies the role of the chief priests and amplifies the consent of the people, while turning Pilate into a quasi-defense attorney for Jesus. I suspect we should discern here something of Luke's own situation reflected in the text, perhaps relating to the post–AD 70 context, when Christians and Jews were battling over who was the true heir of pre–AD 70 Judaism. If so, then Luke is trying to acclaim Jesus as a holy man and righteous king, a victim of intra-Judean machinations, with the Roman prefect vacillating from vindicating Jesus to giving him over to priestly sanctioned violence. That would speak to a context where non-Christ-believing Jews and Jewish Christians were haggling over the borders of Jewish communities when it came to faith in Christ.

The same tendency to blame the Jews and mitigate the role of the Roman authorities occurs in apostolic preaching. Luke emphasizes the culpability of the Jerusalem populace for Jesus' death. Consider the following excerpts from apostolic sermons in Acts:

Table 12.1. The Culpability of Jewish leaders and groups for Jesus' death in speeches in Acts

Peter's Pentecost Sermon (Acts 2:22-23, 36)	Peter's Portico Sermon (Acts 3:13-15)	Peter Before the Sanhedrin and the Reflections of the Church (Acts 4:8-11, 27-28)	Stephen's Speech in Jerusalem (Acts 7:51-53)	Paul's Sermon in Pisidian Antioch (Acts 13:26-29)
22 You that are Israelites, listen to what I have to say: Jesus of Nazareth, a man attested to you by God with deeds of power, wonders, and signs that God did through him among you, as you yourselves know—23 this man, handed over to you according to the definite plan and foreknowledge of God, you crucified and killed by the hands of those outside the law.... 36 Therefore let the entire house of Israel know with certainty that God has made him both Lord and Messiah, this Jesus **whom you crucified.**	13 The God of Abraham, the God of Isaac, and the God of Jacob, the God of our ancestors has glorified his servant Jesus, **whom you handed over and rejected in the presence of Pilate, though he had decided to release him.** 14 But you rejected the Holy and Righteous One and asked to have a murderer given to you, 15 and you killed the Author of life, whom God raised from the dead. To this we are witnesses.	8 Then Peter, filled with the Holy Spirit, said to them, "Rulers of the people and elders, 9 if we are questioned today because of a good deed done to someone who was sick and are asked how this man has been healed, 10 let it be known to all of you, and to all the people of Israel, that this man is standing before you in good health by the name of Jesus Christ of Nazareth, **whom you crucified,** whom God raised from the dead. 11 This Jesus is 'the stone that was rejected by you, the builders; it has become the cornerstone.' ... 27 For in this city, in fact, **both Herod and Pontius Pilate, with the Gentiles and the peoples of Israel, gathered together against your holy servant Jesus, whom you anointed,** 28 to do whatever your hand and your plan had predestined to take place."	51 You stiff-necked people, uncircumcised in heart and ears, you are forever opposing the Holy Spirit, just as your ancestors used to do. 52 Which of the prophets did your ancestors not persecute? **They killed those who foretold the coming of the Righteous One, and now you have become his betrayers and murderers.** 53 You are the ones that received the law as ordained by angels, and yet you have not kept it.	26 My brothers, you descendants of Abraham's family, and others who fear God, to us the message of this salvation has been sent. 27 Because **the residents of Jerusalem and their leaders did not recognize him** or understand the words of the prophets that are read every sabbath, they fulfilled those words by condemning him. 28 Even though they found no cause for a sentence of death, **they asked Pilate to have him killed.** 29 When they had carried out everything that was written about him, they took him down from the tree and laid him in a tomb.

If one takes the combined total of accusations against the Jerusalem residents, then, they are accused of "Christicide," crucifying/killing Jesus, rejecting/denying Jesus, permitting lawless leaders to unlawfully kill an innocent Jesus, and being ignorant about the Scriptures concerning Jesus. What makes their crime so heinous for Luke is that the person they killed was no ordinary bystander but the Lord, Messiah, Isaianic servant, Holy One, Righteous One, author of life, who was sent and authorized by God according to the prophetic script. Plus, at one point, this accusation is broadened from the Jerusalemites to include the entire "peoples of Israel" (Acts 4:27). It was rhetorical denunciations of the Jews for the death of Jesus by Luke, Matthew, and John that led Justin Martyr in the second century to say:

> For other nations have not perpetrated against us and against the Messiah this wrong to such a degree as you [Jews] have done. You who by this act are the authors of a wicked conspiracy against the Righteous One, and against us [Christians] who belong to him. For after that you had crucified him, the only innocent and righteous one, by whose wounds those who approach the Father through him are healed, when you knew that he had risen from the dead and ascended to heaven, as the prophets foretold he would, you not only refused to repent of this wickedness which you had done, but at that time you selected and sent out from Jerusalem specific men through all the land to denounce the Christians as a godless heresy that had sprung up, and to spread many falsehoods about us. So that you are the cause not only of your own unrighteousness, but that of other people too (Justin, *Dial.* 17 [my translation]).

We have to remember that in the first century, at least until the Neronian persecutions in Rome in the 60s AD and mostly before AD 70, Jews and Christians were not distinguishable groups but part of the diverse expressions of common Judaism. Christ-followers were called "Christians" in Syrian Antioch probably by local pagan authorities in the 30s/40s to distinguish the messianic chapter of Jews and their Gentile adherents from the Jewish majority in the city (Acts 11:26). But to the Judean authorities, the early church was a sect, a deviant faction within the Judean constituency, even if they were pushing its boundaries by their faith and devotion to Jesus and shamelessly fraternizing with Gentiles (Acts 24:5; 24:14; 28:22). According to Dulcinea Boesenberg:

> Although Acts 11:26 announces that the disciples were first called Christians at Antioch, the presence of the word "Christian" in Acts should not be taken to indicate a well-developed division between Christians and Jews whether in the time and location described in the narrative itself or in the time and location of its composition. Rather, Acts bears witness to a period in which group identities and the boundaries between and within groups were being negotiated.[3]

Yet Luke's writings, full of invectives and denunciations, seem to accelerate what was later the parting of the ways between Jews and "Christians." Luke is engaged in intra-Jewish sectarian denunciations of non-Messiah-believing Jews (e.g., Acts 7:51-53; 14:2) and in-house debates among Jews about how faith in Jesus relates to the Jewish tradition (e.g., Acts 6:13-14; 15:1-21; 21:20-26; 23:6-10). But Luke also aided in the invention of the category of "Jews" and "Judaism" as a people and a religion who were to be *defined* as "other."[4] In the Lukan narrative the Jews are made culpable for Jesus' death and vehemently opposed to God, and this pattern was accented in later Christian literature such as that by Justin Martyr.

---

[3]Dulcinea Boesenberg, "Negotiating Identity: The Jewishness of the Way in Acts," in *Religion and Identity*, ed. R. A. Simkins and T. M. Kelly (Omaha: Kripke Center, 2016), 59.
[4]See Mitzi J. Smith, *The Literary Construction of the Other in the Acts of the Apostles: Charismatics, the Jews, and Women* (Eugene, OR: Pickwick, 2011), 57-94.

Bleak as this all sounds, I think we need not jump to the conclusion that Luke was proudly inventing the *contra Ioudaeos* (*against the Jews*) tradition. Luke's narration of the forces causing Jesus' crucifixion, as well as his depiction of Jewish figures in the story, is far from one dimensional. For a start, even with betrayal, rejection, and injustice, Jesus goes to the cross to fulfill the Jewish Scriptures (Luke 22:37; 24:44; Acts 3:18; 13:27-29, 33), as has been divinely foreordained (Luke 22:22; 24:6-8; Acts 2:23; 4:28). The cross is part of the plan and purpose of God; it is *necessary* for salvation, a fate Jesus embraces as part of his messianic vocation (δεῖ, "necessary," is repeated). In addition, unique to Luke is that the opposition to Jesus is hatched as a satanic plot. Satan exits the temptation episode in defeat, waiting for "an opportune time" to renew his attack on the Son of God (Luke 4:13). Satan's return is marked with his entering into Judas Iscariot (Luke 22:3), which puts into process the events surrounding Jesus' execution. Jesus' death is more than a miscarriage of justice; it is a deed of diabolic darkness, as Jesus tells the mob arresting him, "This is your hour, and the power of darkness" (Luke 22:53). The priests and rulers act as they do because they are blinded by the darkness and power of Satan (Acts 26:17-18).

It must also be noted that the passion narrative includes various Jewish supporters and mourners for Jesus' death. Many women are lamenting Jesus' sentence to death, and Jesus greets them with an oracle of lament and woe that worse days are coming. For, if men do evil deeds "when the wood is green" (i.e., in times of blessing), then what will they do "when it is dry" (i.e., in times of upheaval; Luke 23:31)? Jesus again grieves and forewarns Jerusalem and its inhabitants of a forthcoming disaster (Luke 23:27-31; see Luke 13:31-35; 21:20-24). Even if the Jerusalem temple ceases to be the locus of the divine presence (Luke 13:35), Jerusalem and its people remain the subject of Jesus' prophetic concern and lament (Luke 13:31-35; 21:20-24). In addition, Jesus is not buried by Gentile supporters, nor by a Roman senator, but by Joseph of Arimathea, a "righteous man," who is "waiting expectantly for the kingdom of God," a member of the Sanhedrin (Luke 23:50-51). Jesus was a Jewish prophet, buried by a Jerusalem leader, with a Jewish burial, according to Jewish customs, on the eve of the Jewish Passover.

What about the indictment of the Jerusalem population for their participation in the Messiah's execution, according to apostolic preaching? It seems as if Luke focuses on the Jerusalem rejection of Jesus in order to explain how it happened. Luke also wants to defend the apostles not so much as standing *against* the Jerusalem populace but as standing *for* God's plan and purposes that transpire through the risen and exalted Lord. The Jerusalem crowd, perhaps filled with partisans of the chief priests, is guilty to the degree that they allow lawless men to do an unlawful act (Acts 2:23). As such, Luke stresses that Pilate, Herod, and the chief priests, even if they act with popular assent, are the primary architects of Jesus' death (Luke 23:25; Acts 4:27; 13:27-28).[5]

Another thing to consider is how Jerusalemite regret and repentance for the act come quickly. Upon Jesus' death, "when all the crowds who had gathered there for this spectacle saw what had taken place, they returned home, beating their breasts" (Luke 23:48). To beat one's own breast was a mark of contrition (see Luke 18:13; Josephus, *Ant.* 4.320; 7.252). Many observers in Jerusalem either felt morally ambivalent or were filled with regret for what they'd seen. Then later, upon hearing Peter's Pentecost sermon, many in Jerusalem are "cut to the heart" and seek to make themselves right with God for their part in Jesus' death (Acts 2:37). Further, Peter's

---

[5] Jon A. Weatherly, *Jewish Responsibility for the Death of Jesus in Luke–Acts*, JSNTSup 106 (Sheffield: Sheffield Academic Press, 1994), 271-75.

second speech does offer mitigating circumstances, "I know that you acted in ignorance, as did also your rulers" (Acts 3:17). Such a claim does not absolve anyone from culpability, but it shows that even the error of executing God's messianic son can be met with divine forgiveness.

Luke never indicts all the Jews for Jesus' death, nor does he write them off for it. Luke has Peter admonish the Jerusalemites for their role in the tragic saga (i.e., "you," in Acts 2:23, 36; 3:13-17), whereas Peter and Paul, in the Diaspora, both refer to what Jerusalemites did to Jesus (i.e., "they," in Acts 10:39; 13:27-29). This is a subtle shift that means that Luke does not hold all Jews responsible for Jesus' death.[6] Even if the "peoples of Israel" are specifically named and blamed at one point (Acts 4:27), this is in the same prophetic tradition as Isaiah, who can denounce Israel's blindness and ignorance (Isaiah 42:19) while also affirming that a remnant will be restored (Isaiah 49:5-6; 50:10).

THE APOSTOLIC MISSION TO JEWS AND GENTILES

It is often assumed that Luke–Acts majors on mission, and by *mission* is meant the mission to the Gentiles. The implication is that Jesus' ministry to Israel and the apostles' ministry to Jerusalem and Judea are just warm-up acts for the main event, which is the apostle Paul preaching to Gentiles. That assumption might have a ring of truth to it, but on closer analysis it does not work.

Mission to the world. There is a mission to the world that is intimated early in Luke–Acts. Simeon testifies that the child Jesus is to be a "light for revelation to the Gentiles and for glory to your people Israel" (Luke 2:32 = Isaiah 42:6; 49:6). Soon after, John the

---

[6]See Steve Walton, "Acts," in *Dictionary of Theological Interpretation of the Bible*, ed. Kevin J. Vanhoozer (Grand Rapids, MI: Baker, 2005), 29; Isaac W. Oliver, *Luke's Jewish Eschatology: The National Restoration of Israel in Luke–Acts* (Cambridge: Cambridge University Press, 2021), 133.

Baptist declares, "all flesh shall see the salvation of God" (Luke 3:6). The Gentile mission is prefigured when Jesus heals the servant of a centurion in Capernaum (Luke 7:1-10) and exorcises the demoniac in the Decapolis (Luke 8:26-39). Concerning the Samaritans, Jesus refuses to call down fire on them despite their failure to receive him (Luke 9:51-56), tells an unexpected parable about a "good" Samaritan (Luke 10:25-37), and later heals a number of Samaritan lepers (Luke 17:11-19). In the parable of the great banquet, the offer of salvation is extended further, and the servants are commanded, "Go out into the roads and lanes, and compel people to come in, so that my house may be filled" (Luke 14:23). The Lukan Great Commission includes the interpretation of Israel's Scriptures to the effect that "the Messiah is to suffer and to rise from the dead on the third day, and that repentance and forgiveness of sins is to be proclaimed in his name to all nations, beginning from Jerusalem" (Luke 24:46-47).

Acts 1:8 provides a table of contents for the spread of the early Christian mission to include Jerusalem, Judea, Samaria, and the ends of the earth. Yet a world evangelistic mission does not happen straightaway; the apostles are preoccupied with local ministry, needs, and persecution. It is with the Hellenists (i.e., Greek-speaking Jewish Christians) that the mission to the nations gets underway, as demonstrated by the activities of Philip the evangelist (Acts 8:4-40), and it is in Syrian Antioch that these Greek-speaking Jewish Christians begin preaching the Lord Jesus to Greek Gentiles (Acts 11:19-21). At the same time, Paul, the designated apostle of the Gentiles, is converted (Acts 9:1-22), and Peter has his own epiphany about God's impartiality prioritized over God's purity laws concerning the Gentiles (Acts 10:1-48). Once the mission to all nations is underway, it is still no easy affair, as it seems to exacerbate Judean and Diasporan rejection of the Messiah, while the question of how Jewish Christians and Gentile Christians live together in a single community is a perplexing topic (e.g., Acts 15). In any case, Paul and Barnabas explicitly see themselves, like Jesus, as "a light for the Gentiles, so that you may bring salvation to the ends of earth" (Acts 13:47 = Isaiah 49:6). By the end of Acts, the gospel has spread to people from as far as Ethiopia and all the way to Rome.

> **Mixed Jewish Responses to the Gospel**
>
> "We have an ambivalence in Acts: incidents that speak glowingly of the growth of Jewish Christianity as well as incidents that show how virulently Jews opposed the mission of Paul."[a]
>
> ---
>
> [a]Joseph B. Tyson, *Luke, Judaism, and the Scholars: Critical Approaches to Luke–Acts* (Columbia: University of South Carolina Press, 1999), 137.

The Jewish mission as linked to the Gentile mission. Yet, also, there is a connection between the Jewish rejection of Jesus and the launch of the mission to the Gentiles. This is intimated in Jesus' sermon in Nazareth, which makes mention of how Israel's rejection of prophets such as Elijah and Elijah led to deliverance and blessings for Gentiles such as Naaman the Syrian and the widow of Zarephath (Luke 4:25-27). In addition, Paul twice turns away from evangelistic preaching to the Jews of the Diaspora because of their frosty response to focus on preaching the gospel to the Gentiles, who prove to be more receptive to the message (Acts 13:46; 18:6). But Luke's pro-Gentile mission perspective and his juxtaposition of Jewish unbelief and Gentile faith do not necessitate that God has voted the Jews off something like "covenant island" or that a mission to the Jews has been abandoned. Much to the contrary, Jewish rejection of Jesus is the occasion for the Gentile mission, but the Gentile mission never substitutes for a Jewish mission. The vast bulk of Luke–Acts features Jews sharing the gospel with other Jews.[7] In those discourses, Jewish Christians such as Peter and Paul address their Jewish compatriots with fraternal language ("brothers"), appeal to shared paternity ("our ancestors"), and refer to investment in a common Israelite identity ("You Israelites").[8] Plus, Gentile audiences, too, can be ignorant, obstinate, and violently hostile, yet Gentile unbelief is not a problem that needs explaining like Jewish unbelief.[9]

It is also clear that the Jewish mission is not merely initiatory but is intrinsic to the Christian mission. The risen Jesus says that the disciples' witnessing starts "beginning from Jerusalem" (Luke 24:47) and includes "in Jerusalem, in all Judea and Samaria" (Acts 1:8). Acts 1–12 is resolutely about the apostolic mission in Judea, which is amazingly successful (Acts 2:41, 47; 4:4; 5:14; 6:1; 9:42; 12:24) and includes even converts from the priests (Acts 6:7) and Pharisees (Acts 15:5). The Pauline mission to the nations is really the Pauline mission to Jews and Gentiles in the lands outside Judea.[10] Among the "nations," Paul spends a lot of time in Jewish synagogues and meets with modest success as far as making converts goes (see Acts 13:42-46 [Pisidian Antioch]; Acts 14:1-2 [Iconium]; Acts 17:5-6 [Thessalonica], Acts 17:10 [Berea]; Acts 18:19-21; 19:8-10 [Ephesus]). The Gentiles/Greeks whom Paul evangelizes are, with a few exceptions, associated with Jewish communities (see "Jews and Greeks" in Acts 14:1; 18:4; 19:10; 20:21).

True, Paul twice abandons his mission to the Jews to focus on preaching to Gentiles (Acts 13:46; 18:6). However, Paul always

---

[7] Oliver, *Luke's Jewish Eschatology*, 135.
[8] Boesenberg, "Negotiating Identity," 62-63.
[9] Jacob Jervell, *Luke and the People of God: A New Luke at Luke–Acts* (Minneapolis: Augsburg, 1972), 49.
[10] See Michael F. Bird, *An Anomalous Jew: Paul Among Jews, Greeks, and Romans* (Grand Rapids, MI: Eerdmans, 2018), 69-107.

returns to Jewish communities to recommence his evangelistic endeavors (Acts 14:1; 18:19-21). The Lukan Paul's summary of his ministry is, "I testified to both Jews and Greeks about repentance toward God and faith toward our Lord Jesus" (Acts 20:21). While in prison, the risen Lord consoles him that just as he testified in "Jerusalem," so also he must soon testify in "Rome" (Acts 23:11). Paul's geographical summary of his ministry is, "first to those in Damascus, then in Jerusalem and throughout the countryside of Judea, and also to the Gentiles, that they should repent and turn to God and do deeds consistent with repentance" (Acts 26:20).

Luke's account of Paul's Christophany with its apostolic commission is, "I [the risen Jesus] will rescue you from your people and from the Gentiles—to whom I am sending you to open their eyes so that they may turn from darkness to light and from the power of Satan to God, so that they may receive forgiveness of sins and a place among those who are sanctified by faith in me" (Acts 26:17-18). Paul even tries to make the Judean king Herod Agrippa II a "Christian" (Acts 26:27-29). As such, we can concur with the verdict of Jacob Jervell:

> The mission to Gentiles is simply part of the mission to the Jews. The command to world mission in Acts 1:8 shows the disciples witnessing in Jerusalem, Judaea and Samaria, and to the ends of the earth. "To the ends of the earth" does not mean the Gentile mission: throughout Acts the mission goes from synagogue to synagogue, ending with a meeting with the Jews in Rome (28:17ff). There is no specific mission to the Gentiles, separated from the mission to the Jews. It is striking that in their speeches to Jews the apostles emphasize the sharing of the Gentiles in salvation, while in their speeches to Gentiles, they mention their commission to Israel.[11]

---

[11] Jacob Jervell, *The Theology of the Acts of the Apostles*, NTT (Cambridge: Cambridge University Press, 1996), 41.

Still Jewish. The other thing to note is that Luke portrays Paul as the Jewish Christian apostle who remains deeply connected to Jewish Christianity. Paul maintains close connections with the churches of Jerusalem (Acts 11:27-30; 12:25; 15:1-5; 16:4; 18:22; 19:21; 20:22; 21:15-26) and Antioch (Acts 11:26; 13:1-3; 14:26; 15:22-23, 30-35; 18:22). In his testimony before the murderous crowd, he declares, "I am a Jew, born in Tarsus in Cilicia, but brought up in this city at the feet of Gamaliel, educated strictly according to our ancestral law, being zealous for God, just as all of you are today" (Acts 22:3), and then describes his apostolic commission in terms of the arresting call of the prophets (Acts 22:3-21). When put before the Sanhedrin, Paul says of himself, "I am a Pharisee, a son of Pharisees. I am on trial concerning the hope of the resurrection of the dead" (Acts 23:6).

Paul appears to be, in Jewish metrics, a Torah-observant and pious Jew who rebuffs the allegation that he teaches "all the Jews living among the Gentiles to forsake Moses, and that you tell them not to circumcise their children or observe the customs" (Acts 21:21; see the accusation in Acts 18:13; 21:28; 24:5-6). Paul repeatedly proclaims his innocence (Acts 23:1; 24:16; 25:8), claiming fidelity to his apostolic calling and belief in the scriptural hopes (Acts 22:3-21; 24:10-20; 26:2-23) as well as denying that he betrays the customs of his people (Acts 25:8; 28:17).[12] In light of Paul's statement to Festus, "I have in no way committed an offence against the law of the Jews, or against the temple, or against the emperor" (Acts 25:8), it seems that Luke is trying to make a thick defense of Paul from both charges of sedition against Rome and infidelity to the Jewish tradition.

---

[12]See e.g., Isaac W. Oliver, "The 'Historical Paul' and the Paul of Acts: Who's More Jewish?," in *Paul the Jew: A Conversation Between Pauline and Second Temple Scholars*, ed. Gabriele Boccaccini and Carlos A. Segovia (Minneapolis: Fortress, 2016), 51-80; Joshua W. Jipp, "The Paul of Acts: Proclaimer of the Hope of Israel or Teacher of Apostasy from Moses," *NovT* 62 (2020): 60-78.

Thus, it is not the case that a Jewish mission is replaced by a Gentile mission or that Jewish Christianity is replaced by Gentile Christianity. In the Pauline mission, the Jewish and Gentile missions are interwoven; in Pauline Christianity, Jews and Gentiles are united together, with Paul himself depicted as a Torah-observant advocate for Torah-light Gentile converts. This makes Acts especially suited as an apologetic work that attempts to assuage Jewish criticism of the apostles, especially Paul, and perhaps even makes something of a tacit or token effort at commending Jesus as the fulfillment of God's purposes to Jews.[13]

"True Israel." One lingering issue is whether Luke thinks that the church replaces the Jews as God's people. Consider these two statements by two European scholars about the church as God's true people in Acts:

> Luke's main interest is to demonstrate *the church as the one and only true Israel*, the unbroken continuation of the people of God in the time of Messiah-Jesus. The Christian message cannot be separated from the religious, political and cultural fate of Israel.[14]

> By depicting the Jewish Christians, including Paul, as essentially faithful to the law, Luke—against the historical situation of his time—is trying to say that the *Christians are the true Israel and that the break with Judaism* (i.e., with the community organized in the synagogue congregations of the Diaspora) was not caused by Christians, but by Jews (Acts 28.26ff.). The Christians had not left the synagogues of their own accord but had been driven out of them by force.[15]

---

[13]See Rebecca I. Denova, *The Things Accomplished Among Us: Prophetic Tradition in the Structural Pattern of Luke–Acts* (Sheffield: Sheffield Academic Press, 1997), 230-31; David A. Smith, "The Jewishness of Luke–Acts: Locating Lukan Christianity Amidst the Parting of the Ways," *JTS* (2021): 738-68.

[14]Jervell, *Theology of the Acts*, 4-5, emphasis added.

[15]Martin Hengel, *Earliest Christianity*, trans. John Bowden (London: SCM Press, 1986), 63-64, emphasis added.

Now, the language of "true Israel" can be highly problematic, if it implies that either the Jews who do not believe in Jesus or Jewish Christians who still observe the Torah are rejected because they are a "false Israel." I just don't think a hardline supersessionism or even a hyper-Pauline contrast of law and gospel maps onto Luke-Acts. That said, we need to note three important things: (1) In Luke-Acts, *Israel* is a prestige term, while "the Jews" are the empirical expression of Israel who are now, tragically, mostly in opposition to Jesus and the apostles. (2) Luke is clear that the story of Israel is continued in the story of the church so that there is continuity in terms of prophetic fulfillment from Israel, to Jesus, to the churches. To be precise, James's adjudication at the Jerusalem Council, with his appeal to Amos 9:11-12 (Acts 15:13-18), is that the churches should understand themselves as the fulfillment of the prophetic promises for Israel's restoration, a restoration that was always intended to include the Gentiles.

Finally, (3) the church, composed of Messiah-believing Jews and Gentiles, is best understood not as the totality of a true Israel to the exclusion of the Jews but as the vanguard of a renewed Israel prepared for the conversion of more Jews and Gentiles. Accordingly, I would argue that in Luke's mind the underlying premise is, *extra Israel nulla salus est*, "without Israel there is no salvation," and, *non est verus Israel sine Iudeis ex Israel*, "there is no true Israel without the Jews from Israel."[16] This is precisely why Luke has Stephen pray for the forgiveness of his murderers, "'Lord, do not hold this sin against them'" (Acts 7:60). The kingdom can never be fully consummated without Israel forgiven rather than estranged from its own messianic promises.

---

[16] Riffing off Jacob Jervell, "The Future of the Past: Luke's Vision of Salvation History and Its Bearing on His Writing of History," in *History, Literature, and Society in the Book of Acts*, ed. Ben Witherington (Cambridge: Cambridge University Press, 1996), 123.

LUKE'S JEWISH RESTORATION ESCHATOLOGY

What I think mitigates Luke's negative depiction of the Jews in his account of the internecine rivalry between Jewish Christians and nonbelieving Jews is the salient place that Luke attributes to Israel in his eschatological scheme.

While a later chapter will cover Luke's eschatology in more depth, I will make an interim statement here. In Luke's telling, Israel's hopes for redemption, rescue, and restoration have come to fruition, at least embryonically, through Jesus and his kingdom (see Luke 2:38; 4:18-21; 7:22-23; 24:21; Acts 1:6; 3:19-21; 13:32-33; 15:13-18). This is evident chiefly in Jesus' performance of signs of restoration, his exaltation, the offer of forgiveness, and the pouring out of the Spirit—all given as proof that the day of salvation is here. But such blessings are more than advance notice of the end or a foretaste of good things still to come. The narrative of Jesus as Israel's kingdom bringer (Acts 8:12; 28:23, 31) and the good news of Israel's restoration realized in Jesus' resurrection and exaltation (Acts 13:32-33) mean that the church now has the task of carrying forward the story of Israel (Acts 15:13-18), to be Israel-for-the-sake-of-the-world, to be just like Jesus himself, "a light to the nations, that my salvation may reach to the ends of the earth" (Isaiah 49:6; Luke 2:32; Acts 13:47; 26:23).[17]

The premise is not that Jesus came to Israel and then Israel rejected Jesus, so they are replaced by Gentiles. That's not the story at all. The story is that a transformed Israel will transform the world. Though many or even most Jews are not at the point of messianic faith, like a mustard seed, like a pugnacious weed, the kingdom of God is growing and sprouting in all sorts of places, in synagogues and agoras.

---

[17]See Michael F. Bird, "'A Light to the Nations' (Isa. 49.6): Inter-textuality and Mission Theology in the Early Church," *Reformed Theological Review* 65 (2006): 122-31.

The early church, in other words, saw itself as the vanguard of Israel's restoration, not trampling on the grave of an Israel vanquished and soon to vanish from the future. Far from it; Israel too still needs redemption, to rejoice like Mary in "God my savior" (Luke 1:47) and to resound with joy like Zechariah when it dawns on them that Jesus is the messianic "dawn" and the "horn of salvation" from the "house of his servant David" (Luke 1:69, 78). Luke's periodic pessimism about Jewish prospects is countered by his emphasis on the Jews as the empirical expression of Israel and as the beneficiaries of God's enduring faithfulness and providence that runs through the narrative. The Lukan description of the apostolic church is that it is an assembly of divine devotion, messianic faith, and spiritual fervor composed of Jews and Gentiles in the eastern Mediterranean who believe and behave in ways that mean that God's kingdom has come in the person of Jesus to Israel, for Israel, beyond Israel, but never to the demise of Israel. Paul himself is bound in chains "for the sake of the hope of Israel" only because God bound himself, in his Son, to make Israel's hopes come true (Acts 28:20).

THE END OF ACTS

If the infancy narrative in Luke 1–2 portrays God as faithful to the Jewish people, then Acts 28 presents the Jewish people as mostly recalcitrant in their rejection of the apostolic message of Jesus as their Messiah. Indeed, in the final section of Acts, the subject of the Jewish reception of Jesus remains unresolved: Will they or won't they get on board with messianic salvation?[18] Paul's arrival in Rome includes his interaction with the Jewish community, which yields a mixed response and climaxes in the jarring denunciation

---

[18]Troy M. Troftgruben, *A Conclusion Unhindered: A Study of the Ending of Acts Within Its Literary Environment*, WUNT 2/280 (Tübingen: Mohr Siebeck, 2010), 179.

of unbelief by way of a quotation of Isaiah 6:9-10 (Acts 28:17-30). Yet, I would argue that this passage is intended as the final explanation of the Jewish rejection of Jesus and the apostles, not to assert the cessation of a Jewish mission, nor as a final rejection of the Jewish people.

First, the Jews in Rome are initially portrayed as open and willing to listen, neither overtly hostile nor giving succor to rumor (Acts 28:21-22).

Second, Paul's message leads to a division among the Jews, with some convinced and others still unbelieving (Acts 28:24-25). This rupture has been known since Simeon's prophecy (Luke 2:32), is a pattern that follows Jesus himself (Luke 4:16-31), and is especially true of Paul's apostolic ministry (Acts 13:45, 50; 14:1-2, 4, 19; 17:4-5, 12-13; 18:5-8, 19-20; 24:19). The normal pattern is that a section of synagogue Jews believe, some God-fearers and Greeks join them, a larger faction of Jews take offense at Paul, then tumults ensue. Acts ends with the same pattern. Some Jews believe, most are unpersuaded.

Third, the quotation of Isaiah 6:9-10 describes the present state of the Jewish people. It does not deny them a part in Israel's future restoration. There is still the hope, the desire, the need for them to "turn and be healed." The Lukan Paul's words are a prophetic and intracovenantal critique of Israel's temporary intransigence, not Israel's normal state or a remark about expelling them irrevocably from the covenant. In addition, dullness of mind is true of many characters in Luke–Acts who still find their way to messianic faith (Luke 2:49-50; 8:9-10; 9:44-45; 24:25). The Jewish opposition is persistent yet partial, tragic but never terminal. In fact, "Although many Jews reject the Christian message, not all do," argues Jon Weatherly. "Israel is divided, not monolithic, in response to Jesus. And that division, far from being inconsistent with Christian claims about the fulfillment of the Jewish Scriptures, is in fact itself a fulfillment of the pattern of Israel's response found in them."[19]

Fourth, Paul's remarks to the nonbelieving Jews are certainly heated: "Let it be known to you then that this salvation of God has been sent to the Gentiles; they will listen" (Acts 28:28). However, these words are part and parcel of a previous pattern of Paul's being either rejected by Jewish audiences or disaffected by their lukewarm response, then turning to the Gentiles, only to revisit a Jewish audience later (Acts 13:46; 18:6). We have no reason to think that Luke expects the future to be any different: Paul will walk away from a hostile Jewish audience but will again return to his evangelistic activities in a Jewish setting.

Fifth, the very final scene of Acts is benign and even somewhat positive. Luke narrates how Paul stayed in Rome for two years, proclaiming the kingdom of God and teaching about the Lord Jesus, and "welcomed all who came to him" (Acts 28:29-30). This is hardly Paul wiping the dust off his feet one last time. Paul, as the proverbial Jesus-freak he was, is pictured as still willing to talk Jesus and the Jewish Scripture with anyone who will listen.

The closing section of Acts, then, demonstrates the gravity of the Jewish failure to communally accept Jesus as the Messiah, their Messiah, even though their obduracy in never regarded as final. That is because Luke–Acts maintains the communal election of Israel, the reception of Jesus by a remnant of Jewish Christians, and continues to see Jesus as the embodiment of the hope of Israel. Neither the influx of Gentiles into the church nor the resistance of the Jews to the apostolic preaching can dissuade Luke from believing that Jesus is the Messiah of Israel and for Israel. What is left for Israel is not judgment but waiting for the revelation of the

---

[19]Weatherly, *Jewish Responsibility for the Death*, 274.

Messiah and having their minds and hearts opened, as was done for other disciples (Luke 24:45; Acts 16:14).

THE VERDICT: IS LUKE PRO- OR ANTI-JEWISH?

As you can tell, Luke's relationship with Judaism is complicated by his historical situation. The church was involved in sectarian and polemical debates with Jewish communities in Judea and the Diaspora, pre- and post–AD 70, and Luke reflects that adversarial debate over Jesus' messianic identity. In addition, Luke seeks to deflect imperial criticism of the church by attributing the tumult and turmoil associated with Jesus' death, as well as the furor that followed the apostles, with their Jewish antagonists. We read Luke in a post-Holocaust context, where antisemitism was the most successful ideology of the twentieth century, finding both fascist and communist expressions, and attains traction even today among certain Islamicists and anti-Zionists. This means that Christians must find ways to read Luke–Acts responsibly, knowing that Luke's writings can be easily converted into the anti-Jewish rhetoric that has characterized so much of the Christian tradition.

Be that as it may, I do not think that Luke can be regarded as straightforwardly or systematically antagonistic to the Jews, nor seeking to engender prejudice against them. Luke polemicizes against Jewish unbelief, even as he affirms that Israel's heritage and hopes find fulfillment in Jesus (see esp. Acts 13:32-33). Luke presents Jesus as Israel's Messiah and the church as a messianic chapter within Judaism, like the Pharisees or Sadducees, that is treated as deviant by some non-Messiah-believing Jews. Thus the church, sociologically speaking, becomes othered and pushed to margins of common Judaism.

First, the culpability for Jesus' death falls on the priestly leadership and Jerusalem crowds, not "the Jews" as a bloc. Moreover, even while that culpability is accented by Luke's redactional activity and framing of his passion narrative, it must be juxtaposed with the infancy narratives, which buttress the view that Jesus is Israel's messianic Lord and Davidic deliver who himself is the expression of God's enduring faithfulness to Israel.

Second, for Luke, the tragedy is the *rupture* within Israel caused by Jesus, not the *rejection* of the Jews, nor the *replacement* of the Jews by Gentiles. Luke's paradox is that he portrays the early church as the heirs of Israel's prophetic promises because they are the preliminary recipients of Israel's messianic deliverance, yet Luke simultaneously laments and lambastes the Jews for their unbelief that messianic salvation has dawned. As salvation is extended to and experienced by Gentiles, it raises the question of the boundary between Jews and Gentiles and of whether messianic faith suffices over Torah observance for salvation and inclusion (Acts 10–11; 15). On this point, Luke certainly attempts to legitimate the identity of Gentile "Christians" as members of God's people, yet he does not do that by displacing the Jews from God's people, nor by emulating the anti-Jewish prejudice of Roman elites, but by postulating the church as an ideal cosmopolitan community, as an *ideal* Israel.[20] In Luke's account Jewishness is not supplanted, and neither is Gentileness superordinated; rather, space within Israel is expanded by the Spirit to include Gentiles as covenant partners with Jews through faith in the Messiah.

Third, Luke's "Christians" are flexibly depicted as a species of Jewish Christianity or Christian Judaism. If Luke hails from and advocates for "Gentile Christianity," then in his own telling, Gentile Christianity is Pauline Christianity. Yet the Lukan Paul is

---

[20]C. R. Stroup, *The Christians Who Became Jews: Acts of the Apostles and Ethnicity in the Roman City* (New Haven, CT: Yale University Press, 2020), 18-20.

depicted as robustly Jewish in his persuasion and piety, which makes Pauline Christianity a type of Jewish Christianity. Even as Luke emphasizes Jewish recalcitrance toward the apostles in both Judea and the Diaspora, it is a foil to emphasize the remnant of Jews who do believe Jesus is Israel's Messiah (Acts 2:41-42, 47; 4:4; 5:14; 6:7; 13:42-46; 14:1; 15:5; 17:5-6, 12) and Jewish opposition itself is sometimes the catalyst for the mission to the Gentiles (Acts 13:45-46; 18:6). The church, in Luke's narration of its founder and apostolic origins, is still within the orbit of Judaism because Jesus of Nazareth is the expression of God's faithfulness to the Jews even as the apostles believe that such faithfulness embraces Jews and Gentiles who have repentance and exhibit faith (see Acts 20:21; 26:19-20). For all the polemics and rhetoric against Jewish unbelief, Jewish Christians deploy familial language when addressing other Jews.[21] The identity of Jesus as Israel's Messiah and the inclusion of Gentiles without circumcision is a divisive affair, but it remains an in-house Jewish family affair. Hence the investigation conducted by the Jews in Rome as to what the fuss with Paul is about in Acts 28.

Fourth, the tension in Luke's narrative is born of Luke's conviction that many prophetic promises intended for Israel have been fulfilled by Jesus, and yet it is now mostly Gentiles believing in Jesus who are enjoying Israel's manifold blessings, not least of which is the Holy Spirit. But the fulfillment is not complete because Lukan eschatology is Jewish restoration eschatology in that a redeemed Israel leads to the redemption of the world. Unless Israel too shares in the age of messianic redemption, God's purposes and plan for the inhabited world can never be truly realized. In this case, then, Luke's eschatology will not permit the

---

[21]Boesenberg, "Negotiating Identity," 64-66.

abandonment of the Jews as God's faithfulness to Gentiles deflects from his first and foremost faithfulness to Israel. In Luke's scheme, there is no *fulfillment* without a *future* for Israel, for Luke's "times of the Gentiles" (Luke 21:24) are an interlude ahead of the redemption, refreshing, and consolation of Israel (Luke 1:68; 2:25; 24:21; Acts 1:6; 3:19).

REVIEW QUESTIONS

1. How would Luke explain that while Jesus crucified according to God's purpose, the chief priests and residents of Jerusalem were culpable for his death?
2. Compare and contrast the Lukan infancy narrative (Luke 1–2) and the Lukan passion narrative (Luke 22–23). What does this tell us about Luke's view of the Jews in God's plan and purposes?
3. If Luke had written one more chapter, Acts 29, how do you think it would have gone?
4. How does Lukan eschatology affect our view of Luke and the Jews?

RECOMMENDED READING

Armstrong, Karl L. "The End of Acts and the Jewish Response: Condemnation, Tragedy, or Hope?" *CurBR* 17 (2019): 209-30.

Cowan, J. A. *The Writings of Luke and the Jewish Roots of the Christian Way: An Examination of the Aims of the First Christian Historian in the Light of Ancient Politics, Ethnography, and Historiography.* LNTS 599. London: T&T Clark, 2019.

Moraff, James F. "Recent Trends in the Study of Jews and Judaism in Luke–Acts." *CurBR* 19 (2020): 64-87.

Schröter, Jens. "Salvation for the Gentiles and Israel: On the Relationship Between Christology and People of God in Luke." In *From Jesus to the New Testament: Early Christian Theology and the Origin of the New Testament*

Canon, translated by W. Coppins, Baylor-Mohr Siebeck Studies in Early Christianity, 227-46. Waco, TX: Baylor University Press, 2013.

Tyson, Joseph B. *Images of Judaism in Luke–Acts*. Columbia: University of South Carolina Press, 1992.

———. *Luke, Judaism, and the Scholars: Critical Approaches to Luke–Acts*. Columbia: University of South Carolina Press, 1999.

13

Turning the World Upside Down

Luke and Empire

CHRIST VERSUS CAESAR?

Empire is a hot topic at the moment.[1] I've read several recent books and listened to many podcasts about the Roman Empire, the Ottoman Empire, the British Empire, the Russian Empire, and the American Empire. World empires leave their mark through conquest, colonization, forced migrations, pogroms and persecutions, slavery and exploitation. You don't have to be a fan of Star Wars to know that *empire* conjures up feelings of tyranny and terror. The histories of India and Armenia alone are enough to tell you what happens when empires do their worst.

Luke–Acts is a book set in the context of the Roman Empire. The story takes place in the Greco-Roman world, where Greek culture interfaced with Roman military power. The story features Roman prefects and proconsuls, centurions and magicians; it takes readers on a journey from Bethlehem to Rome, from a small town in a volatile province to the very heart of the empire itself. In fact, Luke quite explicitly sketches the birth of Israel's new Davidic deliverer

---

[1]The title of this chapter is riffing off C. Kavin Rowe, *World Upside Down: Reading Acts in the Graeco-Roman World* (New York: Oxford University Press, 2009).

and the beginnings of Jesus' public ministry against the backdrop of Roman imperial power by naming the ruling powers of the day:

> In those days a decree went out from Emperor Augustus that all the world should be registered. This was the first registration and was taken while Quirinius was governor of Syria. All went to their own towns to be registered. Joseph also went from the town of Nazareth in Galilee to Judea, to the city of David called Bethlehem, because he was descended from the house and family of David. (Luke 2:1-4)

> In the fifteenth year of the reign of Emperor Tiberius, when Pontius Pilate was governor of Judea, and Herod was ruler of Galilee, and his brother Philip ruler of the region of Ituraea and Trachonitis, and Lysanias ruler of Abilene, during the high priesthood of Annas and Caiaphas, the word of God came to John son of Zechariah in the wilderness. (Luke 3:1-2)

Luke heralds Jesus as the Lord's Messiah (Luke 2:11), and Roman elites knew of the Jewish prophecy about a ruler who would rise from the East to rule the world, whom Jews of the empire longed to see. According to the ancient historian Tacitus, "Some few put a fearful meaning on these events, but in most there was a firm persuasion, that in the ancient records of their priests was contained a prediction of how at this very time the East was to grow powerful, and rulers, coming from Judea, were to acquire universal empire" (Tacitus, *Historiae* 5.13).[2] Suetonius, another ancient historian, declares, "There had spread over all the Orient an old and established belief, that it was fated at that time for men coming from Judaea to rule the world" (Suetonius, *Vespasian* 4.4).[3] Even earlier, the Jewish philosopher Philo referred to Alexandrian mobs taunting the Judean minority with mocking gibes about their so-called coming Messiah

---

[2] Tacitus, *The History*, trans. Alfred John Church, William Jackson Brodribb, and Sara Bryant, ed. for Perseus (New York: Random House, 1873; rprt, 1942).
[3] Suetonius, *Lives of the Caesars, Volume II*, trans. J. C. Rolfe, Loeb Classical Library 38 (Cambridge, MA: Harvard University Press, 1914), 275.

(Philo, *Against Flaccus* 36-39). It is interesting, then, that Luke locates Jesus' Davidic and therefore messianic identity against the backdrop of Roman power. Ultimately it is a question of who the true Lord of the world is. Is it the son of Augustus or the Son of David? The Imperator or the Messiah? Caesar of the Palatine Hill or the Jesus of Palestine? An aristocrat authenticated by the swords of the praetorian guard or a holy man authenticated by the word of the prophets?

The study of the New Testament and empire is always fashionable, since American imperialism and expansionism is often seen as a modern equivalent to Rome's unrivaled military supremacy and its imperial evils. Thus, many are eager to find in Luke–Acts a critique of imperial power, which becomes a quaint mirror of their own rage against the empires of our own day.

Therein lies the problem. Is Luke really against the Roman Empire? Does Luke regard the empire with disdain, treat it with indifference, hope for its overthrow, aspire to fly under its radar, or pray for its redemption? The answer is mixed. The Lukan Jesus is certainly a victim of Roman imperial violence . . . even as Luke plays down Pilate's role in Jesus' death. The Lukan Paul is a victim of corrupt, inept, and unjust Roman officials . . . even as Paul has several positive interactions with Roman officials. Luke notes how Pilate and the Jerusalem leaders crucified Jesus (Acts 3:13; 4:27; 13:28) and how Paul was contravening the emperor's decrees by saying that Jesus was "another king" (Acts 17:7). Yet Paul uses his Roman citizenship to get out of a tight spot (Acts 22:23-29), Paul protests that he has "done nothing wrong against . . . Caesar" (Acts 25:8 NIV), and Herod Agrippa II tells Festus about Paul, "This man could have been set free if he had not appealed to the emperor" (Acts 26:32).

If Luke's purpose is to ingratiate himself to Roman power and seek its benefaction, he fails. If Luke's purpose is to stir up an insurrection against Roman power, he fails at that too. So then, we may ask, what is Luke's view of the empire? Is it a bland backdrop, a benign power, or a belligerent character?[4]

RENDER TO CAESAR

Luke's Gospel does not read like a political manifesto; rather, it is a type of biography, one about Israel's long-awaited Davidic Messiah. That said, there are some tacit anti-imperial themes that emerge across the book if we look closely enough, as well as some positive encounters with Roman officials that complicate the picture.

Mary's Magnificat echoes the prophets and Psalter in Yahweh's contest against the pagan nations and their gods. Mary's song celebrates how "He [God] has brought down the powerful from their thrones, and lifted up the lowly; he has filled the hungry with good things, and sent the rich away empty" (Luke 1:52-53). Luke's hope for the future does not entail a game of thrones played by Roman senators but God's throne with his vice regent establishing a renewed Israelite kingdom (Luke 22:66-71).

In the Lukan temptation sequence, the devil offers Jesus "all the kingdoms of the world" if only Jesus will worship him (Luke 4:5). It's hard not to see here a temptation for Jesus to engage in the caesarization of his messiahship, to adopt the mantle and means of imperial power as his instrument and goal. The devil offers him instant, total, and universal power at the cheap, cheap price of idolatry. The temptation, a shortcut to power, requiring neither service nor sacrifice, is the seduction of anti-God worship. This is a temptation that Jesus rebuffs by an assertion of Israel's monotheistic devotion: "Worship the Lord your God, and serve only him" (Luke 4:8).

---

[4]The scholars diverge on whether Luke is pro- or anti-Roman authorities. The contrast can be seen in Kazuhiko Yamazaki-Ransom, *The Roman Empire in Luke's Narrative*, LNTS 404 (New York: T&T Clark, 2010), who thinks Luke is negative toward the Roman Empire, against Joshua Yoder, *Representatives of Roman Rule: Roman Provincial Governors in Luke-Acts* (Berlin: de Gruyter, 2014), who thinks Luke has a positive view of the Roman system of governance.

Not all is negative between Jesus and Roman figures; several centurions play positive parts in Luke–Acts. There is a remarkable episode where Jesus heals a centurion's slave in the town of Capernaum (Luke 7:1-10). The scene has a Matthean equivalent (Matthew 8:5-10), but there are noticeable differences between the two accounts: (1) In Matthew, the centurion approaches Jesus himself, while in Luke the centurion sends two delegations. (2) Luke's account includes a report by the Jewish elders about the centurion's worthiness to have his request granted since he loves the local people and built their synagogue. (3) Matthew combines the story with a saying about many coming from the East and West to participate in an eschatological banquet, which Luke places elsewhere (Matthew 8:11-13/Luke 13:28-30). Finally, (4) Matthew emphasizes the centurion's faith, while Luke highlights the centurion's belief in Jesus' authority, his faith in Jesus' healing power, and the centurion's worthiness to have his request granted. Most commentators concur that Jesus' willingness to heal the centurion's slave foreshadows the Gentile mission even if Luke mutes the story by locating the saying about the eschatological banquet elsewhere.[5]

> **Roman Peace Was Created and Sustained by Violence**
> Tacitus puts into the mouth of the Pictish king Calgacus words that describe the Romans as purveyors of a rapacious and predacious empire: "They ransack the world, and now that the earth fails to contain their all-devastating grasp, they scour even the sea: if their enemy has wealth, they are greedy; if he is poor, they are ambitious; neither East nor West has satiated their hunger. . . . They plunder, they murder, they rape, in the name of their so-called empire. And where they have left desolation, they call it 'peace'" (*Agricola* 30 [my translation]).

---

[5] Michael F. Bird, *Jesus and the Origins of the Gentile Mission*, LNTS 331 (Edinburgh: T&T Clark, 2006), 116-21.

When Jesus is asked whether it is lawful for a Judean to pay taxes to the emperor, it is not an honest question; it is a trap. If Jesus says, "Yes, pay your taxes to the emperor," he could be accused of complicity with Rome's bloodsucking tax policies. Jewish historian Josephus tells us that some zealous Galileans had a motto, "No king but God," and since paying taxes to the emperor meant recognizing him as king, paying taxes was not just an economic burden, it was a cowardly betrayal of their religious devotion (see Josephus, *Ant.* 18.23; *J.W.* 2.118; 7.410). But if Jesus says, "No, don't pay taxes to Caesar," then he could be arrested on the spot for sedition, precisely the charge that is presented at his trial before Pilate (Luke 23:2). Jesus' response splits the horns of the dilemma and urges that this pagan money—stamped as it was with an idolatrous image of Tiberius as a so-called son of the divine Augustus—be given back to its pagan owner, while what is rightly God's—such as his people—be given back to God.[6]

The Lukan Olivet discourse follows the Markan template by including Jesus' warning that, prior to the siege of Jerusalem, "Before all this occurs, they will arrest you and persecute you; they will hand you over to synagogues and prisons, and you will be brought before kings and governors because of my name. This will give you an opportunity to testify" (Luke 21:12-13). The followers of Jesus will experience intrafamilial betrayal and hostility from Jewish synagogues and will be forced to testify before ruling authorities. Jesus here does not indicate whether those authorities are benign or opposed to the disciples, but the subsequent course of events in Jesus' trial and in the career of the apostles demonstrates that they found themselves arraigned before magistrates and governors who were morally vacuous, corrupt, or unjust. Such a view dovetails

---

[6]Michael F. Bird and N. T. Wright, *The New Testament in Its World* (Grand Rapids, MI: Zondervan, 2019), 52.

with Paul's exhortation to the Galatian churches, "It is through many persecutions that we must enter the kingdom of God" (Acts 14:22). Those persecutions may have started as internecine synagogue debates but soon morphed into pagan mob violence, with imperial authorities either refusing to intervene or else actively scapegoating Christians for the commotions. Yet, such trials provide the providential opportunity for testimony to the gospel.

At the Last Supper, the disciples are found to be bickering over who is the GOAT in their circle, the "greatest of all time." Jesus sternly replies that there is no GOAT in the kingdom, only GITOS, "greater is the one serving." They are not to seek positions as benefactors and lord this over clients and supplicants who request their patronage. This emphasis goes beyond mere circles of wealth and connections and applies to the entire Roman Empire. The empire was a hierarchical system of power and patronage over which the emperor presided. Honor, wealth, and power could be attained by ingratiating oneself into the imperial system of patronage and becoming a patron to one's own clients in that system. But the disciples are not to pursue that endeavor; they are to find greatness in service, not in the ranks of their entourage. According to Joel Green: "When Jesus set his kingdom over against 'the kings of the Gentiles' (22:25) he was not only engaging in an interesting object-lesson. To a degree not often recognized, the values and behaviour for which Jesus calls in Luke are contradictory to and even put in question the existence of the Roman Empire in his day."[7]

Turning to the trial narrative, Pilate is portrayed as vacillating, morally indifferent, but an inadvertent witness to Jesus' innocence (Luke 23:4, 14-16, 22). In the end, he surrenders Jesus to the will of the Jerusalem priests and their spontaneous mob of

---

[7]Joel B. Green, *The Theology of the Gospel of Luke*, NTT (Cambridge: Cambridge University Press, 1995), 119.

supporters (Luke 23:24-25). Later, in Acts, Pilate is remembered as one who is culpable for Jesus' death, even as he acted in collaboration with the Jerusalem leadership (Acts 3:13; 4:27; 13:28). At the crucifixion is a cohort of soldiers, probably drawn from nearby Samaritans and Syrians, who mock Jesus (Luke 23:36-37). Yet among them is a centurion who witnesses the manner of Jesus' death and engages in an act of worship and acclamation. Luke reports how the centurion at the cross "praised God and said, 'Certainly this man was innocent'" (Luke 23:47). Luke swaps out Mark's confession by the centurion of Jesus as "truly this man was the son of [a] god" (Mark 15:39 my translation) for "certainly this man was innocent" (δίκαιος, lit. "righteous") to highlight the unjust nature of Jesus' execution. This centurion, just like Pontius Pilate, is another Roman witness to Jesus' innocence.

The tension is that Luke can affirm the inclusion of tax collectors who were, directly or indirectly, collaborators with Rome and also commend the faith of two notable centurions. But on the whole, the Roman Empire looks like just another pagan empire opposed to God's kingdom, king, and people.

ON IDOLS AND DIVINE EMPERORS

The ancient world was full of gods. Keith Hopkins imagines two time travelers reporting how god-saturated the city of Rome was to observers:

> There were temples and Gods, and humans praying to them, all over the place: at the entrance to the town, at the entrance to the Forum; there were altars at the crossroads, Gods in the niches as you went along, with passersby just casually blowing a kiss with their hands to the statue of a God set in a wall. And of course, here in the Forum, the ceremonial center of the town, there were temples, altars, Gods, heroes just about everywhere we looked. . . . Our end of the square was filled

by the grand Temple to Jupiter, with Vesuvius magnificently snow-capped behind. And all the rest of the buildings looked as though they could be temples too.[8]

What is more, the gods were not above and beyond the world but were the mightiest forces in the world.[9] As Robin Lane Fox notes, "The gods were not simply up in heaven, but rather were all around—in the storm, in sickness, in battle, in the public spaces, in dreams, in stories."[10] Whether bees, beers, war, weather, seas, or trees, the gods were associated with everything in life. The gods were the subjects of myths, poetry, and philosophy; they were consulted through oracles, placated in rituals, praised in temples. There were beliefs about and in gods, but it was far more than that. Ancient religion was concerned with family devotion before images, with prayers and prostitutes at a meal for a trade guild held in a temple, with shouting praises as statues of one's gods were paraded by, with buying a papyrus with secret words to curse an enemy, with making an offering at a temple in want of healing. Ancient cities, such as those visited by Paul, did not think in terms of believing in gods as much as they spoke of "having gods," gods who could be a blessing or bane, because every facet of life and every season of existence was controlled by a power greater than that of mortals.[11]

The Jewish critique of idols and pagan religion is rehearsed by Christians. This is clear in Luke's gag reflex at Herod Agrippa I being acclaimed as a god in Tyre (Acts 12:20-23), the embarrassment of

---

[8]Keith Hopkins, *World Full of Gods: The Strange Triumph of Christianity* (New York: Plume, 2001), 13.
[9]James O'Donnell, *Pagans: The End of Traditional Religion and the Rise of Christianity* (New York: Ecco, 2016), 67.
[10]Robin Lane Fox, *The Classical World: An Epic History from Homer to Hadrian* (New York: Basic, 2006), 50.
[11]Robert Louis Wilken, *The Christians as the Romans Saw Them,* 2nd ed. (New Haven, CT: Yale University Press, 2003), 58.

Paul and Barnabas at being worshiped as earthly doppelgangers of Olympian gods in Lystra (Acts 14:8-18), the exorcism of a slave girl possessed by a pythonic spirit in Philippi (Acts 16:16-18), Paul's disgust that Athens is a city "full of idols" (Acts 17:16), and Paul and his friends' almost bankrupting the silversmith industry and causing affront to Artemis in Ephesus (Acts 19:17-41). The early church resolutely rejected idols made with "human hands" in favor of the worship of the true and living God.

Ephesus is a good segue because, in the mid-first century, it had two major cults, a local one of Artemis and an imperial one for the emperor Augustus and the goddess Roma. What is more, the two were combined, as the Artemesian temple had a sanctuary for Augustus and Roma. This made the deified Augustus and the Roman people *synnaoi* or "temple sharers" with the goddess Artemis. Within a hundred years, Ephesus had several imperial temples to former emperors.[12] Thus, to fill out the religious backdrop of Acts, we need to consider the significance of the imperial cults of the empire. In these cults the emperor's benefactions were reciprocated with varying degrees of divine worship, sometimes demanded by Roman officials as proof of loyalty, other times proposed by local civic leaders to ingratiate themselves to the imperial regime.[13]

Ruler cults were practiced in the ancient Near East and in the Hellenistic period. In the late republic, the Romans gradually began to apply divine honors to revered leaders such as Marius, Sulla, and Julius Caesar. However, it was during the Augustan era that the cult of the emperor began to make strides as the civic religion of the empire. While the emperors gratefully accepted divine

---

[12]See Craig S. Keener, *Acts* (Grand Rapids, MI: Baker, 2012–2015), 3:2551-57.
[13]See Michael F. Bird, *Jesus Among the Gods: Early Christology in the Greco-Roman World* (Waco, TX: Baylor University Press, 2022), 302-17.

honors from their eastern subjects (from public statements of divine benefaction all the way to sacrifices in a temple with a priesthood), they also had to be careful not to appear too eager to request divine honors (less they appear arrogant or neglecting the traditional deities). In any case, by the first century, the various imperial cults, that is, the diverse forms of veneration of living and deceased emperors, were among the most significant aspects of the Mediterranean religious landscape.

The devotion offered to the emperor, his heir, and wider family was neither political flattery nor pious pretense. The emperors were real gods, real within the symbolic universe of the empire. The deceased deified emperors and their living heirs were a real source of benefaction and salvation and thus real gods for those who gave them homage. It is important to note that the imperial cults were not uniform, as they had various forms of expression, many outside the realm of what we would normally call religion. One can find inscriptions celebrating the birth and accession of the emperor, listing his various benefactions and the divine honors granted to him by a city or province. In the provinces, festivals often included parading images of the emperor, choruses singing songs about the emperor, priests singing hymns to the emperor, climaxing with sacrifices either for or to the emperor.[14] City officials and associations venerated the emperor with inscriptions, shrines, libations, and sacrifices for his health, usually as thanksgiving for some type of benefaction such as tax relief or famine assistance. Cities competed for the honor of hosting imperial temples, and civic elites jostled for positions within its priesthood. The best evidence of piety was erecting images of the emperors (Josephus, *Against Apion* 2.73). From

---

[14]S. R. F. Price, *Rituals and Power: The Roman Imperial Cult in Asia Minor* (Cambridge: Cambridge University Press, 1986), 104-5.

Augustus to Marcus Aurelius, the emperor's image was enfaced all over the empire, in banks, booths, baths, gymnasia, graffiti, grottos, villas, coins, temples, shops, markets, taverns, porches, parades, festivals, and windows.[15]

The result of this mass media, propaganda, and religious fervor was that the emperor's veneration was a means of creating "imperial consciousness," that is, bolstering social hierarchy while cultivating provincial loyalty.[16] The imperial cults reinforced bonds of allegiance by the emperor's generous benefactions being reciprocated with ritualized devotion to him by provincial subjects. The result was a mutually reinforcing web of patronage and power laced with religious elements. This was done largely by embedding imperial paraphernalia within preexisting religions and cults. This could look like placing a statue of the emperor within an existing temple or including prayers for the emperor at an annual festival. It is no surprise, then, that the imperial cult became a central sociopolitical and religious fixture of the empire. It did this by marrying together the emperor, elites, provincial clients, pantheon, and people, joining local cults with the goddess Roma and the imperial family, giving the Olympian deities an earthly embodiment, assimilating priestly and political offices, offering benefaction, and inviting supplication. According to Hans-Josef Klauck:

> The emperor cult was not seen as an alternative to the inherited religious, but as a kind of superstructure which could be added onto local cults. It functioned as a kind of institutional metonymy: it evoked the

---

[15]See Paul Zanker, *The Power of Images in the Age of Augustus* (Ann Arbor: University of Michigan Press, 1988); Harry O. Maier, *Picturing Paul in Empire: Imperial Image, Text and Persuasion in Colossians, Ephesians and the Pastoral Epistles* (London: Bloomsbury, 2013).

[16]Oliver Stoll, *Excubatio ad Signa: Die Wache bei den Fahnen in der romischen Armee und andere Beitrag kulturgeschichtlichen und historischen Bedeutung eines militarishcen Symbols* (St. Katharinen; Scripta Mercaturae, 1995), 36.

fact of Roman rule, gave an ideological foundation for it and furthered its social acceptability, at least for members of the leading classes to whom new and honorable careers as provincial priests of the emperor cult were offered.[17]

> **A Dedication to the Divine Emperor**
>
> A first-century BC inscription in the city of Mytilene on the island Lesbos acclaims the emperor Augustus with divine honors and offers to deify him further if any reasons can be found: "We reckon on his magnanimity to see that those who have attained celestial glory, and divine superiority and might, can never stand on the same level with what is humbler by both fortune and nature. However, if something more honoring should be discovered in the time to come, the city's willingness and piety will omit nothing that could contribute more effectively to his deification."[a]
>
> A first-century AD inscription in the city of Myra states, "The people of Myra [honor] the emperor Tiberius, the exalted god, son of exalted gods, lord of land and sea, the benefactor and saviour of the entire world."[b]
>
> A first-century AD inscription in a town called Acraephiae of Boetia includes a statement by an Augustan priest to consecrate an altar to Nero, who is "lord of the entire world."[c]
>
> Notice should also be given of how Festus, in Acts 25:25-26, intends to write to Emperor Nero and describes him as "imperial majesty" (σεβαστός) and "sovereign" (κύριος).
>
> ---
>
> [a]Translated by K. Buraselis in *Orientis graeci inscriptiones selectae*, ed. Wilhelm Dittenberger (Leipzig: Hirzel, 1903–1905), 456.
> [b]Translated by H.-J. Klauck in *Inscriptiones graecae ad res romanas pertinentes*, ed. René Cagnat et al. (Paris: Leroux, 1906–1927), 3:721.
> [c]Translated by J. Fantin in *Sylloge inscriptionum graecarum*, 3rd ed., ed. Wilhelm Dittenberger (Leipzig: Hirzel, 1915–1924), 814.30-31.

---

[17]Hans-Josef Klauck, "The Roman Empire," in *The Cambridge History of Christianity: Origins to Constantine*, ed. Margaret M. Mitchell and Frances M. Young (Cambridge: Cambridge University Press, 2006), 73.

PLANTING THE CHRISTIAN GOSPEL IN CAESAR'S BACKYARD

Christ among the Caesars. What does this intersection of pagan religion and imperial power have to do with Luke's posture toward the Roman Empire? Well, Luke narrates the story of the mission of the apostles and the growth of the church in a context where there was an acute connection between sociopolitical power, religious piety, and civic participation. Luke's critique of idolatry is not partitioned from his suspicions about Roman authority because the two were intertwined.

Considering the nexus between pagan deities and worship of the emperor, let's look at what happened to Paul and Silas in Thessalonica:

> After Paul and Silas had passed through Amphipolis and Apollonia, they came to Thessalonica, where there was a synagogue of the Jews. And Paul went in, as was his custom, and on three sabbath days argued with them from the scriptures, explaining and proving that it was necessary for the Messiah to suffer and to rise from the dead, and saying, "This is the Messiah, Jesus whom I am proclaiming to you." Some of them were persuaded and joined Paul and Silas, as did a great many of the devout Greeks and not a few of the leading women. But the Jews became jealous, and with the help of some ruffians in the marketplaces they formed a mob and set the city in an uproar. While they were searching for Paul and Silas to bring them out to the assembly, they attacked Jason's house. When they could not find them, they dragged Jason and some believers before the city authorities, shouting, "These people who have been turning the world upside down have come here also, and Jason has entertained them as guests. *They are all acting contrary to the decrees of the emperor, saying that there is another king named Jesus.*" The people and the city officials were disturbed when they heard this, and after they had taken bail from Jason and the others, they let them go. (Acts 17:1-9)

A group of Thessalonian Jews accuse Paul, Silas, and their converts of upsetting the social order, acting contrary to Caesar's decrees, and venerating Jesus as a king in competition with the emperor. The allegations are somewhat ironic since the Jews were often accused of the same things—misanthropy, antisocial behavior, disloyalty toward Rome and the emperor, and atheism toward the local gods. It's difficult to determine what precise imperial decree these Christians are allegedly breaking. Perhaps the charge is *maiestas*, that is, sedition against the imperial majesty; maybe it is a ban on forming local associations or consulting soothsayers about successions of imperial power; or it could be that proclamation of Jesus as king violates loyalty oaths that citizens were required to make. Given that Thessalonica had its own imperial temple to the emperor since the time of Augustus, the local Jews might be complaining that Paul had coaxed local Gentiles such as Jason into neglecting veneration of the emperor by showing allegiance to Jesus as a type of rival deified emperor.

Competition with the empire. Some emperors jealously guarded their unique authority and coveted their divine honors. According to Quintilian, Augustus took his divine honors with a modicum of seriousness. The people of Tarraco in Spain built an altar to Augustus and a delegation later told Augustus that a palm tree had miraculously sprung out of it. To this Augustus sarcastically quipped that this proved that they obviously didn't kindle any fires on it. The joke was that a regular application of fire and flesh to the altar would have prevented the palm from growing in the first place (Quintilian, *Institutio Oratoria* 6.3.77). Suetonius tells a story of how Caligula was dining with several kings who had come to Rome to pay him their respects. The kings were discussing their royal pedigree when Caligula purportedly blurted out a quotation from Homer's *Iliad*: "Let there be one lord and one king"

(Suetonius, *Caligula* 22.1). Anything that neglected or deflected from the emperor's divine majesty was bound to be treated as a mixture of sedition, atheism, and antisocial behavior.

A potential rivalry with the Roman emperor is signaled by the evangelical architecture of the Lukan narrative. Jesus, who was sentenced to death by a Roman prefect, had been raised up, had ascended into heaven, and was now enthroned at the Father's right hand. Such a narrative would conjure up in many minds Greek notions of apotheosis or Roman *consecratio*, a king/emperor who died, was deified, and thereafter received divine honors. In this line of thought, Jesus was a rival lord, exalted, co-enthroned with a Most High God, and who commanded the worship and allegiance of Jews and Gentiles in the cites of the empire. There is, then, something of a contest of lordships at work. The gospel of the early church included the acclamation of and allegiance to Jesus as Lord (Acts 2:36; 3:20; 4:33; 8:16; 11:17, 20; 15:11, 26; 16:31; 19:5, 17; 20:21, 24, 35; 21:13; 28:31). Drew Strait comments: "For Luke, Jesus' ascent is the fulfilment of God's promises to Israel and functions to call both worshipers of Yahweh and Caesar to change their posture heavenward toward the Messiah King Jesus in heaven."[18]

> **Who's in Charge?**
>
> "Acts, far from being a humble appeal to Caesar for a little recognition and respect, is a revolutionary manifesto addressed to a church determined to show Caesar that God, not the nations, rules the world."[a]
>
> [a]William H. Willimon, *Acts*, Interpretation (Atlanta: John Knox, 1988), 122.

Israel's God is "Lord of heaven and earth" (Acts 17:24), and now it is precisely through his messianic Lord Jesus (Luke 2:11; Acts 2:36)

---

[18]Drew J. Strait, "Proclaiming Another King Named Jesus? The Acts of the Apostles and the Roman Imperial Cult(s)," in *Jesus Is Lord and Caesar Is Not: Evaluating Empire in New Testament Studies*, ed. Scot McKnight and Joseph B. Modica (Downers Grove, IL: InterVarsity Press, 2013), 136.

that divine lordship is embodied and expressed. The best example here is Peter's speech in the house of Cornelius, "You know the message he sent to the people of Israel, preaching peace by Jesus Christ—he is Lord of all" (Acts 10:36). If you asked a Roman or Greek about a "gospel" of someone who was "Lord of all," it would be taken as a reference to Caesar, since that kind of language was often applied to the emperor. Caesar's lordship (Acts 25:25) was over the "all the world" (Luke 2:1); it was an absolute monarchy that lauded its lordship over the nations (Luke 22:25), complete with pagan boasts of self-deification (e.g., Acts 12:22). Yet Luke finds such language as fit to describe Jesus, who is the true, rightful, exalted, and total Lord, before whom Caesar is an idolatrous, pale, and inferior figure. Jesus is not a usurper of Caesar's lordship, like a calculating nephew scheming in a palace coup; it is the other way around. Caesar has usurped with idolatrous self-exaltation the devotion that is demanded of Israel's God in his Messiah.[19]

Yes, there were other deceased and deified emperors, and yes, other deities could be addressed as κύριος for "lord," such as Serapis and Osiris. But Jesus was more than another god and lord added to the panoply of pagan powers in the heavens. Jesus is Lord, Savior, benefactor who will one day establish a messianic kingdom, who requires contrition and allegiance from all, who will judge the world on the very turf on which Caesar is meant to be worshiped and obeyed as the divinely appointed and divinely powerful lord. This pits the two against each other in some sense. One could attempt to diminish the contrast and conflict by arguing, as Dean Pinter does, that Luke would be happy to say that Caesar is lord and king because Jesus is "Lord of lords" and "King of kings."[20]

---

[19]See C. Rowe, *World Upside Down*, 112-13.

[20]Dean L. Pinter, "The Gospel of Luke and the Roman Empire," in *Jesus Is Lord, Caesar Is Not: Evaluating Empire in New Testament Studies*, ed. Scot McKnight and Joseph B. Modica (Downers Grove, IL: IVP Academic, 2013), 113-14.

This is perhaps true to a point; even a deified emperor was subordinate to the Capitoline triad of Jupiter, Juno, and Minerva. But imagining the emperor as subordinate to the god of a backwater province such as Judea, and subservient to a seditious prophet crucified by a Roman official—that's a big sell to an empire with a keen sense of its own divinely appointed destiny and its own inherent superiority over the subjugated barbarian tribes with their purportedly paltry deities.

Interactions with Rome. The other thing to note is that Luke's description of Roman officials is less than flattering at times. Gallio, the proconsul of Achaia, treats Paul and his friends with moral indifference and turns a blind eye to their injustice (Acts 18:12-17). The Roman governor Felix is the apex of a corrupt Roman official; he keeps sending for Paul in the hope that Paul will try to bribe his way out of trouble, thus proving that he is seeking self-enrichment rather than dispensing justice (Acts 24:24-26). The next governor, Festus, leaves Paul in prison for no other reason than to please the Judean leaders (Acts 24:27). If Christians are allegedly a threat to Roman order, laws, and justice, Luke's complaint is that Romans officials act unlawfully and are unconcerned with injustice.

Yet, we must remember that Luke's depiction of Roman officials and officers is not uniformly negative. There is the conversion of Sergius Paulus, the proconsul of Cyprus, who believes Paul and Barnabas's teachings about the Lord Jesus (Acts 13:4-12). In Ephesus, the Asiarchs, that is, local officials, are friendly to Paul and warn him about facing an angry mob in the Ephesians' theater (Acts 19:31). At several times it is mentioned how Roman officials, even when placing Paul in custody, grant him certain liberties and do not hinder his ministry (Acts 24:23; 27:3; 28:16, 31). Then there are depictions of Roman centurions and tribunes, which complicates the picture even more.

There are two centurions prominent in the Gospel of Luke (Luke 7:1-10; 23:47), and centurions return to the fore in Acts 10–11 with Peter's encounter with Cornelius in Caesarea. Cornelius is described as "a centurion, an upright and God-fearing man, who is well spoken of by the whole Jewish nation" and "a devout man who feared God with all his household; he gave alms generously to the people and prayed constantly to God" (Acts 10:2, 22). What is more, Cornelius, after hearing Peter's sermon, believes the message, receives the Holy Spirit, and is accordingly baptized. The story underscores that God shows "no partiality" (Acts 10:34), because God has bestowed on Gentiles the same gift of the Holy Spirit that Jews have received (Acts 10:47; 11:17). God has made Gentiles clean by the exercise of their faith (Acts 10:15; 11:8; 15:9; 26:18). Therefore, the church concludes, "God has given even to the Gentiles the repentance that leads to life" (Acts 11:18).

The apostle Paul has various encounters and interactions with Roman tribunes and centurions, especially in Jerusalem and on his journey to Rome. It is a tribune named Claudius Lysias who prevents Paul from being lynched by a zealous mob in the temple precinct (Acts 21:27-36), who puts Paul in protective custody (Acts 21:34), and who sends Paul to the governor in Caesarea to foil a plot to murder him (Acts 23:16-25). Paul, in other words, owes his very life to the actions of Claudius Lysias. Furthermore, Paul is sent to Rome with some other prisoners under the supervision of "a centurion of the Augustan Cohort, named Julius" (Acts 27:1). When moored at Sidon, Luke says that "Julius treated Paul kindly, and allowed him to go to his friends to be cared for" (Acts 27:3). Also, during the storm in the Adriatic Sea, Julius stops the soldiers from killing Paul and the other prisoners when they run aground off Malta (Acts 27:42-44). Paul himself assists the centurion's mission by offering counsel to avoid a dangerous voyage (Acts 27:9-12), prevents the sailors from abandoning the ship without the passengers (Acts 27:27-32), and strengthens the crew and passengers with an impromptu act of breaking bread (Acts 27:33-38). In the voyage, Paul is clearly a beneficiary of divine favor; he survives storm, shipwreck, snake bite, and heals a Maltese leader. Julius, the Roman centurion, by preserving Paul, is doing his own part in the divine purpose to enable Paul to testify in Rome.

Luke's portrayal of Roman military personnel appears to have two paradoxical functions. First, the anonymous centurion for whom Jesus performs a healing, the centurion at the cross, and Cornelius of Caesarea are proof that centurions can be exemplars of faith.[21] While that might seem innocuous, we must remember that "faith" (πίστις) entails allegiance, allegiance to God and his Messiah. Luke is aware that a Roman centurion's faith in the God of Israel's messianic agent would prompt some alarm because, as David Garland argues, "If a centurion believes that the God of Israel and the Lord Jesus Christ are more powerful than all other so-called powers and must be obeyed above all others, then Caesar's God-denying world is in danger of collapsing."[22] Second, the tribune Claudius Lysias and the centurion Julius demonstrate several salient points for Roman and Christian relationships. The two men are Roman witnesses to how public tumults are instigated by Jews against Christians and not caused by Christians. They are

---

[21]See esp. Laurie Brink, *Soldiers in Luke–Acts: Engaging, Contradicting, and Transcending the Stereotypes*, WUNT 2/362 (Tübingen: Mohr Siebeck, 2014), who argues that Luke subverts the stereotype of Roman centurions as thuggish and impious and instead presents Roman soldiers as "parabolic exemplars" of a good disciple (26) who furnish "the author's optimistic expectation of imperial benevolence" (175).

[22]David E. Garland, *Acts*, Teach the Text Commentary Series (Grand Rapids, MI: Baker, 2017), 109-10.

also witnesses to how Christians demonstrate commendable citizenship by their collaboration with imperial authorities. Luke's imagery is complex; Christ-believing centurions are a potential "fifth column,"[23] while Christ-believers such as Paul should be exonerated from charges of engaging in anti-Roman activities or causing social disturbances (see esp. Acts 25:8).

Luke's Jesus is something of a rival lord to Caesar, but many subjects of Caesar seem quite fit to be worshipers of Jesus.

LUKE, JESUS, AND THE EMPIRE OF GOD

Luke was probably writing Luke–Acts at the end of the first century around the same time that the Jewish historian Josephus was engaged in his own literary endeavors. Indeed, a comparison of the two is quite fitting.

Luke and Josephus. Josephus was a Judean aristocrat who was a general in charge of the defense of the Galilee during the Roman invasion, but later, when captured, he changed sides and became a propagandist for the Roman Empire. He ingratiated himself to General Vespasian when he allegedly prophesied that Vespasian would one day become emperor, which he did. After the war, while living under imperial patronage in Rome, Josephus wrote an apology for the Romans to Jews, his *Jewish War*, explaining how Israel's God had gone over to the side of the Romans, just as Josephus himself had by changing sides during the conflict. But later on Josephus wrote what were effectively apologies for the Jews to the Romans, defending Jews and Judaism against the vehement anti-Judaism of cultural elites in Rome and Alexandria, his *Antiquities of the Jews* and *Against Apion*. Josephus was trying

---

[23]This is a reference to Spanish Civil War history. It's a common term for the enemies' allies who are in your city but you don't know it yet.

to negotiate fidelity to his ancestral Jewish traditions along with loyalty to his imperial patrons. Was Luke engaged in a similar enterprise?

Did Luke write an apology for Jesus and the church to Romans, to prove that the Jesus movement was no sinister threat to Roman order and power?[24] On top of that, did Luke also write an apology for the Romans to the church?[25] Was Luke trying to persuade Christians that Roman officials, such as Sergius Paulus or Cornelius, were good candidates for Christian faith, and further that the emperor, if given good advice, would leave Christians unhindered to practice their religion? Was Luke trying to say that the Christian kingdom, as Justin and Eusebius later argued, was entirely spiritual and otherworldly, and therefore no threat to Caesar's realm?[26] While giving a defense of the Jesus movement is valid, it is grossly unlikely that Luke was trying to provide a defense of Roman power. Josephus and Luke, even if they were writing apologetic discourses, still embed certain criticisms of Roman power in their respective works. Luke does not write his critique of Roman power in hidden transcripts that only insiders can understand, because, just like Josephus, he feels free to offer a few impolite gibes at Roman power. Luke's apologetic tone does not mean that he is trying to ingratiate the church to the Romans, much less refrain from quite active denunciations of Roman

---

[24]See Barrett: "[Acts] was not addressed to the Emperor, with the intention of proving the political harmlessness of Christianity in general and Paul in particular. . . . No Roman official would ever have filtered out so much of what to him would be theological and ecclesiastical rubbish in order to reach so tiny a grain of relevant apology." C. K. Barrett, *Luke the Historian in Recent Study* (London: Epworth, 1961), 63. Followed by Jervell: "Luke's conception of God, who governs history by means of miracles and mighty deeds and delivers apostles from all prisons and perils, makes it difficult to imagine that it is Luke's desire to petition the Romans for favorable conditions and the opportunity to practice religion for the church." Jacob Jervell, *Luke and the People of God: A New Luke at Luke–Acts* (Minneapolis: Augsburg, 1972), 157-58.

[25]See Seyoon Kim, *Christ and Caesar: The Gospel and the Roman Empire in the Writings of Paul and Luke* (Grand Rapids, MI: Eerdmans, 2008), 168-72.

[26]See Justin, *First Apology* 11; Eusebius, *Ecclesiastical History* 3.20.

idolatry and injustice. Luke, like Josephus, wants his community to live peaceably within Rome. But Luke, unlike Josephus, does not want patronage from Rome. So what does Luke want when it comes to Christian and Roman relationships?

Nuancing Luke's perspective. I think Luke stands somewhere between Romans 13:1-7 (Paul's instructions about giving respect to governing authorities) and Revelation 13:1-18 (John the Seer's vision, which reveals Rome to be a satanic beast).

Luke's Acts is not an apocalyptic narrative about Rome's destruction, as one finds in the Qumran War Scroll (1QM) or John the Seer's Apocalypse of Jesus Christ. Luke is not expecting the immediate abolishment of the Roman Empire, let alone its replacement with a Christianized empire that would eventually become Christendom. Luke has a bit of eschatological fervor (see the next chapter), but he's neither a radical millenarian (believing that the kingdom will fall from heaven with flaming fire and angelic ninjas any day now) nor a postmillennialist (believing that the kingdom of God is brought to you by the same people who made Rome a transcontinental superpower).

Luke's view of Jesus, the kingdom, and the church is not that they are direct threats to Rome's borders or to the succession of leaders—well, at least not in the interim; at the final assize it will all be laid at the feet of Jesus, but that is still to come. Precisely because Christians such as Luke saw a reordering of powers at the end of history, they had no need to be organizing a cabal to overthrow Caesar and to replace him with a more pliable and warmly disposed ruler. Luke did not want to join forces with the Parthians to install Sergius Paulus as the first Christian emperor in order to turn Rome into a Christian nationalist state. Luke was not plotting the defeat of the empire as much as slowly transforming it from the inside out.

> **Christianity as Challenge to the Imperial Cults**
>
> "In any case, the challenge of the Christian movement to Roman religion, and its resistance to the visual propaganda and civic ritual that reinforces Roman rule, was ultimately to subvert, at a deep level, the whole edifice of Roman civilization."[a]
>
> [a] John Barclay, *Paul: A Very Brief History* (London: SPCK, 2017), 37.

Luke's story of the early church is not a desperate attempt to make the church look pro-Roman, for there was no escaping the fact that Jesus was a crucified messianic claimant who was now acclaimed as "Lord of the world," that Peter was a prophetic agitator, that Paul was a dangerously successful sophist who was—I suspect Luke and his readers knew—executed in Rome. Luke knew in his own day that the *delatores* ("informants") and *frumentarri* (the emperor's secret police) could come looking for him and his church and arrest them. Luke's Acts is a politically freighted document that witnesses to God's empire and seeks to construct and embody an alternative and disruptive pattern of life that runs counter to the norms and necessities of the Greco-Roman world.[27] Luke acquits Jesus and the church of the accusation of sedition (Luke 22:52; 23:2; Acts 5:36; 21:38) but embraces the charge of causing mayhem and mania (Acts 17:7; 26:24). Luke envisages a peace (Acts 10:36) and salvation (Acts 4:12; 13:26, 47; 16:17) of a different order from Caesar's because it would involve a transformation of the world around the story and symbols of Jesus until the kingdom of God is established in all its fullness. Luke is perhaps heeding the advice of Plutarch, who notes that community leaders living under Roman hegemony had to walk a fine line between

---

[27] Rowe, *World Upside Down*, 4; see also Amanda C. Miller, *Rumors of Resistance: Status Reversal and Hidden Transcripts in the Gospel of Luke* (Minneapolis: Fortress, 2014), 254-55.

acknowledging the grievances of the people, verbalizing their discontent, but not giving Roman birds of military prey cause to be hawkish, which called for realpolitik and no little rhetorical verve (Plutarch, *Moralia* 801c-805e).[28]

Application for the present. In terms of what Luke's vision of the church vis-à-vis empire means for us today, I think William Willimon captures something of Luke's challenge for us to reflect on:

> Luke's church was not trying to be credible to the Empire or to assure Caesar of its apolitical status. It sought to create an alternative political entity, which became a monkey wrench thrown into the clanking machinery of Caesar's systems. Christianity defeated the Empire, in great part, because it out organized the Empire. The church gave the decaying classical world a vibrant, tightly knit, exclusivist organizational alternative to other secular arrangements. Theophilus' church appreciated not only God's involvement in the world through the Spirit but also God's apartness from even the Empire's best cultural achievements. The *Didache*, our oldest catechism, prepared candidates like Cornelius for baptism by instructing them that they would not kill, would not have sex with other people's spouses, would not abuse young children, would not abort fetuses. In doing so the church put itself on a collision course with some of the Roman world's most widely accepted practices. But our current North American church—as well as some churches in the midst of revolution in Third World countries—so want to be recognized as culturally significant (as Caesar defines significance), so want to have the power to change and improve society without converting and evangelizing it, that we gladly adapt the foolishness of the gospel to the world's standards of wisdom and reduce our social witness to the back-seat status of a general civilizing influence on the empire rather than form a new kingdom loyal to a King who is not Caesar.[29]

---

[28]Steve Mason, "Speech-Making in Ancient Rhetoric, Josephus, and Acts: Messages and Playfulness, Part I," *Early Christianity* 2 (2011): 459.
[29]William H. Willimon, *Acts*, Interpretation (Atlanta: John Knox, 1988), 121.

The church must be constantly reminded not to be seduced with the promise of cultural relevance and political sponsorship to the point that it waters down its message or alters its mission to fit in. There is one king and one Lord to whom allegiance is owed—not to any political party or civil power but Christ and Christ alone.

REVIEW QUESTIONS

1. If faced with a choice, would Luke rather be the emperor's personal chaplain or his executioner?
2. Who is the worst Roman character in Luke–Acts?
3. Which Roman centurion in Luke–Acts do you find the most interesting?
4. Why do some scholars think Luke is writing a defense of Christianity to a Roman official?
5. If Luke had written about how Paul appeared before Nero, what do you think Paul would have said?

RECOMMENDED READING

Ahn, Yong-Sung. *The Reign of God and Rome in Luke's Passion Narrative: An East Asian Global Perspective*. Leiden: Brill, 2006.

Bird, Michael F. "Rome, Roman Empire." In *The Baker Illustrated Bible Dictionary*, edited by Tremper Longman III, Peter Enns, and Mark Strauss, 1446-51. Grand Rapids, MI: Baker, 2013.

Evans, Craig A. "King Jesus and His Ambassadors: Empire in Luke–Acts." In *Empire in the New Testament*, edited by Stanley E. Porter and Cynthia Long Westfall, 120-39. Eugene, OR: Pickwick, 2011.

Kim, Seyoon. *Christ and Caesar: The Gospel and the Roman Empire in the Writings of Paul and Luke*. Grand Rapids, MI: Eerdmans, 2008.

McKnight, Scot, and Joseph B. Modica, eds. *Jesus Is Lord and Caesar Is Not: Evaluating Empire in New Testament Studies*. Downers Grove, IL: InterVarsity Press, 2013.

Petterson, Christina. *Acts of Empire: The Acts of the Apostles and Imperial Ideology*. Eugene, OR: Cascade, 2020.

Rhoads, David E., and Jae Won Lee, eds. *Luke–Acts and Empire: Essays in Honor of Robert L. Brawley*. Eugene, OR: Pickwick, 2011.

Rowe, C. Kavin. *World Upside Down: Reading Acts in the Graeco-Roman World*. New York: Oxford University Press, 2009.

Seo, Pyung Soo. *Luke's Jesus in the Roman Empire and the Emperor in the Gospel of Luke*. Eugene, OR: Pickwick, 2015.

Walton, Steve. "The State They Were In: Luke's View of the Roman Empire." In *Rome in the Bible and the Early Church*, edited by Peter Oakes, 1-41. Grand Rapids, MI: Baker, 2002.

Yamazaki-Ransom, Kazuhiko. *The Roman Empire in Luke's Narrative*. LNTS 404. London: T&T Clark, 2010.

14

A Hope in God

Luke and the Future

DELIVER US, O LORD

I enjoy tracing religious themes in animated Disney movies. One of my favorites is *Hercules* (1997), which is a modern take on an ancient story of the demigod Hercules. The funny thing is that Hercules gets heavily Christianized; he becomes a pagan prototype of Christ. I mean, the opening song is called "Gospel Truth," and Hercules makes a deal with the dark and malevolent god Hades to trade his life for his girlfriend, Megara. Hades gets duped when he realizes that Hercules is a god and he can't keep him enslaved in death. The climax is basically the ransom theory of the atonement, that Christ used his flesh as bait and his divinity as the hook to snare the devil. Another good DreamWorks movie with religious themes is of course *Prince of Egypt* (1998), because it is based on the biblical story of Moses leading the Hebrews out of slavery in Egypt. The opening song is "Deliver Us," about the Hebrews toiling under the yoke of Egyptian oppression and their longing for God to rescue them from it.

What do 1990s animated movies have to do with eschatology, or hope for the future, in Luke–Acts? In many ways, the two movies are good analogies for what Luke might be doing. Is Luke effectively Christianizing some Greco-Roman themes about God, history, and the future? Or is Luke telling a very Jewish story about

Israel's sacred history, telescoped into Jesus, with a dramatic climax at Jesus' return? Then again, as Luke seems to be shaped by the Septuagint (i.e., Greek translation of the Old Testament) and literary culture of antiquity (i.e., ancient rhetoric and historiography), perhaps he is genuinely influenced by a bit of both.

Much of Luke's idea of the future centers on his preferred phrase "kingdom of God," which summarizes much of Jesus' teaching and contains a galaxy of expectations about the future. As you might guess, more debates ensue on that topic. What is the kingdom of God, and what does Luke think of it? Then, underlying the whole discussion about Luke's eschatology is the dreaded "delay of the parousia" (*parousia* means "presence" and is a word used for Jesus' future presence or return). Luke has, so it goes, abandoned hope for Christ's return in the near future, filed it away under "Whenevs," and replaced it with the church's mission and increasingly institutionalized leadership as a way of compensating for the failure of Jesus to return as soon as imagined. Luke became—in the minds of beer-sipping, sausage-munching liberal German Protestants—a theological antihero who traded eschatological fervor, charismatic leadership, and the authentic Pauline gospel for "early Catholicism," an allegedly hierarchical, this-world-focused, hodgepodge unity ticket between Jewish Christianity and Pauline Christianity, destined to descend into the institutional inertia of the Catholic Church.

THE KINGDOM OF GOD AS NOW AND NOT YET

The phrase "kingdom of God" can mean all sorts of things depending whether we are talking about Christian theology or exegesis of Lukan texts.[1] What the kingdom meant for Augustine in the fifth century is far different from what it meant for Adolf von Harnack in the early twentieth century. Many people project into

---

[1] See Michael F. Bird, *Evangelical Theology*, 2nd ed. (Grand Rapids, MI: Zondervan, 2018), 297-317.

the kingdom all sorts of ideals and ideas that they wish to champion, or rather that they wish Jesus to champion for them. But generally biblical scholars think that the kingdom of God in the Gospels refers to God's action as king, the effect of his royal power, God's reign. The kingdom, then, is not just a future realm but the divine reign, not just a place but a power, the kingly power of God rescuing his people.[2]

In Luke's telling, the first aspect of the kingdom of God that stands out in Jesus' preaching is the kingdom's future horizon. Disciples are taught to pray, "Your kingdom come" (Luke 11:2) in the sense of the arrival of a new age. The kingdom is something that comes after and lies beyond Jesus' own death (Luke 22:16, 18) and the sacking of Jerusalem (Luke 21:31). Jesus emphasizes the necessity and difficulty of "entering" the kingdom. This is something that can only be done with the openness and vulnerability of a child (Luke 18:17) and without being seduced by possessions (Luke 18:24-25), and it means leaving behind family and possessions (Luke 9:59-62; 18:29). Indeed, one must seek or strive after the kingdom (Luke 12:31; see Acts 14:22), which is the Father's good pleasure to bestow (Luke 12:32). The kingdom's future consummation can be likened to a banquet for a renewed Israel (Luke 13:28-29), and the disciples will preside over a restored Israel as judges (Luke 19:28-29). This kingdom is equated with eternal life (Luke 10:25; 16:19-31; 18:18, 30), with an inversion of social power making the first last and the last first (Luke 13:30; 16:25), as well as involving the general resurrection (Luke 14:14; see Acts 23:6-8; 24:15) and a final judgment (Luke 10:14; 11:31-32; 13:5; see Acts 10:42; 17:30-31).

Luke also sees a second aspect to the kingdom, that it is a present reality, present in the person of Jesus, the power of the Spirit, and

---

[2]Thus, for Wright, the kingdom is "the action of the covenant god [sic], within Israel's history, to restore her fortunes, to bring to an end the bitter period of exile, and to defeat, through her, the evil that ruled the whole world." N. T. Wright, *Jesus and the Victory of God*, COQG 2 (London: SPCK, 1996), 307.

the mission of the church. This embryonic present-ness of the kingdom is largely due to the Lukan atmosphere of messianic fulfillment. The presence of the kingdom is evident in the demonstrable signs of Israel's restoration straight out of Isaiah, focused on the coming of God as King, the primary subject of Isaiah 40–55 (see next section). When the disciples heal the sick, they are entitled to tell people, "The kingdom of God has come near to you" (Luke 10:9). Also, many parables portray the kingdom as something that appears insignificant and inert but then grows and overtakes everything around it. The kingdom is like a mustard seed, a tiny seed that soon sprouts and consumes everything in its path like an infesting weed (Luke 13:18-19); or it is like yeast, something that works itself through everything it touches (Luke 13:20-21). These word pictures from daily life depict the kingdom as a present reality, and while seemingly inauspicious, it is destined to dominate all before it.

Important as well is the idea that Jesus has won a dramatic victory over Satan. Jesus reports to his disciples a vision of some kind where he saw "Satan fall from heaven like a flash of lightning" (Luke 10:18), perhaps referring to his triumph over satanic temptation in the wilderness (Luke 4:1-12). This victory is further established by his exorcisms of demonic spirits (Luke 7:21; 13:10-17) to the point that Jesus considers himself to be the "strong man" who plundered and ransacked the demonic realm (Luke 11:14-23) as empowered by the Spirit/finger of God (Luke 11:20).

Jesus is King

"Jesus is King, and the reality that attends his life, death, and resurrection is named the Kingdom of God."[a]

[a] C. Kavin Rowe, *World Upside Down: Reading Acts in the Graeco-Roman Age* (Oxford: Oxford University Press, 2009), 100.

More light is shed on the now-ness of the kingdom in Jesus' answer to the Pharisees about the timing of kingdom's arrival: "Once Jesus was asked by the Pharisees when the kingdom of God was coming, and he answered, 'The kingdom of God is not coming with things that can be observed; nor will they say, "Look, here it is!" or "There it is!" For, in fact, the kingdom of God is *among you*'" (Luke 17:20-21). The Greek ἐντὸς ὑμῶν is notoriously difficult to translate; it could be rendered as "in your midst" (CSB, NASB, NIV), "within you" (KJV) "among you" (CEB, NLT, NRSV), or "within your grasp" (NTE). Such ambiguity could be used to think of the kingdom as an interior, spiritual reality residing within a person, hence the Vulgate's rendering of *regnum Dei intra vos est*, "the Kingdom of God is inside of you." While this view was very popular among the church fathers, God's kingdom is not a psychological or spiritual event, for "Jesus speaks of men entering the kingdom, not of the kingdom entering men."[3] Plus, if you read the context, it is unlikely that Jesus is saying that the kingdom resides within the Pharisees, given their opposition to him.[4]

The point is perhaps not the kingdom's interior location but its present manifestation. The Pharisees want to know, "When is the kingdom coming?" Jesus responds in effect with, "What do you think is in front of you?" The kingdom is here, powerful and palpable. True, the Son of Man and his judgment are yet to come, but in the here and now the kingdom's sphere of operation is already active and available in part. In other words, the constellation of hopes grouped under the moniker "kingdom of God"—a new exodus, rescue of Israel, the drama of deliverance—has begun . . . in Jesus.

---

[3] I. Howard Marshall, *The Gospel of Luke: A Commentary on the Greek Text*, NIGTC (Grand Rapids, MI: Eerdmans, 1978), 655. See Tom Holmén, "The Alternatives of the Kingdom: Encountering the Semantic Restrictions of Luke 17,20-21 (ἐντὸς ὑμῶν)," *Zeitschrift für die neutestamentliche Wissenschaft und die Kunde der älteren Kirche* 87 (1996): 223.
[4] David E. Garland, *Luke*, ZECNT (Grand Rapids, MI: Zondervan, 2011), 697.

It is the kingdom in and through Jesus that is precisely Luke's point. Despite the old liberal Protestant mantra that Jesus proclaimed the kingdom and the church proclaimed Jesus, Jesus' preaching in Luke's Gospel has an implicit self-reference.[5] To be sure, the kingdom of God is God's kingdom, and it is theocentric to the max, but it is also happening in and through Jesus, his exorcisms, healings, mighty deeds, defeat of Satan, and even his death. Hence his words, "But if it is by the finger of God that *I* cast out the demons, then the kingdom of God has come to you" (Luke 11:20). It is Jesus' ministry that enacts the new exodus that Isaiah spoke about (Luke 4:18-21; 7:22-23). Jesus is the strong man who plunders and ransacks the demonic kingdom and establishes his own (Luke 11:18-22). Jesus is also the Son of Man around whom the disciples will gather as the leaders over a restored Israelite monarchy, which the Father will confer on Jesus (Luke 22:28-30). Those who witness Jesus' deeds and hear his words are "blessed" because they see what many prophets and kings of Israel's sacred history longed for but did not experience, namely, the fulfillment of God's promises to reveal his kingly power precisely in Jesus (Luke 10:23-24).

It is one's response to Jesus that determines entrance to the kingdom (Luke 10:16; 11:23). When it comes to the kingdom, Jesus is no mere messianic messenger; rather, he is at the center of it, as its chief agent. In fact, Jesus is the messianic King of God's coming kingdom, precisely why the gospel of Jesus can be summed up as preaching the kingdom of God (Acts 8:12; 19:8; 20:25). The early church correlates Jesus and the kingdom, yielding "the kingdom of God and the name of Jesus" (Acts 8:12; see also Acts 28:31). God's kingdom entails the reign of Jesus. In fact, it is quite important that Acts is bracketed by references to the kingdom

---

[5]See Wright, *Jesus and the Victory of God*, 222.

(Acts 1:3, 6; 28:23, 31). This shows that God's saving plan is continuing in the risen and enthroned Jesus, the giving of the Spirit, and the mission of his people.[6]

Luke, then, sees the kingdom of God as God's power and place, a future age to be entered into, something still awaited, but already powerfully present in the person of Jesus, the liberating and renewing work of the Spirit, and the church's embodiment of Jesus' message.

LUKE–ACTS AS JEWISH RESTORATION ESCHATOLOGY

Luke's eschatology is storied, specifically telling the story of the prophetic promises fulfilled in Jesus, being fulfilled by the church, and to be completed at Jesus' return. Luke's eschatology is not Stoic, Platonic, Gnostic, Hegelian, or Marxist. Luke's story of God's kingship and King Jesus is a species of Jewish restoration eschatology.[7]

In Luke–Acts, Jesus is the prophetic and messianic agent of Israel's long-awaited restoration. This restoration had many variations and several different renditions, but it normally encompassed a constellation of hopes including the regathering of the twelve tribes of Israel, the defeat of pagan powers, the satanic rebellion conquered, the rebuilding of the temple, the arrival of a new Davidic king, the renewal of the covenant, agricultural fecundity, priestly instruction in the Torah over all the land, Gentiles flocking to Zion with gifts and offerings (some even becoming proselytes),

---

[6]Alan J. Thompson, *The Acts of the Risen Lord Jesus: Luke's Account of God's Unfolding Plan*, New Studies in Biblical Theology 27 (Downers Grove, IL: InterVarsity Press, 2011), 47-48.
[7]On which see N. T. Wright, *The New Testament and the People of God*, COQG 1 (London: SPCK, 1992), 373-84; Richard Bauckham, "The Restoration of Israel in Luke–Acts," in *Restoration: Old Testament, Jewish and Christian Perspectives*, ed. James M. Scott, Journal for the Study of Judaism Supplement Series 72 (Leiden: Brill, 2001), 435-87; Michael E. Fuller, *The Restoration of Israel: Israel's Re-gathering and the Fate of the Nations in Early Jewish Literature and Luke–Acts*, BZNW 138 (Berlin: de Gruyter, 2006); Thompson, *Acts of the Risen Lord Jesus*, 103-24; and esp. Isaac W. Oliver, *Luke's Jewish Eschatology: The National Restoration of Israel in Luke–Acts* (Cambridge: Cambridge University Press, 2021).

and God's reign over God's people in God's Holy City. This was a hope that could be abbreviated as "the kingdom of God."[8] The apostolic churches believed that Jesus had partly fulfilled this restoration in his life, death, resurrection, and exaltation. The church's most fundamental task was to tell the people of Judea the good news that Israel's restoration was now underway, that these faithful Judeans and Galileans were already experiencing the incipient blessings that it brought, chiefly in the forgiveness of sins and reception of the Holy Spirit. What is more, as the Holy Spirit moved in their midst, it was becoming evident that God was now in the business of cleansing Gentile hearts by allegiance toward Israel's God through Jesus.

The Magnificat and Benedictus touch on the themes of divine strength, Israel's redemption and rescue from enemies, covenant mercy, forgiveness, a reversal between the poor and rich, fecundity and food, a Davidic deliverer, the establishment of an age of holiness, righteousness and peace, and patriarchal promises fulfilled (Luke 1:46-55, 67-79). The righteous Simeon is waiting for the "consolation of Israel" and sees in the infant Jesus the long-promised salvation and "a light for revelation to the Gentiles and for glory to your people Israel" (Luke 2:25, 32). Similarly, the prophetess Anna sees in the child Jesus hope for those "looking for the redemption of Jerusalem" (Luke 2:38). These Lukan songs, rooted in the memory and piety of the Judean and Galilean churches, are as clear a summary of Jewish hopes as one could imagine, suffused as they are with prophetic language and psalmic longing.

---

[8]See further Emil Schürer, *The History of the Jewish People in the Age of Jesus Christ*, rev. and ed. G. Vermes, F. Millar, and M. Black (Edinburgh: T&T Clark, 1973–1986), 2:514-47; E. P. Sanders, *Judaism: Practice and Belief 63 BCE–66 CE* (London: SCM Press, 1992), 289-98; Wright, *New Testament and the People of God*, 299-338; James D. G. Dunn, *Jesus Remembered*, CITM 1 (Grand Rapids, MI: Eerdmans, 2003), 393-96; Richard Horsley, *The Prophet Jesus and the Renewal of Israel: Moving Beyond a Diversionary Debate* (Grand Rapids, MI: Eerdmans, 2012).

Jesus' ministry explicitly enacts the Isaianic script for Israel's restoration. This Isaianic prophetic agenda is evidenced by the Nazareth Manifesto, where Jesus declares that he is the Spirit-bearing prophet sent to preach good news to the poor, captive, blind, and lame (Luke 4:16-30 = Isaiah 52:7; 61:1-2). The Isaianic mission is exemplified by Jesus' reply to John the Baptist's question whether he is the Messiah, that the results speak for themselves, that is, the blind receive their sight, the lame walk, the lepers are cleansed, the deaf hear, the dead are raised, and the poor have good news brought to them (Luke 7:18-23 = Isaiah 35:5-6; 26:19; 29:18-19; 61:1). In fact, I could not think of a clearer way that the Lukan Jesus could declare, "I am the Anointed One who will usher in a new exodus just like Isaiah said" unless he walked around Israel with a flashing neon sign on his head saying, "I am the Anointed One who will usher in a new exodus just like Isaiah said."

Furthermore, Jesus chooses twelve disciples to be his apostles, not because a dozen disciples is a pretty good number of men to use for starting a new religion or setting up the politburo of the Palestinian Liberation Front. No, Jesus chooses twelve disciples because they are to symbolize that Israel's reconstitution is now happening, even if unexpectedly and with opposition (Luke 6:12-16). They are gathered from within Israel to be the "nucleus of a restored Israel."[9] In the end, the disciples will sit on twelve thrones judging, that is, rescuing, Israel (Luke 22:29-30). It is reiterated in parables and prophetic warnings that Israel's God *is* king and is unveiling his kingly power in the mighty deeds, healings, and exorcisms performed by Jesus (Luke 11:20).

But God's kingship brings conflict, against those against Israel and against those who oppose God's "son" sent to Israel, as per the

---

[9]Andrew C. Clark, "The Role of the Apostles," in *Witness to the Gospel: The Theology of Acts*, ed. I. Howard Marshall and David Peterson (Grand Rapids, MI: Eerdmans, 1998), 173.

parable of the wicked tenants (Luke 20:9-19). Thus, a reckoning is coming to Israel, which will need to respond with repentance (Luke 5:32; 10:13; 11:32; 13:1-5; 15:7-10; 16:30) and perseverance (Luke 8:15; 18:1; 21:19), or else the axe of judgment will fall on them, too, even on Jerusalem (Luke 10:14; 11:31-32; 13:28; 19:41-44; 21:20-24). But even then, the judgment that afflicts the people and the city of Jerusalem, coming as a direct result of Jerusalem again rejecting the divinely sent prophet (Luke 13:33-34), is an expression of Israel's covenant with God, not a rejection of it. The covenant promised blessings for obedience and judgment for disobedience (Deuteronomy 30). Thus, "the days of vengeance" (Luke 21:22) testify to Israel's discipline within the covenant, not their dismissal from the covenant.[10]

Jesus was undoubtedly perceived by his followers as a messianic agent (Luke 9:20) and one who would establish a reconstituted Judean kingdom (Luke 17:11, 21; 22:24-27). The triumphal episode in Jesus' career in some minds was supposed to be Roman legions humiliated on the battlefield, followed by bawdy banquets in the Herodian fortress in celebration, then doling out power and perks to his loyal supporters. Yet what happened was that their leader was betrayed by one of their own, disowned by his right-hand man, condemned by the high priests as a false prophet and royal usurper, mocked by Herod as an overrated disappointment, derided by the Roman prefect as lunatic, then nailed to a Roman cross, and abandoned by his disciples in his hour of need.

The despair, dejection, and disillusionment of Jesus' wider circle of followers is epitomized by the two travelers on the road to Emmaus, who are lamenting Jesus' execution—ironically to the risen Jesus—because "we had hoped that he was the one to redeem

---

[10]Willie Jennings, *Acts: A Theological Commentary on the Bible*, Belief (Louisville, KY: Westminster John Knox, 2017), 72.

Israel" (Luke 24:21). Their gloom is entirely explicable; a dead Messiah meant that Israel still languished in its own political and spiritual death. To quote the 1982 Moving Pictures song "What About Me?": it all felt like "Nobody's changed, nobody's been saved." Satan, Emperor Tiberius, and the villains could clink mugs after dispatching another annoying religious enthusiast who filled the masses with empty dreams of a reversal of power. The rich would get richer, the poor would get poorer, Israel would choke with Rome's sandal on its throat, the wicked would prosper, sin would burden the consciences of the pious, and scriptural hopes for the day of the Lord would seem still an eternity away.

The two travelers to Emmaus cannot be faulted for their melancholy. The antidote to it, Luke points out with comical verve, is a messianic revelation and scriptural illumination: the risen Jesus teaching how his death and resurrection were part of the prophetic story all along. The purpose and plan of God was about how it was "necessary that the Messiah should suffer these things and then enter into his glory." And then, "beginning with Moses and all the prophets, he interpreted to them the things about himself in all the scriptures" (Luke 24:26-27). Even these disciples needed their minds "opened" to "understand the scriptures" that "the Messiah is to suffer and to rise from the dead on the third day" (Luke 24:45-46). Jesus was not ambushed by the plot to destroy him; it was part of the plan that the Messiah had to go to Jerusalem, die on the cross, and then be raised to life (Luke 9:22, 43-44; 18:31-33). For, as Jesus taught at his Passover with his disciples, Jesus' body was to be broken and given over to death, his blood poured out as an offering, to secure the forgiveness of sins for Israel and to inaugurate the new covenant for Israel (Luke 22:19-20).

The debris of failed expectations was then transformed by meeting the risen Jesus, so much so that later the disciples could ask the risen Jesus, "Lord, is this the time when you will restore the kingdom to Israel?" (Acts 1:6). Resurrection faith did not entail abandoning hopes for Israel's redemption. Quite the opposite—it intensified them. The Messiah's resurrection meant, some way and somehow, Israel's own restoration and resurrection. Israel's tribal constitution and political restoration could be conceived of as a metaphorical resurrection (Hosea 6:1-3; Isaiah 26:16-19; Ezekiel 37) or include a literal one as its climax (Daniel 12:1-2; Psalms of Solomon 3.11-12). The Messiah's resurrection is the precise validation of those prophetic hopes (Acts 13:32-33). It is why Paul, when testifying before the Sanhedrin, says that it is the central matter of contention and an event bound up with the restoration of the twelve tribes of Israel: "I stand here on trial on account of my hope in the promise made by God to our ancestors, a promise that our twelve tribes hope to attain" (Acts 26:6-7). Jesus' resurrection was not a standalone event, a staccato supernatural stage show; rather, it was part of God's purpose and plan that was bound up with Israel's rescue. According to Isaac Oliver, "In Luke's estimation, to uphold the resurrection of the messiah is to sustain the hope in the resurrection of the dead, which remains indissolubly linked with Israel's eschatological destiny."[11] The Messiah's resurrection implied that Israel's eschatological restoration had been birthed and that the resurrection of the righteous was still to come.

The restoration hopes are certainly for Israel yet go beyond Israel. The Lukan Peter's speech in Solomon's portico to the Jerusalemites puts Israel's restoration at the front and center of who Jesus is and what his exaltation means for them: "Repent therefore, and turn to God so that your sins may be wiped out, so that *times of refreshing*

---

[11]Oliver, *Luke's Jewish Eschatology*, 128. See also Thompson, *Acts of the Risen Lord Jesus*, 77-101; Brandon D. Crowe, *The Hope of Israel: The Resurrection of Christ in the Acts of the Apostles* (Grand Rapids, MI: Baker, 2020).

may come from the presence of the Lord, and that he may send the Messiah appointed for you, that is, Jesus, who must remain in heaven until the time of *universal restoration* that God announced long ago through his holy prophets" (Acts 3:19-21). But there is more to it, since Israel's renewal always had as its sequel the redemption of the Gentiles (Isaiah 2:2-4; Zechariah 8:23; Amos 9:11-12; Micah 4:1-4). Accordingly, the Messiah's death would mean the forgiveness of sins and gift of the Spirit even for the nations (Luke 24:47). So Paul can say, to mixed assemblies of Jewish and Gentile Messiah-believers, that they are "the church of God that he obtained with the blood of his own Son" (Acts 20:28). This is why, at the Jerusalem Council, James cites Amos 9:11-12 (LXX) to justify the inclusion of Gentiles in the church without having to first become proselytes to Judaism. This text expresses the view that, after the restoration of the Davidic kingdom, the prophetic sequel is Gentiles called to be part of God's own people within or beside a renewed Israel (Acts 15:13-18).

Lukan eschatology is not a two-step phase that runs (1) Jesus, then (2) eternal life. Rather, Luke's eschatology is restoration eschatology, which means that the Messiah's resurrection and heavenly enthronement are proofs that God has made good his promises to their ancestors. Israel is on the cusp of experiencing its much-longed-for "times of refreshing," and a transformed Israel will transform the world so that Gentiles too can share in Israel's blessings.

THE DELAY OF THE PAROUSIA

Is Jesus really coming back? Albert Schweitzer famously said that all early Christian theology was trying to wrestle with the fact that Christ's parousia (i.e., his second coming) had failed to materialize in the imminent timeframe that many expected it to happen:

> The whole history of "Christianity" down to the present day, that is to say, the real inner history of it, is based on the "delay of the Parousia," i.e., the failure of the parousia to materialize, the abandonment of eschatology, and the progress and completion of the "de-eschatologizing" of religion. It should be noted that non-fulfilment of Matt. 10.23 is the first postponement of the parousia.[12]

Accordingly, one theory of Christian origins has been that the early church was watching and waiting for Christ's return, something that would supposedly happen within one generation (see Mark 9:1; 13:30; 1 Thessalonians 1:9-10; 1 Corinthians 7:26; Romans 13:12; 16:20; Revelation 22:7, 12, 20). But as it gradually became clear that Christ was not coming back any time soon, the church had to pivot and prepare itself for an indefinite interim period of waiting for history's end.[13] The church abandoned Jesus and Paul's apocalyptic fervor to become the "one, holy, catholic church," and in that task Luke was a key facilitator.

Given that scenario, some argue that Luke–Acts, just like 2 Peter 3, deals with the problem of the inexplicable delay of the parousia to materialize in the time frame that Jesus and the apostles intimated in their urging that the end of the world was nigh. If so, then Luke, himself living and thinking inside this trajectory of end-times enthusiasm being diminished by the realities of the nonoccurrence of the Christ's return, was attempting to recalibrate the church's hopes and reset the church's mission to cope with this indefinite delay. There are subtle indications of this in Luke–Acts.

For instance, the Lukan Jesus tells two parables about slaves awaiting their master's arrival after some delay, with the point keenly made that the slaves have a duty to remain alert, watchful,

---

[12] Albert Schweitzer, *The Quest of the Historical Jesus*, 6th ed. (London: SCM Press, 2000), 328.
[13] For an excellent reflection on this problem, see Christopher M. Hays, ed., *When the Son of Man Didn't Come: A Constructive Proposal on the Delay of the Parousia* (Minneapolis: Fortress, 2016).

and faithful until the master returns (Luke 12:35-58). Luke provides other teachings about perseverance precisely because there is going to be a considerable delay in Jesus' return (Luke 8:15; 18:1-8; 21:19; Acts 14:22). Then, later, when Jesus is drawing "near Jerusalem, and because they [i.e., the disciples] supposed that the kingdom of God was to appear immediately" (Luke 19:11), he tells them a parable about a nobleman who went away to receive a kingdom, and there was some delay in his return (Luke 19:11-27). In other words, the parable is designed to specifically mute their enthusiasm for the kingdom's sudden appearance.

Another interesting feature of Luke–Acts is that history is divided up into the epoch of Israel climaxing in John the Baptist (Luke 16:16); the time of messianic fulfillment (Luke 4:16-21; Acts 10:38); the "times of the Gentiles," which makes room for a Gentile church (Luke 21:24); and the arrival of the kingdom in its fullness (Luke 22:16, 28-30; Acts 1:9-11). The giving of Holy Spirit, then, would be for Luke not a deposit guaranteeing a soonish end (2 Corinthians 1:22; 5:5; Ephesians 1:13; 4:30), but merely divine empowerment for proclamation and perseverance until the end. A corollary of hanging around, as it were, was that the church also had to reach a settlement with the Roman Empire, a political rapprochement with Roman authorities, which allegedly explains Luke's pro-Roman ethos. To that one might add that you do not exactly write the history of the early church if you're expecting the world to end tomorrow.[14]

Hans Conzelmann famously promoted the view that "Luke is confronted by the situation in which the Church finds herself by the delay of the Parousia and her existence in secular history, and he tries to come to terms with the situation by his account of

---

[14]Ernst Käsemann, "The Problem of the Historical Jesus," in *Essays on New Testament Themes* (Naperville, IL: Allenson, 1964), 28.

historical events." That coming to terms for Conzelmann principally meant the church had to understand its place in "salvation history," finding itself in the period of the "authentic manifestation of salvation" based on looking back to Jesus and forward to the future.[15] In other words, the reality of salvation is no longer dependent on the imminence of the kingdom of God to appear with Christ's return.

More recently, Paula Fredriksen asserts, "Luke . . . consistently tamps down and reshapes the vibrant apocalyptic tradition that originally shaped what he had inherited. His Jesus, in stark contrast to Mark's, teaches *against* the idea of an impending kingdom . . . [e.g., Luke 19:11]. No need to wait for the Endtime, teaches Luke's Jesus: the Kingdom is already arrived, available as a present reality."[16] The first generation of Christ-believers thought that they were the world's last generation, with the sense of imminence in Christ's returned carried forward by Jesus' fateful death, his resurrection appearances, the emperor Caligula's near-calamitous effort to paganize the Jerusalem temple (AD 39–40), and the sacking of Jerusalem and the destruction of the temple (AD 70). To all that, Fredriksen says, "Luke's calm narrative smooths out these lived peaks of livid expectation, the valleys of disorienting cognitive dissonance, and the various solutions offered by creative reaffirmations. Luke betrays little of these processes. He speaks, instead, of the founding of the Christian church."[17]

Therefore, much scholarship has argued that Luke was a theologian of eschatological crisis management in that he was dealing with the delay of Christ's return by (1) postponing its occurrence to an indeterminable projected future, (2) calling for perseverance in

---

[15] Hans Conzelmann, *The Theology of Saint Luke* (London: Faber & Faber, 1961), 14.
[16] Paula Fredriksen, *When Christians Were Jews: The First Generation* (New Haven, CT: Yale University Press, 2018), 93, emphasis original.
[17] Fredriksen, *When Christians Were Jews*, 184.

the interim, (3) periodizing history into Israel–Jesus–Gentiles, and (4) urging Christians to come to a polite political arrangement with their Roman masters. This is a neat and tidy approach to Lukan eschatology, which resonates with several aspects of Luke–Acts if placed in a certain arrangement, yet it is by no means so certain.

Luke was not anxious about Jesus' absence. I am not alone in suggesting that the alleged delay of the parousia, as a massive factor driving Luke's theology, is somewhat overstated.

First, the problem of delay was not unique to Luke and the early church, as it was inherited from Jewish tradition.[18] The heartfelt cry "How long, O LORD" is a regular part of the Psalter's experience of feeling abandoned by God or exhorting God to finally act (Psalm 6:3; 13:1; 35:17; 79:5; 80:4; 89:46; 90:13; 94:3). Habakkuk is singularly dedicated to the theme of understanding the delay of God's saving action, while Isaiah 40–55 is also concerned with promising an audience that God has not forgotten them and the royal rescue shall make an appearance in due course. Also, Jewish tradition witnesses to the elastic nature of prophetic materials whereby they can be reinterpreted and reapplied. Jeremiah's seventy years of exile in Babylon (Jeremiah 25) is taken up by Daniel and transformed into seventy weeks of years (Daniel 9). The Qumran commentary on the book of Habakkuk (1QpHab) is a classic case of a sectarian group finding in Scripture both solace to sustain themselves in the present and certainty for their own apocalyptic expectations about the future. Luke imbibes this tradition of dealing with the delay of salvation and the creative reinterpretation of prophecy to address the needs of the community in the present.

Second, the intensity of expectation for an imminent return of Christ appears to consistently ebb and flow over the centuries

---

[18]See Richard Bauckham, "The Delay of the Parousia," *TynBul* 31 (1980): 3-36.

among Christian authors. If Mark's Olivet discourse excited hopes for Christ's return (Mark 13), it might be true that Luke softens the edge of expectation (Luke 21), even as Matthew pours the oil of apocalyptic fervor onto the fire of prophetic promises (Matthew 24–25).[19] In the Didache, which is a probably Syrian manual on discipleship written toward the end of the first century, the exhortation oscillates between vivid anticipation of Christ's return and a realism that much is still to take place first (Didache 10.6; 16.1, 7-8). In contrast to Matthew, the Didachist does not seem to think he is living in the last days.[20] John the Seer, who celebrates Christ's prior victory, who exhorts churches in his present to fidelity, who notes the complaint of the martyrs in heaven, and who hears the Spirit say that Jesus' return is soon, "maintains the typical apocalyptic tension of imminence and delay, now sharpened and characterized in a peculiarly Christian manner."[21]

Turning to the mid-second century, Justin Martyr coined the term "second coming" but is neither paralyzed with expectation nor disenfranchised with disappointment. The Epistula Apostolorum, the apocryphal epistle from the apostles, seems to expect, depending on manuscript variants, Christ to return around AD 150–180 (Epistula Apostolorum 17). Then, at the very end of the second century, the author of 2 Peter is wrestling with the non-occurrence of Christ's return as an apologetic response to scoffers. Not long after, Hippolytus of Rome was writing what we would call the first Left Behind novel with his *Treatise on Christ and Antichrist*, imagining who the antichrist would be and warning that his reign of terror over the empire and the church could be imminent. In other words, there's no single linear phenomenon of

---

[19]See Victoria Balabanski, *Eschatology in the Making: Mark, Matthew and the Didache*, SNTSMS 97 (Cambridge: Cambridge University Press, 1997).
[20]Balabanski, *Eschatology in the Making*, 208.
[21]Bauckham, "Delay of the Parousia," 36.

apocalyptic hopes either gradually being abandoned or being stoked up with millenarian fantasy. We detect both trends over the course of Christian thought in the first three centuries.

Luke shares in this ambiguity of anticipation whereby Jesus' return will occur suddenly—after an indeterminate period of waiting.[22] The proof of this is that Luke deploys the notion of delay in seemingly paradoxical ways. In the parable of the unfaithful slave, the master is delayed in returning (Luke 12:45), while in the parable of the widow and the unjust judge we are told that God will not delay the deliverance of his justice (Luke 18:6-8). Luke's aim is to modulate rather than mute eschatological expectations. To that end, notions of delay simultaneously qualify hopes about the future as they intensify expectations about the consummation of the kingdom precisely because delay creates anticipation. Viewed this way, the Lukan notion of delay undergirds rather than stymies his expectation of the end.[23]

Evidently, then, Luke is not a millenarian in the sense of telling people to pack their things and follow him up a mountain to wait the end of the world; but Luke still believes that "the final events of history have already begun and, although the timing of the final culmination remains unknown, as end-time events continue to unfold it should be constantly anticipated," says Kylie Crabbe.[24] To put it into Luke's own language, the church must constantly ask, "When will this be, and what will be the sign that this is about to take place?" (Luke 21:7) and "Is this the time when you will restore the kingdom to Israel?" (Acts 1:6), knowing that "God [will] grant justice to his chosen ones who cry to him day and night" (Luke 18:7)

---

[22]See Stephen G. Wilson, *The Gentiles and the Gentile Mission in Luke–Acts*, SNTSMS 23 (Cambridge: Cambridge University Press, 1973), 67-77, 80.
[23]John T. Carroll, *Response to the End of History: Eschatology and Situation in Luke–Acts*, SNTSMS 92 (Atlanta: Scholars Press, 1988), 166.
[24]Kylie Crabbe, *Luke/Acts and the End of History*, BZNW 238 (Berlin: de Gruyter, 2019), 333.

on the proviso that God has "fixed a day on which he will have the world judged in righteousness by a man whom he has appointed, and of this he has given assurance to all by raising him from the dead" (Acts 17:31).

Third, Luke's eschatological concerns are not reductionistically tied to the parousia's occurrence or postponement but belong to a wider suite of expectations and exhortations. Luke's emphasis is not an eschatological explanation of a deferred end but on the eschatological momentum in the church's participation in the *missio Dei*. Because the eschatological reality of salvation is partially present, the length of the interval until the consummation is of no real significance. The whole of Lukan eschatology is set within the context of a two-stage manifestation of the kingdom of God, present and future, now and not yet.[25] As such, James Dunn correctly observes,

> What mattered was not the dates and times which remained in the hands of the Father, but that the good news of Jesus' death and resurrection must be attested to the end of the earth by those empowered by the Spirit (Acts 1.6-8). What mattered was not looking for the kingdom as something observable, but living out the kingdom (Luke 17.20-21) and being committed to God's rule (9.62), whatever persecution such commitment would entail (Acts 14.22).[26]

Fourth, Christ's parousia does not disappear from Acts but sets the scene for the church's beginning (Acts 1:9-11) and thereafter is subsumed under an overarching concept of Christ's work as something remembered, still operative, and anticipated.[27] Luke has not abandoned the notion that Jesus will return in judgment (Acts 10:42;

---

[25]E. Earle Ellis, *Christ and the Future in the New Testament* (Leiden: Brill, 2000), 117-19.

[26]James D. G. Dunn, *Neither Jew nor Greek: A Contested Identity*, CITM 3 (Grand Rapids, MI: Eerdmans, 2015), 295.

[27]On which see Young Ho Kim, *Die Parusie bei Lukas: Eine literarisch-exegetisch Untersuchung zu den Parusieaussagen im lukanischen Doppelwork*, BZNW 217 (Berlin: de Gruyter, 2016).

17:30-31), but his interests center on the correct identification of Jesus as the messianic Lord of Israel's prophetic promises and on the continuing acts of the risen Jesus, through the Spirit, whom he sends on his church. The real important matter for Luke is not "When is Jesus returning?" but "Who is Jesus?" and "What is Jesus doing?"[28]

What readers should take away is that Luke–Acts is not an exercise in cognitive dissonance for a failed religious cult, as if Luke were trying to readjust expectations in light of failed prophecies. To the contrary, Luke is magnifying the tension between the anticipation of Christ's parousia as the future and final installment of the kingdom of God, on the one hand, and making sober exhortations toward perseverance under duress and participation in mission, on the other hand.

LUKE AND THE FUTURE OF GOD'S PEOPLE

Besides Luke and genre, it is the issue of Luke and eschatology that has given scholars the most grist for their mill. The idea that Luke was engaged in a concerted process of deeschatologizing early Christianity of its apocalyptic ardor should be dismissed. Luke wants Theophilus, and those after him, to be assured that Jesus is the Davidic king of God's kingdom and that the kingdom has proleptically arrived in the person of Jesus, the giving of the Spirit, and the advancement of salvation until the appointed day of judgment. For God's people, the interim is not a time for spiritualized inertia but instead is meant to be filled with the evangelistic urgency of Paul in the synagogues of Asia Minor and in the Athenian Areopagus. This time should be taken with exercises of compassion like those of Jesus and Peter among widows. The church should be readied to speak gospel truth to political powers like Paul before Sergius Paulus and Herod Agrippa II. The church must make itself

---

[28]See Thompson, *Acts of the Risen Lord Jesus*, esp. 43, 49, 67.

busy nourishing disciples in the ministries of prayer, word, and sacrament as the Jerusalem church did. However long history shall tarry, disciples must persevere and be found faithful when their master arrives.

Luke knows that history has an end, and so Christians are called, in their labor and leisure, through the struggles and seasons of life, in their hearts and hopes, to live under the lordship of Christ Jesus until then, confident that their Lord has not forgotten them. Crabbe has a good take on Luke's perspective on the last things: "In Luke/Acts life is lived conscious of the present time within the final period of history, and with confidence that the remaining end-time events are still unfolding—indeed, the resurrection of Jesus proves that divine action to this *telos* [end] is already underway."[29] Luke's eschatology is not a theory of history but rather a proclamation that history finds its meaning and resolution in God's purposes, which climax in Jesus' life, death, resurrection, ascension, and return.

REVIEW QUESTIONS

1. How would Luke define the kingdom of God?
2. In what ways does Luke reflect Jewish restoration eschatology in his own eschatological scheme?
3. To what extent is Luke–Acts a response to the delay of the parousia?
4. What does Luke believe is the future for God's people?

RECOMMENDED READING

Bock, Darrell L. *A Theology of Luke and Acts: God's Promised Program, Realized for All Nations*. Grand Rapids, MI: Zondervan, 2012. Pages 389-405.

---

[29] Crabbe, *Luke/Acts and the End of History*, 335, emphasis original.

Carroll, John T. *Response to the End of History: Eschatology and Situation in Luke–Acts.* Society of Biblical Literature Dissertation Series 92. Atlanta: Scholars Press, 1988.

Crabbe, Kylie. *Luke/Acts and the End of History.* BZNW 238. Berlin: de Gruyter, 2019.

Fuller, Michael E. *The Restoration of Israel: Israel's Re-gathering and the Fate of the Nations in Early Jewish Literature and Luke–Acts.* BZNW 138. Berlin: de Gruyter, 2006.

Gaventa, B. R. "Eschatology of Luke–Acts Revisited." *Encounter* 43 (1982): 27-42.

Hahn, Scott W. "Kingdom and Church in Luke–Acts: From Davidic Christology to Kingdom Ecclesiology." In *Reading Luke: Interpretation, Reflection, Formation*, edited by Craig G. Bartholomew, Joel B. Green, and Anthony C. Thiselton, Scripture and Hermeneutics 6, 294-326. Grand Rapids, MI: Zondervan, 2005.

Oliver, Isaac W. *Luke's Jewish Eschatology: The National Restoration of Israel in Luke–Acts.* Cambridge: Cambridge University Press, 2021.

Wolter, Michael. "Israel's Future and the Delay of the Parousia, According to Luke." In *Jesus and the Heritage of Israel: Luke's Narrative Claim upon Israel's Legacy*, edited by David P. Moessner, 307-24. Harrisburg, PA: Trinity Press International, 1999.

Wright, N. T. "Hope Deferred? Against the Dogma of Delay." *Early Christianity* 9 (2018): 37-82.

Bibliography

Adams, Sean A. *The Genre of Acts and Collected Biography*. SNTSMS 156. Cambridge: Cambridge University Press, 2014.

Agan, C. D. "Jimmy," III. "Why Study the Book of Luke?" Crossway, May 28, 2019. www.crossway.org/articles/why-study-the-book-of-luke/.

Ahn, Yong-Sung. *The Reign of God and Rome in Luke's Passion Narrative: An East Asian Global Perspective*. Leiden: Brill, 2006.

Alexander, Loveday C. *Acts in Its Ancient Literary Context*. London: T&T Clark, 2007.

———. "The Acts of the Apostles as an Apologetic Text." In *Apologetics in the Roman Empire*, 15-44. Oxford: Oxford University Press, 1999.

———. "Sisters in Adversity: Retelling Martha's Story." In *A Feminist Companion to Luke*, edited by Amy-Jill Levine, 197-213. Cleveland, OH: Pilgrim, 2001.

Andrade, Nathanael. *Tried by Pontius Pilate: Why Did Jesus Die?* Oxford: Oxford University Press, forthcoming.

Arlandson, James Malcolm. *Women, Class and Society in Early Christianity: Models from Luke–Acts*. Peabody, MA: Hendrickson, 1997.

Armstrong, Karl L. *Dating Acts in Its Jewish and Greco-Roman Contexts*. LNTS 637. London: T&T Clark, 2021.

———. "The End of Acts and the Jewish Response: Condemnation, Tragedy, or Hope?" *CurBR* 12 (2019): 209-30.

Atkinson, William P. *Baptism in the Spirit: Luke–Acts and the Dunn Debate*. Eugene, OR: Pickwick, 2011.

Balabanski, Victoria. *Eschatology in the Making: Mark, Matthew and the Didache*. SNTSMS 97. Cambridge: Cambridge University Press, 1997.

Barclay, John. *Paul: A Very Brief History*. London: SPCK, 2017.

Barnett, Paul. *Jesus and the Rise of Early Christianity*. Downers Grove, IL: InterVarsity Press, 1999.

Barrett, C. K. *Acts of the Apostles*. 2 vols. ICC. Edinburgh: T&T Clark, 1994–1998.

———. "The First New Testament?" *NovT* 38 (1996): 94-104.

———. "The Historicity of Acts." *JTS* 50 (1999): 515-34.

———. "Luke/Acts." In *It Is Written: Scripture Citing Scripture: Essays in Honor of Barnabas Lindars*, edited by D. A. Carson and H. G. M. Williamson, 231-44. Cambridge: Cambridge University Press, 1988.

———. *Luke the Historian in Recent Study*. London: Epworth, 1961.

Bates, Matthew. *Salvation by Allegiance Alone: Rethinking Faith, Works, and the Gospel of Jesus the King*. Grand Rapids, MI: Baker, 2017.

Bauckham, Richard. "'The Delay of the Parousia." *TynBul* 31 (1980): 3-36.

———. "James and the Gentiles (Acts 15.13-21)." In *History, Literature and Society in the Book of Acts*, edited by Benjamin Witherington, 154-84. Cambridge: Cambridge University Press, 1996.

———. *Jesus and the Eyewitnesses: The Gospels as Eyewitness Testimony*. Grand Rapids, MI: Eerdmans, 2006.

———. "The Restoration of Israel in Luke–Acts." In *Restoration: Old Testament, Jewish and Christian Perspectives*, edited by James M. Scott, Journal for the Study of Judaism Supplement Series 72, 435-87. Leiden: Brill, 2001.

Beale, G. K. *Handbook on the New Testament Use of the Old Testament: Exegesis and Interpretation*. Grand Rapids, MI: Baker, 2012.

Becker, Eve-Marie. *The Birth of Christian History: Memory and Time from Mark to Luke–Acts*. Anchor Yale Bible Reference Library. New Haven, CT: Yale University Press, 2017.

Beers, Holly. *The Followers of Jesus as the "Servant": Luke's Model from Isaiah from Disciples in Luke–Acts*. London: T&T Clark, 2015.

Bernier, Jonathan. *Rethinking the Dates of the New Testament: The Evidence for Early Composition*. Grand Rapids, MI: Baker, 2022.

Bird, Michael F. *An Anomalous Jew: Paul Among Jews, Greeks, and Romans*. Grand Rapids, MI: Eerdmans, 2018.

———. *Crossing Over Sea and Land: Jewish Missionary Activity in the Second Temple Period*. Peabody, MA: Hendrickson, 2010.

———. *Evangelical Theology*. 2nd ed. Grand Rapids, MI: Zondervan, 2018.

———. *The Gospel of the Lord: How the Early Church Wrote the Story of Jesus*. Grand Rapids, MI: Eerdmans, 2014.

———. *Jesus Among the Gods: Early Christology in the Greco-Roman World*. Waco, TX: Baylor University Press, 2022.

———. *Jesus Is the Christ: The Messianic Testimony of the Gospels*. Milton Keynes, UK: Paternoster, 2012.

———. *Jesus and the Origins of the Gentile Mission*. LNTS 331. Edinburgh: T&T Clark, 2006.

———. "'A Light to the Nations' (Isa. 49.6): Inter-textuality and Mission Theology in the Early Church." *Reformed Theological Review* 65 (2006): 122-31.

———. "Rome, Roman Empire." In *The Baker Illustrated Bible Dictionary*, edited by Tremper Longman III, Peter Enns, and Mark Strauss, 1446-51. Grand Rapids, MI: Baker, 2013.

———. "The Unity of Luke–Acts in Recent Discussion." In *Rethinking the Unity and Reception of Luke–Acts*, edited by Andrew F. Gregory and C. Kavin Rowe, 3-22. Columbia: University of South Carolina Press, 2010.

Bird, Michael F., and Ben Sutton. "Social Memory in Acts." In *Jesus, Skepticism, and the Problem of History: Criteria and Context in the Study of Christian Origins*, edited by Ed Komoszewski and D. Bock, 305-19. Grand Rapids, MI: Zondervan, 2019.

Bird, Michael F., and N. T. Wright. *The New Testament in Its World*. Grand Rapids, MI: Zondervan, 2019.

Bock, Darrell L. "Jesus as Lord in Acts and in the Gospel Message." *Bibliotheca Sacra* 143 (1986): 146-54.

———. *Luke*. 2 vols. Baker Exegetical Commentary on the New Testament. Grand Rapids, MI: Baker, 1994–1996.

———. *Recovering the Real Lost Gospel of Jesus*. Nashville: B&H, 2010.

———. "Scripture and the Realisation of God's Promises." In *Witness to the Gospel: The Theology of Acts*, edited by I. Howard Marshall and David Peterson, 41-62. Grand Rapids, MI: Eerdmans, 1998.

———. *A Theology of Luke and Acts: God's Promised Program, Realized for All Nations*. Grand Rapids, MI: Zondervan, 2012.

Bockmuehl, Markus. *Simon Peter in Scripture and Memory*. Grand Rapids, MI: Baker, 2012.

———. *This Jesus: Martyr, Lord, Messiah*. Edinburgh: T&T Clark, 1994.

Boesenberg, Dulcinea. "Negotiating Identity: The Jewishness of the Way in Acts." In *Religion and Identity*, edited by R. A. Simkins and T. M. Kelly, 58-75. Omaha: Kripke Center, 2016.

Bovon, François. *Luke 1: A Commentary on the Gospel of Luke 1:1–9:50*. Minneapolis: Fortress, 2002.

Brindle, Wayne A. "The Census and Quirinius: Luke 2:2." *JETS* 27 (1984): 43–52.

Brink, Laurie. *Soldiers in Luke–Acts: Engaging, Contradicting, and Transcending the Stereotypes*. WUNT 2/362. Tübingen: Mohr Siebeck, 2014.

Bruce, F. F. *The Acts of the Apostles: The Greek Text with Introduction and Commentary*. Grand Rapids, MI: Eerdmans, 1951.

———. *The Book of Acts*. New International Commentary on the New Testament. Grand Rapids, MI: Eerdmans, 1988.

Bultmann, Rudolf. *Theology of the New Testament*. Translated by K. Grobel. 2 vols. London: SCM Press, 1952–1955.

Byrne, Brendan. "Jesus as Messiah in the Gospel of Luke: Discerning a Pattern of Correction." *CBQ* 65 (2003): 80-95.

Byrskog, Samuel. *Story as History, History as Story: The Gospel Tradition in the Context of Ancient Oral History*. Leiden: Brill, 2002.

Cadbury, Henry J. *The Formation of Luke–Acts*. London: Macmillan, 1927.

———. *The Style and Literary Method of Luke*. Cambridge, MA: Harvard University Press, 1920.

Cagnat, René, et al., eds. *Inscriptiones graecae ad res romanas pertinentes*. Vol. 3. Paris: Leroux, 1906–1927.

Capper, Brian J. "Jesus, Virtuoso Religion, and the Community of Goods." In *Engaging Economics: New Testament Scenarios and Early Christian Reception*, edited by Bruce W. Longenecker and Kelly D. Liebengood, 60-79. Grand Rapids, MI: Eerdmans, 2009.

Carroll, John T. "The Gospel of Luke: A Contemporary Cartography." *Int* 68 (2014): 366-75.

———. *Response to the End of History: Eschatology and Situation in Luke–Acts*. Society of Biblical Literature Dissertation Series 92. Atlanta: Scholars Press, 1988.

Carter, Warren. "Getting Martha Out of the Kitchen: Luke 10.38-42 Again." In *A Feminist Companion to Luke*, edited by Amy-Jill Levine, 214-31. Cleveland, OH: Pilgrim, 2001.

Chen, Diane G. *Luke*. NCCS. Eugene, OR: Cascade, 2017.

Cho, Youngmo. *Spirit and Kingdom in the Writings of Luke and Paul: An Attempt to Reconcile These Concepts*. Milton Keynes, UK: Paternoster, 2005.

Cho, Youngmo, and Hyung Dae Park. *Acts*. 2 vols. NCCS. Eugene, OR: Cascade, 2019.

Clark, Andrew C. "The Role of the Apostles." In *Witness to the Gospel: The Theology of Acts*, edited by I. Howard Marshall and David Peterson, 169-90. Grand Rapids, MI: Eerdmans, 1998.

Coleman, Rachel L. *The Lukan Lens on Wealth and Possessions: A Perspective Shaped by the Themes of Reversal and Right Response*. BIS 180. Leiden: Brill, 2020.

Conzelmann, Hans. *The Theology of Saint Luke*. Translated by G. Buswell. London: Faber and Faber, 1960.

Cort, John C. *Christian Socialism: An Informal History*. Maryknoll, NY: Orbis, 1988.

Cowan, J. A. *The Writings of Luke and the Jewish Roots of the Christian Way: An Examination of the Aims of the First Christian Historian in the Light of Ancient Politics, Ethnography, and Historiography*. LNTS 599. London: T&T Clark, 2019.

Crabbe, Kylie. *Luke/Acts and the End of History*. BZNW 238. Berlin: de Gruyter, 2019.

Crossan, John Dominic, and Jonathan L. Reed. *Excavating Jesus: Beneath the Stones, Behind the Texts*. New York: HarperCollins, 2009.

Crowe, Brandon D. *The Hope of Israel: The Resurrection of Christ in the Acts of the Apostles*. Grand Rapids, MI: Baker, 2020.

Dahl, Nils A. "The Story of Abraham in Luke–Acts." In *Studies in Luke–Acts*, edited by Leander E. Keck and J. L. Martyn, 139-58. London: SPCK, 1968.

Denova, Rebecca I. *The Things Accomplished Among Us: Prophetic Tradition in the Structural Pattern of Luke–Acts*. Sheffield: Sheffield Academic Press, 1997.

deSilva, David A. *An Introduction to the New Testament: Contexts, Methods and Ministry Formation*. Downers Grove, IL: InterVarsity Press, 2004.

Dibelius, Martin. *Studies in the Acts of the Apostles*. London: SCM Press, 1956.

Dittenberger, Wilhelm, ed. *Orientis graeci inscriptiones selectae*. Leipzig: Hirzel, 1903–1905.

———, ed. *Sylloge inscriptionum graecarum*. 3rd ed. Leipzig: Hirzel, 1915–1924.

Doble, Peter. "Luke 24.26, 44—Songs of God's Servant: David and His Psalms in Luke–Acts." *Journal for the Study of the New Testament* 28 (2006): 267–83.

———. "The Psalms in Luke–Acts." In *The Psalms in the New Testament*, edited by Stephen Moyise and Maarten J. J. Menken, 83-117. London: T&T Clark, 2004.

Donaldson, Terence. *Jews and Anti-Judaism in the New Testament: Decision Points and Divergent Interpretations*. Waco, TX: Baylor University Press, 2010.

Dunn, James D. G. *The Acts of the Apostles*. Grand Rapids, MI: Eerdmans, 2016.

———. *Baptism in the Spirit*. London: SCM Press, 1970.

———. *Beginning from Jerusalem*. CITM 2. Grand Rapids, MI: Eerdmans, 2009.

———. "The Book of Acts as Salvation History." In *Heil und Geschichte: Die Geschichtsbezogenheit des Heils und das Problem der Heilsgeschichte in der biblischen Tradition und in der theologischen Deutung*, edited by Jörg Frey, Stefan

Krauter, and Hermann Lichtenberger, WUNT 248, 385-401. Tübingen: Mohr Siebeck, 2009.

———. *Jesus Remembered*. CITM 1. Grand Rapids, MI: Eerdmans, 2003.

———. *Neither Jew nor Greek: A Contested Identity*. CITM 3. Grand Rapids, MI: Eerdmans, 2015.

Ellis, E. Earle. *Christ and the Future in the New Testament*. Leiden: Brill, 2000.

———. *The Gospel of Luke*. London: Thomas Nelson, 1966.

Esler, Philip F. *Community and Gospel in Luke–Acts: The Social and Political Motivations of Lucan Theology*. Cambridge: Cambridge University Press, 1989.

Evans, Craig A. "King Jesus and His Ambassadors: Empire in Luke–Acts." In *Empire in the New Testament*, edited by Stanley E. Porter and Cynthia Long Westfall, 130-39. Eugene, OR: Pickwick, 2011.

Evans, Craig A., and Donald A. Hagner, eds. *Anti-Semitism and Early Christianity: Issues of Polemic and Faith*. Minneapolis: Fortress, 1993.

Evans, Craig A., and James A. Sanders, eds. *Luke and Scripture: The Function of Sacred Tradition in Luke–Acts*. Eugene, OR: Wipf & Stock, 2001.

Fitzmyer, Joseph A. *The Acts of the Apostles*. Anchor Bible. New York: Doubleday, 1998.

———. "Discipleship in Lucan Writings." In *Luke the Theologian: Aspects of His Teaching*, 117-45. New York: Paulist, 1989.

Flemming, Dean. *Recovering the Full Mission of God: A Biblical Perspective on Being, Doing and Telling*. Downers Grove, IL: InterVarsity Press, 2013.

Forbes, Gregory W., and Scott D. Harrower. *Raised from Obscurity: A Narrative and Theological Study of the Characterization of Women in Luke–Acts*. Eugene, OR: Pickwick, 2015.

Fox, Robin Lane. *The Classical World: An Epic History from Homer to Hadrian*. New York: Basic, 2006.

Fredriksen, Paula. *When Christians Were Jews: The First Generation*. New Haven, CT: Yale University Press, 2018.

Fredriksen, Paula, and Adele Reinhartz, eds. *Jesus, Judaism and Christian Anti-Judaism: Reading the New Testament After the Holocaust*. Philadelphia: Westminster John Knox, 2002.

Fuller, Michael E. *The Restoration of Israel: Israel's Re-gathering and the Fate of the Nations in Early Jewish Literature and Luke–Acts*. BZNW 138. Berlin: de Gruyter, 2006.

Garland, David E. *Acts*. Teach the Text Commentary Series. Grand Rapids, MI: Baker, 2017.

———. *Luke*. ZECNT. Grand Rapids, MI: Zondervan, 2011.

Gasque, W. Ward. *Sir William M. Ramsay, Archaeologist and New Testament Scholar: A Survey of His Contribution to the Study of the New Testament*. Grand Rapids, MI: Baker, 1966.

Gaston, Lloyd. "Anti-Judaism and the Passion Narrative in Luke and Acts." In *Anti-Judaism in Early Christianity*, vol. 1, *Paul and the Gospels*, edited by Peter Richardson and David Granskou, Studies in Christianity and Judaism, 127-54. Waterloo, ONT: Wilfred Laurier University Press, 1986.

Gaventa, Beverly Roberts. *Acts*. Abingdon New Testament Commentaries. Nashville: Abingdon, 2003.

———. "Eschatology of Luke–Acts Revisited." *Encounter* 43 (1982): 27-42.

Gempf, Conrad H. "Public Speaking and Published Accounts." In *The Book of Acts in Its Literary Context*, edited by B. W. Winter and A. Clark, 259-303. Grand Rapids, MI: Eerdmans, 1993.

Goheen, Michael. *A Light to the Nations: The Missional Church and the Biblical Story*. Grand Rapids, MI: Baker, 2011.

González, Justo L. *The Story Luke Tells: Luke's Unique Witness to the Gospel*. Grand Rapids, MI: Eerdmans, 2015.

Grant, Jamie A. "Singing the Cover Versions: Psalms, Reinterpretation and Biblical Theology in Acts 3–4." *Scottish Bulletin of Evangelical Theology* 25 (2007): 27-49.

Green, Gene L. "Luke: Historian, Rhetor, and Theologian. Historiography and the Theology of the Speeches in Acts." In *New Testament Theology in Light of the Church's Mission*, edited by J. C. Laansma, G. Osborne, and R. van Neste, 161-80. Eugene, OR: Cascade, 2011.

Green, Joel B. *Conversion in Luke–Acts: Divine Action, Human Cognition, and the People of God*. Grand Rapids, MI: Baker, 2015.

———. *Discovering Luke: Content, Interpretation, Reception*. London: SPCK, 2021.

———. *The Theology of the Gospel of Luke*. NTT. Cambridge: Cambridge University Press, 1995.

Grindheim, Sigurd. *Christology in the Synoptic Gospels: God or God's Servant?* London: T&T Clark, 2012.

Gupta, Nijay K. *Paul and the Language of Faith*. Grand Rapids, MI: Eerdmans, 2020.

Haar, Stephen. *Simon Magus: The First Gnostic?* BZNW 119. Berlin: de Gruyter, 2003.

Haenchen, Ernst. "The Book of Acts as Source Material for the History of Early Christianity." In *Studies in Luke–Acts: Essays Presented in Honor of Paul Schubert*, edited by Leander E. Keck and J. Louis Martyn, 258-78. Nashville: Abingdon, 1968.

Hahn, Scott W. "Kingdom and Church in Luke–Acts: From Davidic Christology to Kingdom Ecclesiology." In *Reading Luke: Interpretation, Reflection, Formation*, edited by Craig G. Bartholomew, Joel B. Green, and Anthony C. Thiselton, Scripture and Hermeneutics 6, 294-326. Grand Rapids, MI: Zondervan, 2005.

Harnack, Adolf von. *Luke the Physician*. New York: Putnam, 1907.

Harris, Sarah. *The Davidic Shepherd King in the Lukan Narrative*. London: Bloomsbury T&T Clark, 2016.

Hays, Christopher M. *Luke's Wealth Ethics: A Study of Their Coherence and Character*. WUNT 2/275. Tübingen: Mohr Siebeck, 2010.

———, ed. *When the Son of Man Didn't Come: A Constructive Proposal on the Delay of the Parousia*. Minneapolis: Fortress, 2016.

Hays, Richard B. *Reading Backwards: Figural Christology and the Fourfold Gospel Witness*. Waco, TX: Baylor University Press, 2014.

Helyer, Larry R. *The Witness of Jesus, Paul, and John*. Downers Grove, IL: InterVarsity Press, 2008.

Hemer, Colin. *The Book of Acts in the Setting of Hellenistic History*. Tübingen: Mohr Siebeck, 1989.

Hengel, Martin. *Earliest Christianity*. Translated by John Bowden. London: SCM Press, 1986.

———. *The Four Gospels and the One Gospel of Jesus Christ*. Translated by J. Bowden. Harrisburg, PA: Trinity Press International, 2000.

———. *Property and Riches in the Early Church*. Translated by J. Bowden. London: SCM Press, 1974.

Henrichs-Tarasenkova, Nina. *Luke's Christology of Divine Identity*. LNTS 542. London: T&T Clark, 2016.

Henze, Matthian, ed. *A Companion to Biblical Interpretation in Early Judaism*. Grand Rapids, MI: Eerdmans, 2012.

Hobart, W. K. *The Medical Language of St. Luke*. Grand Rapids, MI: Baker, 1954.

Holmén, Tom. "The Alternatives of the Kingdom: Encountering the Semantic Restrictions of Luke 17,20-21 (ἐντὸς ὑμῶν)." *Zeitschrift für die neutestamentliche Wissenschaft und die Kunde der älteren Kirche* 87 (1996): 204-29.

Hopkins, Keith. *World Full of Gods: The Strange Triumph of Christianity*. New York: Plume, 2001.

Horsley, Richard. *The Prophet Jesus and the Renewal of Israel: Moving Beyond a Diversionary Debate*. Grand Rapids, MI: Eerdmans, 2012.

Jennings, Willie. *Acts: A Theological Commentary on the Bible*. Belief. Louisville, KY: Westminster John Knox, 2017.

Jervell, Jacob. "The Future of the Past: Luke's Vision of Salvation History and Its Bearing on His Writing of History." In *History, Literature, and Society in the Book of Acts*, edited by Ben Witherington, 104-26. Cambridge: Cambridge University Press, 1996.

———. *Luke and the People of God: A New Luke at Luke–Acts*. Minneapolis: Augsburg, 1972.

———. *The Theology of the Acts of the Apostles*. NTT. Cambridge: Cambridge University Press, 1996.

Jipp, Joshua W. "The Acts of the Apostles." In *The State of New Testament Studies*, edited by Scot McKnight and Nijay Gupta, 350-67. Grand Rapids, MI: Baker, 2019.

———. "The Beginnings of a Theology of Luke–Acts: Divine Activity and Human Response." *Journal for Theological Interpretation* 8 (2014): 23-43.

———. *Divine Visitations and Hospitality to Strangers in Luke–Acts: An Interpretation of the Malta Episode in Acts 28:1-10*. NovTSup 153. Leiden: Brill, 2013.

———. "The Paul of Acts: Proclaimer of the Hope of Israel or Teacher of Apostasy from Moses." *NovT* 62 (2020): 60-78.

Johnson, Luke Timothy. *Prophetic Jesus, Prophetic Church: The Challenge of Luke–Acts to Contemporary Christians*. Grand Rapids, MI: Eerdmans, 2011.

———. *Sharing Possessions: What Faith Demands*. Grand Rapids, MI: Eerdmans, 2011.

Käsemann, Ernst. "The Problem of the Historical Jesus." In *Essays on New Testament Themes*, 15–47. Naperville, IL: Allenson, 1964.

Kee, Howard Clark. *The Beginnings of Christianity: An Introduction to the New Testament*. New York: T&T Clark, 2005.

Keener, Craig S. *Acts*. 4 vols. Grand Rapids, MI: Baker, 2012–2015.

———. *Gift and Giver: The Holy Spirit for Today*. Grand Rapids, MI: Baker, 2001.

Kim, Seyoon. *Christ and Caesar: The Gospel and the Roman Empire in the Writings of Paul and Luke*. Grand Rapids, MI: Eerdmans, 2008.

Kim, Young Ho. *Die Parusie bei Lukas: Eine literarisch-exegetisch Untersuchung zu den Parusieaussagen im lukanischen Doppelwork*. BZNW 217. Berlin: de Gruyter, 2016.

Klauck, Hans-Josef. "The Roman Empire." In *The Cambridge History of Christianity: Origins to Constantine*, edited by Margaret M. Mitchell and Frances M. Young, 69-83. Cambridge: Cambridge University Press, 2006.

Koester, Helmut. *Ancient Christian Gospels*. Philadelphia: Trinity Press International, 1990.

Koperski, Veronica. "Women and Discipleship in Luke 10.38-42 and Acts 6.1-7: The Literary Context of Luke–Acts." In *A Feminist Companion to Luke*, edited by Amy-Jill Levine, 161-96. Cleveland, OH: Pilgrim, 2001.

Kuhn, Karl Allen. *The Kingdom According to Luke and Acts: A Social, Literary, and Theological Introduction*. Grand Rapids, MI: Baker, 2015.

Kümmel, Werner G. *Theology of the New Testament: According to Its Major Witnesses: Jesus—Paul—John*. Translated by J. E. Steely. London: SCM Press, 1974.

Labahn, Michael. "The Significance of Signs in Luke 7:22-23 in Light of Isaiah 61 and the Messianic Apocalypse." In *From Prophecy to Testament*, edited by Craig A. Evans, 146-68. Peabody, MA: Hendrickson, 2004.

Ladd, George E. *A Theology of the New Testament*. Revised and edited by D. A. Hagner. Grand Rapids, MI: Eerdmans, 1993.

Law, Timothy Michael. *When God Spoke Greek: The Septuagint and the Making of the Christian Bible*. Oxford: Oxford University Press, 2013.

Levine, Amy-Jill. "Luke and the Jewish Religion." *Int* 68 (2014): 389-402.

Levine, Amy-Jill, with Marianne Blickenstaff, eds. *A Feminist Companion to Luke*. Cleveland, OH: Pilgrim, 2001.

Lieu, Judith. *The Gospel of Luke*. Eugene, OR: Wipf & Stock, 2012.

———. *Marcion and the Making of a Heretic: God and Scripture in the Second Century*. New York: Cambridge University Press, 2017.

Litwak, Kenneth D. *Echoes of Scripture in Luke–Acts: Telling the History of God's People Intertextually*. London: T&T Clark, 2005.

Longenecker, Richard N. "Taking Up the Cross Daily: Discipleship in Luke–Acts." In *Patterns of Discipleship in the New Testament*, edited by Richard N. Longenecker, 50-76. Grand Rapids, MI: Eerdmans, 1996.

López Rodriguez, Darío. *The Liberating Message of Jesus: The Message of the Gospel of Luke*. Eugene, OR: Pickwick, 2012.

Louw, Johannes P., and Eugene A. Nida, eds. *Greek-English Lexicon of the New Testament: Based on Semantic Domains*. 2nd ed. New York: United Bible Societies, 1989.

Lucian. *How to Write History; The Dipsads; Saturnalia; Herodotus or Aetion; Zeuxis or Antiochus; A Slip of the Tongue in Greeting; Apology for the "Salaried Posts in Great Houses"; Harmonides; A Conversation with Hesiod; The Scythian or The Consul; Hermotimus or Concerning the Sects; To One Who Said "You're a Prometheus in Words"; The Ship or The Wishes*. Translated by K. Kilburn. Loeb Classical Library. Cambridge, MA: Harvard University Press, 1959.

Macchia, Frank D. *Jesus the Spirit Baptizer: Christology in Light of Pentecost.* Grand Rapids, MI: Eerdmans, 2020.

Maddox, Robert. *The Purpose of Luke–Acts.* Studies in the New Testament and Its World. Edinburgh: T&T Clark, 1982.

Maier, Harry O. *Picturing Paul in Empire: Imperial Image, Text and Persuasion in Colossians, Ephesians and the Pastoral Epistles.* London: Bloomsbury, 2013.

Malina, Bruce J., and Richard L. Rohrbaugh. *Social-Science Commentary on the Synoptic Gospels.* Minneapolis: Fortress, 1992.

Mallen, Peter. *The Reading and Transformation of Isaiah in Luke–Acts.* LNTS 367. London: T&T Clark, 2008.

Marguerat, Daniel. *The First Christian Historian: Writing the "Acts of the Apostles."* SNTSMS 121. Cambridge: Cambridge University Press, 2002.

Marshall, I. Howard. "Acts." In *Commentary on the New Testament Use of the Old Testament,* edited by G. K. Beale and D. A. Carson, 513-606. Grand Rapids, MI: Baker, 2007.

———. "The Christology of Luke's Gospel and Acts." In *Contours of Christology in the New Testament,* edited by Richard N. Longenecker, 122-47. Grand Rapids, MI: Eerdmans, 2005.

———. *The Gospel of Luke: A Commentary on the Greek Text.* NIGTC. Grand Rapids, MI: Eerdmans, 1978.

———. *Luke: Historian and Theologian.* 3rd ed. Carlisle, UK: Paternoster, 1988.

Mason, Steve. "Speech-Making in Ancient Rhetoric, Josephus, and Acts: Messages and Playfulness, Part I." *Early Christianity* 2 (2011): 445-67.

———. "Speech-Making in Ancient Rhetoric, Josephus, and Acts: Messages and Playfulness, Part II." *Early Christianity* 3 (2012): 147-71.

Matera, Frank J. *New Testament Christology.* Louisville, KY: Westminster John Knox, 1999.

———. *New Testament Ethics: The Legacies of Jesus and Paul.* Louisville, KY: Westminster John Knox, 1999.

McKnight, Scot, and Joseph B. Modica, eds. *Jesus Is Lord and Caesar Is Not: Evaluating Empire in New Testament Studies.* Downers Grove, IL: InterVarsity Press, 2013.

Metzger, Bruce M. *The Canon of the New Testament: Its Origin, Development, and Significance.* Oxford: Clarendon, 1987.

Metzger, James A. *Consumption and Wealth in Luke's Travel Narrative.* Leiden: Brill, 2007.

Miller, Amanda C. "Bridge Work and Seating Charts: A Study of Luke's Ethics of Wealth, Poverty, and Reversal." *Int* 68 (2014): 416-27.

———. *Rumors of Resistance: Status Reversal and Hidden Transcripts in the Gospel of Luke*. Minneapolis: Fortress, 2014.

Moessner, David P. "The Appeal and Power of Poetics (Luke 1:1-4): Luke's Superior Credentials (παρηκολουθηκότι), Narrative Sequence (καθεξῆς), and Firmness of Understanding (ἀσφάλειαν) for the Reader." In *Jesus and the Heritage of Israel: Luke's Narrative Claim upon Israel's Legacy*, 84-123. Harrisburg, PA: Trinity Press International, 1999.

Moraff, James F. "Recent Trends in the Study of Jews and Judaism in Luke–Acts." *CurBR* 19 (2020): 64-87.

Morgan, Teresa. *Roman Faith and Christian Faith: Pistis and Fides in the Early Roman Empire and Early Churches*. Oxford: Oxford University Press, 2017.

Neagoe, Alexandru. *The Trial of the Gospel: An Apologetic Reading of Luke's Trial Narrative*. SNTSMS 116. Cambridge: Cambridge University Press, 2002.

Neyrey, Jerome H. *An Encomium for Jesus: Luke, Rhetoric, and the Story of Jesus*. Sheffield: Sheffield Phoenix, 2020.

Nolland, John. *Luke*. 3 vols. Word Biblical Commentary. Dallas: Word, 1989–1993.

O'Donnell, James. *Pagans: The End of Traditional Religion and the Rise of Christianity*. New York: Ecco, 2016.

Oliver, Isaac W. "The 'Historical Paul' and the Paul of Acts: Who's More Jewish?" In *Paul the Jew: A Conversation Between Pauline and Second Temple Scholars*, edited by Gabriele Boccaccini and Carlos A. Segovia, 51-80. Minneapolis: Fortress, 2016.

———. *Luke's Jewish Eschatology: The National Restoration of Israel in Luke–Acts*. Cambridge: Cambridge University Press, 2021.

Padilla, Osvaldo. *The Acts of the Apostles: Interpretation, History, and Theology*. Downers Grove, IL: InterVarsity Press, 2016.

Pao, David W. *Acts and the Isaianic New Exodus*. Grand Rapids, MI: Baker, 2002.

Pao, David W., and Eckhard J. Schnabel. "Luke." In *Commentary on the New Testament Use of the Old Testament*, edited by G. K. Beale and D. A. Carson, 251-414. Grand Rapids, MI: Baker, 2007.

Parsons, Mikael C. *Luke: Storyteller, Evangelist, Interpreter*. Peabody, MA: Hendrickson, 2007.

Parsons, Mikael C., and Richard I. Pervo. *Rethinking the Unity of Luke and Acts*. Minneapolis: Fortress, 1993.

Pawlikowski, John. Review of *Mature Christianity*, by Norman A. Beck. *CBQ* 49 (1987): 137-38.

Penner, Todd. *In Praise of Christian Origins: Stephen and the Hellenistic Apologetic Historiography.* New York: T&T Clark, 2004.

Petterson, Christina. *Acts of Empire: The Acts of the Apostles and Imperial Ideology.* Eugene, OR: Cascade, 2020.

Pilgrim, Walter. *Good News to the Poor: Wealth and Poverty in Luke-Acts.* Eugene, OR: Wipf & Stock, 1981.

Pinter, Dean L. "The Gospel of Luke and the Roman Empire." In *Jesus Is Lord, Caesar Is Not: Evaluating Empire in New Testament Studies.* Edited by Scot McKnight and Joseph B. Modica, 101–15. Downers Grove, IL: IVP Academic, 2013.

Pitts, Andrew W. *History, Biography, and the Genre of Luke-Acts.* Leiden: Brill, 2019.

Plummer, Alfred. *The Gospel According to St. Luke.* ICC. Edinburgh: T&T Clark, 1896.

Porter, Stanley E. "Further Comments on the Use of the Old Testament in the New Testament." In *The Intertextuality of the Epistles: Explorations of Theory and Practice*, edited by Thomas L. Brodie, Dennis R. MacDonald, and Stanley E. Porter, New Testament Monographs 16, 98-107. Sheffield: Sheffield Phoenix, 2007.

———. *The Paul of Acts: Essays in Literary Criticism, Rhetoric and Theology.* WUNT 115. Tübingen: Mohr Siebeck, 1999.

———. "Thucydides 1.22.1 and Speeches in Acts: Is There a Thucydidean View?" *NovT* 32 (1990): 121-42.

———. "The Use of the Old Testament in the New Testament." In *Early Christian Interpretation of the Scriptures of Israel: Investigations and Proposals*, edited by Craig A. Evans and James A. Sanders, JSNTSup 148, 79-96. Sheffield: Sheffield Academic Press, 1997.

Powery, E. B. *Jesus Reads Scripture: The Function of Jesus's Use of Scripture in the Synoptic Gospels.* BIS 63. Leiden: Brill, 1999.

Price, S. R. F. *Rituals and Power: The Roman Imperial Cult in Asia Minor.* Cambridge: Cambridge University Press, 1986.

Ramsay, William M. *The Bearing of Recent Discovery on the Trustworthiness of the New Testament.* London: Hodder & Stoughton, 1953.

———. *Pictures of the Apostolic Church: Studies in the Book of Acts.* Grand Rapids, MI: Baker, 1959.

Reid, Barbara E. *Choosing the Better Part? Women in the Gospel of Luke.* Collegeville, MN: Liturgical, 1996.

———. "The Gospel of Luke: Friend or Foe of Women Proclaimers of the Word?" *CBQ* 78 (2016): 1-23.

Reid, Barbara E., and Shelly Matthews. *Luke 1–9*. Minneapolis: Liturgical, 2021.

Rhoads, David E., and Jae Won Lee, eds. *Luke–Acts and Empire: Essays in Honor of Robert L. Brawley*. Eugene, OR: Pickwick, 2011.

Rosner, Brian S. "Acts and Biblical History." In *The Book of Acts in Its Ancient Literary Setting*, edited by Bruce W. Winter and Andrew D. Clarke, 65-82. Grand Rapids, MI: Eerdmans, 1994.

Roth, Dieter T. "Marcion's Gospel and Luke: The History of Research in Current Debate." *Journal of Biblical Literature* 127 (2008): 513–27.

———. *The Text of Marcion's Gospel*. Leiden: Brill, 2015.

Rothschild, Clare K. *Luke–Acts and the Rhetoric of History: An Investigation of Early Christian Historiography*. WUNT 2/175. Tübingen: Mohr Siebeck, 2004.

Rowe, C. Kavin. *Early Narrative Christology: The Lord in the Gospel of Luke*. Grand Rapids, MI: Baker, 2006.

———. *World Upside Down: Reading Acts in the Graeco-Roman Age*. Oxford: Oxford University Press, 2009.

Sanders, E. P. *Judaism: Practice and Belief 63 BCE–66 CE*. London: SCM Press, 1992.

Sanders, Jack T. *The Jews in Luke–Acts*. Philadelphia: Fortress, 1987.

Schnabel, Eckhard J. *Acts*. Zondervan Exegetical Commentary on the New Testament. Grand Rapids, MI: Zondervan, 2012.

———. "The Muratorian Fragment: The State of Research." *JETS* 57 (2014): 231-64.

Schneider, Gerhard. *Die Apostelgeschichte*. 2 vols. Freiburg: Herder, 1980–1982.

Schnittjer, Gary Edward. *Old Testament Use of the Old Testament: A Book by Book Guide*. Grand Rapids, MI: Zondervan, 2021.

Schrader, Elizabeth, and Joan E. Taylor. "The Meaning of 'Magdalene': A Review of Literary Evidence." *Journal of Biblical Literature* 140 (2021): 751-73.

Schreiner, Patrick. *The Mission of the Triune God: A Theology of Acts*. Wheaton, IL: Crossway, 2022.

Schröter, Jens. "Salvation for the Gentiles and Israel: On the Relationship Between Christology and People of God in Luke." In *From Jesus to the New Testament: Early Christian Theology and the Origin of the New Testament Canon*, translated by W. Coppins, Baylor-Mohr Siebeck Studies in Early Christianity, 227-46. Waco, TX: Baylor University Press, 2013.

Schürer, Emil. *The History of the Jewish People in the Age of Jesus Christ*. Revised and edited by G. Vermes, F. Millar, and M. Black. 3 vols. Edinburgh: T&T Clark. 1973–1986.

Schweitzer, Albert. *The Quest of the Historical Jesus*. 6th ed. London: SCM Press, 2000.

Seccombe, David. "Dating Luke–Acts: Further Arguments for an Early Date." *TynBul* 71 (2021): 207-27.

Seneca. *Seneca's Letters from a Stoic*. Translated by Richard Mott Gummere. Mineola, NY: Dover, 2016.

Seo, Pyung Soo. *Luke's Jesus in the Roman Empire and the Emperor in the Gospel of Luke*. Eugene, OR: Pickwick, 2015.

Shellard, Barbara. *New Light on Luke: Its Purpose, Sources, and Literary Context*. London: T&T Clark, 2004.

Sherwin-White, A. N. *Roman Society and Roman Law in the New Testament*. Oxford: Clarendon, 1963.

Smith, David A. "The Jewishness of Luke–Acts: Locating Lukan Christianity Amidst the Parting of the Ways." *JTS* (2021): 738-68.

Smith, E. Elbert. *Church Planting by the Book*. Alresford, UK: CLC International, 2015.

Smith, Mitzi J. *The Literary Construction of the Other in the Acts of the Apostles: Charismatics, the Jews, and Women*. Eugene, OR: Pickwick, 2011.

Soards, Marion L. *The Speeches in Acts: Their Content, Context, and Concerns*. Louisville, KY: Westminster John Knox, 1994.

Spencer, F. Scott. *Acts*. Sheffield: Sheffield Academic Press, 1997.

———. *Dancing Girls, Loose Ladies, and Women of the Cloth*. New York: T&T Clark, 2014.

———. *The Gospel of Luke and Acts of the Apostles*. Nashville: Abingdon, 2011.

———. *Luke*. Two Horizons New Testament Commentary. Grand Rapids, MI: Eerdmans, 2019.

———. *Salty Wives, Spirited Mothers and Savvy Widows: Capable Women of Purpose and Persistence in Luke's Gospel*. Grand Rapids, MI: Eerdmans, 2012.

Spencer, Patrick E. "The Unity of Luke–Acts: A Four-Bolted Hermeneutical Hinge." *CurBR* 5 (2007): 341-66.

Stanton, Graham. "The Fourfold Gospel." *New Testament Studies* 43 (1997): 317-46.

Sterling, G. E. *Historiography and Self-Definition: Josephus, Luke–Acts, and Apologetic Historiography*. NovTSup 64. Leiden: Brill, 1992.

Steyn, Gert J. "Soteriological Perspectives in Luke's Gospel." In *Salvation in the New Testament: Perspectives on Soteriology*, edited by Jan G. van der Watt, 67-99. Leiden: Brill, 2005.

Stoll, Oliver. *Excubatio ad Signa: Die Wache bei den Fahnen in der romischen Armee und andere Beitrag kulturgeschictlichen und historischen Bedeutung eines militarishcen Symbols*. St. Katharinen; Scripta Mercaturae, 1995.

Strait, Drew J. "The Gospel of Luke." In *The State of New Testament Studies*, edited by Scot McKnight and Nijay Gupta, 315-33. Grand Rapids, MI: Baker Academic, 2019.

———. "Proclaiming Another King Named Jesus? The Acts of the Apostles and the Roman Imperial Cult(s)." In *Jesus Is Lord and Caesar Is Not: Evaluating Empire in New Testament Studies*, edited by Scot McKnight and Joseph B. Modica, 130-45. Downers Grove, IL: InterVarsity Press, 2013.

Strauss, Mark L. *The Davidic Messiah in Luke–Acts: The Promise and Fulfilment in Luke's Christology*. JSNTSup 110. Sheffield: Sheffield Academic Press, 1995.

———. "The Purpose of Luke–Acts: Reaching a Consensus." In *New Testament Theology in Light of the Church's Mission*, edited by J. C. Laansma, Grant Osborne, and R. Van Neste, 135-50. Eugene, OR: Cascade, 2011.

Strelan, Rick. *Luke the Priest: The Authority of the Author of the Third Gospel*. Aldershot, UK: Ashgate, 2007.

Stroup, C. R. *The Christians Who Became Jews: Acts of the Apostles and Ethnicity in the Roman City*. New Haven, CT: Yale University Press, 2020.

Suetonius. *Lives of the Caesars, Volume II*. Translated by J. C. Rolfe. Loeb Classical Library 38. Cambridge, MA: Harvard University Press, 1914.

Sutton, Benjamin. "Formulations of the Gospel in the Speeches of Acts: Memory and Historiography." PhD diss., Australian College of Theology, 2015.

Talbert, Charles H. "Discipleship in Luke–Acts." In *Discipleship in the New Testament*, edited by F. Segovia, 62-75. Philadelphia: Fortress, 1985.

———. *Literary Patterns, Theological Themes, and the Genre of Luke–Acts*. Society of Biblical Literature Monograph Series 20. Missoula, MT: Scholars Press, 1974.

———. *Reading Acts: A Literary and Theological Commentary on the Acts of the Apostles*. New York: Crossroads, 1997.

Tannehill, Robert. *The Narrative Unity of Luke–Acts: A Literary Interpretation*. 2 vols. Philadelphia: Fortress, 1991–1994.

Thompson, Alan J. *The Acts of the Risen Lord Jesus: Luke's Account of God's Unfolding Plan*. New Studies in Biblical Theology 27. Downers Grove, IL: InterVarsity Press, 2011.

Thucydides. *History of the Peloponnesian War*. Vol. 1, *Books 1-2*. Translated by C. F. Smith. Loeb Classical Library. Cambridge, MA: Harvard University Press, 1919.

Troftgruben, Troy M. *A Conclusion Unhindered: A Study of the Ending of Acts Within Its Literary Environment*. WUNT 2/280. Tübingen: Mohr Siebeck, 2010.

Twelftree, Graham H. *People of the Spirit: Exploring Luke's View of the Church*. London: SPCK, 2009.

Tyson, Joseph B. *Images of Judaism in Luke–Acts*. Columbia: University of South Carolina Press, 1992.

———. *Luke, Judaism, and the Scholars: Critical Approaches to Luke–Acts*. Columbia: University of South Carolina Press, 1999.

Uytanlet, Samson. *Luke–Acts and Jewish Historiography: A Study on the Theology, Literature, and Ideology of Luke–Acts*. WUNT 2/340. Tübingen: Mohr Siebeck, 2014.

Vanhoozer, Kevin J. *The Drama of Doctrine: A Canonical Linguistic Approach to Christian Theology*. Louisville, KY: Westminster John Knox, 2005.

Varghese, P. V. "The Holy Spirit and the Risen Christ in Luke–Acts." *Indian Theological Studies* 44 (2007): 245-74.

Vermes, Geza. "Bible and Midrash: Early Old Testament Exegesis." In *The Cambridge History of the Bible*, vol. 1, *From Beginnings to Jerome*, edited by Peter R. Akroyd and Craig F. Evans, 199-231. Cambridge: Cambridge University Press, 1975.

Vielhauer, Philipp. "The 'Paulinism' of Acts." *Perkins (School of Theology) Journal* 17 (1963): 5-17.

Vinson, Richard B. "The God of Luke–Acts." *Int* 68 (2014): 376-88.

Vinzent, Markus. *Marcion and the Dating of the Synoptic Gospels*. Leuven: Peeters, 2014.

Wagner, J. Ross. "The Septuagint and the 'Search for the Christian Bible.'" In *Scripture's Doctrine and Theology's Bible: How the New Testament Shapes Christian Dogmatics*, edited by Markus Bockmuehl and Alan J. Torrance, 17-28. Grand Rapids, MI: Baker, 2008.

Walters, Patricia. *The Assumed Authorial Unity of Luke and Acts: A Reassessment of the Evidence*. SNTSMS 145. Cambridge: Cambridge University Press, 2009.

Walton, Steve. "Acts." In *Dictionary of Theological Interpretation of the Bible*, edited by Kevin J. Vanhoozer, 27-31. Grand Rapids, MI: Baker, 2005.

———. "The Acts—of God? What Is the 'Acts of the Apostles' All About?" *EvQ* 80 (2008): 291-306.

———. *Leadership and Lifestyle: The Portrait of Paul in the Miletus Speech and 1 Thessalonians*. SNTSMS 106. Cambridge: Cambridge University Press, 2000.

———. "Primitive Communism in Acts? Does Acts Present the Community of Goods (2:44-45; 4:32-35) as Mistaken?" *EvQ* 80 (2008): 99-111.

———. "The State They Were In: Luke's View of the Roman Empire." In *Rome in the Bible and the Early Church*, edited by Peter Oakes, 1-41. Grand Rapids, MI: Baker, 2002.

Weatherly, Jon A. *Jewish Responsibility for the Death of Jesus in Luke–Acts*. JSNTSup 106. Sheffield: Sheffield Academic Press, 1994.

Wenham, David. "The Purpose of Luke–Acts: Israel's Story in the Context of the Roman Empire." In *Reading Luke: Interpretation, Reflection, Formation*, edited by Craig G. Bartholomew, Joel B. Green, and Anthony C. Thiselton, 79-103. Grand Rapids, MI: Zondervan, 2005.

Wenham, John. "The Identification of Luke." *EvQ* 63 (1991): 3-44.

Wenkel, David. *Jesus the Dayspring: The Sunrise and Visitation of Israel's Messiah*. Sheffield: Sheffield Phoenix, 2021.

———. *Joy in Luke–Acts*. Milton Keynes, UK: Paternoster, 2015.

Wi, MiJa. *The Path to Salvation in Luke's Gospel: What Must We Do?* London: T&T Clark, 2019.

Wilken, Robert Louis. *The Christians as the Romans Saw Them*. 2nd ed. New Haven, CT: Yale University Press, 2003.

Willimon, William H. *Acts*. Interpretation. Atlanta: John Knox, 1988.

Wilson, Stephen G. *The Gentiles and the Gentile Mission in Luke–Acts*. SNTSMS 23. Cambridge: Cambridge University Press, 1973.

Winstanley, Gerrard. "The True Levellers Standard Advanced: Or, The State of Community Opened, and Presented to the Sons of Men." 1649. www.marxists.org/reference/archive/winstanley/1649/levellers-standard.htm.

Wise, Michael Owen, Martin G. Abegg, and Edward M. Cook, trans. and eds. *The Dead Sea Scrolls: A New Translation*. San Francisco: HarperSanFrancisco, 1996.

Wolter, Michael. "Israel's Future and the Delay of the Parousia, According to Luke." In *Jesus and the Heritage of Israel: Luke's Narrative Claim upon Israel's Legacy*, edited by David P. Moessner, 307-24. Harrisburg, PA: Trinity Press International, 1999.

Wright, N. T. "Hope Deferred? Against the Dogma of Delay." *Early Christianity* 9 (2018): 37-82.

———. *Jesus and the Victory of God*. COQG 2. London: SPCK, 1996.

———. *The New Testament and the People of God.* COQG 1. London: SPCK, 1992.

———. "Reading the New Testament Missionally." In *Reading the Bible Missionally,* edited by Michael Goheen, 175-93. Grand Rapids, MI: Eerdmans, 2016.

Yamazaki-Ransom, Kazuhiko. *The Roman Empire in Luke's Narrative.* LNTS 404. New York: T&T Clark, 2010.

Yoder, Joshua. *Representatives of Roman Rule: Roman Provincial Governors in Luke–Acts.* Berlin: de Gruyter, 2014.

Zacharias, H. Daniel. "Dead Sea Scrolls: Messianic Apocalypse." In *Encyclopedia of the Historical Jesus,* edited by C. A. Evans, 138-39. New York: Routledge, 2008.

Zanker, Paul. *The Power of Images in the Age of Augustus.* Ann Arbor: University of Michigan Press, 1988.

Zetterholm, Karin Hedner. *Jewish Interpretation of the Bible: Ancient and Modern.* Minneapolis: Fortress, 2012.

Zyl, Hermie C. van. "The Soteriology of Acts: Restoration to Life." In *Salvation in the New Testament: Perspectives on Soteriology,* edited by Jan G. van der Watt, 133-60. Leiden: Brill, 2005.

General Index

Acts, book of. *See* Luke–Acts
Adams, Sean, 3, 24
Agan, C. D. "Jimmy," III, 3
Agricola, 247
Ahn, Yong-Sung, 268
Alexander, Loveday, 27, 51, 172
Ananias, 115, 146,
    and Sapphira, 152, 197, 208-9
Andrade, Nathanael, 60
Anna the Prophet(ess), 34, 168, 170-71, 277
anti-Judaism, 8, 217-23, 238-41
    contra Ioudaeos tradition, 224
antisemitism, 219, 238
Apocalypse of John, 2, 265. *See also* Revelation (book)
apologetics, apology, 5, 30, 39-46, 50-54, 61, 232, 263-65, 287
Apostolos, the, 31
Arlandson, James, 166
Armstrong, Karl, 27, 241
Atkinson, William, 216
Augustine of Hippo, 69, 207, 271
Augustus (Caesar *or* Emperor), 58, 80, 244, 248, 252, 254, 255, 257
    son of (Gaius Caesar), 47, 60, 245
Balabanski, Victoria, 287
baptism, 102, 122, 149, 151, 180, 181, 214
    of and with the Holy Spirit, 35, 47, 73, 102, 112-13, 209-12, 271-77
    of Jesus, 73, 91, 134, 162, 202-4, 208
    of repentance, 84, 119, 149, 209
Barclay, John, 266
Barnett, Paul, 60
Barrett, C. K., 2, 58, 84, 127, 264
Bates, Matthew, 149
Bauckham, Richard, 55, 131, 276, 287
Beale, G. K., 143
Becker, Eve-Marie, 24
Beers, Holly, 144

Benedictus, 2, 34, 100, 211, 277
Bernier, Jonathan, 144
Bird, Michael F., 24, 27, 75, 111, 131, 180, 208, 210, 229, 247, 248, 252, 268, 271
Bock, Darrell, 10, 60, 68, 78, 80, 120, 123, 140, 205, 216, 291
Bockmuehl, Markus, 82, 148
Boesenberg, Dulcinea, 223, 229, 240
Bovon, François, 23, 56, 60, 79, 178
Brink, Laurie, 262
Bruce, F. F., 46, 58
Bultmann, Rudolf, 69, 95
Burnett, D. Clint, 92
Byrne, Brendan, 90
Byrskog, Samuel, 55
Cadbury, Henry, 18, 26
Caesar, 41, 42, 45, 54, 243, 256-60, 263
Caesarea Philippi, 156, 204, 209, 261-62
Capper, Brian, 198
Carroll, John, 288, 292
Carter, Warren, 172
Celsus, (Greek Philosopher), 183
Chen, Diane, 30, 36, 153, 195
Cho, Youngmo, 211
Christian socialism, 7, 31, 186-87, 199
Christianity, 12, 32, 46, 48, 54, 290
    converts to, 180, 260
    and imperial cults, 250-55, 266-67
    Jewish roots of, 72, 228, 231-32, 239-40, 271
Christology, Lukan, 65, 71-72, 76-80, 89
    in book of Isaiah, 80-81, 136-39
    and Holy Spirit, 102-3, 201-5
    in Old Testament, 6, 125-27, 140
    in the Psalter, 134-36
    and salvation, 97, 106
church, the, 198-99, 290-91
    awaiting return of Christ, 282-88
    inclusion of Gentiles in, 235, 238-40, 261, 282
    mission of, 4, 232-33, 267-68

Clark, Andrew, 278
Clement of Rome, 2
Coleman, Rachel, 192, 199
conversion, conversion stories, 36, 48-50, 147-51, 130, 146, 210, 233, 260-62
Conzelmann, Hans, 69, 284, 285
Cornelius, 156, 209, 261-62
Cort, John, 16, 31
covenant, covenant standing, 150, 156, 188, 239, 276-78
Cowan, J. Andrew, 241
Crabbe, Kylie, 288, 291, 292
Crossan, John, 37
Crowe, Brandon, 281
Dahl, Nils A., 25
Denova, Rebecca, 87, 144, 232
deSilva, David, 66
Diaspora, the, 8, 22, 38, 87, 150, 232, 240
 Diasporan and Judean rejection of the Messiah, 141, 226-28, 238
Dibelius, Martin, 58, 61
Didache, the, 267, 287
Dio Cassius, 59, 62
discipleship, 2-3, 6-7, 15, 73-74, 100, 121, 146-47, 287
 cost of, 147, 152-55, 190-92
 marks of, 97, 155-58, 249
 missional, 158-66
Doble, Peter, 134
Donaldson, Terence, 219
Dunn, James, 24, 151, 205, 277, 289
early church, the, 127, 138, 140, 156
 and communal life, 111, 186, 192, 196-97, 200-201
 and Israel's restoration, 235-41
 mission of, 4, 49, 106, 158-62
 nature of, 131, 138, 197, 201, 217-18, 222-23, 235
 persecution of, 32, 47, 112, 155, 163-65, 182, 222, 227, 243, 248-49, 289
 women in, 166-67
Ellis, E. Earle, 55-56, 289
Emmaus road, 3, 6, 125, 180, 279-80
Esler Philip, 40
Eusebius, 14, 17, 264
Evans, Craig, 144, 219, 268
faith (*pistis*), also belief, 10-19, 149-55, 281
feminist interpretations of Luke–Acts, 7, 171-72, 182-83, 280
Fitzmyer, Joseph, 58, 66, 67, 165
Flemming, Dean, 161, 165
Forbes, Gregory, 168, 169, 179, 184

forgiveness of sins, 33-38, 77-78, 83-85, 117-19, 121, 159-160, 162-63, 175-76, 213, 216, 227, 230
Fox, Robin, 251
Fredriksen, Paula, 285
Fuller, Michael, 20, 276, 292
Gamaliel, (the Elder, rabbi), 44, 61, 231
Garland, David, 188, 262, 274
Gasque, W. Ward, 53
Gaston, Lloyd, 218
Gaventa Beverley, 10, 131, 211, 292
Gempf, Conrad, 63
Gentiles, Gentile church, 8, 32, 49
 inclusion of, 130-31, 282
Gnosticism, 48
God, Yahweh, 90, 99, 103, 133, 258
 faithfulness to Israel, 9, 36-39, 72, 107, 211, 277
 kingship of, 89, 272, 278-79
 mercy of, 34-35, 100-102, 107, 116-19, 159, 169, 212
 saving purposes of, 49-50, 70-72, 76-77, 84-85, 100, 105-6, 214
Goheen, Michael, 163
González, Justo, 200, 212, 214, 216
Grant, Jamie, 136
Great Commission, Lukan, 118, 160, 227
Green, Gene, 75
Green, Joel, 10, 27, 39, 71, 73, 147, 148, 249
Grindheim, Sigurd, 103
Gupta, Nijay, 150
Haar, Stephen, 48
Haenchen, Ernst, 218
Hahn, Scott, 292
Harnack, Adolf von, 18, 271
Harris, Sarah, 103
Harrower, Scott, 169, 179, 184
Hays, Christopher, 191, 199
Hays, Richard, 98, 126
Helyer, Larry, 69
Hemer, Colin, 58, 63, 67, 75
Hengel, Martin, 12, 19, 64, 68, 75, 194, 232
Henrichs-Tarasenkova, Nina, 103
Hippolytus of Rome, 287
Hobart, William, 18
Holmén, Tom, 274
Holy Spirit (or, "the spirit")
 gift of, 9, 84, 103, 156, 209-12, 215-16, 240, 261, 277
 Lukan emphasis on, 3, 8, 26, 72-73, 200-202
 nature and role of, 3, 50, 73, 162-64, 207-9

relationship with and empowerment of
  Jesus, 71-72, 90-91, 102-103, 202-7
 salvation and empowerment for mission
  by, 106, 147-50, 212-14, 284
Hopkins, Keith, 250, 251
Iamblichus, 196
idolatry, 45-46, 114, 117, 246, 251-52
 cleansing from, rejection of, 65, 119-20,
  246-48, 252, 256-60
Ignatius of Loyola, Saint, 191
Irenaeus of Lyons, Bishop, 14, 15
Israel
 covenant with God, 56, 65, 276-79
 redemption of, 89, 108-9, 160, 240-41
 restoration, restoration eschatology, 33-39,
  84-85, 130-31, 232-41, 276-82
 salvation, for and through, 2, 70-72, 108-9
Jennings, Willie, 279
Jerome, 17, 18
Jervell, Jacob, 20, 31, 77, 85, 229, 230, 232, 233,
 264
Jesus
 as giver of the Holy Spirit, 205-7
 as Isaianic fulfillment, 83, 90, 136-39, 137,
  138, 162, 203-4, 222, 278
 and Jewish culpability for death of, 9,
  40-43, 83-85, 218-23
 as Lord of the church, 5, 77, 98-103
 the ordained death of, 65, 70, 84-85, 91-93,
  224
 as prophet and prophetic fulfillment, 26,
  34-36, 40, 77-80, 87-89, 101, 109-10, 175,
  201, 224-25, 233, 244-45
 rejection of, 36-37, 46, 116-17, 141-42, 171,
  222, 228-29, 237-38
 resurrection, physical resurrection of, 30,
  48-49, 65, 72, 83-85, 178
 as Savior, 36-37, 77-78, 85, 91, 105, 259
 Son of God *or* God's son, 71, 89-93, 97-99
 Son of Man, 9, 82-83, 87, 93-98, 116, 135,
  150, 275
 See also Messiah
Jipp, Joshua, 10, 68, 180, 231
John the Baptist, 7, 33, 99, 102, 108, 109, 117-18,
 119, 138, 147, 192-93, 195, 210, 212, 226-27, 278
Johnson, Luke, 88, 199
Josephus, 19, 21, 55, 59, 62, 196, 225, 248, 253,
 263-65
judgment, 89, 102, 115-16, 211
 of Israel, 102, 119-20, 130, 142, 279
Julius Caesar, 29, 62, 252
Julius, Roman centurion, 261-63

Justin Martyr, 69, 222, 223, 264, 287
Käsemann, Ernst, 284
Kee, Howard, 57
Keener, Craig, 210, 252
kerygma (proclamation, preaching), 24, 58, 69,
 131-32
 apostolic, 3, 77, 84-86, 85, 97, 118, 135, 206,
  212, 220-21, 237-38
Kim, Seeyoon, 264, 268
Kim, Young Ho, 289
kingdom of God, 9, 73, 270-77, 290
 as deliverance, destination, and
  discipleship, 35-36, 112-13
 and eternal life, 112-14, 117, 139, 155, 272,
  282
 as Israel's restoration, 86-87, 274-81, 284
 and the Son of Man, 9, 274-75
 See also Luke–Acts: eschatology
Klauck, Hans-Josef, 254, 255
Koester, Helmut, 17
Koperski, Veronica, 173
Kuhn, Karl, 32
Kümmel, Werner, 69
Labahn, Michael, 82
Ladd, George, 69
Law, Timothy, 129
Levine, Amy-Jill, 172, 173, 184, 219
Lieu, Judith, 15, 189
Litwak, Kenneth, 144
Longenecker, Richard, 165
López Rodriguez, Darío, 154
Lucian, 63-64
Lukan narratives
 birth/infancy, 58, 77, 80, 98-99, 107, 117,
  168-70, 178, 211, 235
 passion, 169, 178, 219, 224, 239
 resurrection, 125, 178
 travel, 3, 6, 89, 145-46
Luke (the Evangelist)
 companion of Apostle Paul, 14-18
 as first apologist, 45-46
 as historian and theologian, 5, 23, 54-74,
  200, 202, 215, 285-86
 identification and self-identification, 14-20
Luke–Acts
 audience of, 22-23
 central themes and unity of, 5, 25-27,
  31-36, 39, 50-51
 and Christian socialism, 7, 31, 185-87
 context and dating of, 5, 11, 14-17, 20-22,
  29, 32
 distinctive Christology of, 78-84

eschatology, 73, 116, 212, 234-35, 240-41, 265, 270-71, 282-86, 288-91
genre, 23-26, 127, 290
historicity of, 53-59, 64-67
historiographical narration, 5, 29, 54-57, 62
historiography, 19, 24, 29, 67, 271
in Muratorian Canon (Fragment), 16
present-day applications of, 3, 31, 112, 146-47, 267-68, 290
purposes of (salvific, apologetic, polemical, legitimating), 4, 21-23, 25, 31-33, 39-44, 46-51
speeches and sermons in, 33, 60-64, 71-72, 85, 118, 126, 139, 161, 220-21, 225-26, 230, 259
unique materials in, 2, 4, 77-78, 145-46, 148, 189, 193, 224
Lydia, Gentile convert, 7, 156, 180-81, 195
Macchia, Frank, 207
Maddox, Robert, 31, 52
Magnificat, 2, 34, 47, 107-8, 169, 246, 277
Maier, Harry, 254
Malina, Bruce, 173
Mallen, Peter, 139
Marcion of Sinope, Marcionism, 14-15, 17, 31
Marguerat, Daniel, 52
Marshall, I. Howard, 74, 84, 103, 106, 123, 144, 274
Mary Magdalene, 166, 168, 176-79
Mary and Martha of Bethany, 168, 171-74, 176, 191
Mary, mother of Jesus, 34, 36, 59, 78-79, 89-90, 99, 152, 166, 168-70
Mason, Steve, 45, 267
Matera, Frank, 71, 104, 154
Matthews, Shelly, 10
McKnight, Scot, 268
Messiah, Davidic Messiah, messianic Lord, 42-43, 47, 71-72, 77-87, 97-99, 108, 125-26, 134-35, 140, 202-5, 244-45, 203-4, 244, 259
"anointed one," 80, 83, 203, 214, 278
"horn of salvation," 6, 33, 78-80, 108, 235
and Messianic Apocalypse, 81-82
Metzger, Bruce, 16
Metzger, James, 189, 199
Miller, Amanda, 199, 266
mission, mission to nations, 3, 38, 100, 121, 139-40, 158-65
apostolic, 165, 179, 226-28, 235
and Holy Spirit, 3, 162-64, 214
to Jews and Gentiles, 72, 226-32, 281-82
prayer and provision for, 2, 164

Moessner, David, 56
Moraff, James, 241
Morgan, Teresa, 150, 151, 152
Nazareth Manifesto, 36, 109, 121, 213, 278
Neagoe, Alexandru, 40, 52
new covenant, 72, 87, 109
Neyrey, Jerome, 40
Nolland, John, 60
O'Donnell, James, 251
Old Testament, also Jewish Scriptures, 24, 125-28, 132-34, 206, 218
intertextuality, definition, methods, and techniques of, 127-28, 131-34
Isaiah, use of in Luke-Acts, 136-39, 140-42, 202-3, 226, 273, 278
messianic revelation and reading of, 6, 71-72, 141-43
the Psalter, use of in Luke-Acts, 101, 134-36, 246
Oliver, Isaac, 106, 218, 226, 229, 231, 276, 281, 292
Origen, 183
Padilla, Osvaldo, 10
paganism (Greco-Roman religion), 33, 48-49, 251, 256-57
Pao, David, 138, 144
Park, Hyung Dae, 211
Parsons, Mikeal, 10, 25, 26
Paul, apostle, also Saul of Tarsus
and Apollos, 67, 163, 181
and Barnabas, 49, 163, 191, 195, 197, 208, 212, 228, 252
Christophany and conversion of, 2, 44-45, 49-50, 64, 66-67, 86, 143, 148, 230
commitment to Jewish mission, 45, 231
mission to the Gentiles, 50, 111, 149, 228-30
Pharisee, 231
speeches of, 61-62, 86, 118, 126, 139, 161
trial and defense of, 5, 9, 32, 231, 281
Pawlikowski, John, 218
Penner, Todd, 58
Pentecost, also Day of Pentecost, 73, 201-2, 221, 225, 201-2, 209-212, 214-216
Pervo, Richard, 26
Peter, apostle, also Simon Peter, 16, 48, 190, 266, 290
confession of Jesus, 82-83
conversion of, 148, 152
Lukan emphasis on, 25, 30, 70
mission to Gentiles, 111-12, 130, 149, 179, 208, 227

General Index

mission to Jews, 38, 229
sermons and speeches of, 42-43, 61, 84-85, 88, 137, 150, 204, 214, 221, 259
Petterson, Christina, 269
Philo, 24, 196, 244
Pilgrim, Walter, 199
Pinter, Dean, 259
Pitts, Andrew, 24
Plummer, Alfred, 60
Plutarch, 62, 266, 267
Polycarp of Smyrna, 21
Pontius Pilate, 41-42, 76, 219-20, 225, 244-45, 248-50
poor and outcasts, 2, 8, 74, 89, 109, 188, 193, 278
Porphyry, 196
Porter, Stanley, 63, 67, 132
Powery, Emerson, 143
Price, S. R. F., 253
Quintilian, 257
Quirinius, 5, 58-60, 244
Qumran scrolls, 102, 286
Ramsay, William, 53, 54, 58, 60
Reed, Jonathan, 37
Reid, Barbara, 10, 167, 168, 182, 184
repentance, 117-20, 123, 147-49, 155
Revelation (book). 2, 128, 132, 265, 287
revelation, 68, 100, 160
  to the Gentiles, 43, 66, 72, 214, 277
  messianic, 100, 141-43, 237-38, 280
Rohrbaugh, Richard, 173
Roman Empire
  and the church as 'rival empire,' 47-48, 257-60, 266
  idolatry in, 264-65
  imperial cults of, 250-55, 266-67
  Lukan view of, 9, 243-50, 258, 264-68
Rosner, Brian, 24
Roth, Dieter, 15
Rothschild, Clare, 24, 75
Rowe, C. Kavin, 100, 104, 243, 259, 266, 269, 273
salvation, 6, 33-36, 106-8
  and community of the saved, 36-37
  for the Gentiles, 109, 111, 116
  holistic, 6, 35, 109-12, 121, 123, 213
  for Israel, 33-34, 37-38, 108, 234
  Lukan theology of, 6, 105-6, 117-20, 150
  and reversal of status, 43, 47, 97, 107-8, 110-11, 116, 156-57, 169, 189, 212
  story of, 37-39, 122-23
salvation culture, past, present and future, 120-23, 271-76

Sanders, E. P., 277
Sanders, Jack, 219
Sanhedrin, the, 40, 44, 83, 85, 164, 221, 225, 231, 281
Satan, satanic, 91, 99, 115, 162, 224, 230, 265, 280
  defeat of, 165, 273, 275-77
  also devil, antichrist, 115, 204, 246, 270, 287
Schnabel, Eckhard, 16, 63, 64, 144
Schneider, Gerhard, 61
Schnittjer, Gary, 127
Schrader, Elizabeth, 177
Schreiner, Patrick, 4
Schröter, Jens, 241
Schürer, Emil, 277
Schweitzer, Albert, 282-83
Seccombe, David, 27
second coming, also Parousia, 282
  delay of, 282-88
  and *missio Dei*, 289-91
Seneca, 196
Septuagint (LXX), 19, 79, 101, 128-31, 271
Seo, Pyung Soo, 269
Shellard, Barbara, 52
Sherwin-White, A. N., 58
sin
  liberation from, 213-14
  nature of, 107, 114-15, 162
  See also forgiveness of sins
sinful woman, the unnamed, 118, 152, 175-76
Smith, David, 20, 87, 232
Smith, E. Elbert, 31
Smith, Mitzi, 31
Soards, Marion, 61
socialism, social justice, 7, 74, 89, 111-12, 185-87, 196
Spencer, F. Scott, 10, 157, 160, 161-62, 176, 184
Spencer, Patrick, 28
Stanton, Graham, 16
Sterling, Gregory, 57
Steyn, Gert, 123
Stoll, Oliver, 254
Strait, Drew, 10, 258
Strauss, David, 50
Strauss, Mark, 32, 50, 52, 80, 104
Strelan, Rick, 18, 20, 28, 56
Stroup, Christopher, 239
Suetonius, 244, 257-58
supersessionism, supersessionist theology, 218, 233
Sutton, Benjamin, 68, 75
Tabitha/Dorcas, first female disciple, 179-80, 195

Tacitus, Publius Cornelius, 59, 60, 62, 244, 247
Talbert, Charles, 24, 62, 74, 165
Tannehill, Robert, 10
Taylor, Joan, 177
Theophilus, 16, 19, 22, 26, 30-31, 40, 50, 55-56
  Lukan purposes, for Theophilus and beyond, 146, 158, 267, 290
Thompson, Alan, 30, 276, 281, 290
Thucydides, 62, 63, 64
Tiberius (Emperor), 244, 248, 255, 280
trinitarian theology, 208-9
Troftgruben, Troy, 235
Twelftree, Graham, 159
Tyson, Joseph, 228, 242
Uytanlet, Samson, 25
Vanhoozer, Kevin, 147
Varghese, P. V., 216
Vermes, Geza, 131
Vielhauer, Philipp, 65
Vinson, Richard, 68
Vinzent, Markus, 15
Wagner, J. Ross, 129
Walters, Patricia, 26
Walton, Steve, 64, 68, 199, 226, 269
Way, the, 73, 100, 138, 140, 146-47, 154, 181, 206
wealth and possessions, 2, 7-8, 47, 187, 194
  dangers of, 89, 113, 116, 152, 188-89, 249
  generosity with, 192-95, 197-99
Weatherly, Jon, 225, 236, 237
Wenham, David, 52
Wenham, John, 13, 28
Wenkel, David, 79, 212
Wi, Mija, 124
Wilken, Robert, 251
Willimon, William, 258, 267
Wilson, Stephen, 288
Winstanley, Gerrard, 185-86
Wolter, Michael, 292
women in Luke–Acts, 7, 110, 166-68, 174, 181-83
  exemplary discipleship, 155
  generosity of, 177, 195
  plight of, 109, 166
Wright, N. T., 24, 89, 159, 248, 272, 275, 276, 277, 292
Yamazaki-Ransom, Kazuhiko, 246, 269
Yoder, Joshua, 246
Young, Ho Kim, 289
Zacharias, H. Daniel, 81
Zanker, Paul, 254
Zetterholm, Karin, 132
Zyl, Hermie van, 124

Scripture Index

Old Testament

Exodus
4:31, *101*
15:1-18, *169*
15:20-21, *169*

Leviticus
19:18, *157*

Numbers
24:17, *79*

Deuteronomy
6:5, *99*
13:1-11, *134*
30, *279*

1 Samuel
1–2, *128*
16:13, *203*

2 Samuel
7:8-16, *79*
7:14, *90*
23:2, *203*

1 Kings
17:8-24, *133*

2 Kings
5:1-19, *133*

Ezra
9:5-9, *170*

Esther
8:17, *131*

Psalms
2:1-2, *135*
2:1-3, *84*
2:7, *90, 126, 134, 136, 203*
4, *90*
8:4, *93*
16, *84*
16:8-11, *136*
16:10, *126*
31, *135*
31:5, *135*
77:19, *133*
80:15, *101*
104:30, *103, 206*
106:5, *101*
107:29, *133*
110, *84, 135*
110:1, *83, 92, 97, 99, 135, 136*
118, *135*
118:22, *135*
118:26, *99*

Isaiah
2:2-4, *130, 138, 282*
6:6-9, *139*
6:9, *142*
6:9-10, *47, 128, 141, 142, 218, 236*
7:14, *169*
9:1-2, *132*
9:7, *34*
11:1-2, *203*
11:2, *203*
25:6-8, *138*
25:9, *212*
26:16-19, *281*
26:19, *81, 278*
29:18, *81*
29:18-19, *81, 278*

35:2, *212*
35:5, *81*
35:5-6, *82, 138, 278*
35:6, *81*
40, *99, 138*
40–44, *138*
40–55, *127, 138, 273, 286*
40:3-5, *138*
40:5, *109*
42:1, *90, 203*
42:6, *72, 108, 138, 161, 226*
42:7, *81*
42:18, *81*
42:19, *226*
44:3, *103, 206*
44:18, *138*
44:24-28, *138*
48:16, *204*
49:5-6, *226*
49:6, *72, 108, 138, 161, 226, 228, 234*
50:10, *226*
52:7, *278*
52:11, *137*
52:13, *137*
53, *137*
53:4, *81*
53:4-6, *137*
53:6, *137*
53:7-8, *137*
53:11, *137*
53:11-12, *137*
53:12, *137*
55:3, *126*
59:21, *204*
61, *82*
61:1, *36, 80, 81, 82, 99, 102, 109, 138, 141, 203, 204, 213, 278*

61:1-2, *133, 204, 278*
61:2, *133*
61:10, *212*
66:19, *138*
66:19-21, *130*

Jeremiah
23:5, *34*
25, *286*
25:1-14, *127*

Ezekiel
2:1-2, *204*
2:1-3, *94*
34:23-24, *34*
37, *281*
39:29, *103, 206*

Daniel
7, *94*
7:8, *94*
7:13, *92, 97, 132, 135*
7:13-14, *94*
7:22, *94*
7:27, *94*
9, *286*
9:2, *127*
9:3, *170*
9:20-27, *127*
10:5-6, *94*
11:14, *130*
12:1-2, *281*

Hosea
6:1-3, *281*

Joel
2:28-29, *103, 212*
2:28-32, *206*
2:29-29, *206*
2:31, *99*

Amos
9, *130*
9:1-10, *130*
9:11, *86, 131*
9:11-12, *108, 129, 130, 131, 233, 282*
9:11-15, *130*
9:12, *130*

Micah
3:8, *204, 210*

4:1-4, *130, 282*
5:2, *59*
5:2-6, *169*

Zechariah
3:8, *79*
6:12, *79*
8:23, *282*

Malachi
4:5, *34*

Apocrypha

1 Maccabees
2:50-68, *62*

New Testament

Matthew
4:14, *132*
5–7, *156*
8:5-10, *247*
8:11-13, *247*
8:23-27, *133*
14:22-33, *133*
16:17, *177*
24–25, *287*
24:30, *132*
26:64, *132*

Mark
3:17, *177*
4:35-41, *133*
5:16, *57*
6:45-52, *133*
7:13, *56*
7:24-30, *26, 110*
8:34, *152*
9:1, *283*
9:9, *57*
13, *287*
13:26, *132*
13:30, *283*
14:55-59, *41*
14:61, *41*
14:62, *83, 132*
15:15, *220*
15:32, *41*
15:39, *42, 250*
16:1-8, *178*

Luke
1, *21, 23, 37, 56, 60, 68, 79, 128, 178*
1–2, *7, 34, 235, 241*
1–9, *10*
1:1, *6, 30, 87, 88, 126*
1:1-2, *19*
1:1-4, *26, 29, 30, 54, 56, 69, 75*
1:1–9:50, *23, 56, 79, 178*
1:3, *19*
1:4, *23, 40, 158*
1:6, *73*
1:15, *210*
1:15-17, *204*
1:16-17, *34*
1:17, *78, 99*
1:18-20, *152*
1:25, *110*
1:26-37, *168*
1:28, *168*
1:30, *168*
1:32, *90, 98, 99, 205*
1:32-33, *34, 79, 202*
1:35, *90, 98, 202*
1:38, *152, 168*
1:41-44, *210, 211*
1:42-43, *170*
1:43, *99*
1:46-55, *2, 34, 277*
1:46-56, *169*
1:47, *34, 36, 78, 105, 235*
1:48, *170*
1:50, *117, 159*
1:50-55, *107*
1:52, *47, 115, 157*
1:52-53, *246*
1:53, *187*
1:54, *117*
1:58, *117*
1:67-79, *2, 34, 204, 210, 211, 277*
1:68, *100, 108, 241*
1:68-71, *123*
1:68-75, *108*
1:69, *6, 34, 36, 78, 108, 205, 235*
1:70, *79*
1:72, *117*
1:74, *115*
1:76, *99, 204*
1:77, *118, 213*
1:78, *77, 79, 100, 117, 235*

Scripture Index

1:79, *109, 115, 162*
2:1, *259*
2:1-3, *80*
2:1-4, *244*
2:1-5, *5, 59*
2:2, *59*
2:11, *36, 42, 77, 78, 79, 99, 103, 105, 138, 205, 244, 258*
2:19, *169, 170*
2:25, *42, 211, 241, 277*
2:25-35, *210*
2:26, *42, 77*
2:26-27, *207*
2:26-32, *204*
2:27, *211*
2:29-32, *211*
2:30, *105*
2:32, *72, 108, 138, 161, 214, 226, 234, 236, 277*
2:34, *46, 80*
2:34-35, *35*
2:35, *169*
2:36-38, *170*
2:37, *109*
2:38, *34, 102, 108, 234, 277*
2:49, *98, 170*
2:49-50, *236*
2:51, *170*
3, *215*
3:1-2, *244*
3:3, *119, 147, 213*
3:4, *99*
3:4-6, *138*
3:6, *109, 227*
3:7-9, *116*
3:8, *119, 147*
3:9, *116*
3:10-11, *111*
3:10-14, *108, 192*
3:11, *7*
3:12-13, *195*
3:16, *8, 73, 79, 102, 119, 205, 209, 212, 216*
3:21-22, *162, 204, 208*
3:22, *8, 73, 90, 134, 203*
3:23-38, *91*
3:31, *91*
3:34, *91*
3:38, *91, 94*
4:1, *73, 102, 204, 211, 213*
4:1-12, *273*
4:1-13, *115*
4:3, *91*
4:5, *246*
4:8, *99, 246*
4:9, *91*
4:12, *99*
4:13, *115, 224*
4:14, *102, 204, 207, 211, 213*
4:14-16, *49*
4:14-30, *46*
4:16-19, *133*
4:16-21, *204, 284*
4:16-30, *37, 97, 133, 278*
4:16-31, *2, 236*
4:18, *99, 109, 123, 162, 204*
4:18-19, *36, 213*
4:18-21, *80, 97, 109, 121, 138, 159, 234, 275*
4:21, *88*
4:21-23, *116*
4:22-30, *114*
4:24, *88, 142*
4:24-27, *116, 133*
4:25-27, *228*
4:27, *88*
4:28-30, *134*
4:31-37, *109*
4:36, *204*
4:38, *18*
4:41, *91*
4:43, *70, 89, 112*
5:1-11, *148*
5:8, *99, 114*
5:11, *154, 190*
5:12, *18, 99*
5:12-20, *109*
5:17, *99, 204*
5:21, *76*
5:24, *96*
5:27, *72*
5:27-28, *155*
5:27-32, *195*
5:28, *154, 190*
5:30, *195*
5:31, *159*
5:32, *36, 116, 119, 148, 279*
6:5, *94, 96, 99*
6:9, *109*
6:12-16, *278*
6:17, *156*
6:17-19, *156*
6:17-49, *156*
6:19, *204*
6:20, *109, 123*
6:20-26, *156*
6:22, *96*
6:24, *188*
6:27-32, *157*
6:30, *193*
6:31, *21*
6:35, *193*
6:36, *159*
6:36-38, *21*
6:37-38, *157*
6:39-42, *158*
6:42, *114*
6:43-49, *158*
6:45, *114*
6:46, *99*
6:47-49, *158*
7:1-10, *108, 111, 116, 227, 247, 261*
7:11-12, *109*
7:11-15, *89*
7:16, *88, 101*
7:18-23, *110, 278*
7:19-20, *80*
7:19-23, *81*
7:20, *79*
7:21, *80, 273*
7:22, *82, 109, 123*
7:22-23, *36, 81, 82, 138, 234, 275*
7:22-30, *155*
7:24-28, *79*
7:27, *70*
7:29, *118*
7:30, *114*
7:34, *96, 110, 116, 195*
7:35, *118*
7:36-50, *118, 152, 155, 175, 176*
7:37, *110*
7:37-39, *114, 175*
7:39, *88*
7:40-43, *193*
7:49, *76*
7:50, *35, 109, 123, 150*
8:1, *112*
8:1-2, *35*
8:1-3, *177*
8:1-10, *142*
8:2, *109, 176*
8:2-3, *155, 195*
8:3, *164*
8:9-10, *236*

8:10, *142*
8:12, *35, 115*
8:14, *174, 188*
8:15, *172, 279, 284*
8:22-25, *133*
8:25, *76*
8:26-39, *109, 111, 116, 227*
8:28, *91*
8:36, *109*
8:40-42, *179*
8:40-56, *109*
8:42-48, *110*
8:43-44, *18*
8:46, *204*
8:48, *109, 123, 150*
8:48-50, *35*
8:49-56, *179*
8:50, *109, 123*
9:1-6, *159*
9:2, *35, 113*
9:3, *190*
9:8, *88*
9:9, *76*
9:10, *57*
9:10-11, *159*
9:11, *35, 113*
9:19, *79, 88*
9:20, *77, 82, 148, 279*
9:21-27, *91*
9:22, *42, 92, 96, 280*
9:22-25, *82*
9:23, *152*
9:23-25, *74*
9:25, *155*
9:26, *82, 94, 96*
9:27, *82*
9:30-31, *92*
9:31, *83*
9:35, *91, 134*
9:37-43, *109*
9:41, *114*
9:43-44, *280*
9:44, *42, 96*
9:44-45, *236*
9:51-56, *110, 227*
9:51–19:44, *3, 6, 10, 145*
9:52-53, *146*
9:52-56, *159*
9:54, *99*
9:57-62, *3, 74, 122, 153*
9:58, *95, 96, 190*
9:59-62, *272*

9:62, *154, 190*
10, *172, 173*
10:1-12, *160*
10:1-17, *13*
10:2, *99, 164*
10:3-16, *114*
10:4, *190*
10:8-16, *102, 116*
10:9, *112, 273*
10:13, *89, 148, 279*
10:14, *123, 272, 279*
10:16, *116, 275*
10:17-20, *160, 172*
10:18, *162, 273*
10:21, *102*
10:22, *91*
10:23-24, *275*
10:25, *272*
10:25-37, *110, 193, 227*
10:27, *99, 157*
10:29, *118*
10:30-37, *2*
10:37, *157, 172*
10:38-42, *7, 155, 167, 171*
10:39, *176, 180*
10:42, *191*
11:2, *113, 272*
11:13, *73, 205, 206, 207*
11:14-15, *114*
11:14-23, *273*
11:18-22, *275*
11:20, *35, 73, 89, 112, 213, 273, 275, 278*
11:21-22, *115*
11:23, *275*
11:29-32, *89, 114, 116*
11:31-32, *123, 272, 279*
11:32, *89, 148, 279*
11:34-35, *115, 162*
11:37-52, *114*
11:39, *114*
11:41, *109*
11:42, *114*
11:53-54, *114*
12:1, *114*
12:5, *116*
12:8, *96*
12:10, *96, 209*
12:11-12, *163, 172*
12:12, *208*
12:13-21, *113, 116, 188*
12:15, *47, 188*

12:16, *188*
12:21, *114*
12:22-34, *172*
12:31, *272*
12:31-32, *113*
12:32, *272*
12:32-34, *191*
12:33, *109*
12:35-40, *97*
12:35-58, *284*
12:40, *94, 96*
12:45, *288*
12:49, *46*
12:50, *92*
12:56, *114*
12:57-59, *113*
13:1-5, *89, 116, 119, 279*
13:3-5, *148*
13:5, *272*
13:6-9, *89, 116*
13:10-14, *109*
13:10-16, *110*
13:10-17, *273*
13:15, *114*
13:16, *115*
13:18-19, *273*
13:20-21, *273*
13:22-30, *36, 108*
13:24-27, *113*
13:28, *113, 279*
13:28-29, *110, 272*
13:28-30, *247*
13:29, *9, 113*
13:30, *8, 47, 107, 272*
13:31-35, *224, 225*
13:32, *89*
13:33-34, *88, 279*
13:34, *46*
13:35, *99, 224*
14:1-23, *110*
14:2, *18*
14:7-11, *108*
14:7-23, *35*
14:10-11, *157*
14:11, *110*
14:12, *9*
14:13, *109, 193*
14:14, *113, 193, 272*
14:15, *113*
14:15-23, *108*
14:21, *109*
14:23, *227*

Scripture Index

14:26, *154*
14:26-27, *153*
14:28-33, *154*
14:33, *154, 191*
15, *119*
15:1-2, *195*
15:1-32, *2*
15:7, *148*
15:7-10, *279*
15:10, *148*
15:11-32, *118, 195*
15:20, *159*
16:1-13, *194*
16:9, *113, 194*
16:9-31, *157*
16:10-13, *194*
16:13, *187*
16:14, *189*
16:15, *118*
16:16, *72, 79, 112, 284*
16:19-31, *108, 116, 188, 272*
16:20-21, *106*
16:25, *272*
16:30, *119, 279*
17, *274, 289*
17:2, *21*
17:11, *145, 279*
17:11-19, *109, 110, 155, 227*
17:19, *35, 109, 123*
17:20-21, *274*
17:21, *112, 279*
17:22, *96*
17:22-35, *97*
17:24, *96*
17:24-30, *94*
17:26, *96*
17:26-37, *116*
17:30, *96*
18:1, *279*
18:1-8, *109, 284*
18:2, *114*
18:6-8, *288*
18:7, *115, 288*
18:8, *9, 94, 97*
18:9-14, *108, 118, 152, 195*
18:11, *114*
18:13, *114, 117, 159, 225*
18:14, *110, 150, 157*
18:17, *113, 272*
18:18, *113, 272*
18:22, *109, 191*
18:22-25, *114*

18:23, *188*
18:24, *113*
18:24-25, *272*
18:24-29, *113*
18:25, *189*
18:28, *148*
18:29, *272*
18:29-30, *113*
18:30, *155, 272*
18:31, *42, 88, 96*
18:31-33, *280*
18:35-43, *109*
18:38, *117*
18:41, *99*
18:42, *35, 109, 123, 150*
19:1-10, *97, 108, 155, 195*
19:2-10, *35*
19:8-10, *191*
19:9-10, *97*
19:10, *36, 96, 97, 105, 116, 119, 159*
19:11, *284, 285*
19:11-27, *284*
19:12, *87*
19:27, *47*
19:28, *99*
19:28-29, *272*
19:38, *87, 135*
19:41-44, *101, 116, 279*
19:44, *101*
20–21, *274*
20:1-26, *89*
20:9-18, *116*
20:9-19, *279*
20:17, *135*
20:17-19, *114*
20:21, *73*
20:21-26, *41*
20:36, *114*
20:41-44, *83, 205*
20:42-43, *135*
20:42-44, *99*
20:46, *114*
20:47, *109, 114*
21, *287*
21:1-3, *109*
21:1-4, *155, 190*
21:1-38, *89*
21:5-38, *116*
21:7, *288*
21:12-13, *248*
21:15, *163*

21:19, *279, 284*
21:20-24, *224, 225, 279*
21:22, *279*
21:24, *5, 72, 241, 284*
21:27, *94, 96*
21:31, *113, 272*
22–23, *241*
22:3, *115, 224*
22:16, *272, 284*
22:16-18, *113*
22:18, *272*
22:19-20, *159, 280*
22:20, *72*
22:22, *42, 96, 141, 224*
22:24-26, *114*
22:24-27, *279*
22:25, *259*
22:27, *113*
22:28-30, *275, 284*
22:29-30, *113, 278*
22:30, *108*
22:31, *115*
22:32, *148, 152*
22:33, *99*
22:37, *88, 137, 224*
22:38, *99*
22:48, *96*
22:49, *99*
22:52, *42, 266*
22:53, *115, 162, 224*
22:54-61, *148*
22:62, *148*
22:66, *41*
22:66-71, *76, 80, 246*
22:67, *46*
22:67-70, *92*
22:67-71, *41*
22:69, *83, 96, 97, 135*
23:2, *41, 42, 219, 248, 266*
23:2-3, *87*
23:3, *76*
23:4, *41, 42, 220, 249*
23:5, *98*
23:8-11, *41*
23:10, *219*
23:13, *220*
23:14, *219*
23:14-15, *41*
23:14-16, *220, 249*
23:15, *42*
23:16, *41, 220*
23:18-19, *41*

23:20, *220*
23:22, *41, 220, 249*
23:24, *41*
23:24-25, *220, 250*
23:25, *225*
23:27-31, *224*
23:31, *224*
23:35, *77*
23:36-37, *250*
23:37-38, *87*
23:39-43, *42*
23:41, *41, 42, 220*
23:42, *113*
23:44–24:12, *182*
23:46, *135*
23:47, *42, 87, 220, 250, 261*
23:48, *225*
23:50-51, *225*
24, *37, 83, 134*
24:1-11, *178*
24:6-8, *224*
24:7, *42, 96*
24:8, *178*
24:9, *178*
24:9-12, *155*
24:13-35, *2, 13*
24:17-24, *125*
24:19, *88*
24:21, *42, 72, 83, 108, 125, 234, 241, 280*
24:25, *150, 236*
24:26, *49, 83, 125, 137*
24:26-27, *3, 125, 280*
24:27, *6, 143*
24:31, *180*
24:32, *3, 127*
24:34, *99, 148*
24:39, *48*
24:44, *70, 88, 224*
24:44-48, *142*
24:45, *142, 238*
24:45-46, *280*
24:46, *70*
24:46-47, *83, 227*
24:46-48, *160*
24:47, *83, 108, 111, 118, 119, 206, 213, 229, 282*
24:48-49, *163*
24:49, *8, 26, 73, 102, 206, 207, 212, 214*
24:50-53, *2*

John
1:1, *70*
3:16, *205*
6:16-24, *133*

Acts
1, *289*
1–12, *229*
1:1, *19, 26*
1:1-2, *30*
1:1-11, *2*
1:3, *43, 276*
1:4, *8, 163, 212*
1:4-5, *206, 209*
1:5, *102*
1:6, *42, 113, 234, 241, 276, 281, 288*
1:6-8, *213*
1:8, *108, 111, 138, 146, 160, 163, 206, 207, 209, 214, 227, 229, 230*
1:9-11, *284, 289*
1:16, *207*
1:16-22, *61*
1:21, *99*
1:25, *171*
2, *8, 49, 71, 84, 201, 215*
2:1-42, *206*
2:1-43, *73*
2:1-47, *2*
2:4, *211*
2:14-36, *61*
2:14-41, *148*
2:17-18, *103, 206*
2:20, *99*
2:21, *37, 123*
2:22, *40, 42, 43, 84, 88*
2:22-23, *221*
2:22-36, *77*
2:23, *42, 44, 47, 70, 84, 141, 224, 225, 226*
2:24, *43*
2:25, *80*
2:25-31, *84, 136*
2:27, *87*
2:29, *80*
2:31, *80, 84*
2:32, *84*
2:32-36, *43*
2:33, *84, 137, 206, 207, 209, 212*
2:33-34, *136*
2:33-35, *99*
2:34, *80*
2:36, *43, 47, 77, 84, 99, 114, 221, 226, 258*
2:37, *225*
2:38, *102, 118, 120, 149, 206, 207, 209, 210, 214*
2:38-39, *61, 212*
2:38-41, *84*
2:40, *114*
2:41, *229*
2:41-42, *240*
2:42, *3, 158*
2:42-47, *121*
2:43-47, *43*
2:44, *150*
2:44-45, *186, 196*
2:45, *7, 111*
2:47, *106, 120, 229, 240*
3–4, *136*
3:1-16, *111*
3:7, *18*
3:11-26, *84, 148*
3:12-16, *61*
3:13, *87, 137, 220, 245, 250*
3:13-15, *85, 221*
3:13-17, *226*
3:14, *87, 137*
3:15, *85, 87*
3:16, *44, 85, 151*
3:17, *85, 226*
3:17-24, *213*
3:18, *85, 88, 224*
3:18-20, *70*
3:19, *108, 120, 149, 241*
3:19-21, *234, 282*
3:20, *85, 258*
3:20-21, *38, 42*
3:21, *115*
3:21-22, *85*
3:22-23, *88*
3:22-24, *204*
3:23, *85*
3:24-25, *85*
3:26, *87, 114, 137, 149*
4:4, *151, 229, 240*
4:8, *163, 211, 213*
4:8-11, *221*
4:8-12, *61, 85*
4:8-22, *211*
4:9, *123*
4:10, *44, 47, 85*

Scripture Index

4:11, *135*
4:12, *6, 38, 85, 106, 123, 266*
4:19-20, *61*
4:25, *207*
4:25-26, *84, 135*
4:25-27, *85, 87*
4:26, *77*
4:27, *204, 222, 225, 226, 245, 250*
4:27-28, *221*
4:28, *70, 224*
4:30, *44, 87*
4:31, *163, 207, 211, 213*
4:32, *150, 186, 196*
4:32-37, *111*
4:33, *99, 258*
4:34, *196, 197*
4:36-37, *152*
4:37, *156, 191, 195, 197*
5:1-10, *152*
5:1-11, *197*
5:3, *8, 115, 208*
5:3-4, *209*
5:9, *8*
5:12-16, *111*
5:14, *150, 151, 229, 240*
5:29-31, *85*
5:29-32, *61*
5:31, *38, 77, 78, 85, 87, 99, 105, 118, 136, 137, 149, 206, 213*
5:32, *85, 208*
5:34-39, *44*
5:35-39, *61*
5:36, *266*
5:39, *114*
5:42, *85*
6, *173, 174*
6:1, *229*
6:1-4, *111*
6:1-6, *2, 197*
6:1-7, *44*
6:2, *158*
6:3, *207*
6:4, *171, 173*
6:7, *20, 229, 240*
6:10, *207*
6:13-14, *44, 223*
6:14, *56, 72*
7, *156*
7:2-53, *61*
7:37, *88*
7:41, *49*
7:41-43, *114*
7:51, *208*
7:51-52, *114*
7:51-53, *221, 223*
7:52, *21, 87, 137*
7:53, *114*
7:55, *211*
7:55-56, *99, 100, 136, 211*
7:56, *95, 96, 97*
7:59-60, *100*
7:60, *233*
8, *156*
8:4, *163*
8:4-25, *111*
8:4-40, *227*
8:5, *86*
8:7, *111*
8:9-25, *122*
8:12, *112, 151, 234, 275*
8:15-17, *73, 209, 210*
8:16, *100, 258*
8:18-23, *114*
8:20, *48*
8:21, *21*
8:26-35, *137*
8:29, *208*
8:39, *208*
9, *64, 143*
9:1-19, *45*
9:1-21, *66*
9:1-22, *67, 227*
9:1-30, *2*
9:2, *73, 138*
9:5, *100, 114*
9:15, *66*
9:15-16, *50*
9:20-22, *90*
9:22, *86*
9:22-25, *67*
9:26-27, *67*
9:27, *57, 156*
9:30, *67*
9:32, *208*
9:32-35, *179*
9:32-43, *111*
9:35, *149*
9:36, *179*
9:36-40, *195*
9:36-43, *179*
9:42, *151, 229*
10, *156*
10–11, *111, 214, 239, 261*
10:1-48, *227*
10:2, *261*
10:15, *119, 261*
10:19, *208*
10:22, *261*
10:34, *112, 261*
10:34-43, *61*
10:36, *99, 143, 259, 266*
10:38, *73, 138, 204, 210, 284*
10:39, *226*
10:40, *43*
10:42, *21, 87, 116, 272, 289*
10:43, *118, 137, 150, 162, 206, 213*
10:44, *209, 210*
10:44-48, *73*
10:45, *108, 206, 207, 214*
10:47, *209, 214, 261*
11:5-17, *61*
11:8, *261*
11:12, *208, 214, 215*
11:16, *208, 209*
11:17, *112, 258, 261*
11:18, *108, 112, 120, 149, 261*
11:19-21, *111, 162, 227*
11:20, *99, 163, 258*
11:21, *149, 151*
11:22-27, *156*
11:23, *158*
11:26, *223, 231*
11:27-30, *66, 67, 111, 231*
11:28, *208*
11:29-30, *197*
12:17, *57*
12:20-23, *251*
12:22, *259*
12:24, *229*
12:25, *231*
13, *37*
13:1, *13, 158, 164*
13:1-2, *208*
13:1-3, *231*
13:2, *8, 49, 164*
13:4, *208*
13:4-12, *162, 260*
13:5-12, *49*
13:6-11, *114, 122*
13:7, *45*
13:8-12, *211*
13:9, *163*
13:12, *45, 151, 191*
13:16-41, *61*
13:22, *80*

13:23, *38, 78, 105*
13:24, *147*
13:26, *150, 266*
13:26-29, *221*
13:27, *88*
13:27-28, *225*
13:27-29, *224, 226*
13:28, *220, 245, 250*
13:30, *43*
13:32, *65*
13:32-33, *126, 234, 238, 281*
13:32-34, *6*
13:33, *136, 224*
13:34, *80*
13:34-39, *205*
13:35, *136*
13:36, *80*
13:36-37, *70*
13:37, *43*
13:38, *118, 206, 213*
13:38-39, *119*
13:39, *114*
13:42-46, *229, 240*
13:45, *236*
13:45-46, *240*
13:46, *116, 228, 229, 237*
13:46-47, *113, 139*
13:47, *108, 161, 214, 228, 234, 266*
13:48, *70, 151*
13:50, *236*
13:52, *212, 214*
14, *289*
14:1, *150, 151, 229, 230, 240*
14:1-2, *229, 236*
14:2, *223*
14:4, *236*
14:8-10, *111*
14:8-18, *252*
14:15, *65*
14:15-17, *61*
14:15-18, *49*
14:19, *236*
14:22, *9, 113, 155, 158, 249, 272, 284*
14:23, *170*
14:26, *231*
15, *66, 123, 129, 130, 131, 228, 239*
15:1, *106, 123*
15:1-5, *48, 72, 231*
15:1-21, *223*
15:1-22, *67*
15:1-33, *2*
15:5, *229, 240*
15:7, *151*
15:7-11, *61*
15:8, *112, 214*
15:9, *112, 119, 162, 206, 214, 261*
15:10, *72*
15:11, *38, 100, 106, 123, 150, 258*
15:12-21, *130, 156*
15:13-18, *233, 234, 282*
15:13-21, *61*
15:14-18, *49*
15:15-18, *86, 108*
15:16, *80*
15:19, *149*
15:20, *114*
15:22-23, *231*
15:26, *258*
15:28, *208*
15:29, *114*
15:30-35, *231*
16:4, *231*
16:6-7, *208*
16:6-9, *100*
16:7, *164*
16:7-17, *13*
16:11-15, *156, 180*
16:11-40, *67*
16:12-40, *21*
16:14, *180, 214, 238*
16:14-15, *7*
16:15, *174, 180, 195*
16:16-18, *252*
16:17, *5, 38, 73, 106, 266*
16:18, *111, 162*
16:30-31, *38, 106*
16:31, *100, 120, 150, 258*
16:40, *156, 158*
17, *37*
17–18, *66*
17:1-9, *67, 256*
17:3, *86*
17:4, *150*
17:4-5, *236*
17:5-6, *229, 240*
17:6-7, *80*
17:7, *87, 245, 266*
17:10, *229*
17:12, *240*
17:12-13, *236*
17:15-34, *67*
17:16, *49, 114, 252*
17:22-31, *49, 61, 62*
17:24, *258*
17:30, *120*
17:30-31, *272*
17:31, *87, 116, 289*
18:1-18, *67*
18:2, *67, 181*
18:3, *67*
18:4, *229*
18:5, *67, 86*
18:5-8, *236*
18:6, *45, 116, 228, 229, 237, 240*
18:8, *151*
18:11, *158*
18:12-17, *260*
18:13, *231*
18:17, *45, 67*
18:18-19, *181*
18:19-20, *236*
18:19-21, *229, 230*
18:22, *231*
18:24-25, *73*
18:25, *100*
18:25-26, *73*
18:26, *73, 158, 181*
18:27, *150*
19:1, *67*
19:1–20:1, *67*
19:4, *119*
19:5, *100, 258*
19:6, *209, 210*
19:8, *112, 275*
19:8-10, *229*
19:9, *73, 138*
19:10, *229*
19:17, *150, 258*
19:17-41, *252*
19:19, *49*
19:19-20, *114*
19:21, *67, 231*
19:23, *73, 138*
19:25-27, *61*
19:31, *260*
19:35-40, *61*
20:5-15, *13*
20:7-12, *158*
20:11-12, *111*
20:18-35, *61, 64*
20:20, *158*
20:21, *65, 100, 108, 120, 149, 229, 230, 240, 258*

Scripture Index

20:22, *231*
20:23, *208*
20:24, *65, 100, 258*
20:25, *112, 275*
20:27, *70, 158*
20:28, *208, 209, 282*
20:31, *67*
20:32, *119, 158*
20:33-35, *198*
20:34, *67*
20:35, *21, 258*
21–28, *5*
21:1-18, *13*
21:11, *208*
21:13, *258*
21:15-26, *231*
21:17-25, *156*
21:17-26, *45*
21:20-26, *223*
21:21, *231*
21:21-24, *72*
21:25, *114*
21:27-36, *261*
21:28, *231*
21:34, *261*
21:38, *266*
21:39, *66*
22, *64, 143*
22:1-21, *2, 61, 66*
22:2-5, *50*
22:3, *174, 231*
22:3-21, *231*
22:4, *73, 138*
22:6-21, *45*
22:8, *100*
22:14, *87, 137*
22:15-21, *66*
22:19, *150*
22:23-29, *245*
22:25-29, *66*
22:30, *23*
23:1, *45, 231*
23:1-11, *45*
23:6, *50, 231*
23:6-8, *272*
23:6-10, *223*
23:11, *100, 230*
23:16-25, *261*
23:27, *66*
24:2-8, *61*
24:5, *223*
24:5-6, *231*

24:10-20, *45, 231*
24:10-21, *61*
24:14, *73, 138, 223*
24:14-16, *50*
24:15, *272*
24:16, *231*
24:19, *236*
24:22, *73*
24:23, *260*
24:24-26, *260*
24:25, *116*
24:26, *45*
24:27, *45, 260*
25:8, *45, 231, 245, 263*
25:24-27, *61*
25:25, *259*
25:25-26, *255*
26, *64, 143*
26:1, *161*
26:1-18, *50*
26:2-3, *61*
26:2-23, *2, 66, 231*
26:2-29, *45*
26:4-23, *45*
26:6, *9*
26:6-7, *281*
26:12-23, *45*
26:15, *100*
26:16, *162*
26:16-18, *66*
26:17-18, *224, 230*
26:18, *21, 109, 115, 118, 119, 162, 213, 261*
26:19-20, *240*
26:20, *86, 120, 149, 230*
26:22-23, *109, 161*
26:23, *86, 138, 234*
26:24, *266*
26:27-29, *230*
26:29, *164*
26:31-32, *45*
26:32, *245*
27:1, *45, 261*
27:1–28:16, *13*
27:3, *260, 261*
27:9-12, *262*
27:21-26, *61*
27:27-32, *262*
27:33-38, *111, 262*
27:42-44, *262*
28, *20, 128, 218, 232, 235, 240*
28:1-10, *180*

28:8, *18*
28:16, *260*
28:17, *231*
28:17-20, *61*
28:17-22, *45*
28:17-30, *236*
28:20, *235*
28:21-22, *39, 236*
28:22, *223*
28:23, *112, 234, 276*
28:23-24, *86*
28:24-25, *236*
28:25, *207*
28:25-28, *139, 142*
28:28, *108, 214, 237*
28:29-30, *237*
28:31, *234, 258, 260, 275, 276*

Romans
1:16, *65*
1:18-32, *62*
2:16, *14*
4:6-8, *119*
6:7, *119*
9, *15*
9–11, *128*
13:1-7, *265*
13:12, *283*
15:22-25, *67*
15:25-27, *66*
16:3, *181*
16:20, *283*
16:21, *13*
16:25, *14*

1 Corinthians
1:17-18, *65*
1:18–2:5, *62*
2:1-5, *65*
2:2, *65*
5:7, *65*
7:26, *283*
9:15, *67*
11:2, *56*
11:23, *56*
15:3, *56*
15:35-49, *48*
16:1-3, *66*
16:1-8, *67*
16:12, *67*

2 Corinthians
1:19, *67*
1:20, *65*
1:22, *284*
1:22-23, *213*
2:13, *67*
3, *15*
5:5, *213, 284*
7:5, *67*
9:2-4, *67*
11:7-9, *67*
11:7-8:33, *67*
11:9, *67*
11:32, *67*

Galatians
1:6, *65*
1:16, *66*
1:17, *67*
1:18-20, *67*
1:21-22, *67*
2–5, *15*
2:1-10, *66*
2:11-14, *66*
5:11, *65*

6:12, *65*
6:14, *65*

Ephesians
1:13, *284*
4:30, *284*

Philippians
4:15-16, *67*

Colossians
1:6, *65*
4:14, *13*

1 Thessalonians
1:9-10, *65, 283*
2:9, *67*
2:17–3:6, *66*
3:1, *67*
3:6, *67*

2 Timothy
2:8, *14*
4:11, *13*

Philemon
23–24, *13*
24, *19*

Hebrews
11:32, *57*

1 Peter
1, *102*
2:12, *102*

2 Peter
3, *283*

Jude
3, *56*

Revelation
13:1-18, *265*
22:7, *283*
22:12, *283*
22:20, *283*

Also by Michael F. Bird

*Introducing Paul: The Man,
His Mission, and His Message*
978-0-8308-2897-5